D1570065

THE ATTACK ON CORPORATE AMERICA

The Corporate Issues Sourcebook

THE ATTACK ON CORPORATE AMERICA

The Corporate Issues Sourcebook

Law and Economics Center
University of Miami School of Law
Coral Gables, Florida

M. BRUCE JOHNSON
Editor

McGRAW-HILL BOOK COMPANY

*New York   St. Louis   San Francisco   Auckland   Bogotá   Düsseldorf
Johannesburg   London   Madrid   Mexico   Montreal   New Delhi   Panama
Paris   São Paulo   Singapore   Sydney   Tokyo   Toronto*

Library of Congress Cataloging in Publication Data

Miami, University of, Coral Gables, Fla. Law and
    Economics Center.

    The attack on corporate America: the corporate issues sourcebook.

    Bibliography: p.
    Includes index.
        1. Corporations—United States—Addresses, essays,
lectures. 2. Industry—Social aspects—United States
–Addresses, essays, lectures. 3. Industry and
state—United States—Addresses, essays, lectures.
I. Johnson, M. Bruce. II. Title.
    HD2785.M5 1978   338.7′4′0973   77-20669
    ISBN 0-07-036693-4

1234567890   DODO   7654321098

The editors for this book were W. Hodson Mogan and Joan
Zseleczky, the designer was Elliot Epstein, and the
production supervisor was Teresa F. Leaden. It was set in
Caledonia by University Graphics, Inc.

Printed and bound by R. R. Donnelley & Sons Company.

CONTENTS

The Question of Profits   **245**

EDITOR'S INTRODUCTION

The essays in *The Attack on Corporate America: The Corporate Issues Sourcebook* address the issues and challenges raised by contemporary critics of the large American corporation. The volume was designed to be useful to people in business, intelligent lay readers, and interested students, many of whom are understandably uncertain about the substance and validity of the latest attacks on corporations. The issues explored in the volume naturally represent an assessment of the appropriate range of topics under debate. The essays are concise and free of technical jargon and are accompanied by a consolidated bibliography that suggests directions for further reading and reflection.

The Attack on Corporate America is designed to provide a "quick fix" on the substance of a wide variety of issues. The essays summarize pro and con arguments on issues and indicate the results of thoughtful analyses.

Preparation and publication of the volume was sponsored by the Law and Economics Center at the University of Miami School of Law. A number of Center personnel made important contributions to the volume. Dr. Henry G. Manne, Director of the Law and Economics Center, originally suggested the potential usefulness of such a volume. Professors Allen Hyman, Arleen Leibowitz, and Robert Tollison provided invaluable assistance to the editor in connection with the review, revision, and editing of the collection of essays. Professors Kenneth Clarkson, Louis De Alessi, Donald L. Martin, and James S. Mofsky also gave editorial assistance. Mark Taylor, a John M. Olin Fellow at the Center, spent the major part of the summer of 1976 researching materials pursuant to a compilation of a list of issues. William Weston, consultant to the Law and Economics Center, was a constant source of encouragement throughout the project. Finally, Jeanie Gay Reese provided superb secretarial and copy-editing services with unflinching patience and good cheer.

I must also express my appreciation to the outside contributors—the law professors and the economics professors at various universities around the country. Their willingness to cooperate—as I directed the preparation of the volume, restructured the table of contents again and again, and judiciously suggested modifications and improvements—was most impressive.

Only time (and the market) will tell whether the volume usefully serves the purpose for which it was intended. My goal was, of course, to make a contribution to the current debate over the structure and performance of our contemporary corporate system. However, every effort was made from the outset to develop a level of discourse higher than the strident rhetoric used by many of the corporation's contemporary critics. The analytical approach to the issues places a greater burden on the reader— but not, we hope, without commensurate benefits.

M. Bruce Johnson

PREFACE

Periods of strong, even strident, antibusiness and anticorporate sentiment are not new in American political history. But we have probably not previously experienced the near hysteria that characterizes current attitudes. From those quarters of society charged with developing and disseminating ideas and social attitudes comes the view that the large corporate system is an unmitigated evil.

Some of the charges sparking this highly emotional atmosphere suggest that the structure of large corporations is unsuited to a democratic society; that large corporations manipulate consumer demand to serve their own greed; that profit serves no social purpose; that competitive forces are inadequate to constrain massive private enterprises; and that no political powers are strong enough to tame the beast. Excessive consumerism and environmentalism and undesirable regulatory schemes of all kinds feed on such nonsense.

That anti-free-market attitudes emanate most strongly from political and governmental functionaries should occasion no surprise. It is almost a truism that persons (and governments) bent on increasing their political powers can do so only at the expense of someone in the private sector.

Large corporations provide an ideal target; they seem so impersonal, so big, so pervasive, so easily misunderstood, and so lacking in direct mass voter support. And certainly scandalmongering about ambiguous payments to foreign officials is more titillating to the public's psyche than the non-news of quiet, efficient, productive effort and accomplishment.

The many myths and unproved charges against large corporations stem also, in considerable measure, from the academic and intellectual communities. Such behavior often smacks strangely of biting the hand that feeds, but then government may feed even better, and one must suspect that the hoary moral about paying the piper and calling the tune has some application here. A more important answer may be simply that both academia and the media misunderstand how our modern corporate system is supposed to function and how it actually does function.

While it may surprise some to suggest that broad-based ignorance about the American corporate system exists among the country's intellectual elite, there are some peculiarities about this subject matter worth noting. For whatever odd reason, there does not exist even today in the scholarly literature about the great American corporate system a single volume that sets forth a coherent and integrated economic theory of how large, publicly held corporations, and a corporate system, should operate in a free-market environment.

That is partly because until fairly recently crucial aspects of the complete picture simply were not comprehended even by experts in the field. But this is no longer the case, and study after study has now overwhelmingly vindicated the workings of our large corporations, our capital markets, and the free-market systems in general. Nevertheless, the past ten to fifteen years have witnessed an outpouring of corporate and business criticism as venomous as anything seen since Nazi "scholars" placed responsibility for the ills of an earlier epoch on the Jewish community.

Still, the intellectual picture in America may be improving. Increasingly, the academic air is rent with talk of new and powerful analytical tools—tools such as "efficient market hypothesis," "random walk theory," "market for corporate control," "monitoring function," "information theory," "time costs," "public choice models," and a host of other new ideas to help explain such seemingly disparate phenomena as corporate social responsibility, the selection of corporate directors, the size of firms, advertising practices, tender offers, employment relationships, stock prices, and myriad other aspects of the enormously complex apparatus that is the modern corporation.

Out of all these new scholarly developments has come a serious realization: understanding every aspect of our corporate system is probably too difficult for even the most specialized scholars. Similarly, even for the reasonably well-informed person in business or, for that matter, the dabbler in modern economic and finance theory, the subject is simply too large for one person to master in depth. But this complexity adds greatly to the vulnerability of the corporate system to political or demogogic attack. Who in the business community can respond articulately and with intellectually sound arguments to the variant mass of charges, myths, accusations, partial information, and downright slander that passes today for popular criticism of big business? Few could be found even to claim such an ability, much less to demonstrate it.

The function of this sourcebook, then, is to provide knowledge to that segment of the public interested in becoming familiar with the most modern thinking about the economics of corporate enterprise. The sourcebook is organized so that readers can learn quickly what the most vigorous and unbiased scholarly views are on the most significant topics concerning large corporations. It is not designed as a work of original scholarship, though happily some is included. Nor is it intended to be only a popularization of the best scholarly work extant or a handy reference guide, though again it is both of those things. Rather, it is offered as a work by many authors that has been carefully integrated and edited and that explains how the American corporate system functions in those areas most subject to ill-conceived criticism.

Many persons studying this work will be surprised to learn that the weight of high-grade scholarship about the modern corporate system supports strongly the conclusion that unregulated corporate capitalism functions far more desirably than various louder voices have led us to believe. Among intellectuals actively researching and publishing in this area there is little significant criticism of the manner in which the American corporate system functions—apart, that is, from the distortions introduced by government intervention.

The supreme irony of modern American corporate history may be that just when the intellectual battle about free enterprise has been won overwhelmingly by its proponents, the system is in the greatest danger ever of being destroyed. Hopefully, wider dissemination of this good news about the corporate system can help stave off the malignant alternatives that could replace it.

Henry G. Manne, Director
Law and Economics Center

HOW TO USE THIS BOOK:
A NOTE ABOUT NOTES

This book uses a consolidated bibliography with 464 consecutively numbered entries, as well as a list of legal citations. Numbers that appear in brackets in the text refer to the entry listed in the bibliography. An entry such as "[173]," for example, refers the reader to entry 173, which is Milton Friedman's book *Capitalism and Freedom*. An entry such as "[173: 25-26]" refers the reader to pages 25 and 26 of *Capitalism and Freedom*. An entry such as "[173: 95, n2]" refers the reader to footnote 2 on page 95 of *Capitalism and Freedom*. An entry such as "[173:95–97; 208]" refers the reader to pages 95–97 of *Capitalism and Freedom* and to Garrett Harden's article "The Tragedy of the Commons." An entry such as "[173, SB2]" refers the reader to *Capitalism and Freedom* and to Chapter 2 of the Sourcebook.

At the end of each chapter there appears a list of additional readings, which follow the same format as the bracketed entries in the text. These additional readings refer to entries in the consolidated bibliography and were supplied by the author or editorially.

THE ATTACK ON CORPORATE AMERICA

The Corporate Issues Sourcebook

PART ONE

SOCIOPOLITICAL ANALOGIES AND THE CORPORATION

```
┌──────────────────────────────────────────────────┐
│              CORPORATE SOCIAL                      │
│            RESPONSIBILITY AND                      │
│               ACCOUNTABILITY                       │
└──────────────────────────────────────────────────┘
```

1. Should Corporations Assume More Social Responsibilities?

HENRY G. MANNE
Law and Economics Center
University of Miami School of Law

Editor's Summary   Many corporate executives promote the notion of corporate social responsibility because they believe it is good public relations. Other "corporate statesmen" use the social responsibility argument to secure government protection from competition. But the costs of non-profit-oriented corporate action are ultimately passed on to consumers. Thus, corporate officials who try to shoulder social responsibilities are acting like nonelected officials allocating social costs and benefits, or levying taxes and distributing subsidies, all without the legitimacy of a political mandate. Still, effective profit-maximizing action may generate the paradox of all these seemingly anticapitalist activities.

Misunderstanding of our system of large corporations has been a part of the American social and political scene from its beginnings. Even in colonial days complaints were heard about "soulless corporations." One might think that the absence of a soul would inhibit the argument that corporations should engage in "good works" to "save" themselves. On the contrary, we have been told most stridently in recent years that even when acting within the law, and even while trying simply to maximize profits (or, more correctly, to maximize the present wealth position of the owners), corporations should undertake and fulfill certain social responsibilities. These may be of a traditional, charitable nature, such as making contributions to community chests or universities; or, they may require functions more commonly thought of as governmental, such as providing an education for children of migrant laborers, establishing uneconomically high safety standards, or beautifying the environment.

THE BACKGROUND OF CORPORATE SOCIAL RESPONSIBILITY

The demand that large corporations should act in a socially responsible manner has various implications, depending upon its source. When leaders of large corporations utter this demand, the odds are great that the demand is being used as public relations to overcome the public assertions of corporate evildoings that opponents of corporate enterprise make. Sometimes, however, a demand for corporate social responsibility by a corporate executive smacks strongly of other motives. These motives include an attempt to secure government protection from competition, particularly foreign competition, as when business "statesmen" proclaim the "need" to protect American jobs, by pressuring the federal government for tariffs or import quotas on foreign goods.

Although the notion of corporate social responsibility is today most commonly identified with public figures like Ralph Nader and other admitted opponents of the American corporate system, the origins of the idea can be traced to the business community itself. In the 1930s, when big business was under unusually severe political and social attack, a public relations specialist named Ivy Lee sold American industry on proclaiming that social welfare, not dollar profits, is the real goal of large enterprises.

Undoubtedly, the earliest proponents of this view were realists, or cynics if one prefers. But as academics, especially those associated with the Harvard Business School, picked up the social responsibility notion, executives came rather to like the idea that they had duties other than merely producing profits in a competitive marketplace.

By the early 1950s the law, too, had adjusted to this newer view, and many courts overruled the prior leading precedent of *Dodge v. Ford Motor Company* [204 Michigan 459 (1919)], in which was quoted the quaint expression from an earlier English decision: "Charity qua charity has no seat at the Board of Directors." With the erosion of the decision in *Dodge v. Ford Motor Company,* and thus freed of legal shackles and economic arguments that they should pursue only profits, many managers presumably slept better at night and daily wrestled with issues of how best to support the local symphony or art museum. Little did these managers realize the ominous turn this seemingly innocuous concept would ultimately take.

In the hands of both government officials and nongovernment enemies of corporate capitalism, the phrase "corporate social responsibility" has become a vicious weapon used both as a club to bludgeon individual companies not acting as the particular attacker would prefer and as an effective political argument for additional government regulation of business. One of the principal arguments of corporate opponents was also made often by some persons seemingly sympathetic to the corporate system: that corporations must act in a socially responsible manner to preserve the capitalist system. Much more commonly, however, the identical argument was made by opponents of a free enterprise system as a clear threat: "Unless you act as we dictate, we will not allow you to survive."

Before examining the economics of corporate social responsibility or non-profit-maximizing activity, it is useful to recall that over the years of the existence of this doctrine (and it has gone by other titles, including "corporate citizenship" and "business statesmanship"), the content of what is supposed to constitute corporate social responsibility has changed with considerable regularity.

At the inception of this doctrine, programs such as the community chest, the Boy Scouts, and other close-to-home charities were generally comprehended as constituting the province of the socially minded company (and in many cases corporate contributions were very good business). This idea of appropriate corporate activities, in turn, expanded to include support of basic research, scholarships, and general unrestricted support of universities. In still a later period, corporations were supposed to be the principal patrons of the arts or supporters of fine architecture and sculpture.

More recently the list made popular initially by Ralph Nader began to dominate [328]. This list included such items as product safety, employee safety, and not trading with countries on some person's least-favored-nation list [SB 15]. At the moment of writing, the most active aspects of the corporate social responsibility movement seem to involve racial and sexual hiring practices and environmental issues [SB 3, SB 4, SB 8, SB 10, SB 11, SB 24].

This chapter does not examine the merit, or lack of merit, in each of these particular substantive proposals. It should be noted, however, that there is no underlying theory or philosophy that guides the proponents of corporate social responsibility. Nor is there any necessary consistency in the positions these proponents advocate. These deficiencies alone should be enough to make clear that the concept of corporate social responsibility is fundamentally at odds with a free-market, private property system in which multitudes of individual human beings, making their own free and uncoerced choices, condition the actions of business. More ironies are to follow.

COMPETITION AND CORPORATE ALTRUISM

The first of these ironies is that to the extent that corporations do business in a competitive product market, the use of funds or resources for nonproductive purposes cannot survive the stringent test of the marketplace, unless the government mandates this use for every firm in an industry. Consider, for example, several competing paper companies, each emptying its waste products into the same body of water [SB 3, SB 4]. Suppose one of these companies decides to act "responsibly," but the others do not. The responsible company would soon find itself in serious financial difficulties, or perhaps with a new team of less socially minded managers.

The same result follows if any number less than all the companies act in this manner. But perhaps if all the companies could get together, presumably with a dispensation from the antitrust laws, there would be no difficulty with their agreeing to act responsibly. This answer, however, fails to reckon with our extremely competitive capital markets. Unless other companies in other industries somehow agreed to the same profit restraint, these companies (with all the difficulties and dangers implicit in such private agreements) would find their lower rate of return reflected in a higher price of capital and less investment in their industry. And, therefore, the possibility of insolvency or a takeover would still be present. This analysis, incidentally, remains true regardless of whether the particular company or companies involved are realizing competitive or monopoly rates of return, since the rate of return realized in the financial market, even for shares in companies realizing monopoly profits, will always be the competitive one.

This analysis brings us to the rather surprising posture that corporate altruism does not seem to be an economically viable way of life. Yet we hear constantly of more and more corporations acting in a socially responsible manner. Assuming, as it seems proper to do, that each of these states of affairs actually exists, can they be reconciled logically? They can, and with little difficulty.

The real business purpose served by corporations trying to be socially responsible rests not on a theory of voluntary corporate altruism, but on conventional theories of competition and rational political action. The vast bulk of what could otherwise pass as non-profit-oriented corporate activity has in modern America become an important, indeed crucial, aspect of business public relations. Whether this activity is aimed at acquiring friends or allaying the attacks of enemies, the situation remains the same, and the associated nonproductive expenditures are simply costs of doing business. Like any costs of doing business, these expenditures must be covered, and this is true, like the weather, whether we like it or not. Thus, economists who inveigh against business leaders engaging in this activity are themselves merely second-guessing real business decisions about which they normally would have little or no expertise.

THE INEVITABILITY OF COSTS

Individual companies may often be singled out for attack by self-styled public interest groups or others seeking to publicize a particular social campaign. Inevitably, the companies singled out are those most vulnerable to widespread loss of popularity among the general public. For this reason, we are far more apt to see an attack on certain activities of the Coca Cola Company, or manufacturers of children's pajamas, than on certain activities of industrial construction companies. Coca Cola would be seriously damaged by a relatively small drop in popular market support, say on the order of 2 to 5 percent, while a construction company might hardly notice a ripple in its business if popular attention were turned in its direction, since it does not sell to the broad, mass, public market.

The next important thing to note about the economics of nonproductive expenditures is that the ultimate costs are apt to be borne by persons whom we would probably not choose directly to bear such costs. After all, there is no such thing as a corporation itself bearing any costs. What are termed corporate costs must be passed forward to consumers in the form of higher prices, or back to investors as lower returns, or to suppliers as lower prices or wages. Economists disagree as to exactly what the ultimate incidence of these costs would be (the question is not unlike that of the incidence of certain excise taxes), but the consensus is fairly strong that ultimately the burden falls most heavily upon consumers.

HOW NADER CHOOSES BUSINESS
EXECUTIVES TO GOVERN US

Notice the irony of any of these effects. The very persons, top corporate executives, who are berated for not having their corporations act in a socially responsible fashion—and we should emphasize here that we are not arguing about the legality or moral responsibility of the executives' actions—now find themselves in the position of nonelected officials allocating social costs and benefits, or taxes and welfare, without even the legitimacy of a political franchise. Corporate social responsibility, in other words, demands that corporate executives act like nonelected government officials. But, naturally, popular advocates of corporate social responsibility, such as Ralph Nader, assume that they, or perhaps their favored politicians, and not the corporate officers, will be able to control this social distribution of benefits and costs.

OTHER IRONIES

There is another fundamental economic argument against corporate social behavior that I note in passing: corporate executives must be assumed to have the knowledge necessary to improve upon the free-market allocation of resources and to generate an even more socially desirable result. All evidence, whether from Russia, Cuba, or China, or from the ICC, the CAB, or our other experiences with allocation and price controls, indicates the absurdity of this assumption.

There is yet another irony implicit in the concept of corporate social responsibility. As indicated earlier, some of the best-intentioned defenders of the concept argue that it is necessary to prevent or stave off further government intervention in the private sector. Inevitably, however, the voluntary adoption of socially responsible activity, as it is currently defined, has had precisely the opposite effect.

Consider, again, the single competing paper company whose executives decide that it will no longer pollute the water it shares with others. As economic forces work their inexorable way, that company, to survive, must either reverse its decision or find a way to make that decision mandatory for everyone else similarly situated. The latter course is what seems most often to occur. The self-proclaimed "moral" corporation hies its lobbyists off to Washington to seek to impose on its competitors precisely those standards it has voluntarily adopted (and in which it may be assumed to have some comparative advantage). The competitors are not in a strong position to oppose the request for regulation. Politicians and bureaucrats, naturally, will respond to the argument that they cannot allow the "bad guys" to continue profiting while the "good guys," those who have stopped polluting the water, are being driven out of business.

CONCLUSION

Thus, finally, we see that there is no logic or morality to the idea of corporate social responsibility and that its true implications are almost inevitably the opposite of what they are superficially supposed to be. Yet the talk of moral corporations and socially responsible, non-profit-maximizing activity persists. The most sincere advocates of corporate social responsibility could not want the results it generates, and its most obvious opponents have no choice but to continue advocating it and acting as though it were for real.

ADDITIONAL READINGS: 51, 60, 174, 278, 283, 288, 386, 389, 429.

2. Does the Corporation Discourage Individual Responsibility?

ARLEEN LEIBOWITZ
The Rand Corporation

Editor's Summary   Corporations monitor what their employees do because they are liable for employee actions and because those actions affect demand for the corporations' products. The firm's lower relative cost of internally monitoring employee actions favors the organization of production within a firm as opposed to the organization of production by transactions in external markets. Corporate indemnification of employees does not encourage employee irresponsibility. Because of its own liability, the corporation spends resources to reduce or eliminate irresponsibility. Employees, therefore, have personal incentives to eliminate mistakes just as if they had personal financial liability for their assigned business decisions. Naturally, embezzlement or other illegal acts that enrich the employee directly are illegal in any organization, corporate or otherwise. The dispersion of share ownership acts also to reduce corporate misdemeanors, since shareholders can influence management by selling shares and placing downward pressure on stock prices.

$\mathbf{A}$ superficially plausible though naïve view of the corporation holds that the "corporate entity diffuses roles and decisions, discourages individual responsibility, and hence, encourages individual irresponsibility" [328: 64]. Even if corporations assign responsibility to a specific person, moreover, this naïve view maintains that individual employees can hide from the consequences of their actions behind the screen of the corporate persona. And, shareholders are so dispersed that they cannot effectively monitor management's actions.

On the one hand, some critics believe that because corporations are large, it is difficult to know who fails to monitor product safety or who decides to engage in illegal activities.

> In the old days when a butcher sold you bad meat from an animal he had bought, raised, slaughtered and prepared, the customer at least knew whom to blame. When a bridge collapses, so, usually, does the reputation of its engineer. But who exactly is to blame when a large corporation produces a dangerous drug, engages in political bribery, or tries to overthrow foreign countries? [328: 65]

On the other hand, these same critics assert, paradoxically, that corporations, in spite of their size, are able to shield culpable persons from bearing the consequences of their actions; the corporations rehire these people as consultants if they are forced to resign and reimburse them for any fines that the courts impose.

ACCOUNTABILITY OF INDIVIDUAL EMPLOYEES

Plainly, a corporation's customers may not know which worker is responsible for the faulty design of their cars' brakes, as they would the name of the butcher who sells them bad meat. But, they do know who is responsible for the faulty brakes: the corporation is responsible.

If the consumer cannot name the responsible person, does it follow that the employees of the corporation bear no penalty for irresponsible or even illegal acts? Only someone unaware of how corporations act would believe so. There are clear and purposive lines of authority within the corporation. Exactly because there are many employees, there are also formalized areas of responsibility. Just as employees want responsiblity to be well defined so that they can take credit for worthwhile innovations, so managers want responsibility well defined so that they can replace ineffectual employees. Individual employees are personally accountable to their superiors, even if they are not personally accountable to consumers.

Large organizations find it advantageous, also, to monitor continuously the quality of services that others provide to them. Manufacturers are liable for defective parts under warranty or for contract actions, even if they get the defective parts from subcontractors. The butcher, for instance, is liable for the bad meat sold even if the animal was raised and slaughtered and the meat prepared by someone else.

Indeed, the reduced costs of monitoring product quality and lower transaction costs make advantageous the *internal* organization of the corporation, as opposed to subcontracting in external markets [98]. Because a corporation exercises internal control, employees who impose greater costs than benefits on the firm (and therefore on the firm's customers) are soon discharged. Exercising care by monitoring production is, of course, costly [11]. An employee's failure to monitor that results in costs exceeded by the costs of not monitoring is employee "carelessness." No profit-maximizing firm tolerates employee "carelessness," and firms pay to identify employees who are "careless" in this sense. Firms also monitor employees for potentially illegal acts to preclude the likelihood of large damage claims [SB 18].

CORPORATIONS, NOT INDIVIDUALS, PAY THE FINES

Do corporate employees act irresponsibly because they do not bear the full costs of their actions? If the corporation pays for manufacturing mistakes or indemnifies employees for legal fines, perhaps the employees have no incentive to prevent safety hazards or act legally. But precisely because the corporation is liable, it expends resources to reduce or eliminate potential abuses. The corporation, taking on this duty in its own interest, thus protects the public from the aberrant, illegal acts of individual employees.

If corporation employees were personally financially liable for all their assigned business decisions, they would have to accept a degree of risk equal to that of partners in a partnership, but they would not receive the rewards to which partners are entitled for their risk-bearing activities [SB18]. Employees, in principle, could purchase insurance to cover the costs of consumer complaints and legal actions. But they would then demand higher salaries as compensation for the cost of their liability insurance premiums.

Employee insurance for business decisions is entirely feasible (it would be similar to accountants' malpractice insurance). That such insurance seldom is purchased indicates that it is less costly to shift the risk of bad business decisions to corporations that can monitor employee performance and that can buy insurance for this risk on better terms than can the individual employee. (A 1976 survey shows that 87 percent of the firms questioned provide insurance against directors' and officers' liability [247: 16, n. 31].) The corporation, because it is in a better position to monitor employee actions, can be more effective than an insurance company in eliminating "carelessness." There is little difference, therefore, between personal and corporate insurance. Hence, corporations that accept financial responsibility for their employees' actions are not part of an insidious arrangement.

If either employers or outside insurance companies indemnify employees against consumer complaints, what incentive do the employees have to avoid "carelessness"? Since firms replace "careless" employees with others who are less careless (that is, who impose lower costs on the firms), each employee must choose either to use the optimum amount of care or lose a job.

Corporate officers are sometimes criminally liable for actions they undertake for their firms. Officers of General Electric and Westinghouse, for example, served jail terms for their attempts at price-fixing. This is the kind of nontransferable penalty faced by anyone who commits a crime. One might argue that while the penalty for a given crime is the same whether the form of business organization is a corporation or a partnership, the rewards differ. Actually, there is less incentive for an officer of a corporation to commit illegal acts that increase the present value of the firm than there is for a sole proprietor or a partner in a partnership. The partner or proprietor who engages in legal or illegal actions shares directly in the value changes created by those actions. Corporate managers do not necessarily share the increased value they produce. But the criminal sanctions are the same in either case. This asymmetry implies that there is less of an incentive for illegal acts in corporations than in other forms of organization. Naturally, illegal acts, such as embezzlement, that enrich the employee directly are illegal in any organizational form.

SHAREHOLDER POWER IS TOO DISPERSED TO MONITOR THE "CARE" AND LEGALITY OF CORPORATE ACTIONS

The final aspect of this naïve view of corporations is that shareholders are "so diffused and divorced from genuine corporate control, (they) are far more likely to sell out their shares rather than throw out venal or inept management" [328: 64]. Selling the shares, however, places downward pressure on stock prices, which itself influences management [SB21]. Management salaries are positively related to equity market values [261]. Executives, therefore, knowing that the consequent decline in stock values affects their salaries and jeopardizes their jobs, are less likely to be careless or to act illegally [SB 55, SB 56].

ADDITIONAL READINGS: 115, 460.

3. Does the Corporation Operate without the Consent of Affected Citizens?

ROBERT THOMAS
Department of Economics
University of Washington

Editor's Summary Citizens, municipalities, and other institutions create over one-half of all pollution. Therefore, corporations are not the major cause of environmental problems. Most plants in basic industry are either in compliance with environmental standards or on a schedule to be in compliance, while less than one-half of the nation's municipalities will comply with the 1977 water quality regulations, and only one-half of the designated air quality regions are meeting the 1975 minimum standards. Nonmarket impacts like pollution are serious problems, and everyone causes them. These problems will be solved when the government replaces common property rights. Corporations and citizens will then have incentives to reduce nonmarket effects to acceptable levels.

Corporations historically received from the state certain privileges, such as limited liability, perpetual life, and equal protection under the laws [SB 27, SB 28, SB 29, SB 30]. Firms with these privileges were deemed to be useful. Corporations, too, had substantial freedom to act and to contract because of the *consensual* relationship they had with their customers. A consumer was free to choose whether or not to buy. The corporation could not force anyone to trade with it, and so all transactions were voluntary, both parties consenting freely.

POLLUTION AND VOLUNTARY CONSENT

This "consensual cornerstone," according to some, "has crumbled" [328: 63]. The giant corporation, they believe, often engages in activities that affect other persons without their consent. Chemicals, gases, and particulates foul the environment. A resident of a large city cannot choose not to breathe the air that the local factories of corporate giants pollute. The market activities of the giant corporation thus damage the resident without consent.

Nader et al. report that "industrial pollution today accounts directly for one-third of all solid waste, one-half of all air pollution, and more than one-half of total water pollution" [328: 18]. This finding is not surprising, considering the importance of industry in the United States economy. But it does lead one to ask what persons or institutions account for two-thirds of all solid waste, the other one-half of air pollution, and somewhat less than one-half of all water pollution. Are not these persons or institutions equally "guilty" of acts that have nonmarket impacts, that do not have the consent of affected persons? Clearly, the "guilt" is shared, and, just as clearly, the existence of giant corporations in and of itself does not create nonmarket impacts.

POLLUTION, PRIVATE CHOICE, AND COMMON PROPERTY

These impacts derive from the lack of constraints on *all* public and private economic decision makers. Persons, partnerships, and corporations pollute the environment because it is in their private interests to do so [239]. Consider, for example, a paper mill organized as a corporation [SB 1]. The mill bargains with its customers to determine the price of paper and the quantity to manufacture, and also to get the customers' consent to the exchange. The mill bargains also with labor and the owners of other productive inputs to get resources to produce paper. The mill must bargain with others because they own the resources required to produce paper.

The paper mill, however, need not bargain with the downstream users of an adjacent river to determine how much waste it dumps into the river during manufacture. The mill need not do so because the river is there for all to use. The mill owners need not bargain about pollution even if the waste they emit reduces the value of the river for recreation, for fishing, and for downstream water consumers, because the river is held legally as common property. Everyone has equal access to it; no one is excluded.

A similar case, not involving a corporation, develops when a driver decides to use an automobile instead of other means of transportation. The driver adds to the number of automobiles on the streets and expressways, increasing congestion without the consent of other drivers and thus increasing the possibility of automobile accidents, again without the consent of other drivers. The driver also contributes to air pollution, adding to the discomfort of other citizens and reducing property values in general. The personal use of the automobile is the greatest cause of air pollution in most metropolitan areas [192: 28]. The driver's case is like the mill owners' case in that a decision is made because of personal interests, and other people affected by the decision are not consulted.

The driver and the paper mill owners choose to pollute because it is in their personal interests to do so. And, it is their legal right to do so. They inherit, along with everyone else, the right to use resources such as rivers, streams, and the air. The legal right of equal access to a resource is termed a common property right. Common property rights are in sharp contrast with private property rights. Private property rights are exclusive rights granted to owners to enjoy what they own and to exclude others from using what they own. The owners may sell or transfer these rights to others. Under common property rights, everyone is equally entitled to use a resource; no one can be excluded from using it; hence, there is nothing over which to bargain. A person who wants to use a common property resource does not have to get the permission of other owners, as would be the case if the resource were held privately.

If a good is not scarce relative to the amount of demand for it, common property ownership does not result in substantial costs to society. But if a common property resource becomes scarce, people tend to overutilize it [208]. Overutilization seldom occurs if a resource is privately owned, since a potential user must first bargain with the owner to get permission to use it, just as the paper mill must first bargain with workers to get their labor to make paper.

PROPERTY RIGHT CHANGES CAN REDUCE POLLUTION

The problem of most nonmarket impacts stems not, as some suggest, from the existence of giant corporations but rather from the existence of resources that remain as common property. The ultimate solution to environmental problems *is not* to place more fetters on large corporations, which account for only some pollution. The solution *is* to eliminate the common property ownership of water and air.

Only the government, which is responsible for creating and enforcing property rights, can do this. The government has many alternatives for resolving nonmarket impacts. The government could grant individual citizens or institutions private property rights to resources now held as common property. Failing that, the government could declare these resources to be publicly owned and either limit access by imposing standards upon *all* users or charge each user in proportion to the damage done or the cost that the private use of the resources places on others.

The government can eliminate common property aspects simply by redefining the rights to the air and water and assigning to individual citizens or institutions private property rights over these resources. The new owners of these resources would require all potential users to bargain for the right to discharge a certain amount of waste products into the resources; they would allow those who are willing to pay the most the right to use the resources. The new owners would have the same incentives as the private owners of other resources and goods. These new owners would now have an incentive to use their assets optimally. In short, they must allow the optimal amount of pollution.

Alternately, the government could require that common property resources become publicly owned resources available only to users who meet certain standards. This is the route followed now in the United States. Economists, however, generally favor a third alternative: the imposition of an effluent charge. Each user of a resource would be charged for waste disposal according to the amount and relative harmfulness of the wastes discharged, balanced by the relative value of the goods produced. This method provides incentives for the resource user to reduce both the amount and harmfulness of the discharge. A National Academy of Science study for the National Commission on Water Quality estimates that concentrating abatement efforts where they cost the least, rather than uniformly everywhere, would save 40 percent in capital costs [*Fortune,* Nov. 1976: 284]. A system of effluent charges would do just that. This method works well in the Ruhr River Basin [240].

Whatever method we use, the solution to nonmarket impact problems lies in eliminating common property rights to resources, not in proposals to "tame" giant corporations. This property rights change is precisely what the tough Clean Air Act amendments of 1970 and the Water Pollution Control Act amendments of 1972 were intended to accomplish. And, to some extent, they worked. Nevertheless, the Environmental Protection Agency, which is responsible for enforcing these laws, meets stiff opposition—not just from industry but also from local municipalities. Less than one-half of the nation's municipalities will comply with the 1977 water quality regulations, and one-half of the designated air quality regions are violating the 1975 minimum standards. By contrast, 80 percent of the plants in basic industry are in compliance or are on schedule [13]. Hence, the main continuing source of nonmarket impacts is not industry or the giant corporation but the private citizen and the municipality in which the citizen lives.

CONCLUSION

Nonmarket impacts remain a serious economic and political problem in the United States. Their existence stems not from the existence of giant corporations but from the absence of appropriate property rights. The agents of government can solve the problem by specifying appropriate property rights. When they do, corporations and individual citizens alike will have an incentive to reduce significantly or to eliminate such impacts.

ADDITIONAL READINGS: 99, 140, 191.

4. Should Corporations Ignore Social Goals?

KENNETH CLARKSON

Law and Economics Center
University of Miami School of Law

Editor's Summary   Corporate decision makers, like everyone else, do the best they can in the face of existing laws and regulations. If the law fails to create or enforce a property right to water, air, or other scarce resources, for example, pollution results. Pollution is the result of rational decision making in the legal setting that government establishes. Tighter controls on corporate activities will result in increased consumer prices, diminished investment, and lower pay for workers.

Critics of corporations often claim that these organizations ignore, or even create through their activities, such undesirable outcomes as air and water pollution [328]. This claim accompanies the belief that corporations generally ignore social objectives by failing to contribute financially to charitable and other nonprofit organizations. To understand this claim, one must ask: What is the major purpose of a corporation? What aspects of corporations create these "undesirable" outcomes? Are there now adequate remedies to correct these outcomes? And, what are the costs and benefits of increased *corporate* attention to objectives such as reducing pollution and increasing charitable contributions?

THE VIRTUES OF CORPORATE ENTERPRISE

Corporations have emerged because the cost of conducting some exchange and production within an organization is lower than the cost of operating exclusively in the marketplace [SB 2]. Part of the lower cost derives from the advantages of assigning tasks to and monitoring the performance of many persons who contribute jointly to a firm's output [11, 98]. More importantly, the limited liability, equal protection, and perpetual life provisions of incorporation allow a firm to lower the costs of financing, producing, and marketing its products. The limited liability provisions, for example, permit an enterprise to offer a wider range of risk and rate-of-return financing options to potential investors. Perpetual life provisions encourage a firm to plan for the long term and to develop name brand identification, which lowers information costs to consumers. These and other provisions of incorporation make possible an improved environment for organizing production and conducting exchange.

BLAMING THE CORPORATION

Some people believe, however, that these same legal provisions of incorporation are the root of many of today's problems. They believe that corporations' incentives discourage or prohibit desirable actions. Existing common law, they maintain, is inadequate to alleviate these problems, especially the parts of common law that cover property and tort actions. Ostensibly in the interest of improving corporate performance, they have lobbied successfully for many new federal and state laws. The additional constraints in these statutes impose new rules and liabilities governing actions thought to have "social impacts." The National Environmental Policy Act of 1969, for example, imposes new constraints on both governmental and corporate decision makers. Administrative bodies, also, have received broader discretion to promulgate rules and regulations that have severe effects on decision makers in corporations and other business firms.

In spite of these constraints, there remain many harmful environmental consequences and a general lack of corporate activity to reduce them. A closer examination of the events that lead to such consequences reveals one plain phenomenon: the decision makers are operating systematically within the context of existing rules and regulations. Thus, in case after case, the lack of or inadequate enforcement of a property right to water, air, or other resources causes pollution. In the remaining cases, the polluting party has an explicit legal right to pollute. Even more startling is the extent to which this phenomenon goes beyond corporations and permeates all forms of organizations within every society. Municipal governments, for example, cause many of the most serious cases of pollution [*Platt Bros. & Co. v. City of Waterbury*, 72 Conn. 531, 45 A. 154; *City of Valparaiso v. Hagen, et al.*, 153 Ind. 337, 54 NE 1062]. Simple arithmetic reveals that persons and nonindustrial institutions are responsible for two-thirds of all solid waste and roughly one-half of the air and water pollution [328: 18].

In societies where the state owns all resources, one finds even more extensive damage to the environment and neglect of social problems. Thus, a comparison of pollution in the United States with pollution in the Soviet Union reveals that Soviet *public* firms cause more extensive damage than their *private* counterparts in the United States [191].

EXISTING REMEDIES

The problem, then, becomes one of identifying the alternatives or level of adequate remedies for reducing the undesirable consequences of corporate and noncorporate decision making. An examination of the common law reveals many situations in which public and private parties have access to the courts for constraining undesirable environmental and nonenvironmental actions. Such access may rest on the theories of negligence, absolute liability, trespass, inverse condemnation, or on the public trust doctrine. Administrative agencies or existing federal, state, or local statutory law or constitutional provisions also allow legal action. The existing common law and statutory law remedies for reducing undesirable actions have the added advantage of jurisdiction over both public and private institutions.

THE COST OF ADDITIONAL REMEDIES

These remedies, along with individual incentives, create the present pattern of private and public costs and benefits. How do these costs arise and benefits change if one adds even more laws and regulations? To answer this question, insofar as corporations are concerned, one must investigate the costs and benefits of increased corporate attention to "social" objectives. One can say little about the specific outcomes of increased corporate attention to these objectives unless one knows the preferences and constraints of the corporate decision makers who are responsible for actions that contribute to "social" objectives (such as reducing pollution and increasing gifts to charities) [SB 1].

Corporations, like other business organizations, are merely institutional arrangements that facilitate exchange and production among consumers, stockholders, and workers. Hence, the impacts on these parties of requiring corporations to increase social actions must be understood if one wishes to predict the additional costs of new laws and regulations.

Suppose, for example, that workers must bear part of the cost of diminished pollution and increased charity in the form of lower salaries. If workers are generally opposed to increasing the amount of resources for "social" objectives—if they would work elsewhere if their pay were reduced—one would expect that consumers would bear the cost of such diversions in the form of higher prices. And stockholders would bear the cost in the form of lower dividends and equity prices.

Plainly, overall investment will decline with increased constraints on corporate decision makers. Investors already have the alternative of placing their funds in the form of bonds, mortgages, real property, or other financial instruments of nonprofit organizations. Additional constraints will mean that less capital is available to corporations for investment in new productive activities. Since many existing corporate investments already yield external "social" *benefits,* the costs of decreased investment levels are evident. Several United States firms, for example, recently invested millions of dollars in developing deep-seabed mining techniques to reach the untapped riches of the ocean. In their search for new profitable ventures, these firms will yield substantial benefits to humanity in the form of lower costs for scarce resources.

One should recognize that stockholders and workers in corporations are likely to have lower returns and take-home pay if corporations must provide specific social outcomes. A potential result of lower returns is diminished voluntary contributions to private charitable organizations. Increased attention to social objectives by corporate decision makers also reduces the ability of noncorporate persons to reward the social organizations and activities they prefer most, since corporate decision makers will have greater control over the particular social objectives chosen.

A varied set of constraints and remedies for pollution and other problems is available under the current legal system. Furthermore, since one can finance social objectives with revenues from corporate taxes or volunteer contributions from stockholders or workers in corporations, there is little to be gained from imposing social objectives directly on the corporate decision-making process. The costs of such mandatory social engineering are likely to reduce economic activity significantly.

ADDITIONAL READINGS: 15, 20, 99, 140, 192, 208, 278, 283, 289, 318.

5. Are Corporations Undemocratic, Private Minigovernments?

ARLEEN LEIBOWITZ
The Rand Corporation

Editor's Summary   Is the analogy drawn between large corporations and governments legitimate? Some large corporations indeed may have larger budgets than some states. But this does not imply that it is desirable or feasible to make day-to-day corporate decisions by counting explicit votes from shareholders, workers, and consumers. Although shareholders may now vote on only the most important corporate issues, only a small minority vote at all. Since the costs of getting information to cast an informed vote exceed the value of that effort, it is easier for shareholders to register dissatisfaction with management decisions by selling their shares. Similarly, workers can withdraw their labor if their wages or working conditions are unsatisfactory. And unhappy consumers can refuse to buy a corporation's products.

The *political* view of the modern corporation draws an analogy between a corporation and a political system: shareholders are the citizens, directors are the legislators, and managers constitute the bureaucracy. This analogy pictures consumers, bondholders, and workers as disenfranchised citizens. This analogy is not new. Writing in 1932, Adolph Berle and Gardiner Means proclaimed that corporations are not run democratically by (or for) the shareholders [52, 284, 285, SB 17, SB 21]. The belief that corporations are political, rather than economic, organizations persists today and now includes popular demands to "enfranchise" workers, consumers, and shareholders.

These demands rest on the implication that since someone *believes* that the corporation is a political organization, this belief alone provides sufficient justification for the democratization of the corporation. Thus, since corporate activities affect employees, consumers, shareholders, directors, and managers, all these people should be able to vote on the corporation's activities. Judged by this standard of democracy, most modern corporations fail the test. No modern corporate management formally polls its employees or customers. Management seeks information from these persons through collective bargaining and market research. But present practices are not at issue here. The question is, rather: is it legitimate and useful to consider the corporation as a private minigovernment, and does corporate democracy require that all parties affected vote on all issues?

SHAREHOLDER VOTING AND THE POLITICAL ANALOGY

Some corporate democracy proponents seek to impose on shareholders a level of involvement characteristic of the traditional New England town meeting. There is a fundamental contradiction, of course, in the proposition that because some corporations are as big as states, they should be run like small towns! The New England town meeting, with its practice of participatory democracy, can work because there are few issues at stake, and because the voters are few in number, in close communication, and geographically localized. But even in small communities the town meeting is disappearing as a form of government; because of the complexities of the issues and the number of voters involved, it is more efficient for the voters to elect representatives who, in turn, reflect and vote on the complicated issues at hand.

Representative democracy, in which voters elect the persons who formulate policy, characterizes the governance of most corporations as well. Richard Posner emphasizes that the political metaphor in the phrase "corporate democracy" is appropriate because corporations already are representative democracies. "Voters do not manage the government, but political entrepreneurs can use the electoral process to wrest control from the incumbents and this possibility helps keep the incumbents on their toes" [356: 183].

This electoral process in government is similar to the system of governance in corporations, except that in corporations the market for corporate control is the "possibility" that "helps keep the incumbents on their toes." Proposals for shareholders to vote on product mix, prices, or a variety of other issues would impose a town meeting level of involvement on the shareholders. This level of involvement is as totally inappropriate for shareholders as it would be for the citizens of New York. It would be impractical, to say the least, to have the citizens of New York vote on zoning variances, building permits, and who should be hired by the fire department.

Viewed as citizens in a representative democracy, shareholders do seem extremely casual about exercising their existing voting rights. Most stockholders do not take the trouble to inform themselves about the issues, vote for directors, or attend annual meetings [SB 16, SB 17, SB 19, SB 22]. By abdicating their "responsibilities" in this way they allow power to be concentrated in the hands of management. To pursue the analogy, shareholders probably use the same benefit-cost calculations that citizens use in real world politics. Since 1932, only about 41 percent of the voting-age population has cast ballots in midterm congressional elections.

Proposals to reinvigorate corporate democracy would have little effect on voter participation because shareholders are content to retain the present managers as long as they are satisfied with their financial returns.

If they are not satisfied, it is cheaper for them to change stockholdings than to change managers. Stockholders can sell their shares. Henry Manne puts it thus:

> As shareholder dissatisfaction grows, there is no need for complicated and inefficient political paraphernalia. Market forces, working invisibly and automatically, provide the correct solutions. Dissatisfied shareholders will sell their shares, thereby lowering the market price of the company's shares. As that price declines to a crucial level, outsiders will find tremendous opportunity to make large gains by taking over the corporation and managing it efficiently [283: 535].

It is not so much that stockholders are *prevented* from taking an active role in the decision-making process of corporations as it is that they are *unwilling* to bear the costs of decision making [11]. One advantage of stock ownership is the ease with which an investor can diversify investments and redirect them among various corporations. Because of this diversification, no single investor is willing to spend great amounts of resources to make management decisions.

Enhanced shareholder decision making would not only impose costs on individual investors: it would also impose additional costs on each corporation. If all stockowners participated in the corporate decision-making process, large costs and substantial delays would result before a corporation could take any action at all. No stockowner would find it worthwhile financially to become well informed about the issues at hand, since the cost of being informed would be constant for stockowners regardless of the number of shares each owns. But, the losses a bad decision creates are spread over all corporate shareholders.

A much more practical method of control is to have a corporation's stockowners agree to transfer corporate decision-making power to a smaller group, which manages the corporation. The kinds of issues stockowners vote on reflect this delegation of authority. Typically, owners do not vote on the placement of a new plant, on the hiring and firing of workers, or on the amount spent on pollution control equipment. Rather, their decisions are limited to approval of the board of directors and to approval of mergers, consolidations, and dissolutions. Even so, very small proportions of stockowners vote on these issues, since for most stockholders the cost of acquiring enough information to make an informed vote exceeds the personal value of their individual efforts.

VOTING RIGHTS FOR OTHERS

Should bondholders, workers, or consumers have voting rights, or at least representation on a board of directors? Board members now have a single goal: to see that management maximizes the profitability of the firm over the long run. What goals should workers' directors, public directors, or bondholders' directors pursue? If these directors are to represent *their* constituencies, they must advocate goals favoring workers, the public, or bondholders. One can pursue such goals only at the expense of share-holders. The conflicting aims of an enlarged board of directors, elected by various constituencies, would lead to disputes, compromises, and vote-trading in the board room.

If boards of directors use voting in board meetings to arrive at deci-sions, there is a good possibility that the voting outcomes of *enlarged* boards will make no sense at all. Suppose, for example, that a board has three members—a stockholder representative, a labor representative, and a consumer representative—and that each has one vote. They are to vote on three proposals: A, B, and C. The stockholder representative prefers A to B and B to C. The labor representative prefers B to C and C to A. And the consumer representative prefers C to A and A to B. The stockholder and labor representatives combine against the consumer representative and vote for A over B. Hence, the board chooses A over B by a vote of 2 to 1. Similar calculations show that proposal B defeats proposal C by the same vote. But C also defeats A, which means that board voting is inconsistent: proposal A defeats proposal B; proposal B defeats proposal C; and proposal C defeats proposal A. There is no stability in this procedure.

Duncan Black and Kenneth Arrow show that this result is far more general than this brief example might imply [19, 54, 55]. In this case, majority rule leads to endless cycling. Further, if voter preferences vary in intensity, and if vote trading is prohibited, the gains of the winning majority can be less than the minority's losses [78].

Appointing directors for the various groups that corporate decisions affect may be impractical. But how then should these groups find repre-sentation? Mintz and Cohen argue, with regard to workers, that corporate government is "private government without the consent of the governed" [316: 22]. Workers, like consumers, however, are not the *subjects* of the corporation [SB 8]. Their position is more nearly analogous to that of another "state" engaged in commerce with the "corporate state." They can decide to engage in mutually beneficial exchange with the corporation if the terms of trade are satisfactory. And if the terms are not satisfactory, they can trade elsewhere. Through union bargaining power, workers can hope to get the best terms of trade possible. But there is no justification for voting rights similar to those of stockholders.

One purpose of stockholders' voting rights is to ensure that stockhold-ers receive in dividends a fair share of profits. Workers can withdraw their labor if their wages are too low. Consumers can refuse to buy a product if the price is too high. Stockholders, of course, have an analogous power over corporations: they can sell their shares. Recognition of this power leads some distinguished economists to question even the right of shareholders to vote. Alchian and Demsetz treat bondholders, owners of preferred and convertible preferred stock, and owners of common stock as simply different classes of investors [11]. These investors differ in their willingness to accept risk, in their beliefs about the size of a firm's future earnings, and in their certainty about those beliefs. Owners of common stock are merely more optimistic than bondholders about the prospects of a firm, and therefore they are willing to take a share of whatever profits materialize as compensation for advancing capital. Alchian and Demsetz ask why stockholders should be regarded as owners distinct in any sense from other financial investors, such as bondholders who receive a fixed return on their investment.

CONCLUSION

Complete and extensive shareholder voting on all management decisions is not the only (or least costly) method for shareholders to use to make known their dissatisfaction with management. Very few shareholders vote because the benefits to be gained are not worth the costs of becoming informed about the issues. It follows that workers and consumers, with even less at stake than shareholders, would be even less likely to vote in corporate elections. They have much more direct and less costly means of making their preferences known. And, their participation would substantially destabilize the useful governance of the corporation.

ADDITIONAL READINGS: 98, 116, 117, 287, 288, 289.

6. Do Multinational Corporations Escape Political Oversight?

DENNIS E. LOGUE
Amos Tuck School of Business Administration
Dartmouth College

Editor's Summary   Multinational corporations, like domestic firms, seek to maximize shareholder wealth, subject to economic and legal constraints. Hence, they are motivated to allocate resources in the most efficient manner. Although some critics believe that multinational corporations are beyond the reach of competitive market forces, that they misuse shareholders' funds, and that they consciously break laws, the evidence in support of these allegations is largely anecdotal. The theoretical arguments that multinationals do not create resource misallocations are tighter than the vague models of market imperfection implicit in the critics' beliefs. Policies to restrict multinational corporate activity are more likely to lead to inefficient resource allocations because mistaken government policies are less amenable to correction by natural market forces.

Multinational corporations generally are large multiproduct firms whose suppliers and customers are not contained entirely within the boundaries of any one country. Although most multinational corporations began as small businesses in the United States, are largely owned by United States investors, and are headquartered in the United States, several major firms are of Japanese and European origin. Despite the widely held traditional view that multinational corporations contribute to world economic prosperity, there is today a growing concern that these firms no longer adequately perform this useful function. Some critics see the multinational corporation as a power unto itself, too large to be disciplined by markets and too rich and powerful to be controlled effectively by most nation-states.

DISTORTION OF RESOURCE ALLOCATION

A common argument is that multinational corporations distort the domestic and international allocation of resources. Logically, this argument must rest on at least one of three presumptions. The first presumption is that multinational corporations are beyond the reach of competition. Hence, they can control market forces. The second presumption is that multinational corporations epitomize the problem of the separation of ownership and control in large firms. Hence, they misuse shareholders' funds [52,

SB 3, SB 5, SB 21]. The third presumption is that multinational corporations consciously and routinely violate the laws of their host countries. Evidence to support each of these presumptions is largely anecdotal. And anecdotes should not constitute the basis for policies with potentially broad implications.

Regarding the first presumption, there is little evidence to suggest that market forces fail to control multinational firms. In most instances, the products of multinational corporations have close substitutes, sold either by domestic firms or by other multinational corporations. Prices are not monopolistic, unless there is collusion among all the suppliers and potential suppliers of a particular product. This collusion is highly unlikely, if for no other reason than that international collusive arrangements that are not officially sanctioned are difficult to enforce [SB 53].

Regarding the second presumption, the possibility that dissident stockholder groups may take over publicly owned multinational firms and bring about a mass firing of managers serves generally as an adequate brake on management's disregard for stockholders' welfare. This threat limits the scope of unprofitable investments or excessive expenditures solely for the benefit of management.

Concerning the third presumption of illegalities, policing accompanies legislation in most countries. If any misallocation of resources occurs because of crimes, in principle the host nation can easily eliminate them.

MULTINATIONAL CORPORATIONS AND CURRENCY MANIPULATIONS

Another belief about multinational corporations is that they manipulate currencies, thus contributing to, or in some cases causing, international currency crises. Under fixed exchange rates, for example, as pressure mounts on the par value of a currency, corporations switch into or out of that currency depending upon the direction of the pressure. (The anecdote cited most often is the British devaluation of 1967. Prior to that many multinational corporations shed their sterling balances and even borrowed sterling for conversion into United States dollars or deutsche marks.) The general notion is that a multinational corporation has sufficient resources at its disposal to affect significantly the foreign exchange market. The notion may be true regarding small, developing countries, but it seems implausible when considering the major currencies.

Multinational corporations have a responsibility to their shareholders to maximize long-run profits. If the firms anticipate a major currency realignment, as was often the case under the Bretton Woods fixed exchange rate system, they have an obligation to do what is necessary to protect owners' assets from the adverse effects of exchange rate shifts.

Indeed, under a fixed rate system in which there is little risk of guessing wrong about the direction of any impending exchange rate change, there is justification for speculation in currency markets.

Currency fluctuations, however, whether with fixed or floating exchange rates, are less the result of a *multinational's* speculative buying and selling than of a *government's* pursuit of monetary and fiscal policies that are out of line with those of the rest of the world. To the extent that multinational corporations recognize the divergencies in domestic policies early and, through their actions, cause these divergencies to be reflected quickly in exchange rates, they are contributing to, rather than hindering, an efficient allocation of global resources: an allocation dependent upon a set of prices, including exchange rates, that reflects all economically relevant, available information.

To assert that multinational corporations consciously manipulate foreign exchange markets (temporarily move rates away from true equilibrium) requires the assumption that no one can profit by speculating against a multinational firm. If a multinational corporation begins to sell a currency with the expectation of forcing the rate down, encouraging other sellers, and then buying before the market pushes the rate back up to where it should be, it is assuming implicitly that it can fool the foreign exchange market. It is profitable to foreign exchange dealers, and indeed to many others, to keep from being fooled and to prevent such manipulation. Therefore, the belief that multinational corporations manipulate currencies makes little sense.

MULTINATIONAL CORPORATIONS AND DOMESTIC JOBS

Barnet and Müller, in their influential indictment of multinational corporations, *Global Reach,* provocatively title one chapter "The Obsolescence of American Labor" [36]. They present evidence suggesting that as United States corporations locate production facilities abroad, jobs shift from the United States to foreign lands. Firms engaged in maximizing shareholder wealth will produce widgets in Barbella instead of Indiana if it is more profitable to do so. Those who are involved in the domestic production of widgets will find themselves unemployed, at least in the short run. The permanent loss of domestic jobs is a popular belief of organized labor in the United States, and, not surprisingly, the suggested remedy is the enactment of strict controls on direct foreign investment.

Evidence and arguments are not lacking on the other side, however. A recent survey by Business International offers support for the position that United States investment abroad creates jobs here [*Commercial and Financial Chronicle,* 10 May 1976: 23]. But volumes of evidence on jobs miss the real point that available capital should be put to its most efficient use. If the combination of foreign labor and United States capital results in the least-cost method of producing a particular good, that allocation is an efficient one. The returns from the employed capital, moreover, accrue to the capital-exporting country. Hence, the United States really does not lose.

Paradoxically, if capital were not put to its most efficient use but, rather, were employed so as to maximize domestic employment, that assuredly would constitute an inefficient allocation of resources. Indeed, it might lead to further distortions of resource allocations, such as those that accompany import restrictions to protect internationally inefficient industries.

MULTINATIONAL CORPORATIONS AND TAX AVOIDANCE

A third argument concerning multinational corporations is that they practice wholesale tax avoidance by shifting profits among countries so as to minimize their effective tax burdens. This practice, however, may not create distortions. Recall that it is desirable that multinational firms maximize shareholder wealth. Promoting shareholder interests requires that tax payments be as low as legally possible. That a particular government loses tax revenues does not imply that a misallocation of resources exists; it means, simply, that the government must either spend less or convince the international capital markets that the projects it wishes to undertake are worthwhile economically so that it may borrow to finance them. If it cannot make the case for borrowing, its *lost* tax revenues contribute to, rather than detract from, the efficient international allocation of resources.

Another aspect about taxes is worth considering. There are many countries with onerous tax burdens. If multinational firms could not escape the full burden, they might never make initial investments. A country could then be worse off than if it could impose its complete tax burden. And the country would impose that burden on a much lower investment base.

MULTINATIONAL CORPORATIONS AND DOMESTIC DEVELOPMENT

A fourth belief about multinational corporations is that they often invest in less-developed countries, bid up the prices of capital and labor, and thus make it impossible for those countries to undertake infrastructure investments in roads, schools, and dams. Once again, if these projects are economically worthwhile to a country as a whole, funds for them should be available from international markets.

Indigenous factors of production, notably labor, tend to find employment in their highest-valued uses. If domestic workers can earn higher wages on the payroll of a multinational corporation, preventing those workers from doing so or paying higher wages than a project merits constitutes not an efficent use of resources but a distortion of the kind that should be eliminated.

A second aspect of this argument about multinational corporations is their lack of environmental concern. As in the case of pollution by purely domestic firms, so with multinationals: there is no basis for suggesting that the prevailing legislation, the political reflection of how much a country is willing to pay for clean air and clean water, is routinely ignored [SB 3, SB 4]. Further, if firms did more than was legally necessary, that excess would be contrary to shareholder wealth maximization and efficiency, just as any investment made solely for management's sake would be.

MULTINATIONAL CORPORATIONS AND BRIBERY

As recent hearings in the United States Senate make all too clear, some multinational corporations have engaged systematically in the bribery of foreign officials. While bribery is not to be condoned, bribery *per se* is not evidence of a misallocation of resources [SB 14].

Bribery tends to be a response to nonmarket allocation situations. In New York and other cities, for example, where a large portion of available rental housing is under rent control programs that keep the rental prices lower than they would be in a free market, it is not unusual for a prospective renter to pay a rental agent "key money" to get to the top of a waiting list. Paying key money is a rational response to exchange in a controlled market. The person for whom an apartment has the greatest value ultimately gets the use of the apartment by paying key money. An efficient allocation of resources results.

In transactions with governments, in which the decisions to purchase goods or services or allow particular kinds of activities often are highly political, the scope for capricious decision making is great. Bribery is a rational response to this capriciousness. If firms compete among themselves with their bribes, the producer with the lowest costs will normally be able to offer the highest bribe. Awarding a contract to this producer constitutes an efficient allocation of resources, not a distortion, even though bribery is clearly unethical.

MULTINATIONAL CORPORATIONS AND "TARIFF FACTORIES"

Also at issue in the international allocation of resources by multinational corporations is the existence of what Yeager and Tuerck refer to as "tariff factories" [463]. The willingness of corporations to invest in different nations fosters competition for investment capital among countries. Some countries offer highly concessionary tax breaks while others declare their desire to protect their domestic markets for foreign firms with domestic production facilities by adopting highly restrictive import policies. If multinational corporations respond to these kinds of policies, they are acting in the interest of their shareholders. Of course, competition to attract investment may result in a distortion in the allocation of resources among countries. But it is erroneous to blame the multinationals for this phenomenon. They *respond* to national policies; they do not *make* them.

The concern for tariff factories, however, raises a much broader question. Individual countries, even when they are not competing for investment, intentionally often pursue policies that distort domestic resource allocation relative to the international economy. Trade and tax policies ultimately might have this effect. That multinational corporations take advantage of such differences seems to be less a cause for concern than if they did not. As nominal differences among countries are exploited, moreover, there is a tendency to equalize the real effects of these policies across countries. This equalization tends to promote the efficient international allocation of resources.

CONCLUSION

The evidence about the effect of multinational corporations on the domestic and international allocation of resources is mixed. The theoretical arguments in support of the view that multinational corporations do *not* cause a misallocation of resources seem, however, to be tighter than the vague models of market imperfection implicit in arguments to the contrary. Unfortunately, policies that would hamper the activities of multinational corporations are now being considered at the United Nations and in other international organizations. Ill-conceived official policies, however, are much less likely to yield economically efficient allocations of resources than any set of private decisions, largely because resulting misallocations will be considerably less amenable to correction through natural market forces.

ADDITIONAL READINGS: 135, 451.

7. Do Corporations Violate Employees' Civil Rights

THOMAS E. BORCHERDING
Department of Economics
Simon Fraser University

Editor's Summary   People considering employment positions in which their civil rights will be restricted can weigh the benefits and costs of such actions. The common law assumes that an employee is competent to trade a "bill of rights" for a "bill of goods" on advantageous terms. Monitoring employees on the job curbs the tendency to reduce work effort, promotes increased productivity, and leads to higher returns for employees and the corporation. An employee bill of rights that curtailed the amount of monitoring below the optimum would result in lower productivity, wages, and profits. Competitive product and labor markets and vigorous markets for corporate control are the best guarantees that employees will not trade their rights without adequate compensation.

Corporate employers, according to recent critiques, violate with impunity the civil rights of their employees. Corporations dismiss employees without due process and for capricious reasons, including eccentric hairstyles, unacceptable personal life-styles, and radical political utterances. Corporations violate employees' rights to privacy by searching lockers, by paying other employees to inform on their fellows, by engaging detectives to pry into employees' work and into employees' private lives, and by requiring polygraph examinations.

ONE VIEW OF CORPORATION-EMPLOYEE RELATIONS

Nader, Green, and Seligman argue that the modern "giant" corporation is a social behemoth analogous to a "giant" government [SB 8]. "By employing thousands of individuals, it possesses the power to rule them. It can establish employment rules restricting their conduct; grant or withhold financial rewards otherwise unavailable; or effectively destroy the career of a specialist in a monopoly or near monopoly industry" [328: 181]. They believe that such power must be controlled. Otherwise, "How can a Constitution, which fully restrains all levels of political government from invading the rights of citizens, *then* permit *every* business corporation to do so [328: 181; emphasis added]?"

Since the Supreme Court generally has not seen fit to limit how a corporation uses its property in the area of employee civil rights, Nader, Green, and Seligman urge that Congress step in to curb what they believe are abuses of corporate power [328: 183]. "It makes no meaningful difference to those who lose their 'inalienable' rights to freedom of speech or due process of law that they were victimized by a giant corporation rather than by a giant government. In either case the purpose of the Constitution has been frustrated, and the Bill of Rights reduced to a bill of goods" [328: 183].

These authors present several examples of alleged abuses, based on specific actions of "giant" corporations, to substantiate their accusations. One example is that of a Lockheed employee who was demoted for publicly decrying gross inefficiencies associated with supplying the C-5A transport plane [328: 184]. A second instance is afforded by Vance Packard's interviews with executives in two major private investigation firms. These interviews assured him that at least one-fifth of the labor force was, at the time of his study, subject to surveillance by means of peepholes, hidden microphones and cameras, one-way mirrors, and other snooping devices [328: 188]. A third datum is that 80 percent of the largest corporations subject job seekers to tests that require them to reveal reading habits, their relationship to parents and friends, sexual preferences, their degree of marital fidelity, and the like [328: 186]. Polygraph tests are commonly administered to job seekers to detect whether they have "tendencies" toward dishonesty, homosexuality, dangerous habits, gambling, the keeping of mistresses on the side, and so forth [328: 186–188].

Nader, Green, and Seligman believe that management has two motives that explain these intrusions. The first motive, which they seem to dismiss with little comment, is the need to assess a person's honesty, reliability, loyalty, habits, responsibility, emotional stability, and ability to interact well with others [328: 186–191]. The second motive is the desire of managers to run the "giant" corporation in their own interests, not in the interests of the stockholders. The strategies the managers choose to please themselves without maximizing shareholder wealth often take the form of the pursuit of idiosyncratic political and social preferences [328: 193–194].

AN EMPLOYEE BILL OF RIGHTS

Nader, Green, and Seligman, therefore, wish to extend the protection that the Constitution's Bill of Rights and civil rights laws provide to the relationship between employer and employee. Hence, they urge that a federal chartering act require a corporation—in every "transaction, practice, or occurrence" with its employees—to preserve the employees' civil rights as enumerated in the Bill of Rights, to respect the employees' rights to privacy, and completely to avoid discrimination on the basis of race, color, religion, or sex [328: 194–195].

To understand how the Employee Bill of Rights might operate, consider a firm and the case of one of its employees who communicates information to the firm's board of directors, or to some arm or agency of government, about unethical, or possibly illegal, company actions. Currently such a "whistle blower" can be fired. Under the Employee Bill of Rights, the employee would have the right to sue for reinstatement, and the government agency charged with supervising the Employee Bill of Rights could act in this employee's behalf.

Briefly, there are other alleged abuses that the Employee Bill of Rights might correct. Mandatory polygraph tests would become illegal. Hidden cameras and microphones would be proscribed. Preemployment testing that digs into a person's private life would be subject to restraint. An employee's personnel files, containing reports and references, would be open to the employee's scrutiny. Discrimination would be prohibited, and rights would be defined broadly enough to ensure that federal actions would not be unduly limited. Monetary damages could be assessed against corporate violators, and injunctive relief could be used to halt certain proscribed practices. A court could order a corporation to pay an injured employee's legal fees, and it could have the responsible executives or employees transferred, or even dismissed.

THE PROBLEM OF CORPORATE OWNERSHIP AND CONTROL

Do alleged abuses of employee civil rights make any sense at all, or are they indeed the result of a "separation" of corporate ownership and control? To answer this question, one must investigate the separation hypothesis as first proposed by Berle and Means [52]. They argue that in a very large corporation with widely held shares, stockholders' detection of waste is very unlikely, since few shareholders have an incentive to acquire the relevant information. Furthermore, the shareholders' ability to alter management's negligent policy and move it in the direction of more efficient courses of action is limited for the same reason: wide dispersion of ownership.

What Berle and Means fail to consider, however, is specialization of ownership [SB 1, SB 2, SB 5, SB 21]. Since shares are freely transferable, comparative advantage dictates that among the owners a nonnegligible fraction can critically assess the performance of a corporation's management.

There are two factors that serve as severe constraints on managerial incompetence and on the pursuit of non-wealth-oriented ends. The first is the transferability of a corporation's stock. The second is the presence of informed specialists whose business it is (and whose fortunes depend upon their ability) to assess the actual and potential prospects of a firm under its existing or alternative management. If specialists agree, even implicitly, that a corporation's performance is substandard, the price of the firm's stock declines. Note, however, that a profit accrues to the group that owns stocks, fires the incompetents, and brings in more efficient managers. The tender offer, proxy fight, and merger are just three important tools that aid this market in corporate control and ensure that management is concerned with stockholders' well-being, that is, with the maximization of shareholder wealth.

Internally, stock options, bonuses, and profit sharing act as "carrots" to encourage corporate management to maximize shareholder wealth, and they complement the external "stick" of the market for corporate control. Just as important, competition for managerial positions within a firm ensures that those willing to offer the most managerial competence for a given salary and amenities get the right to "control" the corporation. A good "track record" in terms of the profitability of a division or section is a valuable asset for a corporate manager; it ensures greater viability for the manager in the struggle to get and keep superior-level positions [SB55, SB56]. Thus, it is safe to assume that corporate policy is best characterized as the pursuit of shareholder wealth. (Dramatic empirical proof of this assertion is not yet available. But conditions are propitious for such a direction of corporate policy and decidedly unfavorable for those who wish a firm not to maximize shareholder wealth.)

EMPLOYEE RIGHTS AND SHAREHOLDER WEALTH

It follows from the preceding discussion that managers who wish to remain managers must consider their "abuses" of employees' civil rights in economic terms. If it is sensible in wealth-maximizing terms for a manager to worry about certain aspects of an employee's character and actions on or off the job, even if the firm is not interested in politics, morals, or social matters, the manager will do so.

The reasons for this concern are obvious. First, an employee is associated contractually with a firm, but the contract is necessarily more implicit than explicit. No written document could possibly cover all the contingencies of future work life. Nor would such completeness be desirable, even if it were possible to prepare such a lengthy document, for it would be difficult for management to try to monitor each and every specified dimension. Given this contractual difficulty, shirking, chiseling, and slacking are ever present options for a less scrupulous employee [11]. On the other hand, an employee who is team-spirited, loyal, trustworthy, honest, responsible, diligent, discrete, and able to "get along" is more valuable for certain jobs than one who lacks these qualities. The ability to seek out these desirable qualities is beneficial to both a firm *and* the employee who has them [270].

Second, other methods such as clandestine security measures, polygraph tests, and locker searches ensure that those dimensions of the contract that management *can* monitor to prevent chiseling, negligence, and theft will be monitored efficiently. Monitoring also ensures a higher productivity of labor and again raises the returns to both the corporation and the employee [11, SB 2].

People who are considering corporate positions in which their civil rights might be restricted can weigh the benefits and costs of such actions. The common law, on the whole, has seen fit to assume that the employee is competent to make this calculation and trade a "bill of rights" for a "bill of goods" on advantageous terms. Only in those cases in which employees disagree with, and are not compensated for, intrusion on their privacy or the taking of their civil rights by a firm do the courts come in to relieve them.

One anecdote, attributed to Steven Cheung, compels the conclusion that if management did not perform a monitoring function, employees might provide it for themselves. The anecdote reports that in pre-Maoist times, along a particular stretch of river in China, boats were dragged by a very large gang of coolies. A visitor noticed that the gang's overseer was going up and down the line, beating some of the men with a whip. The visitor protested to his host about this cruelty but was quickly informed that the enterprise was a cooperative effort of all the coolies. *They* had hired the overseer to look out for shirkers [307].

The Employee Bill of Rights, counter to the common law tradition, implies that the individual employee is incompetent to sell (or rent) civil rights because of ignorance or deception and that perhaps a sale somehow violates the rights of others. Nader, Green, and Seligman do not offer evidence for either of these implications; nor will they be able to do so in the great majority of real world cases, since the takings voluntarily are agreed upon and involve no losses to third parties.

In the particular cases in which abuses are associated with ignorance, deception, or losses to third parties, the courts are not reluctant to act. The Marsh case decision, which permitted the distribution of religious

literature in a company town against the wishes of the owning corporation, is such a judicial incursion [*Marsh v. State of Alabama,* 326 U.S. 573
(1944)]. That the court is reluctant to apply the Marsh decision without
care reflects its belief that one should not interfere with the contractual
relationship between corporation and employee without evidence of overwhelming social purpose.

One consequence of the Employee Bill of Rights is that the real
productivities, and hence wages, of employees must fall, since information
ascertaining their true "tastes" will be lacking, or certain formerly agreed
upon constraints on their actions will be prohibited. Furthermore, the
prices of the products they produce will rise. The consumption of goods
produced by the private and public noncorporate sectors will increase,
since these sectors are not covered by the Employee Bill of Rights. The
demand for labor not subject to Employee Bill of Rights constraints will
also grow. One should examine these unconsidered consequences in
greater detail before supporting the Employee Bill of Rights. After such a
study, it may well appear that certain abuses of civil rights are not fully
compensated by offsetting gains to employees or to other third parties.
These losses ought then to be handled by specific legislative acts, not by
the meat-ax approach of the Employee Bill of Rights.

A competitive, efficient product and labor market and a vigorous
market for corporate control and managerial positions are the best guarantees that the civil rights of all parties will not be abused or taken without
adequate compensation. This concept presupposes, however, a certain
intelligence and perception on the part of employees, employers, and
shareholders. If that intelligence is lacking, how can we expect the citi-
zenry, the very same people, to monitor efficiently the actions of politicians and bureaucrats who supposedly will guard their rights? Examining
the conditions of employment in a "giant" corporation seems a far easier
task than finding out what a legislator or administrator is doing or will do
to improve conditions and what improvements will really cost.

The Bill of Rights was designed to protect the individual citizen from
abuse by a government that was otherwise deemed likely to indulge in
such abuse. This protection was based upon a theory of state action that
recognized that "interest" and "faction," not social costs and benefits,
make up the stuff of political life. When the Bill of Rights becomes
obsolete because consummate innovations in social engineering have
made governments responsive to individual citizens as persons, not just as
members of crucial coalitions, the time for the Employee Bill of Rights will
have come. Of course, it will be totally unnecessary then, but it will at least
do no harm.

ADDITIONAL READINGS: 3, 24, 282, 284, 285.

8. Is an Employee Bill of Rights Needed?

DONALD L. MARTIN
Law and Economics Center
University of Miami School of Law

Editor's Summary   Corporations are accused of being tyrannical
industrial governments that tread on their employees' civil liberties.
But, the industrial democracy analogy surely is false. The Bill of Rights
in the United States Constitution protects citizens from government's
tyrannical, but otherwise legitimate, use of force. These rights are
important, since the costs of avoiding force or switching citizenship are
extraordinarily high. But corporations have no such powers; the costs
of fleeing one firm for another in response to unacceptable working
conditions are relatively low. The absence of workplace civil liberties
identical to those in the United States Constitution is not the result of
corporate tyranny. Observed differences among firms are the result of
mutually beneficial arrangements among employers and employees,
negotiated arrangements that improve both productivity and
employee earnings.

The perception of the corporation as an industrial form of government
in which management plays the role of the governor and labor the role of
the governed has been particularly popular since the end of World War
II. "Industrial democracy" has been the slogan of the labor movement in
the industrial relations community. This analogy has recently given rise to
demands for an "Employee Bill of Rights" [328: 180–197]. Such a bill
would guarantee the worker the same *due process* that the Constitution
guarantees the citizen. It would protect the worker from the arbitrary and
inequitable exercise of managerial discretion [SB 7].

WHERE THE INDUSTRIAL DEMOCRACY ANALOGY FALTERS

But, the industrial democracy analogy surely must be false. Two important considerations obviate it. First, a crucial distinction between government at any level and private economic organization, corporate or otherwise, is the right entrusted to government to exercise legitimate and
reasonable force in its relations with its citizens. Second, the cost to a
citizen of switching affiliation between governments is far greater than the
cost to an employee of switching affiliations between firms. Since governments will surely violate public trust through their police powers, and

since the costs to citizens of changing leaders or residences are relatively high, citizens will seek institutions to insulate themselves from the arbitrary and exploitative use of such powers by their elected and appointed representatives. These institutions include the first ten amendments to the United States Constitution (the Bill of Rights) and the Fourteenth Amendment (guaranteeing due process).

THE PROBLEM OF THE MONOPSONISTIC LABOR MARKET

Something close to an analogous use of exploitative power in the private sector occurs in the world of monopsonistic labor markets. In those labor markets, would-be employees have few, if any, alternative job opportunities, either because of an absence of immediate competitive employers or because of the presence of relatively high costs of moving to available job alternatives in other markets. With few or no job alternatives, workers are more likely to be the unwilling subjects of employer prejudice, oppression, and personal discretion than if labor market competition prevails.

No one would claim that the American economy is completely free of monopsony power. There is not a shred of evidence, on the other hand, that such power exists in the large American corporation of today. Indeed, there is impressive evidence to suggest that monopsony is not likely to be found in large, private corporations. Robert Bunting's examination of labor market concentration throughout the United States among large firms, for example, finds that employment concentration (measured by the fraction of total employees in a geographic area who are employed by the largest reporting firm in that area) is related inversely to labor market size, while firm size is correlated positively with labor market size [79, 80].

It is well known that monopsonistic powers reside in the collusive owners of professional sports teams, precisely because these powers are exempt from antitrust laws in the United States [332]. Professional sports firms, however, do not number among the large corporations at which "Employee Bill of Rights" proposals are directed.

Interestingly, monopsonistic power in the labor market may be a significant factor at the local government level. Evidence of monopsony exists in such fields as public education, fire and police protection, and nursing [132].

THE NATURE OF EMPLOYER-EMPLOYEE AGREEMENTS

The Constitution of the United States does not extend the Bill of Rights and the due process clause of the Fourteenth Amendment to the private sector unless agents of the latter are performing public functions [*Marsh v. State of Alabama,* 66 S. Ct. 276 (1946)]. Instead of interpreting this limitation as an oversight of the founding fathers, the preceding discussion suggests that the distinctive treatment accorded governments reflects the conscious belief that market processes, more than political processes, yield a degree of protection to their participants that is closer to levels that those participants actually desire. It also suggests that this inherent difference justifies the institutionalization of civil liberties in one form of activity (political) and not in the other form (market).

This interpretation is consistent with the repeated refusal of the United States Supreme Court to interfere with the rights of employers and employees (corporate or otherwise) to make mutually agreeable arrangements concerning the exercise of civil liberties (otherwise protected under the Constitution) on the job or in connection with job-related activities. (The obvious legislative exceptions to this generalization are the Wagner Act of 1935 and the Taft-Hartley Act of 1947. These acts proscribe the free speech rights of employers with regard to their possible influence over union elections on their own property, while allowing labor to use that same property for similar purposes.)

In the absence of monopsonistic power, the substantive content of an employer-employee relationship is the result of explicit and implicit bargaining that leaves both parties better off than they would be if they had not entered into the relationship. That both are better off follows because each is free to end the employment relationship at will—unless, of course, contractual relationships specify otherwise. Americans have demonstrated at an impressive rate a willingness to leave current employment for better pecuniary and nonpecuniary alternatives. During nonrecessionary periods, employee resignations contribute significantly to turnover statistics. In an uncertain world, the workers who resign generate valuable information about all terms and conditions under which firms and would-be employees can reach agreement.

THE COSTS OF WORKPLACE CIVIL LIBERTIES

If information about each party to employment and information about potential and actual performance are costly, both firms *and* employees seek ways to economize. Indeed, the functions of a firm, from the viewpoint of employees, are to screen job applicants and to monitor on-the-job activities. A firm's final output is often a result of the joint efforts of workers rather than a result of the sum of the workers' separate efforts. This jointness of production makes individual effort difficult to measure, and on-the-job shirking becomes relatively inexpensive for any given employee. The reason is precisely that all employees must share the cost of one employee's "goldbricking." As a consequence, shirking, if done excessively, threatens the earning opportunities of other workers. Other white collar crimes, such as pilfering finished products or raw materials, have similar consequences [SB 7].

To protect themselves from these threats, workers use the firm as a monitoring agent, implicitly authorizing it to direct work, manage tools, observe work practices and other on-the-job employee activities, and discipline transgressors. If employers function efficiently, the earnings of workers will be higher than if the monitoring function were not provided [11].

Efficient *employer* activities, however, may appear to others, including some employees, to be flagrant violations of personal privacy from the perspective of the First, Fourth, Fifth, and Ninth Amendments to the Constitution. These employer activities, on the contrary, are the result of implied agreements between employers and employees, consummated by demand and supply forces in the labor market. The reduction in personal liberty that workers sustain in a firm has a smaller value for them, at the margin, than the increase in earning power that results. Thus, limitations on personal liberty in a firm, unlike such limitations in governments, are not manifestations of tyranny; they are, instead, the product of a mutually preferred arrangement.

It should not be surprising that higher-paying firms and firms entrusting more valuable decision-making responsibility to some employees would invest relatively more resources than would other firms in gathering potentially revealing information about the qualifications of prospective employees and about the actions of existing employees. Since the larger a firm is, by asset size or by employee number, the more likely it is to be a corporation, it should also not be surprising that corporations are among the firms that devote relatively large amounts of resources to gathering information of a personal nature about employees.

Prohibiting the gathering of such information by superimposing an "Employee Bill of Rights" on the employment relationship has the effect of penalizing a specific group of employees. This group is composed of those persons who cannot otherwise compete successfully for positions of responsibility, trust, or loyalty because the high cost of information makes it unprofitable for them to distinguish themselves from other workers without desirable job characteristics. Thus, federal protection of the civil liberties of employees in the marketplace may actually harm those who wish to waive such rights as a less expensive way of competing.

Under an "Employee Bill of Rights," the process of searching for new employees and the process of managing existing employees are relatively more costly for an employer. This greater cost will be reflected not only in personnel policy but also in the cost of producing final outputs and in the prices consumers pay for them. An effect of an "Employee Bill of Rights" would be limited dimensions on which employees may compete with each other. Although there are precedents for such limitations (for example, federal minimum wage laws), it is important to recognize that this kind of protection may have unintended effects on the welfare of large numbers of employees. The anticompetitive effects of institutionalizing due process and civil liberties have long been recognized by trade unions. These effects constitute an important reason for the interest unions have in formalizing the procedures employers use in hiring, firing, promoting, demoting, rewarding, and penalizing union employees. It is false to argue, nevertheless, that an absence of formal procedures and rules in non-unionized firms is evidence that workers are at the mercy of unfettered employers, or that workers are more likely to be exploited if they are located in corporations rather than in noncorporate forms of organization.

Even the most powerful corporations must go to an effectively competitive labor market for their personnel. Prospective employees see arbitrary and oppressive personnel policies as relatively unattractive working conditions requiring compensation of pecuniary and nonpecuniary differentials over and above what they would receive from alternative employments. Those workers who want more certainty in the exercise of civil liberties pay for that certainty by forgoing these compensating differentials. This reasoning suggests that the degree of desired democracy in the labor market is amenable to the same forces that determine wages and working conditions. There is neither evidence nor persuasive arguments that suggest that workers in large corporations somehow have been excluded from the process that determines the degree of democracy they want.

ADDITIONAL READINGS: 24, 460.

9. Are Corporations Indifferent to Worker-Job Alienation?

DOUGLAS K. ADIE
Department of Economics
Ohio University

Editor's Summary   If production process complexity and organization size cause worker alienation, the corporation, *per se,* is not responsible for it. Employees seek both monetary wages and job satisfaction. An employee must trade off one for the other under any system of economic organization. Opportunities for better pay *and* better working conditions are exploited quickly in a free and open labor market. Consequently, as long as workers are mobile and willing to change jobs in response to changes in the trade-off between financial compensation and job satisfaction, they will switch to positions that are most satisfactory to them personally. Indeed, the free and open competition among employers for workers and the competition among workers for jobs is the mechanism that generates the best available mix of pay and job satisfaction.

Authors, both ancient and modern, have commented on alienation. Adam Smith and J. B. Say, among the ancients, decried the harm done to workers by minutely specialized tasks [402: 734–735, 373: 98]. More recently, Erich Fromm, Robert Tucker, and Daniel Bell have blamed the modern corporation for the assembly-line processes causing worker-job alienation [179: 43–58, 441: 234–243, 41: 335–368]. Everyone, however, faces these problems to some degree. The typing pool secretary, the waiter or waitress at McDonald's, the auto mechanic, the insurance agent, and the government-employed teacher all believe at times that they have no power over the process in which they operate. Almost everyone, depending on personality, fails to perceive the coherent pattern of cause in a job. Adam Smith's pin factory, however, is not a corporation, and not all workers who experience alienation work for corporations.

ALIENATION AND THE CORPORATION

What is the additional potential for alienation for which the corporation is responsible? The two aspects of the corporation singled out as sources of alienation are, first, technological processes requiring specialization of functions and, second, hierarchical managerial control requiring centralized decision making. While Ernest Mandel and Stephen Marglin blame the hierarchical form of control, Louis Hacker and Yale Brozen blame the development of technology [202: 71–72, 76: 541]. Marglin and Mandel contend that the purpose of specialization is to subjugate the worker rather than increase efficiency [293: 72, 274: 159–172]. Smith, however, notes the increased efficiency of specialization despite the iniquitous effect on workers; so, the belief that the intent of specialization is merely to subjugate workers hardly seems justified [402].

Alienation is not caused solely by the corporate form of organization in a free enterprise system. Production processes in the Soviet Union produce the same result. Critics of the corporate system advocate the Yugoslav labor-managed firm in which workers control production and determine the technological and social organization of the work process through an elected workers' council. Since policy decisions are made through voting, however, a minority of workers in each firm are forced to accept policies they do not like. Since the labor-managed firm tends to restrict employment, moreover, there is little mobility and little information about existing employment opportunities. Alienation apparently exists also in the Yugoslav system in which workers "own" the residual and can contract, determine rates and the quality of output, set levels of employment and investment, and hire and fire [182: 228–234, 183: 196–197, 223].

SOLUTIONS TO THE ALIENATION PROBLEM

There is agreement among critics and supporters of the corporate system concerning the damaging effects of alienation on workers. The loss of control over the work environment and the depersonalization of jobs leave many workers ripe subjects for psychiatric help. The repetitive performance, under seemingly arbitrary circumstances, of minute functions having vague goals can lead not only to frustration but also to decreases in productivity. Centralized organizational forms can cause workers to have attitudes that are less conducive to further productivity advances; they can create low morale and diminished incentives.

Is there a solution to the problem of alienation short of reversing technological developments? Modern technology *can* "rehumanize" the work process. Instead of turning skilled artisans into cogs in a machine, new techniques substitute machines for workers in the performance of repetitive tasks. Since these techniques require skilled engineers to manage and repair machines, they put more decision-making responsibility into the hands of workers and increase the workers' directing roles. New administrative methods that increase responsibility and the importance of jobs can also increase productivity, since workers' attitudes are important for productivity.

J. D. Elliott of Detroit Edison believes that "output takes a wallop unless the worker gets a kick out of his job." Detroit Edison reduced office costs by making clerical jobs more complicated, less repetitive, and more interesting. At Lincoln Electric, increasing opportunities for initiative through decentralization had the effect of raising productivity [76: 541]. Corporations such as General Electric, Allis-Chalmers, and Sylvania have replaced giant plants employing tens of thousands of workers with scattered plants employing a few hundred workers. General Motors and Sears, Roebuck and Company have given more decision-making power to division managers. Suggestion systems and incentive pay plans can increase productivity, since they give workers an opportunity and a reward for exercising initiative. Initiative, morale, and output may be increased by choosing techniques for administration and production that rely on decentralized decision making.

WORKPLACE QUALITY, MONETARY INCOME, AND PRODUCTIVITY

What is the motivational process by which alienation is reduced, particularly when productivity gains are not obvious in a corporation? Critics claim that since there are no nonalienating jobs, workers have no other alternatives, and so they adjust their aspirations to the available alternatives. The critics are wrong in assuming that workers do not choose less alienating work. No convincing evidence exists that workers do not respond to working conditions in moving between jobs [5]. Workers prefer both higher wages and greater job satisfaction, and they are willing to exchange some income for more desirable working conditions involving less alienation if the terms are satisfactory. If some workers would like to exchange income for less alienation, it may be advantageous for an employer to respond to this desire and pay less. In response to worker dissatisfaction with dirty and unattractive jobs, for example, foundries adopted automatic sand-pouring and mold-packing equipment, which eliminated dust and dirt from the shops. Thus it became easier to recruit workers and retain them at economical wages. As employees compete in seeking attractive, easy, secure, or meaningful jobs having less alienation, substitution occurs among the various facets of jobs so that the total remuneration, monetary and nonmonetary, for comparable jobs tends to equalize.

A corporation has an incentive to provide a "quality" work environment for its employees subject to given technology and market prices. A corporation does not dictate the quality of a work environment; instead, it responds to workers' preferences for less alienation and higher wages. Corporations adjust if doing so reduces their costs. Workers can have less alienating jobs at the expense of wages. A lower wage might not even be necessary if a worker's outlook is improved enough by a change in the work environment to make the worker sufficiently more productive.

At some point, however, the costs of reducing alienation become real because alienation is an aspect of scarcity that one can never eliminate completely. Workers will always desire less alienation. If corporations are to remain successful, they must respond to workers' desires to reduce alienation, and the terms of trade between alienation and income must allow for feasible adjustment. The action of labor unions in the United States suggests that corporations have responded to workers' desires for less alienation and that workers are not greatly dissatisfied with existing work environments [139: 1304–1305].

The problem of alienation seems more pressing today than in earlier times, even though a larger fraction of the work force is in nonmanufacturing industries, and working conditions have improved immensely. I suggest three reasons for this. First, perhaps the elimination of alienation is a luxury good, and therefore we desire increasingly more of it as our income increases. Second, remuneration in the form of the elimination of alienation escapes taxation, and therefore it is relatively more desirable today because of our higher tax rates. Third, the welfare of those who are not in manufacturing industries is influenced positively by the perceived welfare of those who are, and this consideration supports legislation governing working conditions.

ADDITIONAL READINGS: 41, 71, 73, 75, 77, 138, 183, 223, 257, 294, 314.

10. Do Corporations Discriminate against Minorities and Women?

DONALD L. MARTIN
Law and Economics Center
University of Miami School of Law

Editor's Summary   Large corporations are alleged to be particularly guilty of having hiring practices that discriminate against minorities. These arbitrary practices are asserted to be a result of the economic market power that such organizations enjoy. "Separation of ownership from control" supposedly permits managers to indulge their tastes for discrimination at the expense of profits that would otherwise go to stockholders. Federal chartering is said to give government another weapon to combat industrial job discrimination. The market power argument is badly misunderstood. The logic of the correct argument does not predict that large corporations should be expected to discriminate against blacks or women relatively more (or less) than other business firms do. Not surprisingly, the latest evidence bears this out.

For almost two decades, serious scholarship has been directed toward estimating and explaining differences in earnings among American workers. One important part of this effort has been the focus on earnings differentials among racial groups and between males and females. After accounting for such socioeconomic differences as years of formal schooling, on-the-job training, occupational choice, experience, geographic location, and even health, significant earnings differentials between whites and nonwhites and between males and females remain [170, 336, 456]. These residual differences were quickly pronounced the product of racial and sexual discrimination in the marketplace.

Discrimination in the labor market is usually broadly defined to mean the use of job-irrelevant criteria such as race, sex, national origin, or religion in determining different wage rates for persons with similar qualifications and productivities. Another closely related definition of discrimination focuses on the use of job-irrelevant criteria such as those just mentioned for hiring and promoting from a set of persons with similar qualifications and productivities.

TWO HYPOTHESES ABOUT DISCRIMINATION

There are at least two competing hypotheses of employer discrimination in the labor market. One hypothesis, the discretionary hypothesis, states that racial, sexual, and religious discrimination are reflections of employer "tastes" or preferences for certain kinds of workers. The other hypothesis, the screening hypothesis, states that employers use race and other personal characteristics as economical proxies for information about productivity differences among would-be and existing employees.

In the discretionary hypothesis, tastes are taken as given and may be expressed in wage differentials favoring one group of workers over another. The wage differentials are such that they cannot be explained by differences in qualifications and productivities; they relate to the possession of desired, but job-irrelevant, characteristics by one group of workers. Employer tastes may also be expressed in the virtual exclusion of unfavored groups from employment and promotion. (These tastes may affect the values of employers' customers, employees, or employers themselves. Here, for the sake of brevity, I consider only employers' values [40].) Excluding unfavored groups means that employers forsake the profits that could have been theirs with no loss of productivity had they hired the less desirable persons at lower, discriminatory wage rates.

Some writers suggest that the existence of job discrimination, in contrast to wage discrimination, is incompatible with competitive markets. More specifically, competitive firms would not survive for long if they ignored opportunities to hire labor at lower wage rates without sacrificing productivity. The firms that did hire less-favored groups would enjoy a competitive advantage in production and drive out firms that practice job discrimination [21, 392]. Thus, job discrimination can be financed only from profits generated by market power.

FEDERAL CHARTERING AND JOB DISCRIMINATION

Supporters of federal chartering for corporations have seized upon this conclusion to suggest that discrimination is the conscious policy of large corporations with market power. Their position is that the managers of large corporations in highly concentrated industries wield discretionary power over hiring and promoting personnel. The absence of competition and the "separation of ownership from control" allegedly permit these managers to indulge their tastes for discrimination at the expense of profits that would otherwise go to owners. Federal chartering would give the government an additional weapon in its arsenal to combat job discrimination in industry [328]. If the incidence of job discrimination is highly correlated with the size of firms and corporate organizations, the threat of charter revocation may be sufficient to reduce significantly this form of discrimination in the marketplace.

DOES MARKET POWER PERMIT DISCRIMINATION?

Before considering the evidence bearing on the relationship between firm size and discrimination, it is appropriate to examine the validity of the market power–discrimination hypothesis.

Wielders of market power, as opposed to owners of competitive firms, should not find it relatively less costly to indulge their own tastes for discrimination at the expense of profits. In the absence of special assumptions, to be discussed later, economic theory does not distinguish between the intensities of the profit-maximizing interests of entrepreneurs in competitive, as opposed to monopolistic, firms. Surely, action aimed at maximizing something other than profit (unless ubiquitous) would threaten the survival of the competitive firm more than it would the survival of the firm protected by some sort of entry barrier, the firm with market power. But, the cost of forsaking each dollar of profit is identical for competitors and monopolists alike, unless one introduces special auxiliary assumptions.

One particularly important assumption is the attenuation of private property rights. If profits are regulated so that positive differences between revenues and costs above some arbitrary number must, by law, either be returned to customers or be reinvested in the business, the trade-off of profits for more job discrimination will be less costly to the profit-attenuated firm than to other firms. Public utilities and other regulated firms are often under such profit constraints. They are also protected by legal entry barriers that give them market power. Some evidence does exist to suggest that these firms practice job discrimination [12].

This analysis may be extended to firms that fear government intervention and regulation if profit-maximizing activity produces conspicuously large profits. But before one predicts job discrimination at the large-firm level in the drug industry, the automobile industry, the oil industry, the sugar industry, the computer industry, and other industries that have come under government scrutiny, it should be made clear that the logical implication from the market power model, given our auxiliary assumption, is definitely that such firms should be expected not to practice job discrimination against nonwhites or females.

The correct implication is that it is less costly, beyond some profit level, for decision makers in these firms to pursue personal preferences in hiring at the expense of profits. This means that especially socially conscious employers, or employers faced with personal pressure from civil rights groups, unions, or the government, will find it no more costly to discriminate in favor of minorities and women than it is for other employers, with the same profit constraints, to discriminate against them. William G. Shepherd finds some support for this implication in his study of market power and racial discrimination. He concludes that the percentage of blacks holding white collar jobs in regulated firms is exceptionally variable. Some regulated firms almost completely exclude blacks from these positions (for example, airlines and shipping firms in many cities), while others have relatively high percentages of minority members. Shepherd reports that the fraction of white collar jobs that blacks hold in electric and gas utilities, urban transit firms, and banks varies sharply from city to city. "As a whole, regulated firms do not lie above the average association, even though they have high market power and have been regulated for decades. . . ." [392].

Another auxiliary assumption, closely related to the attenuated property rights assumption, focuses on the costs to owners of detecting deviations from profit maximization by managers. If these costs are relatively high, and if the managers are not also important stockholders, the managers have opportunities to exercise personal hiring criteria inconsistent with profit maximization. In the absence of knowledge of the particular tastes of the decision maker, this auxiliary assumption, like the previous one, cannot predict which groups will be the subject of job discrimination. Thus, economic theory in general, and the discretionary model in particular, cannot predict that firms with market power are more likely to discriminate against nonwhites and women than are firms without such power.

What is the evidence that large firms, suspected of having market power, practice job discrimination relatively more than other firms do? In an early study Becker analyzed 1940 patterns in thirty-eight industries and found that the nonwhite share in employment in these industries was generally lower under monopolistic conditions than under competitive conditions [40]. In a later study Shepherd concluded, "Most large firms apparently discriminate more than smaller firms especially in their higher echelon" [392]. Unfortunately, these studies were based on extremely crude statistical techniques and suffered from data limitations. More recently, there have been more sophisticated attempts at testing the large firm–job discrimination hypothesis [102, 394].

These studies, however, cannot support the large firm–job discrimination hypothesis. The Shepherd and Levin analysis covers about 200 of the largest United States industrial enterprises. Their analysis focuses on white collar employment patterns, using employment data for 1966 and 1970 broken down by race and sex. Shepherd and Levin try to explain variations in black male officer and manager employment as a percentage of all male officer and manager employment, as well as variations in female officer and manager employment as a percentage of all male officer and manager employment. They use three market power measures as explanatory variables. These are a firm's average market share, its asset size, and its advertising expenditures as a percentage of sales. Several other explanatory variables are also used [394, 413].

Interestingly, the Shepherd and Levin results show that there is a significant and *positive* relationship between asset size and the percentage of blacks in official and managerial positions. That is, the larger the firm, measured by asset value, the more likely it is that it will not practice job discrimination against blacks at higher management levels. Another market power variable, market share, is also related positively to the fraction of blacks occupying official and managerial positions. These results, however, are not statistically significant. The same findings are reported for female workers. Both asset size and market share are positively but insignificantly associated with the fraction of females in official and managerial positions [394: 416–417]. These results clearly reject the large firm–job discrimination hypothesis.

William Comanor's study produces mixed results [102]. Using two statistical models that differ in their assumptions, Comanor tries to measure the effect of firm size and market power on racial and sexual discrimination across American industry. With respect to the large-firm effect on discrimination, Comanor's first model shows a small but significant relationship between firm size (measured as the share of total industry assets accounted for by firms with assets exceeding $250 million) on the one hand and his measure of racial and sexual discrimination by occupational category in 1966 on the other hand. Comanor's second model, however, suggests that there is no significant relationship between firm size and job discrimination. The market power variable is measured by the profit rate, or the ratio of after-tax profits to stockholder's equity in each industry in 1966.

Comanor reports that there is a large, significant, and positive relationship between profit rates and job discrimination by race and sex in *both* models. This he interprets as evidence consistent with the discretionary theory of discrimination. Profit rates, however, are a poor index of market power, especially if measured at a point in time. Profit rates and firm size, moreover, are not highly correlated. At any moment in time, small firms in highly *competitive* industries can register profit rates that are higher than the rates of the largest of firms in highly *concentrated* industries. Thus, this finding, though interesting, does not bear upon the large firm–job discrimination hypothesis.

Finally, both the Shepherd-Levin and Comanor models are notably poor as predictors of discrimination across industries. That is, the Shepherd-Levin analysis cannot explain more than 50 percent of the variations in discrimination across industries, while the Comanor analysis cannot explain more than 23 percent of the total variation in discrimination across industries. Obviously, there are factors other than firm size, profitability, and market share that are relevant to explaining earnings and employment differentials by race and sex in American industry.

THE FILTER HYPOTHESIS

An alternative view of job discrimination in United States industry suggests that employers use race and other personal characteristics as proxies for information about differences in employee productivity. Employers use these proxies because productivity information is costly to get, and employers wish to economize on search costs. That is, employers use personal and group characteristics as screening or filtering devices. The number of degrees or the number of years of formal schooling completed, for example, often are used as a screening device in hiring and promoting in lieu of individualized interviews, tests, and character checks. This theory completely ignores the personal tastes of employers, their market power, and the size of their firms [21].

Job discrimination for the purpose of screening or filtering need not be related closely to job performance. In a world of costly information, however, that employers think the screening characteristic conveys productivity information to them is sufficient explanation for their use of it. This observation suggests that if more relevant information is less costly, or if the returns from gathering more relevant information are higher, job discrimination by race or sex will not be used.

The screening hypothesis actually is more consistent with the finding of Shepherd and Levin that larger firms are less likely to discriminate against blacks and women at higher management levels. This result follows because the returns from gathering more expensive and specific information about individual prospective officers and managers should be higher for larger firms, in which executives are responsible for larger amounts of wealth, than for smaller firms. Thus, race and sex will be used relatively less as screening devices for these positions. Daniel Dick and Marshall Medoff, who examined the employment of blacks and whites in seventeen two-digit (SIC) industries for the years 1940, 1950, 1960, and 1970, provide a more general test of the screening hypothesis. Their findings support the notion that job discrimination against blacks in the American manufacturing sector is consistent with the screening or filtering hypothesis [134: 153–154].

CONCLUSION

An examination of the logic and evidence of the large firm–job discrimination hypothesis suggests no support for the view that large firms discriminate any more or less than small firms do. Hence, the belief that federal chartering of large corporations will significantly improve the employment prospects for nonwhites and women in corporations is baseless. Whatever the merits of federal chartering, they appear to have little to do with job discrimination in American industry.

ADDITIONAL READINGS: 3, 24, 79, 80, 139, 234, 409.

11. Should EEOC-mandated Affirmative Action Programs Be Expanded for Corporations?

DONALD M. ATWATER
University of California
Los Angeles

JOHN COGAN
The Rand Corporation

ALLEN HYMAN
Southwestern University School of Law

Editor's Summary   Sponsors of the 1964 Civil Rights Act were concerned with individual cases of discrimination, not with a work force balanced among the races and sexes. The EEOC, however, uses Title VII of the Civil Rights Act to impose de facto quotas, and employers are put in a double bind. If they do not initiate affirmative action programs to match the composition of their work force with that of the population, they can be prosecuted, even though they do not engage in discriminatory practices. If they initiate affirmative action programs, they may violate their union contracts, and they may be subject to reverse discrimination lawsuits by employees not in currently fashionable minority groups. Independent studies find that the EEOC generates widespread litigation and enormous expense in a program that fails to increase minority participation in covered job categories and that fails to increase minority wages.

While we endorse the concept of equal employment opportunity and approve of the motives and good intentions behind Title VII of the Civil Rights Act of 1964, we are critical of many actions of the Equal Employment Opportunity Commission (EEOC). These actions impose great costs without furthering the cause of any minority.

THE DILEMMA OF COMPLIANCE WITH EEOC RULINGS

The EEOC, having received broad discretionary power, has no reservation in using that power to its fullest, regardless of any adverse results that such use might generate. EEOC abuses seem at times as damaging as the harm that the agency is supposed to prevent. Considering the EEOC, one must agree with Justice Robert H. Jackson: "[I]t appears that the administrative body has become a fourth branch of government which has deranged our three-branch system" [*Federal Trade Commission v. Rubberoid Company*, 343 U.S. 470 and 478 (1952)].

While striving to obey EEOC directives, businesses often face conflicting administrative rulings and court cases, broad EEOC policies based on very tentative evidence, and EEOC-mandated programs that impose considerable costs upon both the employee and the employer. Many of these costly programs and guidelines are imposed with no finding that they improve equal employment opportunity.

One example of the employer's dilemma is the case of *Daniel McAleer v. American Telephone and Telegraph Company* [416 F. Supp. 435 (1976)]. American Telephone and Telegraph tried to comply with a court-ordered EEOC affirmative action program when it promoted a female employee over a male, even though the female had fewer years of experience. AT&T believed that the court decree allowed (and, one could reasonably argue, mandated) it to ignore seniority in its promotion policies concerning minorities so that it could meet the goals and timetables of the affirmative action program. The male employee brought suit against AT&T under the Equal Employment Opportunity Act (the same act that fostered the original court order that he be passed over), and he won a judgment against AT&T for lost promotion pay. Such cases indicate that regardless of any firm's good-faith actions in trying to comply, no company is safe from prosecution.

Employers who *fail* to institute an affirmative action program to remedy past discriminatory practices can face prosecution despite their present nondiscriminatory practices. Yet, if employers proceed with an affirmative action program, they face two problems. First, they may violate their union contracts. Second, they may be subject to reverse discrimination lawsuits.

The EEOC is only one of many federal agencies administering the Civil Rights Act. The Labor Department, the Department of Health, Education, and Welfare, and the Justice Department, as well as the EEOC, investigate and prosecute discrimination cases. Following an approved course of action required by one federal agency in no way protects an employer from being sued on the very same course of action by another federal agency or by a private citizen. Indeed, federal agencies have sued one another under this act.

One dilemma that EEOC regulations cause, therefore, follows from too little "integration" of guidelines, agency actions, and lawsuits. Hence, employers often simply cannot comply with conflicting requirements. A second dilemma follows from firms' trying to comply with costly and sweeping EEOC-imposed policies, which are based upon very tentative, and often ambiguous, statistical studies.

Surely there are many individual *cases* of discrimination that Title VII of the Equal Employment Opportunity Act can and should remedy. Yet, the EEOC imposes broad guidelines based not on individual cases but on certain statistical studies and inferences that have little basis in theory or in fact.

These guidelines impose great expenses upon businesses in that they increase the costs of screening and testing employees and administering employment programs. The added costs are reflected in higher prices for goods and services.

THE EEOC PROVIDES NO BENEFITS

Perhaps these costs are well worth paying if the onerous EEOC guidelines improve employment opportunities. Yet, several studies indicate that these expensive regulations do not accomplish what they are supposed to achieve. (The regulations are expensive in two ways, since taxpayers' dollars create and enforce them, and consumers' budgets bear the burden of the higher product prices that they create.)

Title VII actions are often based upon a finding that there is a higher percentage of minorities in the general population than there is employed in a particular job classification in a particular business in a particular area. A disparity between the percentage of a minority employed by a local company and the percentage of the minority in the local population is normally considered sufficient to indicate a violation of the Civil Rights Act [see *Jones v. Tri-County Electric Cooperative,* 512 F. 2nd 1 (1975); this rule is modified in *Stone v. F.C.C.,* 466 F. 2nd 316 (1972)].

One independent study examines EEOC directives to find out if they had any positive effect on relative minority employment in the communities in which actions were brought [3]. The study reports that EEOC actions, although costly, do not significantly increase minority participation in the job categories that the directives cover. Another study examines the Office of Federal Contract Compliance directives to find out if those directives enhance minority employment [403]. The study finds no evidence of greater wages in industries that are relatively more dependent upon government contracts and relatively more liable to intervention by the Office of Federal Contract Compliance than other industries.

One analyst finds that EEOC efforts in the area of employment testing impose great costs on the nation's employers and leave them in virtually indefensible positions with regard to employment testing [190]. Apparently, the EEOC guidelines for employment testing raise considerably the cost of testing for many employers.

Thus, the EEOC appears to have no effect on increasing minority wages. EEOC rules and regulations, despite their appealing sound, simply result in the imposition of guidelines and burdens on industries at considerable expense to taxpayers and consumers.

REAL GAINS AND IMAGINED GAINS

Many affirmative action programs, though they do little to advance the position of minorities, women, and others, create the impression that they are the reason that such persons receive better jobs. This impression is doubly tragic.

During the 1960s, before affirmative action, the incomes of black citizens in the United States rose at a faster rate than the incomes of white citizens, and the proportion of blacks in colleges and in skilled and professional occupations grew rapidly [409]. The proportion of black families below the poverty line declined at an unprecedented rate in the 1960s. Black income as a percentage of white income reached its peak in 1970, the year before the installation of numerical goals and timetables. The percentage has since declined. Thomas Sowell observes that "what many Affirmative Action programs have done is to destroy the legitimacy of what had already been achieved by making all black achievements look like questionable accomplishments or even outright gifts" [409: 64].

THE ORIGINAL INTENT OF THE 1964 CIVIL RIGHTS ACT

Some of the problems we listed earlier result from the change in presumption of the EEOC law from what the framers of that law intended initially. The legislative history of the 1964 Civil Rights Act shows that the framers of the act believed prosecutions would be based upon a showing of intent to discriminate by an employer. This express requirement of finding an intent to discriminate in individual cases was included in the law to prevent inadvertent or accidental conditions from leading to court actions.

In a memorandum to the United States Senate, the act's main supporters, Senators Clark and Chase, stated the matter thus:

> There is no requirement in Title VII that an employer maintain a racial balance in this workforce. On the contrary, any deliberate attempt to maintain a racial balance, whatever such balance may be, would involve a violation of Title VII because maintaining such a balance would require an employer to hire or refuse to hire on the basis of race. It must be emphasized that discrimination is prohibited as to any individual . . . the question in each case would be whether that *individual* was discriminated against. [Emphasis added; 110 Congressional Record 7213, 8 April 1964.]

At the same time, the Department of Justice also submitted a statement regarding the interpretation of the proposed act.

> Finally, it has been asserted that Title VII would impose a requirement for "racial balance." This is incorrect. There is no provision, either in Title VII or in any other part of this bill, that requires or authorizes any federal agency or federal court to require preferential treatment for any *individual group* for the purpose of achieving racial balance. [Emphasis added.].

> No employer is required to hire an individual because that individual is a Negro. No employer is required to maintain any ratio of Negroes to whites, Jews to gentiles, Italians to English, or women to men. [110 Congressional Record 7207, 8 April 1964.]

Although the supporters of the bill made it clear that the burden was to be on the EEOC to prove by a preponderance of the evidence that an employee discharge or other personnel action was because of race, and despite the clear congressional intent of both the supporters and opponents of the 1964 Civil Rights Act, the actual administration of that law has taken precisely the direction the law's sponsors considered impossible. The burden of proof is now on the employer whose work force composition by race or by sex is not satisfactory to federal agencies.

The EEOC takes the position that any discussion of equal employment opportunity programs is meaningful only if it includes a consideration of the results, or lack of results, in terms of actual numbers of jobs for minorities and women. Numbers and percentages are used repeatedly to "show" discrimination without any reference to individual cases or individual qualifications. Percentages below the EEOC's expectations are considered violations of the law! But, under whose authorization does the EEOC impose costly quotas? Certainly the imposition is not under congressional mandate.

EEOC pressure to change existing occupation and compensation patterns for minorities, women, the aged, and the disabled is not likely to ease in the near future. The Equal Employment Opportunity Commission processed 47,000 charges in 1972 and 84,000 charges in 1975, and it is projected that it will process 152,000 claims in 1980 [152]. This is an enormous amount of litigation and expense for a program that has *failed* to increase minority participation in covered job categories and that has failed to increase minority wages. Perhaps EEOC activities should be curtailed rather than expanded.

ADDITIONAL READINGS: 12, 21, 24, 40, 79, 80, 102, 139, 170, 234, 328, 336, 392, 456.

┌───┐
│   │
│   POLITICAL ISSUES   │
│   │
└───┘
```

# 12. Do Corporations Wield Great Political Power?

**W. MARK CRAIN**
*Department of Economics*
*Virginia Polytechnic Institute and State University*

*Editor's Summary*   The rapid growth of government power over previously private decisions leads to greater competition for political favors among all economic agents, including corporations. Businesses must engage in political activities to survive. Thus, firms support candidates in exchange for political influence. The corporate sector, however, is not a unified coalition. The market for political influence has many participants with diverse interests. A single agent may have a smaller impact than believed. The solution to the problem may be to reduce the favors Congress has to "sell."

The belief that corporations exercise great influence over public policy has become commonplace in the modern press. Although this belief is not limited to a particular industry, a recent statement about the petroleum industry provides an illustration. "The power wielded by the industry since 1946, when the NPC [National Petroleum Council] was established, is certainly one of the more important means of maintaining oil industry hegemony over the United States government and gives new life to the dubious principle, with modification, that what's good for the oil industry is good for the United States" [313: 19]. One can even find more "authoritative" assertions by political scientists: "In fact the actual 'political' role of business is wider than that which has been held proper for governments under Western [political] theory" [439: 110].

This chapter offers a broad perspective on the competition for political influence. First, I discuss the emerging intermingling of private and
```

public decisions and how this development relates to growing demands for political influence. Second, I investigate the general competitiveness of the market for political influence and, in particular, address the issue of corporate domination of the competition for political influence. Finally, I offer some concluding remarks.

POLITICAL INFLUENCE AS A COMMODITY

Milton Friedman offers this assessment of the many revelations, appearing in the media, about payoffs in exchange for political favors: "What the current rash of cases illustrates is that some government officials (who, after all, spend other people's money) are tempted to use their position for personal gain, that private enterprises are tempted to accommodate them, and that those enterprises that resist the temptation may well lose profitable business" [176: 73]. As Friedman's statement suggests, the direction of causality in the exchange between interest groups and politicians is not clear. This ambiguity, of course, characterizes any market transaction; suppliers and "demanders" mutually determine the terms of trade.

Plainly, however, the political process today is an important alternative to the market system. As a result of this development, it is not too surprising that the value of decisions in the political process has increased. Surely, the number of headlines about corporation "slush funds" is correlated highly with the importance of political decisions in affecting who gets what.

The electoral process itself is a market for exchange between votes and public policy. Because of one-man-one-vote rules, however, other kinds of exchanges develop in this market. Since political decisions about the economy have vastly different impacts on different persons, one would expect varying degrees of concern about these decisions. Thus, persons or groups may seek to register different intensities by supporting candidates with campaign contributions. The contributions are given in exchange for "more" political influence, and it is at this level that corporate actions receive criticism. It is useful, then, to examine more closely this aspect of the political market in which campaign contributions instead of votes express political preferences.

HOW COMPETITIVE IS THE MARKET
FOR POLITICAL INFLUENCE?

One important clue to the degree of competitiveness in any market is the number of buyers and sellers. Even if one considers the corporate sector as a unified coalition, there seem to be many worthy rivals in the market

for political influence. The relative amounts of campaign funds that
different sectors contribute to political campaigns are evidence of this
rivalry. In the 1976 elections, for example, the two biggest contributors of
"special interest" money to congressional candidates were, respectively,
organized labor and the medical profession [*Washington Post*, 24 October
1976: A-2]. Recent disclosures, moreover, indicate that even foreign
countries are quite active in the competition for influence [*Washington
Post*, 24 October 1976: A-1].

A recent study provides some quite specific evidence about the role of
groups other than corporations in the market for political influence [396].
This study examines the voting patterns of members of Congress concerning legislative action in 1973 to amend the Fair Labor Standards Act.
The bill being voted on was designed to increase the hourly minimum
wage and extend its coverage to about 6 million workers. The most
important determinant of individual voting patterns was the amount of
campaign contributions each member of Congress received from organized labor. "It is not surprising that union interests had the largest
influence. Unions felt intensely about passage of a strong minimum-wage
bill and contributed significant amounts of campaign funds to representatives" [396: 326].

Evidence about the relative impact that corporations have on public
policy concerns the rather broad implications of the Federal Election
Campaign Act of 1974 and its subsequent amendments [Pub. L. No. 93-
443, 88 Stat. 1263]. This legislation places limits on the monetary contributions that individual citizens or groups may offer to candidates. Since
the limitations do not affect all exchanges in the market for political
influence, an element of discrimination appears.

> Clearly not all individuals and organizations are equally capable of mak-
> ing the types of contributions which by their nature are unaffected by the
> amendment's restrictions. Labor unions, for example, are one type of
> organization which is particularly adept at influencing elections without
> running afoul of the new limitations. They are generally capable of
> mobilizing their own sizable memberships and of conducting public
> educational campaigns of considerable impact [232: 528].

This legislation, therefore, clearly reduces the role of the corporate
sector in the market for political influence. That such far-reaching legislation could ever pass, moreover, is powerful evidence against claims that
corporations exercise hegemony over public policy.

Finally, it is somewhat naïve to treat the policy interests within the
corporate sector as homogeneous. That is, even within the business community, the kinds of policies that one industry or firm may support are

not necessarily desirable to other industries or firms. What is good for General Motors is not necessarily good for United States Steel. Policies concerning tariffs or import restrictions on foreign steel, for example, have quite opposing effects on each of these two corporations. While there is some evidence of a relationship between campaign contributions and industry concentration, the magnitude of this effect is small [352]. Further, there appears to be no significant difference between the contributing activities of regulated enterprises and those of nonregulated enterprises [352: 77].

CONCLUSION

In sum, the market for political influence is characterized by a large number of "demanders" with diverse interests, even within the corporate sector. The presence of competition among these rival interest groups suggests that the preference of any single agent may have a smaller impact on the market as a whole than is typically alleged. The recent restrictions placed on monetary campaign contributions, moreover, will reduce the impact of the corporate sector and thus enhance the bidding power of other interest groups. There is considerable doubt as to the relative dominance of corporations over public policy before legislation, and the extent to which corporations can compete in the future is even more cloudy [SB 13, SB 49].

ADDITIONAL READINGS: 19, 55, 173.

13. Do Corporations Capture Local Communities?

ARLEEN LEIBOWITZ
The Rand Corporation

Editor's Summary   Before moving a plant to another community, a corporation tries to negotiate for low taxes, special public services, and special subsidies through low-interest development bonds. The community, in turn, tries to secure as much revenue in taxes as it can and provide as few public services and subsidies as it can, without changing the corporation's decision to locate in the community. Competition among corporations and communities effectively limits the costs that corporations can impose on local communites.

Although some people believe that corporations capture local communities, some communities seem to believe that they have captured corporations. Many communities advertise in national magazines, promoting the advantages of their locations and promising substantial tax benefits and subsidies through low-interest development bonds. Clearly, communities (or their leaders) must find the net benefits of corporations locating in their areas high enough to justify these advertisements and financial inducements. Communities accept a certain amount of spillover effects, such as pollution, in exchange for the benefits that corporations bring SB 3, SB 4, SB 5].

One student of the corporation and the local community puts the matter this way: "Cities and towns as well as states and nations seek to protect and improve their economic base. Mercantilism is not just a national phenomenon" [264: 125]. Yet, critics of corporations argue that these firms control public opinion, impose spillover effects, avoid taxes, and manipulate local political activities.

> Perhaps the most obvious hostages of corporate power are those communities who depend on large companies for their existence, even as these companies tax these communities in numerous ways. Local plants can provide employment—and pollution, as Gary, Indiana understands about United States Steel. Subsidiaries of giant firms can exploit and damage local services. . . . Large companies possess and often exploit their leverage to bargain down the amounts of local tax they must pay [328: 12].

THE EXCHANGE BETWEEN COMMUNITIES AND CORPORATIONS

Why should communities compete so vigorously for the right to be controlled, polluted, underfinanced, and manipulated? It is clear why unemployed workers would seek to attract a corporation to their area. But, why would other citizens wish to spend public funds for this purpose? Communities are anxious to attract new businesses to their areas primarily because of the direct impact new firms have on local employment and on the demand for locally provided services. But there are indirect, as well as direct, benefits. Greater employment is desirable not only because it reduces unemployment but also because it improves business activity generally. A corporation's workers spend their wages and salaries, and this improves the entire business climate. The incomes of storeowners, dentists, and property owners rise. Through the multiplier effect virtually everyone becomes better off.

Naturally, before locating in a community, a corporation tries to extract the best terms from the community leaders. It tries to negotiate for a low tax bill, special public services (such as roads), and low interest rates. The community, in turn, tries to secure as much revenue in taxes as it can, provide as few public services as it can, charge the highest interest rates it can, without chasing the corporation away.

COMMUNITIES AND EXISTING FIRMS

Once located in a community, a corporation continues to seek the best terms. Now, however, the community and the corporation are in a bilateral monopoly position. There is only one town, and it has jurisdiction over the land the company's factory occupies; relocating will impose costs on the firm. Hence, the community has the opportunity to extract revenues having a present value that is no more than the present value of the cost of the corporation's move to a new location. The corporation, in turn, has some monopoly power with respect to the town. Town leaders might not be able to find another employer that will provide a package of benefits, taxes, and costs having as great a value to the community as the "package" of the present employer. The difference between the value of the package available from the next best firm and the value of the present firm's package determines the limits within which the present firm can impose costs on the town. Norton E. Long summarizes this situation.

> Economic decisions have political consequences and vice versa. The holders of economic power must seek to influence the political environment, and the holders of political power must seek to manage the economic environment to pursue their ends. We readily recognize this at

the national level, though we debate over the appropriate scope of interference and which spheres' objectives should receive priority. What is true at the national level is only to a less degree true at the local level [264: 125].

Traditional market analysis would point to the firm's option to relocate if it wanted to change the characteristics of its environment. A. O. Hirschman calls this option "exit" and identifies an alternative option: "voice" [217]. "Voice" is the tactic of attempting to influence behavior in a political manner, and it is sometimes a lower-cost substitute for "exit."

A COMPLEMENTARITY OF INTERESTS

In trying to control local political activities, corporations protect not only their profits but also their employees. Clearly, "what is good for General Motors is good for Michigan." Local communities there have suffered greatly as a result of a decline in the demand for automobiles in the early 1970s. The unemployment rate in Michigan in 1974 reached 8.5 percent, while the average national rate was 5.7 percent [Bureau of Labor Statistics, Monthly Labor Report 452: 2]. To protect their own interests, Michigan citizens are unlikely to vote for regulations that raise car prices, decrease the demand for automobiles, and therefore diminish employment and incomes throughout Michigan. They oppose these measures not because they are "captured" by the automobile companies, but because it is in their own interests to do so.

A community determines through the political system the amount of pollution and other spillover effects it will tolerate in return for the benefits of having a corporation in its location. It may not be economically or politically feasible to insist that all pollutants be eliminated, especially if obeying this requirement becomes so costly that the corporation is driven out of business. No pollution then accompanies no employment. That most corporations sell their products in competitive markets and that communities compete for the benefits of corporations locating in their areas put effective constraints on the costs that communities can impose on corporations. That various firms compete for the locational benefits different communities provide constrains the costs that corporations can impose on communities.

ADDITIONAL READINGS: 65, 141, 149, 150, 151, 306, 328, 443.

14. How Important Are Corporate Payoffs and Bribes?

G. WARREN NUTTER
Department of Economics
University of Virginia

Editor's Summary   Corporate payoffs are self-defeating because rivalry in the market for influence leads to the dissipation of excess profits. If a corporation is a monopolist, it could secure a higher price by offering a kickback. In the more likely situation, however, different corporations compete with each other. Competition among suppliers leads them to offer a maximum bribe—one just great enough to dissipate the excess profits from a transaction. In this way the benefit the payoff generates is shifted from the corporation to the bribed official. With rival bribery, corporations earn the same returns with and without bribes and payoffs. The magnitude of such abuses, in any case, is self-limiting. While local bribery is usually blatant and crass, it is also of limited scope. Large gains would require a mammoth conspiracy, and there would be an increased risk of disclosure. The scope of payoffs is self-limiting, and competition for influence makes payoffs self-defeating.

A bribe, one distinguished dictionary says, is "a price, reward, gift, or favor bestowed or promised with a view to pervert the judgment or corrupt the conduct of a person in a position of trust, as an official or a voter." Corruption in this usage means betrayal of trust: the selling of favors and privileges in a manner contrary to the fiduciary relation between a public official and the ultimate sovereign body. It follows that the possibilities for bribery, in its literal sense, vary with the nature of a society.

PAYOFFS, BRIBES, AND FORMS OF GOVERNMENT

In some societies, the government itself is sovereign and bears no responsibility to any broader constituency. The ruler does not serve as a trustee for others or rule on behalf of others. This person rules according to personal interest. The ruler is both the government and the sovereign, personally entitled to everything pertaining thereto.

This is merely to say that an absolute dictator, having no trust to betray, is not bribable. A payment to the dictator in exchange for valuables received takes on the character of a normal market transaction between property owners. It is a payoff but not a bribe. Such a transaction is part and parcel of the political system itself, rendering it no more immoral than it already is. What would constitute bribery in a dictatorship would be the sale of favors by any one of the dictator's subordinates in a way that strained the subordinate's loyalty to the dictator. But, such bribery has a connotation different from that in the normal case.

There are many forms of government other than dictatorship and despotism in which the sale of governmental favors is inherent in the political system. In the Orient and in the Middle East, public officials enjoy their own islands of power, encompassing the right to dispense special favors and privileges within defined limits. This right implies a right to charge for services rendered, and the baksheesh given in payment is a part of the way of life, a cost of doing business applicable to all, a surrogate for taxes that would otherwise be levied. Once again, the practice involves payoffs but not bribes.

Let us use the term "payoff" to designate any payment to a public official for a service rendered. A bribe, then, is a special kind of payoff inducing betrayal of trust.

Bribery in the fullest sense occurs in societies with democratic, aristocratic, or other constitutional forms of government. Officials in these societies are subject to venal corruption because they serve in positions of trust, governing on behalf of their constituents. At the same time, these societies construct the strongest barriers against corrupt behavior by restraining the power of individual officials and by relegating decision making to various depersonalized institutional structures. That is to say, no matter how well the officials in a sophisticated democracy might be bribed, it is not easy to find one who is in a position to deliver very much.

In the United States, for example, the most lucrative targets for bribery are likely to be officials in local and state governments that have failed in one way or another to circumscribe the power of those officials to grant favors. Corruption at the local level is usually blatant and crass, but it is also limited in magnitude. Except for such possibilities as corrupting a court of law so that it will render a favorable decision in a particular case, bribery on a national scale by a single corporation for the purpose of achieving a significant gain would generally cost far more than it would be worth. Imagine the cost of trying to buy a majority vote in Congress, if indeed one could tailor any bill to the advantage of a single corporation [396]. And, it is not easy to see what good it might do for a corporation to bribe the President or some other high official in the executive branch, given the institutional constraints on the decisions of that branch.

We may distinguish three different cases in which a corporation might contemplate a payoff, a bribe, or some other political involvement to further its self-interest, taking it for granted that a corporation is motivated solely by its own desire for profit.

THE FIRST CASE: CORPORATIONS SELL TO GOVERNMENTS

A corporation has a product to sell to a government. Perhaps it is a commercial airliner appropriate for a government-owned airline, or some item of military equipment. What the corporation may need to do to sell the product depends on whether or not it has rivals. If the corporation is a monopolist, it may be in a position to increase its profit from the sale by offering a kickback to an official who has the power to get the corporation a higher price than it otherwise could charge. This possibility exists only if the official does not have quite enough power to appropriate governmental funds for personal use without such a subterfuge. There is little point in pressing this case further, however, because it is difficult to think of any interesting examples of such a strong monopolistic position.

Normally, any one corporation has rivals also seeking a sale, and the existence of rivals rules out most opportunities for gain through payoffs. The size of any contemplated payoff depends, in the first place, on the profit expected from the sale, and the greater the competition, the smaller the expected profit. Suppose that the anticipated profit from the sale of an airliner to country X turns out to be higher than normal because a governmental official in X can manipulate the price. Suppose, further, that three firms—A, B, and C—have qualified airliners to offer for sale. If payoffs are solicited, and if bargaining for them is essentially uninhibited, competition among the firms will set the final payoff high enough to eliminate a higher-than-normal profit for at least two of the firms. If A is the only firm that would end up with a normal or higher than-normal profit after the payoff, it will make the payoff and get the sale. If A and B would just have a normal profit after the payoff, while C would not, the purchaser would choose between A and B on some other ground, and the winner would make the payoff and get the sale. And so on.

What has happened, in any event, is that any potential excess gain from the sale has been transferred from the seller to the buyer. In technical economic language, the payoff has shifted economic rent from the seller to the buyer. The payoff does not bring a higher profit to the selling corporation. It merely buttons down the sale. An alternative course of action for the purchasing government would be to reduce the price paid for the airliner by an amount equivalent to the payoff, in which case the benefit would go to the government's treasury instead of to the recipient of the payoff.

THE SECOND CASE: CORPORATIONS SEEK RIGHTS

A corporation wishes to acquire property rights in a country in the expectation that these rights will reduce the costs of production. If a payoff is necessary to acquire these rights, the corporation will consider making one, provided that it does not exceed the present value of the anticipated reduction in production costs. As in the preceding case, in a situation of competition and uninhibited bargaining the payoff would tend to a level that eliminates above-normal profits. Economic rent would shift from the corporation to the recipient of the payoff. If the corporation has no rivals, the economic rent would be divided in some unpredictable way between the corporation and the recipient of the payoff.

Conditions may combine, in rare instances, to bring about the banana-republic case: a small and poor country is heavily dependent for its welfare on a single export that is produced by a monopolistic corporation. If the corporation becomes wealthier than the government of the country, it may come to dominate the government. But, today this is a rare exception.

THE THIRD CASE: CORPORATIONS SEEK TO MAINTAIN RIGHTS

A corporation is threatened with the loss of existing property rights. A typical example here is the threat of confiscation of property without adequate compensation. The maximum payoff the corporation is willing to make is the value that it expects its property to have after it has gained whatever protection the payoff provides. To the government contemplating confiscation, the payoff is the present value that it attaches to the property when owned by the government. From the strictly commercial point of view, there are two reasons why the present value the government anticipates should be lower than the present value to the corporation if its property rights were not disturbed. First, government enterprise is less efficient than private enterprise. Second, the time horizon of government officials is likely to be shorter than that of the corporation. Hence, there seems to be room to bargain if commercial considerations alone are at stake.

Unfortunately, the confiscation of property, particularly that owned by foreigners, is usually politically motivated in the sense that it builds popular support for government in many parts of the world. A government, therefore, will normally attach far more value to confiscation than a simple commercial calculus would dictate, and the possibility of a mutually acceptable payoff will normally be ruled out.

An alternative course for a corporation might be to spend a sum equivalent to an acceptable payoff to support political forces opposing confiscation. But given the social setting that stimulates a movement for confiscation in the first place, it is most unlikely that such a political effort would offer much prospect for long-run success.

In any event, whatever a corporation does in this case is designed to minimize losses, not to generate additional profits. Whatever it pays out in the hope of protecting existing property rights diminishes its profit stream commensurately. It tries, simply, to avoid something worse. But in the end the payments may do no good, and good money will have been sent after bad.

CORPORATIONS AND GOVERNMENTS
IN PAYOFFS AND BRIBERY

Whatever corporations might spend trying to acquire political influence over particular governments, the sums are bound to be trivial compared to what some governments will spend for the same purpose. Large countries are willing to spend billions of dollars a year in the form of clandestine and open foreign aid in an effort to gain influence over all sorts of activities in other countries. The stakes simply are far higher than they could ever be for corporations as a group. Countries desiring aid also are willing to spend large sums to influence legislators and other officials in the United States, as we witness from recent revelations about South Korean payments to members of Congress. Similar actions are no doubt true of other countries dependent on the United States for support.

The primary difference between corporations and governments in this respect is that corporations have no interest in wielding political control as such. A corporation has an interest in influencing political affairs only to the extent that these affairs impinge on the property rights of the corporation itself; a corporation has no interest in furthering a political or ideological cause. The most that any corporation can hope for, in general, is to preserve existing rights. There is little a corporation can do in political channels that will increase the profitability of its endeavors.

ADDITIONAL READINGS: 135, 176, 463.

15. Should Corporations Invest in or Trade with Internationally Unpopular Countries?

DENNIS E. LOGUE
Amos Tuck School of Business Administration
Dartmouth College

Editor's Summary   Beyond the problem of defining what a "pariah" country is, reducing American economic ties with pariah countries would mean reducing the welfare of American consumers, workers, and stockholders. American firms would lose exports and would face higher import costs. All parties would end up worse off economically. The curtailment or elimination of trade and direct investment would hurt workers, consumers, and capital owners in the pariah countries. Such a policy may prove damaging to those who already suffer most in the nations that would bear the brunt of our government's or corporations' arbitrarily distributed wrath.

During the halcyon days of student activism, one of the more popular demands was that a college endowment fund should divest itself of the securities of firms trading with "pariah" countries. Despite the return of peace to campuses, the notion persists that corporations that trade with or invest in internationally unpopular countries should be either punished or brought under less tolerant social control. This notion remains strong particularly among the corporate social conscience elite [SB 1]. However, the argument that United States corporations should not trade with pariah countries is not generally intended to promote debate as to the pros and cons of such activity [SB 6]. Rather, the argument is meant to evoke revulsion and discussion of policies designed either to halt such corporate "irresponsibility" directly or raise corporate social consciousness to the level at which corporations will stop such activity voluntarily. Unfortunately, the more important issues are those that are not meant to be raised.

"PARIAH" AN AMBIGUOUS DESIGNATION

Initially, one should recognize that there is no unambiguous definition of "pariah" country. At first glance, those countries guilty of wholesale violations of human rights might fall into the "pariah" class. This classification, however, is not exclusive enough, for there are many countries that violate human rights rather routinely yet receive warm welcomes in such international settings as, say, the United Nations. Rarely do other nations denounce in public forums countries such as the People's Republic of China and the Union of Soviet Socialist Republics. Powerful countries, no matter what their regard for human rights, or in spite of their neglect of human rights, seem not to fall into the pariah class. Rather, it seems that the only countries that are generally viewed as pariahs are those that violate the human rights concepts of a large portion of the world and that, lacking great military power, have few natural allies. Nations such as South Africa, Rhodesia, and Chile come to mind, but their designations as pariahs appear to have less to do with their violations of human rights than with their lack of nuclear weapons, or their lack of a protector who has such weaponry.

DOMESTIC PROBLEMS OF STOPPING EXCHANGE

Though the designation "pariah" seems capricious, some nations bear the label and hence, in the judgment of many, deserve to be severed economically from the rest of the world. But, if United States firms were to respond, misguidedly, to the demand they do not trade with pariah countries, official American foreign policy would be hindered severely, and American consumers, workers, and shareholders would be harmed.

Reducing economic ties to such countries might eventually harm them and perhaps accelerate moves to eliminate the conditions prompting violations of human rights. In the short run, however, the persons who would be affected most adversely would be the citizens who are presently the least advantaged. Life would be made toughest for those for whom our compassion is greatest.

To deny that American firms trade with pariah countries would be foolhardy. In 1975, for example, American trade with South Africa exceeded $2 billion, and American trade with Chile approximated $700 million. American firms have also placed billions of dollars in these and other countries. Curtailing trade or abandoning investment would do little good, except to those whose consciences are concerned more with form than with substance.

American firms must comply with a variety of rules and regulations established by the State Department, the Department of Defense, the Department of Agriculture, and several other government agencies. These rules and regulations specify the countries with which firms can trade as well as the kinds of products that may be traded. To the extent that American firms comply with these constraints, they fulfill the letter of the law. To the extent that the federal agencies coordinate their policies, moreover, it is possible to achieve the foreign and domestic policy objectives of the agencies' programs.

If corporations develop their own foreign policies, however, the coordinated objectives of official policy may be undermined. If one firm decides that France and Germany are pariah nations, for example, and if another firm decides that Australia and Great Britain belong to the pariah class, American foreign policy, having been taken over by eclectic private views, rather than politically determined public views, could quickly become unworkable [SB 1].

Similarly, the socially motivated actions of one firm may seriously affect other firms. Suppose, for instance, that two firms are selling dissimilar products in a foreign country whose central authority makes most trading decisions. If one firm decides to stop selling to this country, the central authority may punish the firm's home country by refusing to buy from the second firm.

If American firms jointly do not trade with or make investments in so-called pariah countries, firms in other nations will take their place. So, although the pariah nations will then have to import less desirable goods at higher prices, they probably will not be severely harmed. If export firms in all nations collude to eliminate all sales to pariah countries, world trade will decline by a considerable amount. Hence, world economic welfare will decline. Such worldwide collusion among firms, however, would likely prove impossible to coordinate.

If a single American firm, as opposed to *all* American firms, declines to export goods to a pariah country, an American competitor may take the business. The pariah country will not suffer. But the nonexporting firm will lose sales, profits, and jobs, and investors in that firm will ultimately suffer. There is thus a severe, competitive disincentive for any single American firm to resist selling to a pariah country.

Regarding imports from pariah countries, if American firms were to eliminate them, substitute materials would be either procured elsewhere or produced at home. In either case, however, the cost would be high. The United States would commit itself to higher prices or inferior sources of supply, thus reducing its level of domestic economic welfare. Reducing or eliminating trade with pariah countries would result in the loss of jobs in export industries and higher prices for import substitutes. Laborers and consumers as well as the owners of domestic industries would suffer. In any event, if individual citizens hold strong beliefs about imports from pariah countries, in our society they are free to refuse to purchase those goods.

FOREIGN PROBLEMS OF STOPPING EXCHANGE

Focusing on the pariah country, if it loses exports, imports, and foreign investments, it will suffer economically. However, a country tends to *export* certain kinds of goods. The production of such goods involves the intensive use of resources that are relatively abundant in the country. This tendency drives up the prices or wages of the abundant resources. Similarly, a country tends to *import* goods that are produced through the intensive use of resources that are relatively scarce in the exporting country. This tendency drives down the domestic prices of the resources.

In most pariah nations, the chief exports are labor-intensive. Gold and diamonds, for example, are large export items for South Africa, and the production (mining) of these goods employs masses of blacks in the labor force. If exports of these goods were curtailed, blacks in the labor force would suffer more than proportionately. Similarly, the imports of countries such as South Africa tend to be high-technology items. If imports were eliminated, those who can produce them—the technologically elite—would benefit, since the goods would still be needed, and the producers would no longer face foreign competition. Accordingly, in the short run the least advantaged would be hurt most. One may analyze the issue of direct investment in much the same way. Curtailing direct investment would mean enriching the owners of indigenous capital at the expense of nonowners.

Cessation of trade with pariah countries, in the long run, may accelerate social progress by making the pressures for reform less resistible. But, this is an uneasy argument. An equally likely outcome of growing economic pressures is that the response on the part of the ruling parties will be to increase the kinds of social repression that prompted the initial designation of their countries as pariahs. This possibility urges caution in prescribing corporate policy for social goals.

SUMMARY

It seems to be poor policy to encourage private firms to develop their own foreign policy objectives. These objectives may run counter to our legitimate national interests. Similarly, coercing companies to apply high social conscience to their trade and investment decisions would reduce American economic welfare and may prove counterproductive to those who already suffer most in the nations that bear the brunt of our arbitrarily distributed wrath.

ADDITIONAL READINGS: 36, 107, 135, 248, 451, 463.

PART TWO

CONTROL OF
THE CORPORATION

MANAGEMENT ISSUES

16. Are Managers an Elite Clique with Dictatorial Power?

H. E. FRECH III
Department of Economics
Harvard University
and
University of California, Santa Barbara

Editor's Summary Managers' compensation depends on corporate performance and hence is tied to the interests of stockholders. The owners of firms, moreover, monitor the performance of managers both directly and through securities markets by shifting among shares and abandoning one set of managers for another. The clearest examples of arbitrary managerial power exist in the nonprofit sector (charitable and educational foundations, hospitals, and universities) and in heavily regulated industries (public utilities and transportation companies). In contrast to ownership rights in profit-making, "unregulated" contemporary corporations, ownership rights in nonprofit and regulated organizations are so diffuse as to render owner monitoring of management prohibitively costly and, hence, ineffective. Less government regulation, the elimination of the corporate income tax, and the elimination of special privileges for nonprofit firms would strengthen the ability and incentives of owners to monitor the performance of their organizations' managers. In all cases, the best defense against arbitrary managerial power is the strengthening of the property rights of stockholders.

Do modern corporate managers have too much power? Are they too free to act in ways that benefit themselves but harm others, including stockholders? Affirmative answers to these questions would suggest that either additional government regulation is needed to check the power of managers, or the conversion of the present system to one of government ownership is necessary.

THE ILLUSION OF MANAGERIAL POWER

The view that managers have great power rests partially on an illusion that many managers probably believe. This illusion is that the *announcement* of a change is confused with the *cause* of that change. Suppose, for example, that the president of a steel corporation announces a price increase. That action seems to indicate that the president has the power to raise prices. Underlying that announcement, however, are the actual causes of the price increase. The cost of iron ore, coke, and labor may have risen. If the steel corporation's president did not announce a higher price, another firm's president would do so. And, in any case, if the first firm did not raise its prices, it would lose money, and this would lead to the president's early retirement. So, observers, perhaps even including the steel corporation's president, may believe that a corporation's president has great power to raise prices. More likely, the president may merely be announcing and formalizing the results of market forces outside of personal control.

HOW MANAGERS ARE CONSTRAINED

Managers often have strong ownership positions in their firms, or their salaries and other incomes may be tied strongly to the wealth of the stockholders and to accounting profits [SB 55, SB 66]. Hence, managers may best serve themselves by serving their stockholders. Even so, managers cannot pursue common interests unconstrained.

The constraints on managerial action take two forms. The first set of constraints depends on the market in which a firm operates. Market constraints prevent managers from charging too high a price or from offering workers or suppliers payments that are too low [SB 9, SB 21]. Further, the interest of managers in their own wealth leads them to avoid offers that are far from the wealth-maximizing ones for their firms.

Monitoring actions by the owners of firms provide the second set of constraints on managers [11]. Monitoring is imperfect simply because information is costly. Indeed, monitoring is too lax because of government policies that reduce the incentive for owners to examine carefully the performance of their firms. Managers, in a sense, do have too much power. As I argue later, the corporate income tax, government regulation, and the policy bias toward nonprofit firms are the most important examples of policies that reduce incentives for owner monitoring.

Still, owners do have incentives to monitor managers. If one set of owners does a poor job, others can gain by purchasing the firm and improving the monitoring [SB 2, SB 5]. The job of monitoring sounds terribly difficult in the abstract. The job is made simpler, however, by specialization in ownership and by competition of two sorts. The first is the competition of other managers for managerial positions in the firm [SB 55, SB 56]. It pays for lower-level managers who have inside knowledge that top management is making mistakes to reveal this information to the owners of the firm. The objectives of the competing potential managers are simple. They would like better positions. It is a little-recognized fact that the managers of a firm are not a solidly organized class with identical interests. Indeed, the interests of different managers in a given firm may be sharply divergent.

The second kind of competition is competition in the product market. This kind of competition eases monitoring information requirements. If producers of competing products are doing well at given price levels, and if one's own firm is losing money, one might begin to suspect that something is amiss with one's management. Further, the prices of competing products and services, when compared with one's own cost figures, may give a good idea of where and how the managers are underperforming [SB 22].

The result of these varieties of competition is that institutional settings greatly constrain managerial freedom. Further, to the extent that their own incomes and wealth (salaries, bonuses, stock options, and so on) are related to the performance of their firms, managers have a strong, direct interest in efficiency.

To see this, consider for a moment the effect of managerial actions that diminish the wealth of a firm. The managers bear the consequences of these actions to some extent, since their compensation packages in part reflect the firm's performance. The owners of the firm, of course, bear much more of the impact of managerial actions. Through the monitoring of the managers, the owners try to change the situation, possibly by firing the responsible person. Irresponsibility, in the sense of seeking one's own welfare at the expense of the owners of the firm, is limited.

The abuses of managerial responsibility have a direct impact on the financial position of the owners, and thus the owners have a strong incentive to monitor managerial actions. As a result, one would expect that the incentive of the affected owners to safeguard their own private wealth would limit the ignoring of owner interests in the management of the firm. Thus, managers are far from a position of having dictatorial power.

THE REAL SOURCE OF DISCONTENT

Much of the concern expressed by the belief that managers are too powerful derives from a different source. It is not so much that managers have dictatorial power and act irresponsibly from the point of view of their firms' owners. Properly understood, the problem is that managers are all too responsible and indeed make correct decisions as agents of the owners of the firms. But, the actions that benefit the firms' owners may be inconsistent with the tastes of some observers; in some cases, those actions may even be damaging to those not involved directly in the firms' fortunes.

A clear example of this phenomenon involves pollution. Firms pollute because managers are acting in the interests of owners, not because managers are ignoring those interests. In the absence of well-defined property rights that allow market determination of the correct level of pollution, the owners have no incentive to consider pollution [SB 1, SB 3, SB 4]. Whatever slippage there is between owners and managers may be irrelevant to this problem. The problem with pollution is that the owners, and thus the managers, have no incentive to consider the damage caused by pollution. The remedy has nothing to do with the independent power of managers. Rather, the remedy is the creation of an explicit legal and regulatory environment that forces firms in their decision making to consider the cost of pollution. Examples of regulatory practices include establishing property rights to basins subjected to pollutants, imposing legal liability for damages caused by pollution, establishing regulatory standards, and taxing firms in relation to the extent of pollution (effluent taxation) [239, 240, SB 3, SB 4].

The pollution example provides a key to understanding the notion that managers are too powerful. If one were to go behind the objection to managerial power that critics of modern corporations make, one would find that most, if not all, of the specific actions objected to are those that managers are carrying out in the interests of owners. Independent managerial power is irrelevant.

OTHER POSSIBLE CONSTRAINTS ON MANAGERS

The belief that managers are too free, in any case, is not sufficient to indicate a sound rationale for public policy. One must face the matter of alternatives. How can managers be further constrained? What are the side effects of additional constraints? If the side effects are costly, will additional constraints be worth the expense? Or, are the costs too high? Most government regulations have the effect of weakening the property rights of the owners of firms. As a result, the owners' incentives to monitor carefully the managers of their firms are weakened considerably [SB 21]. Thus, most government regulations have the effect of making managers more powerful, and less constrained by owners and by markets. Regulated firms and legally nonprofit firms have the most powerful managers.

In principle, direct government regulation of day-to-day managerial decisions can reduce managerial power. Some reflection indicates, however, that the difficulties of this approach are overwhelming. For one thing, monitoring managerial decisions requires tremendous effort and expense. The reason that owners of firms do not do *more* monitoring is that it is too costly, even to *those with a powerful financial stake in the outcome.* A government agency, of course, has far weaker incentives for monitoring than the owners have. The government can impose rules and restrictions to ease its monitoring tasks, much like civil service and government enterprises in general. But, it takes little insight to recognize the losses in efficiency and flexibility inherent in that approach [SB 40]. The alternatives to shareholder monitoring are not very promising.

There *are* beneficial policy prescriptions, however, for reducing the arbitrary power of management. The basic requirement of a policy for reducing managerial power is that it provide strong incentives for owners of firms to monitor the managers of their firms. An example of such a policy is the elimination of the corporate income tax, so that a dollar of corporate income lost because of managerial action has more bite in reducing the wealth of owners. Another change would be the reversal of current policies that favor regulated firms and nonprofit organizations.

SUMMARY

Complaints about managerial power are generally misguided. Much apparent managerial power is illusory. Management officials are more constrained than even they believe by competition for products, resources, and managerial jobs, and especially by the monitoring actions of the owners of firms. Many managerial actions that give rise to criticism of managerial power actually reflect responsible managerial decisions that promote the interests of owners. Most regulations, furthermore, weaken the interest of owners in monitoring their firm's performance, thus increasing managerial power rather than decreasing it. Policies that would weaken managerial power somewhat in a beneficial way include the elimination of the corporate income tax, *less* regulation, and the elimination of special privileges for nonprofit firms.

ADDITIONAL READINGS: 7, 8, 12, 52, 96, 123, 169, 216, 282, 299, 341, 401, 458, 459.

17. Should Management's Control of the Corporation Be Weakened and That of the Shareholder Strengthened?

MICHAEL P. DOOLEY
University of Virginia School of Law

Editor's Summary Many critics argue that the rights of stockholders are insufficient, even though a minority shareholder has many rights in his or her relationship to management. But, those who propose change fail to realize that the present system limits nuisance suits and gives control to those who have a real stake in a firm's fortunes. Small shareholders receive the benefits of the large shareholders' monitoring of corporate activities. The "Wall Street Rule" and takeover threats operate as mutually beneficial constraints on all parties involved.

There are several proposals to change the present system for nominating and electing corporate directors. The justification for these changes is invariably put in terms of "revitalizing corporate democracy" and restoring to shareholders the degree of control to which their ownership interests entitle them. The present system, some argue, creates a "management autocracy" in which shareholders are deprived of meaningful participation in corporate governance, boards of directors are supine, and management's power is unchecked.

PROPOSALS TO WEAKEN MANAGEMENT CONTROL

Nader, Green, and Seligman propose radical changes to correct these perceived shortcomings [328: 75–251]. They attribute management's power to its effective control of the proxy system and to its consequent ability to dictate the selection of board members. They believe that shareholders can nominate rival candidates—but only if the shareholders are willing to engage in a full-scale proxy fight. They believe also that management's access to corporate funds gives it an unfair advantage over any insurgent group. To support these beliefs, they cite the infrequency of contested corporate elections and the "Wall Street Rule," which is the general tendency of dissatisfied shareholders to sell their shares rather than mount electoral challenges to incumbent managers.

The critics of present corporate governance seek to make corporate governance more "democratic" by increasing shareholder and director participation in decision making, and by severely limiting the role of management. They propose a nine-member board of directors. Each member would have special responsibility for some aspect of the firm's business, such as employee welfare, community relations, compliance with the law and, perhaps as an afterthought, management efficiency [SB 2]. Board members would devote full time to their duties, and each would have extensive staff support. Shareholders owning at least one-tenth of 1 percent of the outstanding stock, or representing a group of at least 100 shareholders, would have the exclusive right to nominate candidates for the board. Present managers, however, could not serve on, or even nominate candidates for, the board, regardless of the number of shares they hold.

Candidates would campaign for directorships on the basis of statements of qualifications sent to the shareholders, and the corporation would bear all campaign expenses. Only beneficial owners would be allowed to vote, and institutional investors would have to "pass through" voting rights to beneficial owners or, if this is impractical, provide for committees that the beneficial owners elect to decide how to cast the votes.

THE NATURE OF THE PRESENT SYSTEM

Although management enjoys some advantages under the present system, those advantages are neither as one-sided nor as undesirable as some observers might believe. Under existing law, management's right to reimbursement for proxy contest expenses is limited to those contests involving policy issues in which the expenditures are reasonable and necessary to inform shareholders about the issues. Admittedly, there are difficulties in distinguishing "policy" issues from "personality" issues, or "information" from "persuasion." But the evidence of undue advantage has force only if one can show that management consistently outspends insurgents in contested elections. The available data, however, indicate that the courts administer legal tests in such a way as to permit management to meet, but not greatly exceed, the amounts insurgents expend.

Existing law, moreover, does not completely preclude insurgents from being reimbursed. They may be reimbursed if they are successful, and if the shareholders vote to reimburse them. Although some argue for more liberal reimbursement rules for insurgents, it is readily apparent that providing automatic reimbursement would mean putting a real drain on corporate treasuries. Similarly, limiting reimbursement to successful insurgents lessens the possibility that someone will mount a challenge for the purpose of extorting a bribe.

LARGE AND SMALL SHAREHOLDERS
AND CORPORATE CONTROL

There is little doubt that the existing system makes changes in corporate control expensive, and thus the system is "undemocratic" in the sense that corporate critics use. The holder of 100 shares does not have the same opportunity to control corporate affairs as the holder of 100,000 shares. The existing system ensures that only those with a significant economic stake in an enterprise will find it worthwhile to displace incumbent managers. But, this is as it should be because those who seek to control a corporation will also bear the value consequences of their control.

Finding out which shareholders bear which consequences reveals the fundamental flaw in the proposals for changing corporate control systems: these proposals simply do not recognize that the process of "managing"—acquiring information, detecting undesirable actions, and enforcing desired actions—is costly and that there is little incentive to engage in a costly activity such as management unless a "manager's" personal welfare is significantly related to improvements in corporate performance [11]. Therefore, those who own 100 shares have little incentive to "manage" the corporation efficiently because they can capture only a minuscule portion of any increase in the profitability of the firm. Such owners fail to "control," not because they are demoralized or because managers are autocrats, but because it is more profitable for them to delegate control over their investments to others, subject to the strictures of fiduciary duties. If such owners were to be put in positions of control, they would be likely to shirk or to indulge personal preferences at the expense of firm profitability.

It is worthwhile for large shareholders, by contrast, to manage the firm efficiently, since they will capture a significant portion of any increase in profitability and bear a proportional diminution of personal wealth if there is inefficient operation. One can explain the relative infrequency of proxy contests, then, not by pointing to undue management advantage, but by realizing that it is not worthwhile for a shareholder or group of shareholders to assume control unless the individual or the group already has a sufficient economic stake in the corporation and will enjoy substantial benefits from improved management.

THE "WALL STREET RULE" AND SHAREHOLDER CONTROL

For the vast majority of shareholders in larger corporations, it is less costly, and hence more efficient, to express dissatisfaction by selling shares. Although the proponents of radical change point to the "Wall Street Rule" as an example of shareholders' lack of power, this rule and its implied market remedy are effective checks on managerial actions. As more shareholders in a corporation express their dissatisfaction by selling, the market price of the corporation's shares declines, and outsiders are alerted to the possibility of gains to be secured from new and improved management [SB 21]. The threat that outsiders will launch a takeover bid by purchasing shares is a powerful incentive for management to operate the firm in a manner that enhances shareholders' interests [SB 20]. To the extent that managers themselves are substantial shareholders, moreover, declining stock prices will diminish their personal wealth [SB 55, SB 56].

The impact of these market restraints largely will be lost if the critics' proposals are adopted. There is no reason to believe that small shareholders will be willing to incur the substantial information and monitoring costs necessary to identify and elect the "most qualified" candidates, or even that the candidates will be chosen on the basis of their managerial abilities. A plausible supposition is that candidates will be selected on the basis of idiosyncratic preferences or that, given shareholders' traditional and understandable reluctance to participate actively in corporate governance, no one will be nominated.

OTHER PROBLEMS WITH PROPOSED CHANGES

With respect to the other details of the proposed reforms, it should be pointed out that the vast increase in board powers and responsibilities would result, simply, in the creation of another level of management, except that the top level would be composed of persons who would be less likely to have the specialized management skills needed to discharge their duties. The existing system provides ample flexibility for redefining the role of corporate directors to meet changing conditions, as witnessed by the growing acceptance of audit committees and other specialized monitoring functions for outside directors.

Finally, the insistence on restricting voting rights to "beneficial" owners is manifestly impractical. We are given no assistance in determining how to identify beneficial owners, how "financial intermediaries" such as insurance companies are to "pass through" voting rights, or even who the "beneficial owners" of institutional investors are.

In sum, the proposed changes in corporate elections are certain to be costly, likely to result in decreased efficiency, and unlikely to be of any benefit to anyone with a legitimate interest in corporate governance.

ADDITIONAL READINGS: 7, 92, 146, 214, 282, 285, 305, 362, 381.

18. Should Corporate Managers' Liability for Third-Party Injuries Be Expanded?

ROLAND N. McKEAN
Department of Economics
University of Virginia

Editor's Summary   If liability for unintended damages shifts from the corporate entity to the individual corporate executive, the anticipated reduction in subsequent damages will entail unanticipated costs. Managers will bargain for higher salaries to help offset their additional risks and personal insurance premiums. Managers will become persons who specialize in a mixture of management and risk bearing, replacing those who specialize in management functions alone. The stock market's ability to provide an automatic mechanism for shifting risks to those with a comparative advantage in shouldering them will be crippled. And, more resources will be devoted to shifting liability within the management structure itself. Because of the resulting reduction in efficiency, the shift of liability from the corporation to the individual manager will yield higher costs, higher prices, lower rates of return, lower levels of investment and saving, and lower future production levels.

Some observers regard the penalties on corporations as woefully inadequate, yielding insufficient deterrence of crime and of other spillover costs. Hence, these observers believe that executives should be held personally liable for damages and violations resulting from corporate activities [328: 102–108]. I do not question here the desirability of punishment for specific persons who commit willful criminal offenses, whether those persons be executives or janitors. I wish to concentrate on liability for unintended damages, not on punishment for criminal activities.

THE GENERAL CHARACTER OF LIABILITY

The possibilities for liability are many, including liability for a firm's contribution to damage from toxic substances, liability for environmental deterioration, and liability for injuries to health [SB 3]. Laws and court decisions have been moving toward assigning liability to corporate officers, even when those officers do not know about the actions leading to damages [*Business Week,* 10 May 1976: 110–116]. Some urge that executives should be liable, whether or not damages occur, if the people they supervise violate federal or local regulations.

Individual responsibility and accountability generally are commend-able. Assigning liability to corporate officers instead of to corporations, however, would bring certain disadvantages, and these should be weighed against the advantages. The issue is: which liability assignment seems, on balance, to be better?

In a hypothetical world without costs for making transactions, the liability assignment would make no difference from the standpoint of achieving economic efficiency. (This world would have to include risks of accidental damage but a perfect market for insurance.) Consumers, stock-holders, managers, and workers would pool resources and hire each other to act efficiently so that, for instance, those who were least averse to risk would bear the risks. This arrangement would produce the optimal degree of safety. As long as arrangements could be made more efficient, it would pay people to agree with others to produce the more efficient arrangements. They would split up the resulting benefits among them-selves to make some persons better off and no one worse off.

THE EFFECTS OF MAKING CORPORATIONS LIABLE

In the real world, in which transactions are costly, liability assignment *does,* of course, affect efficiency. First, consider placing liabilities on the corpo-ration (through either lawsuits or fines). This may sound as though each person involved is able to pass the buck, yet in truth the risks and damages are assigned to an identifiable set of persons: the stockholders. Various monitoring costs prevent them from forcing managers to act exactly as they wish, but these owners are not helpless [11]. The always present *threat* of proxy fights makes management listen to coalitions of major shareholders [SB 17, SB 21]. Perhaps most important of all, stockholders who do not like the risks to which management is exposing them can sell their shares and move their resources to less risky corporations. Those managers who consequently find it difficult to get fresh capital suffer in comparison with other managers [7].

Given these pressures on managers, what will happen if liability for damages is placed on corporations? Investors will adjust in various ways. Since the change will affect all corporations, investors will not find ven-tures in which they are free of such liability. They will shift to some extent toward industries that threaten less damage. They will move to some extent toward consumption instead of saving. And, to some extent, they will have managers purchase liability insurance for corporations. They will also put pressure on managers (through normal market forces) to be more cautious in conducting business.

Officers, in turn, will reduce the risks of damages for which their corporations would be liable. They will reduce such risks by monitoring employees more carefully, obtaining more spillover-abatement equipment, making products safer, reducing the production of relatively hazardous chemicals and drugs, channeling research and innovations toward the development of safer products and processes, and so forth. If liabilities were for actual damages, the managers would concentrate their efforts mainly on damage-reducing steps. If there were also fines for violating regulations, managers would include steps to reduce violations, even if the laws foolishly established standards not closely related to prospective damages.

THE EFFECTS OF MAKING DIRECTORS AND OFFICERS LIABLE

If we now shift the liabilities to directors and officers, they will try to adjust in various ways. One step would be to get more liability insurance. Because of "moral hazard" (created by the inability to estimate risk) and monitoring costs, however, there will be exclusion clauses, and coverage will be incomplete. Coverage that is offered, moreover, will be expensive, and if managers have to pay even a portion of the premiums, they will prefer not to buy complete coverage but to adjust partly in other ways. Another step that managers will take is to bargain for higher salaries to help reimburse them for extra insurance premiums and to compensate for the extra risks that they will now face.

Because of transaction costs, however, management is certain to end up bearing more of the risks. Even if the corporation increases salaries fully to compensate the executives, the effect would be to hire the executives to take on risks: to accept the chances of variable outcomes, including the possibility of crippling lawsuits. The officers could not pass all the risks back to the shareholders unless the corporation could legally reimburse them for all judgments against the officers, which would mean legally nullifying the assignment of personal liability to the executives. This reimbursement would be too expensive, mainly because it simply would be illegal to work out such agreements.

The stockholders, moreover, would not in fact fully compensate the officers for accepting personal liability. The original preference of those who bought shares was to pay less to executives and shoulder the risks themselves. If the price of (liable) managers rises, the stockholders will demand less management—that is, they will settle for officers who will bear some additional risks, yet who will adjust partly by adopting more cautious policies, and who are less specialized and skilled in management. Also, the menu of risk-earnings mixtures available to investors will narrow.

It becomes more difficult, therefore, for those most willing to bear risks to assume those risks. If there is corporate liability, the stock market provides a mechanism for automatically placing the risks on those with a comparative advantage in shouldering them. If there is executive liability, however, this mechanism is crippled. (Corporations, of course, will continue to shoulder the residual risks of damage awards that bankrupt the officers responsible for damage. Otherwise, personal officer liability would be ineffective and unfair to those damaged; individual executives simply would not have enough resources to cover a Kepone or Hudson River PCB award. And, they might even protect themselves by placing their resources in their spouses' names.) When the dust settles, furthermore, a different kind of executive will emerge: a person who is somewhat less averse to risk (or somewhat more prone to risk), a specialist neither in managerial tasks nor in risk bearing, but in some mixture of these responsibilities. Thus, risks would be borne to a smaller extent by those least averse to bearing them. And, managerial duties no longer would be assigned to those with the greatest comparative advantage in managing. Because of the resulting reduction in efficiency, in the long run one could expect higher costs, higher prices, lower rates of return, lower levels of investment and saving, and lower future levels of production.

As usual, though, the adjustments would involve giving a little in all directions. Managers would accept somewhat higher personal risk (and be less efficiency-minded), but at the same time they would move toward greater caution and its accompanying higher costs. Presumably, this is the impact that the advocates of officer liability desire. Whether this impact by itself would be an improvement depends on how much extra caution would result from executive liability and on how much one values additional "safety."

Since managers would now face risks that formerly were spread among many (and more willing) risk bearers, they would go further with each adjustment than they would under corporate liability. Probably, they would reduce total research and development (other things remaining the same), focus research and development on a search for relatively safer products, and tend to avoid venturesome innovations. Industries with risky outputs or processes, as opposed to safer industries, would be discouraged to a greater extent than under corporate liability.

To reduce the risks of damage suits, top executives would set up more reporting systems, double checks on employees, bureaucratic rules, penalties on personnel for deviating from the script, and so on. Corporation presidents would try to shed some risks by contracting with employees for the assumption of liability for selected hazard-generating operations. (Indeed, new FDA regulations will sometimes require pinpointing responsibility for specific activities.) In one observer's words, "The President would appoint a Vice-President in Charge of Going to Jail." At first blush, this may seem like an outrageous waste, yet such adjustments might actually alleviate the uneconomical assignment of risks and managerial responsibilities.

Vulnerable executives would also use up resources in other efforts to dodge penalties, such as putting their assets in someone else's name. What would happen to total litigation costs and damage awards is hard to foresee. Executives would surely devote fewer resources to litigation than would corporations, and corporations would usually be barred, I assume, from paying litigation costs for corporate officers. Undoubtedly, however, there would be frequent lawsuits against officers *and* back-up suits against corporations. Not only would individual defendants be unable to meet large claims; courts might also be reluctant to penalize flesh-and-blood managers as heavily as they would "wealthy and impersonal" corporations. (Indeed, if the personal liability arrangement is poorly enforced because of sympathy for managers, it might actually *reduce* the deterrence of potential damage.)

Managers and stockholders might even find it economical to restrict the size of corporations more than they would under corporate liability so as to cut the costs of monitoring lower echelons and distant branches. By reducing the corporation's size, they might sacrifice economies of scale for for the sake of greater safety. One cannot be sure, however, since conventional economies of scale are not the only variables that determine corporate size. Some might welcome any size reduction as a benefit if, for example, they judge that economies of scale in buying political influence are the major advantage of great size [SB 12].

Except in connection with monitoring employees, on the other hand, it seems likely that extra risks placed on management might especially handicap small corporations. For them, the difficulties of attracting people having the desired management skills and the costs of the greater emphasis on safety might be severe handicaps. In the end, the shift to personal executive liability might reduce the variability in corporate size and, by handicapping bold innovations, aggravate the difficulties of entry by small new companies, thus yielding a less competitive framework. Some of these impacts, of course, are probably minor or relatively speculative.

SUMMARY

What are the major consequences of moving from corporate liability to officer-director liability? If risks are shifted effectively to managers, subsequent damages will tend to be reduced, although naturally this would entail costs. Risks, however, less often would be borne by those most willing and able to bear them, and managers would become persons who specialize in a mixture of management and risk bearing rather than persons who specialize in management tasks alone. These are the major sources of extra inefficiency, compared to putting liabilities on corporations. (Both the burden of paying for extra "safety" and the "excess burdens" from losses in efficiency largely would be shifted to consumers, though portions would be borne by owners of productive resources whose amount supplied does not vary substantially with prices for these resources.) We may willingly accept sacrifices further to reduce spillover threats to health, safety, and the environment. It seems likely, however, that increased corporate liability for damages would involve fewer inefficiencies than would a shift to personal officer-director liability.

ADDITIONAL READINGS: 20, 53, 239, 429.

19. Are Shareholders' Remedies for Improper Acts of Corporate Officials Insufficient?

THOMAS D. MORGAN
College of Law
University of Illinois

Editor's Summary   Corporate law critics argue that managers enjoy too many advantages in relations with shareholders. Under existing law, managers can be reimbursed for the costs of proxy contests, and this dissuades minority shareholders from engaging in corporate political activity and from contesting corporate elections. Existing law, however, does not completely preclude insurgents from being reimbursed for the costs of proxy fights; insurgents, if they win, can receive reimbursement. A considerable percentage of stockholder suits, moreover, are brought on behalf of lawyers and stockholders because of the nuisance value of such suits. Many of these suits do nothing more than provide legal fees for lawyers. They do little to help either the average stockholder or the corporation. Society bears considerable costs as a result of this nuisance litigation.

That corporate officers and directors have a duty to act in the best interest of the corporation is well accepted. Any failure to act in that best interest tends to diminish the corporation's earnings, and the value of the shareholders' stock. It may seem to follow, therefore, that shareholders should have a tough, readily available remedy for improper, or even negligent, acts of major corporate officials.

EXISTING SHAREHOLDER REMEDIES

There are several shareholder remedies now available. One remedy is the suit by an individual shareholder to redress a violation of shareholder rights, such as the right to see a stockholder list [14, 212]. A second remedy is the shareholders' class action to enforce personal rights that shareholders have in common, such as the right to force payment of certain dividends [*Knapp v. Bankers Securities Corp.*, 230 F.2d 717 (3d Cir. 1956); *Dodge v. Ford Motor Co.*, 204 Mich. 459 (1919)]. A third remedy is private action for damages, which has been held available under the proxy rules if, for example, the terms of a merger are misrepresented [*J. I. Case Co. v. Borak*, 377 U.S. 426, 84 S. Ct. 1555, 12 L. Ed. 2d, 423 (1964)]. A fourth remedy is action under SEC Rule 14a-8 in response to a shareholder's request to force a firm to put particular shareholder proposals in its proxy material. A fifth remedy lies in suits to recover short-swing profits from corporate insiders under Sec. 16(b) of the 1934 Securities Exchange Act [*Blair v. Lamb,* 314 F.2d 618 (2d Cir. 1963); 106]. When one looks at all these shareholder remedies, one may legitimately question the basis of concern about limits on other actions.

Concern usually centers, however, only on the shareholder derivative action, a suit that one or more shareholders bring in the name of the corporation to get something due the corporation. If officer or director mismanagement causes the corporation to lose money, for example, this remedy makes it possible to recover the sum. In form, the action is unusual: one sues to enforce not one's own rights, but those of the corporation. But superficially, the idea is reasonable, and if existing rules relating to such a suit adversely affect the shareholder role, perhaps change is due.

PRACTICAL LIMITS TO SHAREHOLDER ACTIONS

The desirability of a corrective role for shareholders, nevertheless, should be challenged. In very small corporations, the shareholders may also be the managers, and thus they are in a position to review the merits of decisions. One of the significant benefits of the corporate form, however, is the possibility of specialized roles for capital providers (shareholders) and capital managers (officers and directors). If shareholders want to be managers and have the necessary skills, they can go into business for themselves [284].

Shareholders in almost any large corporation, however, are suppliers of investment capital who bet that hired management has the skills to use that capital effectively. Far from pilfering their authority from unsuspecting shareholders, corporate managers are performing tasks that shareholders would find expensive and inefficient to perform themselves. Managers thereby allow shareholders to diversify their investments without becoming decision makers in all the enterprises in which they invest. Allowing shareholders to elect directors subjects management to the risk that shareholders might someday sell out to a group that could choose new managers [SB 55]. But apart from the value of such an ultimate sanction, it is reasonable to suggest that most corporate shareowners hold, and should hold, their shares in hopes of getting dividends and capital gains, not to manage the company or file shareholder suits against those who do.

The threat of such suits as a remedy, furthermore, is not without its costs. The loss of potential managers unwilling to assume the risks of suit is difficult to document but potentially serious. Likewise, the costs of a defensive strategy by managers seeking to be able to justify a decision (for example, securing the opinions of outside counsel, independent auditors, and other consultants) may be far from trivial. And, shareholders themselves involuntarily will bear the added costs.

Some remedy short of a complete change in management, however, is probably necessary to deter, and obtain compensation for, serious wrongs done the corporation by dishonest or inept officials. The question is what the nature of that remedy should be. Since officers and directors are probably reluctant to sue each other, and since establishing a public prosecutor of corporate officials is not an attractive option, shareholder suits may seem an inevitable part of corporation law.

THE DAMAGE OF "STRIKE SUITS"

But, important qualifications are necessary. Shareholder suits are potential "strike suits": suits filed solely to coerce a settlement that is financially rewarding to either the plaintiffs or their attorneys, or to both. For example, around the turn of the century one professional stockholder conducted campaigns against at least twenty-three corporations involving over forty suits and personally received several million dollars in settlements. One study shows that in a ten-year period, shareholder actions recovered for corporations less than 5 percent of the amounts claimed [*Cohen v. Beneficial Industrial Loan Corp.*, 337 U.S. 541, 69 S. Ct. 1221, 93 L.Ed. 1528 (1949);153].

That strike suits serve no corporate purpose is obvious. It is easy to understand, also, that in the case of a large corporation and a large damage claim, it may be cheaper for an officer or a director to settle rather than fight. A corporation that is trying to attract managers will ultimately bear the cost in the form of higher salaries, indemnity insurance, or lower-quality personnel [SB 18]. In that case, all the shareholders in the company will be the losers.

Procedural impediments to shareholder suits, in this context, become easier to understand. Several states have adopted security-for-expenses legislation, which requires that a shareholder bringing a derivative action post security against the need to pay the expenses of the corporation, including attorneys' fees, if the suit turns out to be without merit [14, 143]. This requirement may discourage some legitimate suits, but it makes blackmail more costly. If the plaintiff can make a case, the corporation, in most instances, will bear the cost of the plaintiff's bond, and the plaintiff will lose nothing. In some states, if a sufficient number of small shareholders join the plaintiff's case, the requirement of posting security may be waived. Security-for-expenses legislation certainly is far from perfect, but it is an attempt to discourage ill-considered or fraudulent suits while minimizing the potentially adverse impact on legitimate claims.

WHO SHOULD PAY LEGAL FEES?

Some critics describe the failure of courts automatically to order payment of all stockholder-plaintiffs' attorneys' fees as an impediment to suits. A court may order such payment, but usually it will not do so, even in the cases of successful plaintiffs, if the lawsuits do not bring "substantial benefit" to the corporations [205]. Given the theory that a derivative suit is brought on behalf of a corporation, it may be reasonable that a corporation should pay the fee of its "champion."

Because a corporation does not initiate such a suit, however, the "substantial benefit" rule has been developed to discourage self-appointed and self-aggrandizing attorneys who file suits primarily to enrich themselves. Payment is to be made only in cases in which a corporation truly is better off as a result of a suit. Actual financial recovery is not required, but theoretical benefit is not enough. This result is unsatisfactory to professional corporate watchdogs, but their own interests in the issue are not hard to discern. As a means of balancing the various interests involved, the approach seems eminently reasonable.

THE ALLEGED EFFECTS OF MANAGER INSURANCE

Indemnification of officers and directors by insurance that corporations pay for, while technically not an impediment to suits, is viewed as another means of protecting senior managers from accountability to shareholders. Such insurance usually covers expenses for defending officials in shareholder litigation related to alleged misconduct that falls short of self-dealing. Critics charge that the insurance diminishes the corporate officers' incentive to be careful [53, 241, SB 18].

That same charge, of course, is made against medical malpractice insurance and even against auto insurance, and the answer to the charge remains the same. The incentive for being careful is not wholly the fear of a legal judgment; an officer's or a director's reputation is as much at stake in meritorious shareholder litigation as is a doctor's in a malpractice case. The kind of mistake that justifies a judgment against a director is the kind that ruins a career. Insurance can remove only the short-run financial loss resulting from a negligence judgment and the cost of defending baseless suits. These effects are not insignificant; a company that fails to bear those costs would certainly have to compensate its officers and directors in other ways having equal or greater financial value. But, indemnification of senior officials is unlikely to eliminate their concern about good performance, and it should reduce significantly their concern about the financial consequences of baseless suits.

SUMMARY

Reliance on shareholder suits as a primary means of controlling the actions of officers and directors is both shortsighted and naïve. The positive rewards, financial and otherwise, that are associated with good performance and the internal corporate sanctions associated with the failure to perform up to standard are likely to be a senior official's greatest concerns [7]. Shareholder suits can never be more than a backup if all internal controls fail. While the availability of shareholder suits is a necessity, the possible abuse of such suits should be a matter of concern to all associated with corporations. In that perspective, the law's limitations on shareholder remedies are both understandable and desirable.

ADDITIONAL READINGS: 227, 247, 281.

20. Do Tender Offers Damage Stockholders?

ROBERT SMILEY
Graduate School of Business
Cornell University

Editor's Summary   Although takeover bids, or tender offers, are often criticized as the tools of corporate raiders, they benefit both consumers and shareholders. Takeover bids typically are aimed at unprofitable, sluggish companies. Everyone concerned, except the inefficient managers, benefits from a management change. Takeover bids facilitate the liquidation of assets and the shift of resources to other, more highly valued uses. Acquiring firms do not make abnormal profits through takeovers, and stockholders in acquired firms tend to be better off after the takeovers. Takeover bids and tender offers promote the efficient operation of corporations. Instead of following regulatory policies that increase the costs of takeover bids (the Williams Amendment), public policy should recognize that takeover bids tend to yield lower prices and better products for consumers and higher returns to shareholders, as corporate assets are used more efficiently.

What assurances do consumers and shareholders have that corporations are managed in a responsible and efficient fashion? There are several market forces that operate to induce managers to be effective. One is the takeover bid, or tender offer. The managers of a corporation with dispersed ownership must continuously be concerned that someone will make a takeover bid if they do not perform satisfactorily. (A takeover bid is an attempt to acquire control of a corporation through the purchase of stock on the open market and/or through a publicized tender offer.) In this chapter four common beliefs about the effects of takeover bids are listed and described, and the merits of these beliefs are examined. Then, the benefits consumers and shareholders derive from takeover bids are considered. The chapter ends with a discussion of several public policy issues.

CRITICISMS OF TAKEOVER BIDS

One of the most common criticisms of takeover bids is that they are undertaken by young upstarts who have little or no experience in the management of modern enterprises. These young upstarts, then, are seen as casting able managers out onto the streets. Indeed, Senator Harrison

Williams introduced a bill to restrict the use of takeovers in the United States because, as he claims, "In recent years we have seen proud old companies reduced to corporate shells after white-collar pirates have seized control" [210: 108].

Are the targets of takeover bids typically well-managed, proud old companies? In reviewing the economics literature, particularly with respect to the targets of takeover bids, Steiner concludes, "Studies of mergers occurring in the period from 1955–1965 tended to produce a uniform picture of merger targets as relatively unprofitable, sluggish, over-liquid firms, often with the history of static or declining earnings and dividends" [413: 185]. The evidence behind this statement is documented most carefully in Hayes and Taussig, Austin and Fishman, and Singh (for the United Kingdom) [210, 25, 399]. It simply is not true that the targets of most takeover bids are well-managed, fine old firms; they are much more often poorly managed firms—firms in which everyone but the ousted managers would benefit from a management change.

Another criticism of takeover bids is that the liquidation of "fine old firms" often follows successful takeover bids. The first response to this criticism is, of course, that there is nothing inherently wrong with the liquidation of a firm. If groups of assets are more highly valued when they are separated, instead of combined in a firm, that is a clear signal that they should be separated. Indeed, institutions that stand in the way of easy liquidation of asset groupings are deemed almost universally to be undesirable. Imagine the situation if a buggy whip company of the nineteenth century (or an ice company of the early twentieth century) could not be liquidated. One should not condone the milking of firms in a manner unfair to the minority shareholders. But, there are separate business practice laws to solve this problem; the solution is not to outlaw the takeover bid.

There is important evidence about whether or not liquidation is a primary motive for acquisition in takeover bids. Using a sample of twenty-four companies that made successful cash tender offers, Hayes and Taussig found that within the first five years after the mergers, "two-thirds of the companies reported selling off less than 6 percent of the acquired assets," and twenty-one of twenty-four firms "liquidated less than 26 percent" [210: 110]. Hence, even though liquidation is not, on the surface, undesirable, the issue does not appear to arise with great regularity in takeover bids.

A third set of criticisms of takeover bids involves the financial positions and motivations of the acquiring firms. These criticisms assert that the acquiring firms make huge speculative gains at the expense of the shareholders of the target firms. If this is the case, acquiring firms should show abnormally large profits from merger activity. Before looking at the evidence, however, it is useful to recall that competition in the market for corporate control (that is, competition to acquire the control of firms), if sufficiently intense, will preclude acquiring firms from making abnormally large profits. The price at which a firm can be acquired will be bid up by rival bidders to a level at which no profits are possible.

The empirical evidence bearing on this question is mixed. A number of studies—most notably one by Gort and Hogarty and one by Reid—find that, on balance, acquiring firms do not earn abnormal profits from mergers [196, 364]. Weston and Mansinghka, and Lev and Mandelker, on the other hand, find, after allowing for risks and other factors, that acquiring firms do earn abnormally large profits [457, 255]. In the most comprehensive study to date, Mandelker concludes, "Stockholders of acquiring firms seem to earn normal returns from mergers as from other investment-production activities with commensurate risk levels" [275: 303]. While this question deserves further empirical study, it is by no means clear that acquiring firms make speculative gains. Indeed, with a competitive market for the acquisition of takeover targets, there should not be excessive profits.

A final criticism of takeover bids is that the shareholders of the acquired firms are treated shabbily. One can view this criticism as a relative question: How well were they treated by the incumbent managers? Smiley finds that "the value (at the time of the decision to tender) of total wealth losses of tendered firms is 50 percent of what the firm would have sold for had its management maximized profits throughout the ten-year period prior to the offer. Alternatively, the market price of the firm is one-half of what it would have been, had the firm maximized profits" [401: 30].

But, do the stockholders of the acquired firms benefit from the takeovers? Gort and Hogarty provide some evidence bearing on this question. They found, after studying twenty-seven cases, that stockholders of sixteen of the acquired firms benefited by the exchange of stock in the acquired firms for stock in the acquiring firms. They also found that the average gain in all twenty-seven cases was positive and large [196]. Mandelker found that "stockholders of acquired firms earn abnormal returns of approximately 14 percent, on the average, in the seven months preceding the merger" [275: 323]. These findings are consistent with Smiley's evidence regarding abnormally high share price appreciation for targets of takeover bids. [401].

BENEFITS OF TAKEOVER BIDS

A discussion of takeover bids should involve more than a mere defense of them against criticisms. Takeover bids constitute a very important market force in our economy, a force that benefits society at large as well as shareholders. To understand this function one must ask: What forces or constraints act in the American economy to ensure that the managers of corporations (in which ownership is dispersed among many shareholders) will perform effectively? What assurance is there, furthermore, that a corporation will be managed efficiently, in the interest of shareholders and (*at least* to the degree that management will conserve resources) in the interest of society at large, rather than merely in the (perhaps whimsical) interests of the executives currently in control of the corporation?

Constraints and incentives other than takeover bids include competition in the product market, pressures from current shareholders, and the desire for higher salaries or greater stock option returns from better managerial performance. Takeover bids, however, are essential elements of the complementary sets of incentives and constraints on managers that serve to ensure good performance. A manager who performs poorly, either because of a conscious misallocation of the company's (and, eventually, the consumers') resources or because of inadequate skills, must constantly worry about the threat of a takeover. It is precisely this threat that managers consider when they are contemplating the diversion of large amounts of resources from stockholders to themselves. (This diversion may result in higher product prices.) The modern manager must constantly look over his or her shoulder for fear of a takeover bid.

The mechanism works thus. If a manager performs poorly for one reason or another, the returns to shareholders decline, and the stock price drops. If the stock price drops below the level achievable by an efficiently managed corporation, the stage is set for a takeover bid. If the stock price drops enough so that the transaction costs of the offer (for example, brokerage and legal fees) can be recovered through stock price appreciation after the corporation's management is reformed (such appreciation will reflect the market's anticipation of higher earnings from better management), the acquisition of control of the corporation becomes profitable to a bidder, and a bid can be expected to be forthcoming. When the stock price of a corporation drops by an amount in the neighborhood of the transaction costs, the incumbent managers should be concerned. It is this concern that society ought to encourage because it ensures efficient corporate performance.

A critical question, one for which there is empirical evidence, is: How large are these transaction costs? Put another way, how concerned must incumbent managers be about the threat of a takeover? Using a sample of ninety-five tender offers from 1956 through 1970, Smiley estimated that transaction costs are approximately 14 percent of the market value of a firm after an offer takes place [401].

Perhaps more important than the absolute magnitude of transaction costs is the effect of public policy action on these costs. Using the same sample, Smiley estimated that the Williams Amendment to the Securities

Exchange Act, which was passed in 1968 and which severely restricts the use of cash tender offers, increased the cost of tender offers 13 to 27 percent [400]. The Williams Amendment, though it may have had other beneficial aspects, clearly has diminished the extent of protection for investors and for society at large that derives from the takeover mechanism. It is by no means clear that a cost-benefit analysis of the Williams Amendment would show that the benefits from its enactment have overcome these associated, additional costs.

PUBLIC POLICY CONCERNS ABOUT TAKEOVER BIDS

The question of what constitutes an appropriate antitrust policy for the United States economy (whether federal or state) encompasses many other issues besides those discussed here. One issue that is usually neglected, however, is the effect of antitrust policy prohibitions against horizontal and vertical mergers on the efficacy of the takeover mechanism. To see the connection, one need merely ask these questions: Of all potential bidders, which subset is most likely to have the best information about the effectiveness of the incumbent managers of a firm? And, who is in the best position to know if managers are particularly ineffective, whether consciously or not? Manne asserts that the corporations in the best position to know which firms are poorly managed are precisely those corporations that are precluded from takeover bids and mergers by American antitrust policy [282]. A firm's competitors (since the managers continuously face the same kinds of problems), and to a somewhat lesser degree the purchasers of the firm's products and the sellers of products to the potential target, are indeed in an advantageous position to gather information about the degree of inefficiency of the firm's management group. Manne suggests that we reexamine our antitrust policy in this light.

ADDITIONAL READINGS: 12, 103, 154, 156, 211, 227, 286, 379, 458.

21. Is Corporate Ownership Divorced from Control?

H. E. FRECH III
Department of Economics
Harvard University
and
University of California, Santa Barbara

Editor's Summary   Diffuse stock ownership decreases the benefits that individual stockholders receive from monitoring management decisions and also increases the costs of monitoring. But, diffuse ownership of stock provides easier access to risk capital. The right to buy and sell equities and thus to move toward a more or less diffused stockholder structure is valuable to stockholders. There is an incidental advantage of diffused stock ownership, furthermore, which encourages efficient management. Because ownership of less than 10 percent of the stock of a firm may be sufficient for control, it is easier for an outsider to purchase a controlling interest in a corporation with diffused ownership, especially when the outsider believes that the firm is poorly managed. Thus, dispersed ownership reduces the costs of control and makes it easier to take control from owners who are lax in monitoring their managers, to change managers, and to realize the appreciation of the value of shares. There is less careful monitoring in regulated firms. So, the managers of these firms can divert some resources to their own ends. The stockholders of these firms have less of an incentive to monitor, since they cannot claim the full residual income if it exceeds a government-imposed ceiling on the rate of return.

That the managers of a modern corporation act in their own interests rather than in the interests of the firm's owners is a widespread belief. This belief rests, largely, on a series of confusions but stems most directly from the observation that share ownership in many modern corporations is widely dispersed [52, 299, 341]. The popular argument holds that this dispersion of ownership over large numbers of stockholders, especially in the absence of a dominant individual stockholder, allows the control of a firm to pass from the stockholders to the managers. As a result, so the argument goes, managers make decisions in their own interests, and at the expense of stockholders' wealth.

THE FACT OF DIFFUSION

First, one should consider the element of truth in the claim. Diffuse ownership of stock does weaken each stockholder's incentive to monitor managerial performance to assure that managers make decisions in the owners' interests. As De Alessi suggests, "More diffused ownership not only implies greater transactions costs, including greater costs of collecting and disseminating information regarding the efficiency of the managers' decisions, but also a smaller return to each stockholder from seeking to police inefficiencies" [123: 842].

One cannot conclude from this statement, however, that the firm's owners have somehow been robbed, that somehow they have lost something valuable. For, in an important sense, the stockholders themselves have chosen freely the degree of diffusion of ownership. No matter how diffuse ownership is, nevertheless, the stockholders of a corporation are the holders of private property rights in the firm. To understand the meaning of this point, consider what the analysis of private property rights implies for the issue of control versus ownership.

THE RIGHTS OF OWNERSHIP

Private ownership of a firm has nothing to do with diffusion of stock ownership. Rather, it refers to a situation in which the right to make decisions about the use of a resource, including its transfer (for example, its sale), is vested exclusively in one person. Most fundamentally, private ownership implies that the decisions an owner makes about the use of a resource affect the owner's wealth. To make rational use of a resource, the owner must have the right to delegate authority over the use of the resource in whatever manner is advantageous. This relationship between rights and rational use becomes clear in the case of a person who rents the use of a physical asset—say, an automobile—to another person. The delegation or assignment of authority through the rental agreement leads to less active owner participation in the decisions pertaining to the use of the automobile, but it does not make the owner any less an owner. The owner prefers the rental income to the day-to-day use and control of the automobile.

In much the same way, in an industrial corporation, dispersion of ownership involves the delegation of authority. Delegation that derives from dispersed share ownership does make it more difficult for a single shareholder to revoke unilaterally the transfer of authority to the existing managers (for example, by firing them). But, the rights of an owner in a private property rights system include the right to decide how much authority to delegate, the right to decide how to delegate authority, and the right to set the terms on which one can cancel the delegation. Diffuse ownership of stock is simply a permissible contractual arrangement that can be entered into by those owning the rights.

RISK SPREADING, CAPITAL, AND CONTROL

As observed earlier, however, diffuse ownership increases the costs and decreases the benefits of careful monitoring of management officers. These changes could lead to lower wealth for stockholders if managers become less concerned about stockholders' wealth. Here, a paradox seems to exist. Why would owners voluntarily allow ownership rights to become diffuse? Why, indeed, would an individual owner ever sell equity shares to others and thus raise monitoring costs?

To ask the question in the second, stronger form is to answer it, or at least give a clear hint of the answer. Shareholders agree to a more diffuse ownership pattern to raise capital. Clearly, there are advantages to markets in risk bearing that publicly traded shares of stock make possible. It is easier to raise capital if the risk is spread in efficient ways, as investors view them. The individual investor faces less risk if he or she can hold a balanced portfolio of shares in several firms—ideally, firms operating in distinctly different product markets, so that the prices of the stocks held are less likely to move together.

This reduction in an individual owner's risk that results from the diversification of stock ownership has implications for the least-cost method of financing a firm. From the point of view of the stockholders of a firm who are considering the possibility of issuing new stock, thereby making ownership more diffuse, the benefit of a stock issue is that they can raise capital cheaply. They can sell relatively small amounts of stock to widely varying persons so that each person has a reasonably balanced portfolio.

Owners have the choice of keeping the ownership of a firm concentrated, or of allowing it to become more diffused. That the owners of most modern corporations allow shares to become more widely held is strong evidence that the benefits to owners outweigh the costs. Further, owners make this choice continually in the modern economy. Many closely held corporations go public each year, indicating again that the optimal mixture of incentives for monitoring and access to inexpensive capital involves great diffusion of ownership. Also, the current owners of any stock can choose to make ownership more concentrated by purchasing more stock themselves. That they choose not to do so indicates that they believe they have an optimal position in the trade-off between good monitoring incentives and access to inexpensive equity capital.

The ability to sell or buy equity, and thus to move toward a more or less diffused stockholder structure, is a valuable right for the owners of firms. Far from being hurt by a more diffuse ownership, the owners benefit from the easier access to risk capital that accompanies wider diffusion.

There is another, incidental advantage of diffuse stock ownership, which works in the direction of efficient monitoring. If stock ownership is widely dispersed, it is easier for an outsider who perceives that a particular firm is poorly managed to purchase enough stock to get control, change management, and realize appreciation. Ownership of less than 10 percent of the stock, in many corporations, is sufficient for control. Thus, dispersed ownership reduces the costs of the capital market for control, making it easier to take control from owners who are lax in monitoring their managers.

In sum, owner monitoring of managers is without doubt more lax now than in the past when large stockholders held larger percentages of the stock of firms. Far from being an unfortunate development from the point of view of stockholders and the economy in general, however, this change represents a movement toward a new, efficient combination of incentives and risk spreading. That the original stockholders approved the stock issues that led to the dispersion of ownership and that many closely held modern firms are also moving toward more diffused stock ownership constitute strong evidence for regarding this change as desirable. The benefits of widely dispersed ownership for efficient risk bearing must balance the losses from less intensive monitoring.

REGULATED FIRMS

A source of some confusion is the related issue of the kinds of property rights held by the stockholders of a firm. In the case of regulated firms, especially firms subject to rate-of-return regulation, stockholders do not participate fully in the residuals (profits) of the firms. Property rights are not fully private, and so stockholders have less incentive to monitor the actions of managers. In this situation, one cannot achieve the optimal trade-off between monitoring and risk spreading. Thus, regulated firms have managers who pursue their own interests to a larger extent than in the case of private property firms.

As Alchian and Kessel observe, furthermore, many firms that are not formally regulated are regulated informally by the fear of antitrust action or direct regulation [12]. Consequently, these firms essentially *are* regulated. Their stockholders cannot appropriate the full residual income, since the resulting high profits would attract the punitive attention of the government. Thus, managers of both formally and implicitly regulated stock firms are monitored less carefully. This laxness in monitoring is not caused by the separation of ownership and control through widespread stock ownership. Rather, it is a matter of a lack of private property rights. This problem should not be confused with the effects of diffuse stock ownership in a private property situation.

ADDITIONAL READINGS: 7, 11, 96, 169, 216, 282, 401, 458, 459.

INFORMATION AND CORPORATE CONTROL

22. Do Investors Need More Information?

ARTHUR B. LAFFER
Department of Finance and Business Economics
University of Southern California

Editor's Summary   Scholarly research produces overwhelming evidence that securities markets are efficient in the sense that market prices accurately reflect all past and present information and serve as optimal predictors of future share performance. Using past and present stock prices, corporate financial statements, and government statistics, researchers, find no rule that could have been used in the past to perform better than "the market." This "efficient market hypothesis" means that each and every shareholder receives the full benefits of the information collected by researchers or disseminated by corporations. Thus, the securities market is a fair game.

In any discussion of information as it relates either to the stock market or to companies whose shares are traded on the major exchanges, one is led into a consideration of the efficiency of markets. Over the past century, a body of scholarly research aimed at testing the so-called efficient market hypothesis has emerged from academic institutions, as well as from other sources. This research focuses principally on individual company issues traded in the American stock market, but it has also encompassed bond markets, foreign exchange markets, foreign stock markets, futures markets, and commodity markets [154].

THE EFFICIENT MARKET HYPOTHESIS

The efficient market hypothesis states, in its simplest form, that the current market's evaluation of an asset accurately reflects all past and present information. Market prices, therefore, are the optimal predictors of future performance. The implied expected yields on assets have been arbitraged to the point where there are no exceptional expected returns available. (The discussion here assumes that assets are equally risky. The incorporation of assets with different risks, however, in no way alters the propositions in this chapter [155].) One implication of the efficient market hypothesis is that the actual prices of any specific asset relative to the market aggregate follow a random walk. Yields on that asset relative to the market are random or, more precisely, represent a fair game.

THREE FORMS OF TESTING THE EFFICIENT MARKET HYPOTHESIS

All research on the efficient market hypothesis consists of three forms of testing. The first form is called the *weak* form. The proposition tested under the weak form is that the pattern of actual past price performance is helpful in predicting future price performance. Thus, if we know how well one stock, one group of stocks, or even one managed fund has performed historically, the question asked is whether this knowledge offers any insight as to how well the stock, for instance, will perform in the future.

The second form of testing the efficient market hypothesis incorporates all past and current information about other data series readily available to the marketplace. The question asked under this *semistrong* form is whether other series, such as the money supply or data on fiscal policy, allow one to predict the relative performance of assets in the marketplace.

The final form of testing looks explicitly at insider information. The question asked under this *strong* form of testing the hypothesis is whether there is *any* information, no matter how well guarded, that would enable one to predict the relative performance of assets in the marketplace. Insider information would include the knowledge that corporate executives might have about their companies, or even familiarity with the buy-and-sell bids in floor traders' books.

The specific method of analysis used in each of these forms of testing the efficient market hypothesis is to search past data for any kind of filter rule that consistently could be used to predict yields that are higher than the average yield of the market. With 100 percent hindsight, the data available to the researchers include observations on what actually occurs. The data base for these studies is massive and includes all quoted stock prices, corporate financial statements, and government statistics.

TESTS OF THE EFFICIENT MARKET HYPOTHESIS

The results are as impressive as the data base is massive, for from this enormous endeavor, scholars everywhere cannot find any major deviation from the efficient market hypothesis in the actual patterns of past price data. In its weak form, the test of the efficient market hypothesis holds up extraordinarily well. What this means is that there is no way to beat the market by knowing how well a stock or group of stocks has done in the past. This weak form of the test aroused an extraordinarily adverse response from a number of portfolio managers.

Almost all the work on the semistrong form of testing the hypothesis, similarly, reveals that the notion of pure efficiency is an exceptionally good description of the real world. Virtually all the tests on readily available data reveal that these data, no matter how transformed, add nothing to one's ability to forecast the performance of asset prices. The semistrong form, again, encountered an exceptionally hostile response from members of all sorts of groups who believed that they had the key to stock market success. This was true especially for the monetarists, who believed that one could predict stock market performance by using the money supply data.

If insider information exists, the efficient market hypothesis shows itself to be unrepresentative of the actual performance of asset prices. People with inside information appear to be able systematically to do better than the market. This finding is what one would intuitively expect.

It is important to mention here a number of studies focusing on the prices of or yields on assets other than stocks. One implication of efficient markets is that interest rates should forecast inflation rates without systematic error [251]. This result appears to hold. Also, one should be able to use the interest rate term structure to forecast future short-term rates [312]. This result, again, appears to hold.

In an efficient market it is highly unlikely that there will be lags in the effects of monetary policy [250]. Many studies fail to uncover systematic lags. Risk, to the extent that it carries a premium in the marketplace, should be related more to aggregate market movements than to individual asset variations. Forward currency and commodity prices should be accurate forecasters of future spot currency and commodity prices. Exchange rate changes should be associated closely with differential rates of inflation, and so on. The implications of efficient markets are both comprehensive and deep. The breadth of empirical support in many highly diversified areas is quite astounding.

CONCLUSION

In all, then, the efficient market hypothesis remains unrefuted save in the case of specific insider information. Disclosure laws, as well as stock acquisition laws for corporate officers, safeguard the average investor from exploitation resulting from insider information. Additional requirements for the production and dissemination of information appear at best to be redundant. At worst, of course, additional requirements will add to the already burdensome administrative and compliance costs. This additional burden will tend to make everyone worse off, with no compensating improvement anywhere.

ADDITIONAL READINGS: 108, 156, 157, 158, 242, 267, 268, 281, 372.

23. Should Line-of-Business Reporting Be Expanded?

GEORGE J. BENSTON

Graduate School of Management and
The Center for Study of
Financial Institutions and Securities Markets
University of Rochester

Editor's Summary   Proponents of expanded, mandatory line-of-business reporting claim that it would benefit investors and others, since investors would have more detailed information on the profitability of particular business segments and would be able to make "better" investment decisions. These decisions, they believe, would lead to a more efficient resource allocation and to more effective government antitrust activity. But, there are costs associated with line-of-business reporting. Securities markets now appear to operate efficiently with available financial information. The problems in line-of-business reporting would, at best, allow this kind of reporting to make only a marginal contribution to useful financial information. Where line-of-business data are meaningful, disclosure may give more useful information to an enterprise's competitors than to investors. The cost to corporations of providing added data would be considerable, since corporations do not, and perhaps cannot, maintain their records according to the FTC's categories. Thus, line-of-business reporting may cause shareholders to bear extra costs in return for trivial benefits.

BACKGROUND

The merger movement and growth of conglomerates in the middle 1950s and early 1960s elicited increased pressure from economists, security analysts, legislators, and others for disclosure by corporations of financial information on individual lines of business (LBs). The call for detailed information, such as revenues, expenses, and assets or capital used in LBs, was raised in 1965 hearings before the Senate Subcommittee on Antitrust and Monopoly. Witnesses before the subcommittee testified that investors, the Justice Department, and the Federal Trade Commission (among others) were unable to get "vital" information that was buried in the aggregate figures that conglomerates and vertically integrated corporations published. Consequently, witnesses claimed that the capital market does not allocate resources efficiently and that government antitrust activities are impeded. These hearings gave rise to expanded reporting requirements by the Securities and Exchange Commission (SEC); a statement (No. 14) that the Financial Accounting Standards Board (FASB) adopted on December 14, 1976, which requires "financial reporting for segments of a business enterprise"; and a line of business report program of the Federal Trade Commission (FTC), which is being contested in the courts.

PRESENT REQUIREMENTS

The Securities Exchange Act of 1934 required all corporations with over $1 million in assets and over 500 holders of a single class of equity shares to disclose rather detailed financial statements. Companies registering under the securities acts had to disclose the relative importance of products or services (but not net profits) that generated more than 10 percent of gross volume (15 percent for companies having a volume of less than $50 million). Disclosure was in the narrative or text portion of the registration statement. In 1969, this requirement, as well as a requirement for disclosure of lines of business that showed losses of 10 percent or more of income before taxes and extraordinary items, was extended to the annual financial reports (10K). An additional requirement is a statement of the net profits (or losses) that each line of business generates, if the calculation is practicable.

The SEC's line of business (LB) disclosure rules are not as extensive as some would wish. Besides the 10 percent (or 15 percent) criterion, no more than ten LBs need be delineated. Management, furthermore, has the discretion to define a "line of business." (The bases for this choice must be described.) And, the net income for each LB need not be presented if management decides that the calculation is not practicable.

FASB Statement 14 applies to all "business enterprises," including those not publicly held. It requires those doing business in more than one industry to report revenue, income, and asset data for each significant segment. Also, companies must report on their foreign operations, export sales, and dependence on one or a few major customers. Minimum disclosure includes revenue, operating profit or loss (revenue less "reasonably" allocated operating expenses other than corporate office and interest expenses), and identifiable assets. The rules for identifying lines of business are similar to those that the SEC adopted.

The FTC's LB report program is to be applied initially to the 450 largest manufacturing corporations. It differs from the other programs in specifying the lines of business to which corporations must assign all revenues, expenses, and assets. This requirement is imposed so that data from many corporations can be combined to produce average profit rates on sales and averages on assets and on other aggregated data.

ARGUMENTS FOR LB REPORTING

The SEC and FASB LB reporting requirements are designed to give shareholders and investors more information about the operations of individual corporations. Without such information, proponents claim, shareholders cannot adequately monitor the managers of corporations. LB reporting makes it more difficult for managers to avoid censure for unsuccessful operations, and LB reporting also permits a more effective analysis of a corporation's operations. Proponents argue, furthermore, that the reported profits (or losses) of conglomerate and vertically integrated corporations, in particular, may derive primarily from one or more business segments, customers, foreign operations, and so forth. Without information on the profitability of business segments, for example, one cannot estimate effectively the profitability and risk of such enterprises. Nor can one pass judgment on their respective managements.

The FTC lists five reasons for collecting LB data by well-defined categories [essentially standard industrial code (SIC) groups]. These are, first, more effective government antitrust activity; second, the improvement of macroeconomic policy (particularly control of inflation); third, a more efficient allocation of resources in the economy as investors learn which are the best profit opportunities; fourth, improved studies of economic performance; and, fifth, the provision of useful information to business, labor, and investors. The Commission claims that revenues, fully allocated costs, and assets, aggregated by SIC product groups, will enable regulators and investors to identify the products and markets in which above "normal" profits are being earned. Unless this information is reported, the FTC believes, monopoly pricing and similar misallocations of resources will continue to damage the economy. The economics staff of the FTC also wants profitability data by line of business for studies on the relationship of profits to concentration, expenditures for research and development, and advertising.

ARGUMENTS AGAINST LB REPORTING

One can challenge on several grounds the contention that LB data should be required of individual corporations. First, there is little evidence to indicate that the stock markets were inefficient, or would be inefficient, without LB disclosure. A large body of theoretical and empirical evidence supports the belief that the stock markets were efficient, and are efficient, with respect to financial information, in the sense that share prices very quickly discount this information and are unbiased estimates of intrinsic values [44: secs. 4.2.5–4.2.6; SB 22]. Many studies find that accounting reports, when published, do not appear to affect share prices, either because the data are ignored or because the informational content is already known. In particular, the evidence is consistent with the belief that required publication of data by the SEC does not measurably affect investors' expectations.

Only one defensible study finds some evidence to the contrary. Daniel Collins develops a trading rules model to find out whether investors might have benefited from knowing the segment profit data that the SEC first required companies to report beginning with fiscal year 1970 [101]. (These data were reported in 1971 retrospectively for the years 1968, 1969, and 1970.) His findings are mixed. He reports average, positive abnormal returns (18 percent) for 1968 and 1969 (compared to returns on investments in alternative, equivalently risky shares), small and statistically insignificant abnormal returns for 1970, and no significant abnormal returns for the period as a whole.

Bertrand Horwitz and Richard Kolodny further examine the question [219]. They compare changes in the security prices and market measures of risk of companies that reported segment income data for the first time during 1971 with those of a sample of companies that did not report such data. They conclude that their "results provide no evidence in support of the universally accepted contention that the SEC required disclosure furnished investors with valuable information" [219: 247].

The second argument against LB reporting is that the assignment and allocations of revenues, expenses, and assets to individual lines of business are subject to considerable measurement errors and conceptual problems. Most multiproduct corporations are not simply aggregates of individual enterprises. Generally, the several lines of business are operated to take advantage of economies of scale in management, production, distribution, and financing that make it less expensive to produce the "lines" together, rather than separately. Jointly determined demands for and costs of the products produced, furthermore, make it conceptually impossible to find out the separate profitability of individual products. Inter-LB transfers, in addition, are priced by different methods, which makes it difficult to ascertain LB profits. Thus, while management can estimate the contribution to profit of individual products, these estimates are not precise and generally cannot be carried to "the bottom line." Therefore, the LB data are likely to be incorrect, and if they are taken seriously, they may be misleading.

The third argument against LB reporting is that where the LB data *are* meaningful (generally, revenues and directly assigned expenses qualify), disclosure of these data may give more information to an enterprise's competitors than to investors. Competitors often are more knowledgeable than investors about the environment to which these data pertain. Disclosure, then, may be detrimental, on balance, to shareholders.

The SEC and FASB LB disclosure requirements at least permit managers to identify the lines of business that are relevant to their enterprises. The FTC's designation of LBs, though, results in groupings that are meaningless for most corporations [61]. Consequently, the numbers reported are not related to market-determined or management-determined groups of products. Additionally, because the FTC's LB categories are narrower than those required by the SEC and FASB, the revenue, expense, and asset measurement and allocation problems are exacerbated considerably. Therefore, it is very doubtful that profits and rates of return by LBs will be estimated meaningfully. How, then, can the benefits of better antitrust enforcement, more efficient resource allocation, and improved industry studies, as well as other benefits that the FTC envisions, be accomplished? The cost to corporations of providing the required data, furthermore, is considerable, since corporations do not maintain their records according to the FTC's categories [46].

CONCLUSION

A complete benefit-cost analysis of LB reporting would reveal few benefits and considerable costs. There appear to be some benefits from the LB data that the SEC mandates. There are considerable, general limitations of financial statements. But, it is apparent that revenues and directly assigned costs that are related to managerially determined lines of business and that are reported on a consistent basis over time may beneficially inform investors and motivate corporate officers. The costs to shareholders of informing competitors, dysfunctionally motivating managers, and having data prepared by the corporations must also be considered.

The FTC's LB reporting program is much more expensive, since corporations rarely record the required data. The data collected, at best, would be meaningless. Nevertheless, there is a fairly high probability that the data, once published and available, will be accepted as being reliable. As a consequence, activities will be misdirected, incorrect conclusions will be drawn about market performance, and corporations may alter otherwise preferable activities to avoid penalties. And, if past experience is a guide, once the program is instituted, it will continue and be expanded, regardless of evidence that demonstrates its fallibility.

ADDITIONAL READINGS: 154, 155, 156, 157, 158.

24. Should Corporations Be Required to Disclose Income and Employment Data by Race and Sex?

DONALD L. MARTIN
Law and Economics Center
University of Miami School of Law

Editor's Summary   Forced disclosure of information by race and sex
relevant to employment in aggregate job and income categories can
easily be misinterpreted. Since the geographical distribution of
minority groups is not uniform, some corporations will be accused
unjustly of discrimination. Because incomes vary with differences in
hours worked, experience, schooling, and other factors, furthermore,
unadjusted job data will misrepresent the true situation. Public
disclosure of the ethnic composition of occupations, finally, may
violate the privacy rights of minorities and possibly lead to the abuse
of, and discrimination against, those minorities "overrepresented" in
particular professions.

Should corporations publicly disclose data by race and sex relevant to
employment in aggregate job and income categories? Those who recom-
mend such disclosure believe that the resulting public opinion and the
threat of government action will pressure those corporations that might
otherwise practice discrimination to employ a workforce that more nearly
represents the race and sex composition of the population.

PROBLEMS OF INTERPRETATION

What is the likelihood that this ploy will be successful and beneficial to
employees? Several factors cast doubt on the efficacy of such a policy.
First, the geographical distribution of minority groups in the labor force is
not uniform; thus, some corporations would appear to be relatively more
discriminatory than others, even though geographical preferences and
historical accident may be more important determinants of differences in
the racial composition of employment across corporations.

Second, labor force distributions by race and sex differ from population distributions. In a given week in 1975, for instance, 47 percent of all
women and 79 percent of all men were in the labor force. If each
corporation tried to fill job categories so as to mirror the sex composition
of the population, it would soon find this mathematically impossible to
achieve (at least in the short run) without offering significant discriminatory wage differentials. Differences in education and on-the-job experi-

ence between nonwhites and whites and between males and females, moreover, also will place constraints on achieving "representative" employment distributions. Corporations that are required to post their "track records" without the benefit of the many legitimate qualifications that are the determinants of those records may thereby be singled out unjustly as discriminatory [SB 10, SB 11].

Third, reporting income by race and sex poses interpretation problems similar to those associated with employment data. Incomes vary because of differences in length of workweek, experience on the job, and schooling, and because of regional cost-of-living difference. For income differences by race and sex at the corporate level to be understood, the data would have to be adjusted to account for these causal variables. Thus, the requirement that corporations publish income data is more complicated than one at first might expect. Should the firms themselves adjust nominal differences in income by race and sex? Will this lead to tampering with statistics? If government is to be entrusted with this task, will it be necessary to give it greater powers to acquire information about employee characteristics from corporate personnel records?

PROBLEMS OF CORPORATE RESPONSE

Whether or not government regulates the adjustment of corporate income differences by race and sex, the requirement that these data be published at the corporate level will encourage firms to redefine or alter job categories for reporting purposes. If income comparisons are made *within* job categories, it will not be surprising to find that firms establish job categories that differ by race and sex so that income differences appear *between* job classifications rather than *within* them. Indeed, there is some evidence that firms may find this a relatively inexpensive way to appear nondiscriminatory. In a recent study of one large corporation, researchers found substantial pay differences between men and women of similar characteristics across job categories but not within a given job level [273: 704]. The effect of this practice ostensibly is to eliminate income differences in one important dimension. Job categories may be merged and redefined to smooth out apparent earnings differences *within* them. Alternatively, job categories may be defined in such a way as to remove earnings differences *between* them.

PROBLEMS OF EMPLOYEE SENSITIVITIES
AND OTHER ADVERSE REACTIONS

Fourth, the publication of wage and salary data by corporations may have a perverse effect on worker earnings. Illegal agreements among firms to avoid wage and salary competition for workers usually are more successful if firms cannot keep secret their actual levels of remuneration [SB 53]. Requiring the publication of such data for all to see, including rival employers, may result in employees being paid less than the competitive rate. Co-conspirators would have less of an incentive to compete clandestinely for workers by offering wage increases if they were certain this information would be published and made available to their competitors.

The fifth and final reason for doubting the wisdom of requiring the publication of corporate personnel data by race and sex concerns the threat to privacy that the policy implies. If government requires the publication of data dealing with the *ethnic* composition of occupations so that it is possible to identify those occupations with the highest concentration of Irish, Jewish, Italian, and Catholic workers, and so forth, it will not be surprising if such a requirement is denounced as discriminatory and as a violation of privacy by those who will regard themselves as being exposed. Not all occupations enjoy the same status in society. Those persons in "desirable" occupations who are members of a group that is "overrepresented," relative to the population, may become exposed or threatened, and thus they may become the targets of abuse. Members of groups that are "highly" concentrated in "less desirable" occupations will be exposed to stigma and likewise will perceive a threat.

If the activities of firms are to be monitored, more refined measures of discrimination and a more sensitive policy will have to be devised to ensure meaningful results.

ADDITIONAL READINGS: 12, 24, 40, 190, 464.

25. What Kind of Controls on Insider Trading Do We Need?

HENRY G. MANNE
Law and Economics Center
University of Miami School of Law

Editor's Summary   Recent developments in the theories of efficient markets and the random walks of stock prices provide convincing evidence that the stock market is a "fair game," the SEC's alleged desire to regulate insider trading notwithstanding. Although competition for access to information may not be as efficient as desired, there appears to be no serious insider trading problem. It is logically impossible to deter insider trading significantly. And, the costs of enforcing SEC rules should be balanced against the expected benefits of additional regulations. The SEC has displayed a cavalier attitude toward individual citizens' constitutional rights. A fair and objective observer must conclude that the existing regulations and their enforcement present worse evils than the problems they were designed to cure.

An often-voiced belief about the stock market is that in the absence of certain Securities and Exchange Commission regulations, it would not present a "fair game" for small investors. Corporate insiders would use information to their own advantage rather than allow shareholders to learn about that information and benefit from it in the market. The same insiders would also have an increased incentive to manipulate corporate financial affairs so that they could profit from trading in a corporation's stock, rather than profit from properly managing a company.

Insider trading often is claimed to be not only inherently manipulative but also damaging. Critics say that it can lead to a loss of investor confidence in the stock market, thus making people unwilling to invest in American enterprise. Full disclosure of material information before insiders can trade in their companies' shares is legally and popularly viewed as the correct antidote to this financial skulduggery.

Like so many notions about modern corporate affairs, the idea of corporate insiders trading to the general detriment of investors in the market is more remarkable for its perseverance than for its logic or supporting evidence. One can be sure, when rules of law survive in spite of stronger arguments against them than for them, that there are significant interests at stake in the preservation of the suspect rules. In the instant situation, the likely interests are those of the staff of the Securities and Exchange Commission and those of a small band of highly paid private securities lawyers, all of whose power and income would drop significantly if a more reasoned and reasonable approach to the topic were taken.

THE DEVELOPMENT OF INSIDER TRADING RULES

Restrictions on insider trading did not result from any popular hue and cry. The subject was only *made* to sound scandalous during the congressional hearings that led to the federal securities laws of 1933 and 1934; insider trading had not been a secret before that. Even so, Congress adopted a quite restrained provision dealing with the subject. This is the well-known Section 16(b) of the Securities and Exchange Act of 1934, which requires directors, officers, and 10 percent shareholders in a corporation to pay over to the corporation any short-term trading profits: those made from a buy and a sale within six months of each other.

During its hearings on this provision, a Senate committee was presented with a draft outlawing any trading by "anyone" with inside information. This would include any trading known to be done on the basis of information that had not yet been made public. The history of that provision, which would have covered members of Congress, speaks eloquently to the negative intent of Congress on the matter of a rule broader than Section 16(b). The threatening provision was dropped from the next draft of the bill as completely and silently as if it had been a provision to repeal the Declaration of Independence. No one has ever seriously doubted the committee's real view of this effrontery.

The legal history of this topic suggests that there could not have been much demand for a broad ban on insider trading. The courts had long before developed a common-law doctrine known as the "special facts" rule. This doctrine was designed to cover situations involving share trading in small corporations—situations in which the potential for fraud was as great as the difficulty of proving it. But no court, at least before 1968, ever saw reason to apply that rule in the case of a corporation with publicly traded shares. As we shall see, the judicial sense of the economics of the situation was quite correct.

Through a rather tortuous, legally strained, and arguably unconstitutional series of moves between 1942 and 1965, the SEC managed to promulgate precisely the rule that Congress explicitly had declined to accept. The period begins in 1942, the date of adoption of Administrative Rule 10b-5, under which all insider trading cases are now brought, and culminates in 1965 with the well-known *Texas Gulf Sulphur* litigation [*United States v. Texas Gulf Sulphur*, 401 F.2d 833 (2d Cir., 1968); *cert. denied*, 394 U.S. 976 (1969)]. Indeed, in a concurring opinion in the *Texas Gulf Sulphur* case, Judge Henry J. Friendly, the distinguished Court of

Appeals judge, gave the SEC a rather sharp slap on the wrist for the administrative techniques it had used. The SEC has received other rebukes since, but there has been no further serious claim made in litigation that 10b-5 as a rule against insider trading is invalid, though there is strength in the argument.

THE PRACTICAL CASE AGAINST THE RULES

Quite the opposite is true, however, if one looks at the overwhelming weight of the economic arguments offered against the rule. First, one might look at what some wags term the "SEC's Confidence Game," the argument that shareholders would lose confidence in the stock market if they thought that insider trading was occurring regularly. There are at least three (and probably more) things wrong with this notion.

First, if the SEC allows shareholders to believe that it does effectively prevent insider trading, it is practicing a shameful deception. Or, alternately, the market is composed of a greater number of idiots than we have any reason to believe.

Second, individual confidence is *not* shaken by the belief or knowledge that insider trading occurs. During the frenzied period of popular participation in the stock market in the 1920s, news about pools using undisclosed information was published regularly in the financial press, with no apparent loss of investor confidence. Third, it is well known that the one and only thing that does cause investors to lose confidence is losses. After any period of significant downturn in market prices, the number of investors regularly declines, and there seems to be no other factor significantly influencing this variable.

THE ECONOMIC ARGUMENT AGAINST THE RULES

A proper economic excursion into the rather complex subject of insider trading necessitates a brief detour to explain two developments in modern finance economics. One of these is called the "efficient market hypothesis" and the other the "random walk theory" of stock prices. Each of these notions has been the subject of an enormous amount of high-quality scholarly research, analysis, and testing. It is unquestionably safe to say that no "discovery" of modern economic theory has ever received the genuine, unanimous agreement accorded these two related notions. And, while the implications of these notions may disturb the SEC and other more explicit critics of the free-market system of corporate capitalism, no one has come up with any countermanding evidence.

An "efficient" stock market is one that rapidly and correctly evaluates new information and integrates that information into the market price of shares. Study after study demonstrates the almost unbelievable efficiency with which our major stock markets perform this function. Indeed, no matter at what point econometricians test to see whether a given new development has yet impacted a share price, the impact always seems to have already occurred. This finding has even led some slightly incredulous researchers to conclude that the stock market instantaneously reflects any available information relevant to stock price.

Since stock prices do rapidly and correctly reflect new developments in a corporation's affairs, the movements of stock prices (apart from general industry or market movements and certain other oscillations or "noise" not relevant here) should follow a course dictated by these exogenous events. But, as Paul A. Samuelson shows in an important writing on this subject, one cannot imagine anything happening much more randomly than such events [372, SB 22]. They would include, for instance, with infinitely varying degrees of severity and with no predictable pattern, reactions from competitive products, changes in demand, changes in political rulings, international events, changes in the weather, managerial changes, and production difficulties.

These two theories, the efficient market hypothesis and the random walk theory, suggest two problems in connection with the subject of insider trading. The first problem is how the market can possibly be as efficient as has been suggested, and the second is how, if stock prices follow a random movement, shareholders can be injured by insider trading.

The answer to the first question, why the market is so efficient, probably relates in some fashion to insider trading, though the exact nature and characteristics of this relationship have not been clearly isolated or described. It does seem apparent, however, that information in most instances develops an increasing probability of its assumed impact as the time of the event draws closer. That is, the probability that the value of unanticipated earnings actually will be realized only becomes 100 percent on the day that the board of directors announces the fact. But, many weeks earlier those earnings may have appeared to some people to have a 20 percent probability of occurring. Such people include accountants or financial analysts who have information that could not, in and of itself, be said to be significant or material inside information. This information might include, for example, knowledge of an increase in sales, a disabling power struggle within a competitor company, or an important but early technological breakthrough. If this increasing-probability-of-truth hypothesis is correct, the closer one reaches to the actual development, the greater will be the extent to which the assumed value of the information has already been incorporated into the share's price. This reasoning helps to explain why we often see that an important news announcement meets with little or no change in the day's stock price quotations.

Whatever the mechanism by which information is being impacted efficiently into share prices, so long as the information generates a random movement of those prices, there is really no way in which insider trading can injure shareholders, even though shareholders are not privy to the information. This is not to say, of course, that shareholders could not be richer if they had the information. But, that is merely a truism. What it does suggest is this line of reasoning. First, people trade anonymously in an organized stock market. Second, by definition, prior (random) price movements tell "outsiders" nothing about subsequent price movements. Therefore, that a subsequent movement may have been predicted by an "insider" cannot affect the average rate of return investors realize from trading in corporate securities. Whether an insider was on the other side of the trade or not is utterly irrelevant to the noninsider's calculations about whether the stock market is a fair game.

But, one still may complain that there seems to be an immoral windfall profit gained by the insider in these situations. Thus, some believe that insider trading allows corporate officials to secure greater gains than they bargained for, or are entitled to. This argument would have merit if—and only if—the availability of possible trading gains resulting from access to information could not be known or recognized by others. That possibility, to say the least, is very unlikely. Once it is recognized that a special possibility for gain inheres in a given position, competition necessarily will drive down the total remuneration for that position to the competitive level indicated by the discounted value of all future income, including both salary and trading profits.

This observation about competition and bargaining for remuneration is relevant to the charge that allowing insider trading encourages manipulation and lessened attention to business affairs. If profitable opportunities for such activities were common, there should be considerably fewer corporate financial scandals today than there were, for example, in the 1920s. Yet, the evidence points the other way. A rational market theory of corporations reinforces the view that an unregulated corporate system's incentive structure generates efficient (and therefore honest) managerial action. This is not to say, of course, that dishonesty, fraud, and embezzlement do not occur. But, it does mean that the amount of such criminal activity is not a function of the insider trading rule.

There is tremendous uncertainty and variability, of course, in opportunities for profits from insider trading. And, while this uncertainty and variability mean that the competition for access to information is not as efficient as we might like, they also indicate that the entire topic may hardly be worth the posturing and moralizing it has engendered. Even if one agrees that there is a fundamental issue of business morality involved with insider trading, the seriousness of the problem, the possibility of correcting it, and the costs of enforcing rules against the practice still must be taken into account before a rational policy can be adopted. We seem to have evolved, instead, regulatory positions far worse than the evils sought to be cured.

HOW THE SEC VIOLATES CONSTITUTIONAL RIGHTS

The SEC has systematically displayed a cavalier attitude toward both the letter and the spirit of the constitutional rights of those it investigates or regulates. Brokerage offices, for instance, must employ "compliance officers" (generally, former employees of the SEC), whose job it is to report, to the SEC if necessary, violations of securities laws. The SEC's enforcement branch long has condoned (and, of course, denied) compliance officers' listening in on telephone calls between security salespeople and customers to find out whether sales talk regulations are being properly adhered to.

On one occasion, when confronted with charges of these and other dubious practices, the present director of the Enforcement Division of the SEC replied, "Well, you forget, these are the fat cats we are dealing with." A remark like this represents a totalitarian mentality that should be thoroughly expunged from any democratic political structure. Unfortunately, the remark is characteristic of the views of many SEC staff members, and much of the development of this attitude can be traced directly to their enforcement of Rule 10b-5.

TWO KINDS OF INSIDER TRADING

There is an ultimate irony in connection with the SEC's self-proclaimed moral crusade against insider trading. The prices of any goods, as anyone with a modicum of economics training knows, are functions of the demand to acquire additional goods, in this case securities, and also of the demand by present holders of existing goods to keep what they have. This notion of a demand by present holders sometimes is referred to as the "demand to hold," and it is generally signified by reference to a person's "reservation price," the price at which the person is indifferent between continuing to hold or sell the security in question. For a variety of reasons, which space limitations preclude exploring here, it is likely that the demand to hold, rather than the demand to acquire, dominates price changes in securities listed on major stock exchanges.

Given that the supply of outstanding shares remains constant, price, then, becomes primarily a function of the reservation prices of persons who already hold shares. These investors obviously are those most likely to pursue new information about their companies. Consequently, a person who mentally raises his or her reservation price for a given share from $70 to $80 because of becoming privy to new information about the company has gained $10 per share just as effectively as would a person who went out and purchased shares at $70. The gain in the former case was generated by knowing when not to sell rather than by knowing when to buy and hold. Economically speaking, there is no difference between the two cases.

But, notice the difference from the point of view of the poor, confused SEC. There is simply no way the gain realized by an increase in a reservation price can ever be called a result of insider trading, since it involves only a mental act, not a purchase or sale of shares. The real economic gain results from the knowledge that leads to changing one's mind about the price at which a share should be sold. Until it develops mind reading powers, even the SEC can hardly argue that acting on such knowledge constitutes a violation of Rule 10b-5.

ADDITIONAL READINGS: 39, 45, 47, 48, 108, 127, 156, 171, 214, 249, 266, 277, 279, 280, 281, 284, 379, 380, 421, 444.

26. Are State Securities Laws (Blue Sky Regulations) Beneficial or Harmful?

JAMES S. MOFSKY
Law and Economics Center
University of Miami School of Law

Editor's Summary   The proponents of blue sky regulations argue that society needs a more paternalistic form of regulation that empowers state securities commissioners to examine the merits of an offering and to deny registration to those issues of securities that they deem to be too risky for the public. The full-disclosure aspects of the blue sky laws are subject to the same criticism leveled at the federal securities laws: All known information about a firm is reflected very quickly in stock prices *well before* the disclosure required by the securities laws occurs. Thus, detailed disclosure of past information in a firm's history is valueless to investors in forming expectations of future stock prices. Merit rules give more seasoned firms a comparative advantage in raising capital over newly promoted ventures, some of which may never come to market because of these regulations. Thus, the blue sky laws have an adverse effect on competition.

State securities regulation, the so-called blue sky laws, preceded federal securities regulation by more than twenty years, having initially been enacted in Kansas in 1911. In response to populist sentiment, state securities regulation spread first among the Southern and Western states, and later, after World War I, to the East. Today, all the states, the District of Columbia, and Puerto Rico have some form of securities law.

From their inception, the blue sky laws have been based on a paternal istic objective that goes well beyond the full disclosure standard underlying the federal laws. Besides requiring the same disclosure that federal rules also mandate, state laws empower securities commissioners to examine the merits of an offering and to deny registration to those issues of securities they deem to be too risky to warrant investment by members of the public. This form of regulation never was intended to focus on larger companies with substantial operating histories. Indeed, with only a few exceptions, its burden falls on unseasoned firms.

Merit regulation always has been advocated on the grounds that government regulators are somehow in a better position to evaluate the investment risks associated with newly promoted firms than are participants in the market. Merit regulation proponents also argue that because of the lack of a seasoned market for the securities of such firms, there is sufficient likelihood that fraudulent conduct may accompany the offer and sale of those securities. This asserted likelihood warrants this kind of direct government involvement.

The blue sky laws try to alter the terms of public offerings so that public public investors are placed on a more nearly equal plane with the promoters or insiders of a firm than would be the case in the absence of regulation. Merit regulation, accordingly, most often has taken the form of rules: regulating the maximum expenses of public offerings; requiring a minimum equity investment by promoters; regulating the price that insiders must pay for their stock relative to the proposed price for public investors; regulating securities offering prices in relation to earnings ratios; regulating the amount of warrants and options granted to officers, key employees, and underwriters; establishing minimal shareholder voting rights; and regulating interest and dividend coverage with respect to senior securities (preferred stock and debt securities).

EFFICIENT MARKETS AND BLUE SKY REGULATIONS

Increasingly, observers argue that state securities regulation, like federal securities regulation, has generated net costs for society. This argument contains several lines of analysis, one of which is similar to a recent economic evaluation of the federal securities law [47]. Mandatory disclosure under the blue sky laws is not materially different from that required by the federal statutes. Since it turns out, upon empirical testing, that the full disclosure provisions of the federal securities laws generate more costs than benefits from the social point of view, analogous conclusions safely can be drawn with respect to the disclosure provisions of state securities regulation.

The "efficient market hypothesis," a central aspect of this analysis, maintains that all known information about a firm is reflected very quickly in stock prices, *well before* disclosure required by the securities laws occurs [SB 22, SB 25]. Detailed disclosure of past information in a corporation's history, therefore, already is reflected in current stock prices, and knowledge of that information is valueless to investors in forming expectations of future stock prices [288: 23–103]. Benston shows, moreover, that mandatory financial disclosure does not reduce the amount of fraud occurring in the securities markets [47]. The effect of mandatory disclosure, under both federal and state laws, has thus been to create higher costs for raising capital than would exist in the absence of such regulation. Mandatory disclosure does not generate commensurate benefits for investors, either through greater predictability of future stock prices or through reduction of fraudulent conduct. Finally, state-mandated disclosure usually creates information revealing nothing more than that which already has been processed and filed with the United States Securities and Exchange Commission. Hence, it is unnecessarily duplicative and wasteful.

ANTICOMPETITIVE EFFECTS OF BLUE SKY REGULATIONS

Beyond the "efficient market" criticism, the merit rules have been challenged because they give to seasoned firms, not subject to the rules, a comparative advantage in raising capital over newly promoted ventures. Newly promoted companies must either adjust the terms of their offerings to the merit rules or be precluded from publicly offering their securities under state law. Some entrepreneurs, as a result, gain more by selling their innovations to an existing company or by simply giving up a venture rather than by complying with state securities laws.

No empirical study considers the degree to which the merit standards diminish competition. The consequences of these laws are important, however, since they are related intimately to the amount of existing business competition. And, competitiveness in turn bears on the level of the prices everyone pays and on the quality of the goods and services everyone consumes. The harmful effects stemming from the blue sky laws, while never intended by the regulation's advocates, nontheless are real disadvantages that must be accounted for in deciding whether merit regulation is, on balance, socially beneficial.

A brief examination of the markets in which new businesses usually raise capital illustrates the manner in which the state securities laws foster adverse effects. At the outset, financial institutions such as banks, insurance companies, and pension funds often are inappropriate sources for capitalizing newly promoted enterprises. The federal government through the Small Business Administration, furthermore, furnishes very little aid in capitalizing such ventures if the organizers are without assets. Indeed, the equity securities market often is the most appropriate source for capitalizing new or speculative ventures, since that market meets the needs of both investors and organizers of business. Transactions in this market allow a promotor to retain control and management of a firm while sharing the risks with a number of investors. While there are other ways to raise capital, in most instances they are either too costly or impractical. Thus, promoters of new businesses and owners of small firms often are led to the equity market.

At this point, the distinction between the private and public sectors of the equity securities market becomes important. At first blush, private financing has more appeal than a public offering, since regulatory expenses and time delays can be avoided. But, the state and federal private placement exemptions, under which securities usually are offered if they are to escape the registration process and its high cost and time delays, are highly restrictive. The blue sky laws of many states, for example, restrict the number of offerees in a private placement to not more than ten to twenty persons. Therefore, an organizer of a new firm cannot, without violating the securities law, approach more than a limited number of persons. And, these offerees, under some private placement exemptions, must qualify as financially sophisticated persons. The organizer of the firm, however, may not know enough people to raise capital in this manner.

Of course, a private placement specialist who knows venture capital investors would be helpful to such an entrepreneur. But that possibility is precluded because the blue sky laws, in many jurisdictions, prohibit the payment of commissions in connection with the sale of privately placed securities; and, it goes without saying that private placement specialists do not offer their services free. There are other aspects of the private placement exemptions that make them highly restrictive. However, they are too detailed for exploration here. Suffice it to say that in some instances business people cannot or do not wish to avail themselves of these exemptions. Thus they are forced to explore more carefully the possibilities of a public offering of equity securities.

For small and newly promoted firms, the merit rules applicable to public offerings present many regulatory hurdles and may make such offerings more costly than business people often can afford. During the period 1971–1972, for example, average total costs of public offerings below a million dollars actually exceeded the cost limitations imposed under the blue sky laws of most states [321, 448]. Similarly, in some jurisdictions the prevailing cost of underwriters' compensation and other expenses incurred in connection with small offerings of securities exceeded then current state standards. There are strong reasons to believe that since 1971–1972 the disparity between the actual costs of small public offerings and permissible limitations under the blue sky laws has been increasing.

But, the direct limitation on the costs that may be incurred in connection with public offerings is only one form of merit regulation that comes to bear on this problem. Indeed, before deciding to go forward with a public offering, business people generally consider the total impact of all rules rather than the consequences of a single restriction. The organizers of a firm, for instance, must contend with the requirement in some states that they contribute to the equity of their firm a sum representing some percentage (for example, 15 percent) of the amount they seek to raise publicly. Their equity contribution on a per share basis will then be measured against the price being charged the investing public. If the result exceeds permissible ratios (sometimes as low as 3 or 4 to 1), the offering will be deemed "unfair" and will not be permitted. Thus, the organizers of a new firm must themselves contribute proportionately more to the equity of the firm to raise greater amounts in the public markets.

There will always be some entrepreneurs at the margin who, for financial and other reasons, are unable or unwilling to commit sufficient personal resources that will permit them to raise the requisite capital sought in the public markets. And, in that case, they will decide not to sell securities in a public offering. If less costly alternatives for tapping the capital markets are unavailable, new firms simply will not be promoted. All other aspects of merit regulation, of course, are subject to this same kind of analysis.

EVIDENCE ABOUT EFFECTS OF BLUE-SKY REGULATION

No empirical study has examined the extent to which the blue-sky laws contribute to diminishing the total number of new businesses being developed in our economic system. But, in the absence of reliable data, there is no more basis for concluding that the number is substantial. With respect to other aspects of the merit rules, however, a recent empirical study by R. Clifton Poole finds that those rules have not accomplished their presumed benefit: lessening the risks for public investors [353]. For the states of South Carolina, North Carolina, and Virginia, this study compares a sample of securities denied registration with a sample of securities that were registered. The study asks whether the securities denied registration generate returns over different time periods that are lower than returns for the sample of registered securities. On the basis of computations of returns on investment for holding periods of one, two, and three years, the study finds no statistical difference in rate of return between the two samples.

It is interesting to note that statistical differences *are* found with respect to the financial information contained in the balance sheets and income statements for the two samples. The securities commissioners applied the merit rules to deny or permit registration on the basis of the differences contained in the financial statements. Since the financial statements of newly promoted firms often tend to exhibit greater financial risks than the financial statements of more seasoned companies, it should come as no surprise that the securities commissioners denied registration to the firms that (on the basis of financial statements) apparently were more speculative. When the securities of those firms came to market in states other than South Carolina, North Carolina, and Virginia, however, differences in performance did not occur. Thus, on balance, returns on securities denied registration are as high as returns on securities that are registered. This finding is perfectly consistent with the efficient market hypothesis, a corollary of which is that one cannot predict future stock prices from past financial information [SB 22].

The Poole study findings are opposed to those generated by the deputy commissioner of securities for Wisconsin in a study of his state's merit rules [195]. The Wisconsin study is based on a comparison of the performance of securities registered in Wisconsin with the performance of securities denied registration there. The study uses three indices of performance: price, book value, and dividend distribution. Based on a very small sample for a highly limited period, 1968–1971, the Wisconsin study concludes that, on the average, issues denied registration do not perform as well as issues granted registration.

This writer, along with Robert Tollison, recently criticized the methodology underlying the Wisconsin study [323]. First, the use of dividend distribution and book value as measurements of performance is meaningless and misleading. With respect to dividends, a dividend payment does not alter a shareholder's wealth, except to the extent that the dividend may be taxable in the shareholder's hands but not when left in the corporation's undistributed earnings. Dividends are paid when earnings have a greater utility in the hands of shareholders than when left in the corporate treasury.

Second, book value, also, reveals little valuable information about shareholder and corporate wealth. Generally accepted accounting principles contain an inherent conservative bias. Assets, for example, must be carried at their cost or market value, whichever is less. Thus, unrealized appreciation on a firm's assets generally is not recognized in the firm's financial statements. For an ongoing business, the value of assets lies in the stream of earnings they produce; the value of assets is not an inherent one reflected in accounting versions of book value.

Third, in the market, securities prices are based on a present value determination of an expected flow of future earnings, not upon the historical cost of assets as reported in balance sheets. Thus, the comparative performance of firms, based on dividend distribution or book value, establishes no useful information regarding shareholder protection. With respect to the measurement of price performance in the Wisconsin study, the criticism of that study identifies the flawed methodology.

SUMMARY

Unfortunately, the merit rules have been the subject of only two empirical tests of which this writer is aware. As I suggest earlier, however, probably there are substantial costs in the form of anticompetitive effects that flow from those rules. And, the presumed benefit of those rules in the form of investor protection is shown not to exist, at least in the Carolina and Virginia study. The application of the efficient market hypothesis to the blue sky laws should make it abundantly clear that this form of regulation is, on balance, more costly to society than it is beneficial.

ADDITIONAL READINGS: 108, 154, 155, 156, 157, 158, 267, 286, 372, 379.

PART THREE

STATE VERSUS FEDERAL CHARTERING OF CORPORATIONS

27. Have State Regulations Led to Corporate Monopoly Power?

ROBERT B. EKELUND, JR.
Department of Economics
Texas A&M University

Editor's Summary   The historical evolution of incorporation laws in the United States has been a reasoned reaction to the mercantile, or government-sponsored, monopoly concept of enterprise. The emergence of strict enforcement of contract and the states' general incorporation laws, to which the joint-stock company apparatus was a prelude, enhanced competition, promoted easy entry, and provided incalculable benefits to American society. The pervasive controls of the mercantile era (roughly 1500 to 1776), as well as the regulatory systems of contemporary America, provide a basis for predicting the probable effects of the proposed federal legislative chartering and control of business enterprise. Federal chartering represents a return to the old, tried, and rejected system under which government confers monopoly privileges to the favored few.

The historical evolution of corporate chartering provisions in the United States has been a reasoned reaction to the mercantile, or state-supported, monopoly concept of enterprise. The emergence of strict enforcement of contract and general incorporation laws, to which the joint-stock company apparatus was a prelude, was of incalculable benefit to American society. Whether or not these laws emerged as a result of market pressures seems irrelevant when assessing their overall effects. Both the mercantile era (roughly 1500 to 1776) and the regulatory systems of contemporary America provide evidence of the probable effects of federal legislative chartering and control of business enterprise.

THE ORIGINAL MONOPOLY CHARTERS

The contemporary corporate form is the product of many centuries of development. One early form of special interest is the continental system for the provision of public goods. As early as the sixteenth century, the French, for example, used the "undertaker" system (the term acquired its contemporary meaning only in the nineteenth century). Originally, the construction of public works such as military fortifications, public roads, and reservoirs was "undertaken" by individual entrepreneurs called undertakers. They bid competitively for the exclusive right to build public works. (This method survives in the contemporary form of defense contracting, or in some forms of cable television supply.)

In contrast to the French system, the English approach to public provisions rested squarely on common-law concepts of franchise, contract, and "common callings." The mercantile era witnessed a proliferation of franchises. Adam Smith, inveighing against mercantile monopoly, defined its unique characteristic as the *legislative right* to grant exclusive franchises in charters. These franchises all contained some provisions for performance (duties or obligations in the manorial analogy), with alterations possible at the will of the legislative body. In return for the "satisfactory performance" of duties, an enterprise was granted a "trading company" or manufacturing monopoly.

Direct taxation in the post-Revolutionary period could not meet America's need for social overhead capital (capital for bridges, canals, water improvements, roads, defense, and so forth). The joint-stock company (really a copartnership) of limited life, and often (but not always) characterized by unlimited liability on the part of investors, was ill-suited for the provision of much-needed public works. Because of investors' reluctance to pledge their savings (under unlimited liability), the joint-stock company was hard to organize. The state-chartered "quasi-public" corporation with limited life emerged as the legal-institutional framework within which public goods were provided.

This framework, which echoed the old mercantile system, was more nearly the forerunner of the modern, quasi-public, regulated enterprise as found in communications, transportation, and banking than it was of the typical corporation. Today, of course, legislatures delegate many franchising powers to commissions—in violation, one might add, of Locke's good-government dictum that a "delegated power cannot be [further] delegated." Most important, the early post-Revolutionary charter franchises granted monopoly power in the form of entry control and monopolistic privilege in return for the provision of public goods.

MODERN CHARTERS WITHOUT PRIVILEGE

Gradually the legal and legislative system began to reshape the corporate institution. In the 1780s and 1790s, states such as New York and New

Jersey passed general incorporation statutes for religious and educational institutions, and Massachusetts and New York, in 1809 and 1811, respectively, passed the first statutes relating to some kinds of manufacturing. The development of the *private* corporation was facilitated by several landmark Supreme Court cases concerning the privacy of contracts—for example, *Fletcher v. Peck* [10 U.S. 87, 3 L. Ed. 162 (1810)] and, more crucially, *Dartmouth College v. Woodward* [17 U.S. 518, 4 L. Ed. 629 (1819)]. State interference in private contracts was held to be unconstitutional, and private contracts were effectively distinguished from public contracts.

Most important, monopoly-charter restrictions began to fade away as elements of the corporate form. Charter exclusivity, which prohibited all entry, was effectively challenged in 1837, in *Proprietors of the Charles River Bridge v. Proprietors of the Warren Bridge* [36 U.S. 420, 9 L. Ed. 733 (1873)]. President Jackson's famous opposition to the First Bank of the United States stemmed from his fear that the corporation was gaining power over the public good because of the special privileges granted to it by charter. The final result of public pressure against the special franchise form of incorporation, as noted earlier, was the movement toward general incorporation statutes. This movement toward general legislation began in New York in 1811. The main rush to general legislation by the states came during the years 1837 and 1838.

The movement toward general incorporation statutes that were without monopoly provisions and, most important, that were open to all comers was a public reaction to mercantilelike charters. In the well-founded fear that corporations gained monopoly power through special acts, many states, before the Civil War, passed general incorporation laws. By 1875 the vast majority of the states sponsored such "free-entry" charters with very minimum restrictions. This movement came to an end in 1882 when Massachusetts, the only state without general incorporation laws, passed its own statutes.

THE CRITICS' VIEW OF HISTORY AND CORPORATE CHARTERS

Nader, Green, and Seligman, however, regard the removal of special-interest monopoly-charter restrictions as a step backward, or as an emasculation [328]. Somehow, they reason, the "competitive environment" went amok and produced monopoly power with no effective legislative checks. (One should note that they do not regard antitrust legislation as an effective check.) What are the arguments for this proposition?

First, contrary to what I argue, Nader et al. view American economic development in the post-Civil War era through the 1920s as a unidirectional movement toward nationwide monopoly control. Their arguments rest squarely upon the railroad transport revolution and the extension of the corporate form to trusts and holding companies around the turn of the century [328: 38–45]. Implicit in their indictments is the supposed "fact" that a national system of railroads enhanced the possibilities of monopoly power in manufacturing and, especially, in raw materials production. Nader et al. allege further that, in their quest for dominance, robber barons such as J. P. Morgan used every power at their command to further their own economic interest, which comprehended the "control of competition." The trust or holding company charter thus was developed for business monopoly.

Though the jury is still out, modern research in economic history strongly questions some of the quasi-literary accounts of railroad and trust developments of the era between the Civil War and World War I. As the more prescient economists of the time recognized, the most important feature of railroad development was the reduction in costs of transportation to farmers, and to industries using railway services. As Nader et al. argue, transport facilities permitted markets to expand. But, Nader et al. view this expansion as an untoward development fostering national monopoly.

Surely this view is a distortion of the historical record that becomes apparent if one considers supply conditions before widespread rail development. Because of costly entry and because of high transport costs, local and regional markets were strongly monopolized. Lowered costs of transportation and, with them, relatively more production for national markets probably reduced as much monopoly power as they made possible—or even more such power than they made possible. As the returns from technological innovations increased, moreover, vast private resources were devoted to effecting reductions in the cost of production. Capital markets and financial intermediaries, as Lance Davis emphasizes, were a direct result of institutional developments in the corporate holding company form, especially that of limited liability [119, 120].

One can view the trust movement, alternatively, as the result of a failure of the legal process rather than as the result of the pure pursuit of monopoly. Throughout the nineteenth century and into the early 1900s, state incorporation laws were characterized by restrictions on the size of a firm. The 1811 New York laws, for example, restricted the corporation to a capitalization not to exceed $100,000. This limit finally was raised in 1881 to $2 million. These limits were the rule and not the exception in corporate law: Massachusetts retained an 1882 limit of $1 million until 1903; Vermont, until 1911, had a limit of $1 million; and Pennsylvania imposed a limit of $500,000 in 1863.

This period was characterized by rapid economic growth. Thus, the corporations of the period were at a dead end. Efficiency required that they expand, but at the same time their charters forbade any internal growth, leaving external growth the only viable alternative. The result was the great trust movement. Had the states realized the value of expansion, both in size and in product lines, and had the states removed the restrictions, the trust movement might have been averted, along with the third-party damages that arose during that period.

Nader et al. decry the failure to resort to federal chartering in 1890 with the passage of the Sherman Antitrust Act, and again during the New Deal. Roosevelt's NIRA, they think, was a tentative step (unconstitutional, it turned out) in the direction of federal chartering. The essential question is whether this kind of legislative control over business was then, or is now, desirable, let alone necessary. Here, Nader et al. merely *assert* that the existence of trusts meant that competition was eliminated. "Monopoly power" is not conferred automatically by market situation or by the existence of a single or few suppliers; rather, "monopoly power" means "no threat of a competitive or rivalrous response." High profits, also, may signify the return to more efficient productive means or distributional devices, that is, innovation, as well as the return to monopoly in the market.

When the matter of monopoly is so understood, were the "robber barons" earning monopoly returns? Though the question is far from settled, many modern economic historians cast strong doubts upon the received notions of the muckrakers of the period. The Rockefellers, Carnegies, and Morgans may well have been enlightened innovators who led the competition in innovations and who reaped high returns while their competitors tried to catch up. Yet, with the rapid diffusion of technology and the ease of acquiring corporate charters, pervasive national monopoly was short-lived. "Unfair competition," that is, the temporary lowering of price to drive competitors out of the market, was rendered far less likely by the freedom to enter markets, a freedom that general incorporation laws gave. Unquestionably, these laws *encouraged* competitive responses to attempts to monopolize.

PRECURSORS TO FEDERAL CHARTERING

The reactions of some trusts in the 1865–1914 period and during the New Deal (exemplified by the attempts of producers to cartelize some 300 industries through the NIRA) are very instructive with regard to business incentives and organization. Obviously, the failure of the railroads' attempts to cartelize (the last attempt collapsed in 1884) led to an incentive for official governmental cartelization of the industry in 1887. But, the railroads' involvement in the creation of the ICC is yet to be fully documented [244, 410]. One should not overlook the similarity between the effects of legislative regulation and the chartering by federal legislators of business enterprises. One might argue that the entire history of federal legislative regulation presents quite a massive case study of what society could expect with federal chartering and "common-law control" of corporations.

Examples of what one can expect from federal charters exist in Adam Smith's *The Wealth of Nations*. In particular, Smith traces the history of the Royal African Company, the South Sea Company, the Hudson's Bay Company, and the Turkey Company. These histories are replete with instances of the companies being granted special favors by the Crown: taxes on other traders; subsidies; permission to discontinue socially valuable but, for the companies, unprofitable routes; and guaranteed government loans. The results were entirely predictable, given the nature of the government charters [402: 690–716].

Federal chartering with special charter regulations and provisions represents a return to the old, tried, and rejected system of controlling enterprise. Regulatory and policing costs would be fantastic, and one might argue that Congress recognized this in setting up the commission form in 1887.

CONCLUSION

As long as businesses demand, and all levels of government supply, regulation, monopoly and special privileges will defeat the public interest [361]. Federal chartering, as proposed by Nader et al., has more potential for supplying to businesses special privileges and entry control, the only viable sources of monopoly, than any legislative act since the mercantile era. The social and economic stultification which that period produced is well known to historians, and the specter of these possible effects should not escape those who claim to champion the "public interest" in the present century. President Hopkins of Dartmouth College (with only slight overstatement) once evaluated Roosevelt's attempts to cartelize major portions of American industrial production during the New Deal as the substitution of a "specious security" for competition, innovation, and, ultimately, the public interest. He knew, as did Adam Smith, that while large-scale business enterprise may not always please the social critic, large-scale business enterprise regulated, supported, and protected by large-scale government definitely would worsen the social condition.

ADDITIONAL READINGS: 100, 201, 220, 221.

28. Have State Incorporation Laws Established Monopolies or Promoted Competition?

JAMES S. MOFSKY
Law and Economics Center
University of Miami School of Law

Editor's Summary   Early state business chartering conferred monopoly rights on applicants on a case-by-case basis and, simultaneously, made it illegal for rivals to engage in the same activity. The development of state general incorporation laws began in the early nineteenth century as a reaction to, among other things, the special privileges and limited access associated with ad hoc state chartering. From the very beginning, the general incorporation laws of the states conspicuously omitted provisions that conferred monopolistic benefits on business firms. State incorporation laws encourage open entry to business activity and consequently satisfy a necessary condition for competitive economic performance among corporations.

One of the principal criticisms being leveled today against the modern corporation is based upon the notion that state incorporation laws are so business-minded that corporations are, in effect, granted monopoly privileges. This criticism maintains that the permissive nature of the corporation laws facilitates a business attitude that is unresponsive to the needs of other segments of society. Indeed, the concept of federal chartering arises out of a belief that the states, for various reasons, will not through their laws impose constraints on the actions of corporations and that, therefore, restrictive legislation at the federal level is necessary. Distrust of the state corporation laws stems from the argument that the states have competed to enact increasingly permissive general incorporation laws for purposes of generating greater tax revenues. If the states are responding solely to profit motives, so the argument goes, society, on balance, is being damaged.

It may well be that the states have competed to liberalize their general incorporation laws for purposes of attracting more incorporations, and thus raising revenues. However, it is ironic that corporate critics should associate monopoly privileges with that activity, since it was the advent of the general incorporation laws that stopped state legislatures from their earlier practice of conferring monopoly privileges in corporate charters [SB 27]. This little-recognized fact is borne out by an analysis of the provisions contained in early corporate charters granted prior to the enactment of general incorporation laws [137]. The irony comes into clear relief when the reasons for the development of the corporation in America are placed in historical context.

EARLY FORMS OF BUSINESS ASSOCIATION

There are certain concepts that today are generally associated with the corporation. Among these concepts are, for example, the division of capital into shares, free transferability of interests, centralization and delegation of the powers of management, holding property in a firm name, and suing and being sued as a firm rather than as individuals.

It is interesting to find that those concepts were known and used in noncorporate arrangements in the United States as early as 1760. Although most ventures during the middle of the eighteenth century were conveniently conducted as partnerships and sole proprietorships, there were a number of enterprises at that time that required a relatively large pool of capital to commence business. These businesses included certain land merchandising, banking, insurance underwriting, mining, shipping, and textile promotions. Since capital was contributed for some of those businesses by what was then a significant number of persons who did not contemplate engaging in management activities, the norms now associated with the modern corporation even then were important.

Thus, well before the corporation evolved as the principal means of generating these benefits, organizers of firms began devising a business form that eventually became known as the "joint-stock association." The association was not an innovation that sprang up full-blown. Instead, it evolved over a period of time as business people and their lawyers experimented with various contractual arrangements that eventually became corporate norms.

That corporate concepts were thus known and used through the joint-stock associations as early as 1760 seems inconsistent, on its face, with the reality that firms in certain specialized activities (namely banks, insurance companies, and public utility firms) began seeking corporate charters in large numbers in 1792—inconsistent, that is, unless some benefits conferred through the charter were otherwise unavailable through contractual arrangement. It was such other benefits that explain why no fewer than 66 canal, 77 turnpike, 69 toll bridge, 32 water supply, 29 bank, and 33 insurance company charters were granted in the United States by 1800 [137: 366].

Most of these enterprises required substantial initial capital (that was contributed, in many instances, by investors who did not participate in management). For that and other reasons, the corporate form was more appropriate than the partnership. But, as already indicated, the corporate norms contracted for in certain nonchartered land promotions, mining ventures, shipping businesses, and large-scale textile operations already were known to entrepreneurs and lawyers. Indeed, before 1792, some banking and insurance underwriting businesses were conducted without the benefit of corporate charters.

It is argued, often, that the legislative grant of limited liability in corporate charters explains the phenomenon that some firms opt for the corporate form. While there is some evidence that limited liability was important to the more speculative insurance company ventures, it does not seem that it was a critical factor with respect to banks, almost all of which were immediately successful, and with respect to public utility companies [137: 209, n. 22]. In Massachusetts, for example, a "vigorous agitation" for limited liability did not occur until 1828 [137: 209, n. 22]. Although uncertainty about the judicial treatment of unincorporated businesses that tried to adopt corporate norms may have contributed to the application for charters by some promoters, this factor, too, does not appear to have been critical. Unincorporated banks and insurance companies were formed before the rush for charters, and private banks were established after incorporation became common for these ventures [137: 205].

EARLY INCORPORATION AND SPECIAL PRIVILEGES

The primary motivation for incorporation, at that time, probably came from the special privileges granted to certain companies in their charters. With respect to banking, charters granted monopoly rights to engage in that business, and legislative acts were passed quite early in several states making it illegal to engage in that activity without a charter. Monopoly rights were also granted to insurance companies. As long as the Massachusetts Hospital Life Insurance Company paid one-third of its life insurance profits to the Massachusetts General Hospital, for example, it was granted the exclusive privilege of insuring lives [137: 224].

The few manufacturing companies that sought corporate charters during that period were granted special privileges. For example, the Beverly Cotton Manufactory was granted a trademark for a label on its goods, state lands in the District of Maine, exemption of foremen from poll taxes, and tickets in a state lottery [137: 226]. Toll bridge, turnpike, and canal companies were granted the power of eminent domain, as well as franchises to collect tolls. In addition to other exclusive franchises, many of these companies were granted tickets in the state lottery. These are only a few examples of the many monopolistic and special powers granted these early business organizations. These special privileges, it is submitted, probably provided the most significant underlying reason for incorporation at that time.

GENERAL INCORPORATION LAWS
AND THE LOSS OF PRIVILEGES

Those firms that did not seek special grants but that desired the advantages of the corporate form devised their own unique business structure by borrowing corporate norms. Indeed, the cost of obtaining a corporate charter probably was quite high, if for no other reason than that a considerable period of time was required to get one. Thus, business people fashioned for themselves devices to fit their needs. It was not until technology had advanced considerably that there developed significant pressures for an inexpensive and quick method of securing the benefits usually associated with the corporate form. It was at that point that sufficient demand was generated for the general incorporation laws. This demand was associated primarily with the growth of the railroads and textile mills.

The first general incorporation laws were enacted as early as 1809 in Massachusetts, and 1811 in New York. Thereafter, they began to spread throughout the other states. It was not until 1875 that the first modern, "liberal" general incorporation act was passed. That occurred in New Jersey. The other states quickly followed suit. Delaware enacted a statute of its own, and when New Jersey modified its laws to be more restrictive, Delaware became, and remains today, among the most popular states in which to incorporate large-scale, interstate businesses.

From the inception of the general incorporation laws, it was noticeable that those statutes did not contain any of the monopolistic benefits that were associated with the early corporate charters. On the contrary, the general incorporation acts have not restricted in any way the nature of a firm's business activities as long as some minimal description of the chosen activities appeared in the certificate of incorporation. That kind of open entry is hardly consistent with the monopoly privileges found in early corporate charters. It is ironic, therefore, that today claims are made that monopoly privileges stem from state corporation laws, since these very laws replaced a system that did indeed produce such privileges.

ADDITIONAL READINGS: 56, 88, 93, 118, 263, 408.

29. Have Delaware's Incorporation Laws Set a Bad Example for Other States?

MICHAEL P. DOOLEY
University of Virginia School of Law

Editor's Summary   If the trend toward greater flexibility for
management is undesirable, why have many states modified their laws
to follow the example of Delaware, which provides flexibility? The
critics claim that states want to attract corporate residents. Yet, why
would corporations want to move to states where their minority shares
(and majority shares as well) would sell for less? The critics never
answer this question but merely claim that state corporate law abuses
the interests of minority shareholders. Hence, a system of federal
chartering statutes. But substantive legislation is a more appropriate
vehicle for regulation. Nader et al. seem to be the only ones who want
federal chartering. The states are happy, as are corporate managers
and shareholders. Apparently, the real motive of Nader et al. is to
impose their views on everyone else.

A principal argument for a federal incorporation act is that the several
states have proved incapable of providing responsible corporate regulation. Their incapacity is attributed to greed: anxious to attract or to retain
incorporation fees and franchise taxes, one state is quick to adopt the
statutory changes that another state enacts lest its domestic corporations
be induced to incorporate in the other, more "favorable" state. This
competition, so the argument runs, produces a "race for the bottom," with
the leading incorporation state, Delaware, naturally ahead.

Nader, Green, and Seligman document the influence that the Delaware
General Corporation law has had on the corporate statutes of other states
[328: 50–61]. They also infer a strong promanagement bias in the statute
because the drafting committee for the major 1967 revision of the Delaware law was composed of persons engaged in the practice of corporate
law [328: 55–57].

THE UNIFORMITY OF CORPORATION STATUTES

It is certainly true, as Nader et al. argue, that there has been a trend
toward greater uniformity in state corporation laws and that, allowing for
isolated exceptions, there is relatively little difference between the basic

approach, scope, or policy of the Delaware statute and that of the New York Business Corporation law, the Model Business Corporation Act, or the law of any other state. It is also true that innovations in one state have been adopted by others, that the Delaware law has been the most influential, and that the process of corporate law reform generally has been delegated to drafting committees composed of corporate lawyers.

Standing alone, however, none of these propositions is either remarkable or significant. The development of corporate legislation is part of a broad trend toward uniformity in American law, which has produced a number of uniform codes for diverse subjects, including commercial transactions, adoption, gifts to minors, and probate. One hardly would expect a contrary trend in an increasingly interdependent and mobile society. Indeed, the failure of states to achieve some measure of uniformity in corporate regulation undoubtedly would produce pressure for federal legislation. But, in that event, the pressure would come from the business community, not its critics. It is reasonable to suppose, also, that most of the uniform codes in other areas have been produced by drafting committees dominated by lawyers practicing in the areas to be regulated. The presence of these persons on such committees can be accounted for not only by their self-interest or that of their clients but also by their experience in the subject of legislation.

If the trend toward uniformity is itself unobjectionable, the critics' case must rest on the direction of the trend. That is, the critics must believe that state legislation is developing in undesirable ways. Here, the attack runs into difficulty, for the critics cannot provide a documented bill of particulars in support of their criticisms. It is quite likely, on the contrary, that the trend toward enabling charter legislation has produced more efficient allocations of capital and other resources than would be realized under a more highly regulated system such as the critics propose.

CORPORATE CHARTERS AND THE SOCIAL IMPACTS OF CORPORATIONS

While criticism of the existing state corporation law system is diffuse, it does seem to have two parts. The first part concerns the social, economic, and environmental impacts of the activities of large firms; the second part concerns the relationship between the prerogatives of management and the rights of shareholders.

First, corporate statutes are said to be inadequate because they fail to regulate and control the business activities of large firms "in the public interest," a term which one may define as the personal value preferences of a particular critic. Prominently mentioned are the anticompetitive practices of large businesses and the adverse impact on the environment of noxious emissions or other negative side effects produced by manufacturing activities [SB 3, SB 4]. While these are important problems, they are not the proper concerns of business organization law. With respect to competition, there exists a panoply of federal antitrust laws. If these laws are inadequate, it is obviously preferable to direct attention to their improvement; and, the call for a federal incorporation statute to ameliorate this alleged condition seems to be a non sequitur [SB 57, SB 58, SB 59, SB 60, SB 61]. The problem of side effects is not unique to corporations or even to the capitalistic system: a Soviet pulp plant presumably produces as much pollution as its American counterpart, and remedial efforts in both instances are better directed to the specific problem than to the form of organization in which the pollution-producing activity is carried on [191, SB 3, SB 4].

The goals of business organization law, whether partnership or corporate, are important, but much more limited. The goals are to enhance the efficient operation of a firm and to ensure the equitable treatment of those who have an interest therein. It is on the basis of these criteria that the existing legislation should be judged. Here, Nader, Green, and Seligman advance two principal arguments. First, the general trend in corporate legislation has been away from a system in which the state made limited grants of power to specific firms to engage in specified activities. The present system comprehends general enabling acts available to anyone who wishes to engage in business activity that the state does not expressly prohibit. Second, the state statutes are insufficiently "regulatory" in nature and favor management interests to the disadvantage of shareholders.

CORPORATE CHARTERS AND SHAREHOLDER RIGHTS

Except for their general preference for more regulation, it is difficult to take seriously the critics' objection to the basic notion of enabling statutes. Given the variety of economic activities today, a return to specific grants of power obviously is impractical. With respect to the belief that the statutes are insufficiently regulatory, one may concede readily that the general trend in corporate legislation has been to give management greater flexibility with respect to the internal operations of corporations. But, it does not necessarily follow that this development has had an adverse impact on shareholders.

According to the critics, the dilution of shareholders' rights is not a recent development; it is a long-term trend that began before the turn of the century [SB 17, SB 19]. By 1912, for example, a majority of states had adopted provisions permitting businesses to be organized for any lawful purpose, permitting the issuance of stock for property, authorizing mergers and consolidations, and eliminating requirements that directors be residents of the state. It is not at all clear why these changes are believed to have an impact on shareholder rights. And, one is reminded of an earlier critic who objected to the 1899 revision of the Delaware law on the ground that it permitted corporations to own land located outside the state!

Later identified milestones include permitting the elimination of mandatory preemptive rights and cumulative voting, neither of which is of any use to shareholders in corporations with widely dispersed holdings, and permitting the issuance of shares in different classes. In no case do the critics demonstrate that these changes adversely affect shareholder interests. One would expect that there is relatively little market for preferred shares with low dividend rates and weak or nonexistent security features.

Fundamentally, if the course of corporate law has been consistently antishareholder for as long as the critics claim, one would suppose that there would no longer be an interest in corporate investments and that the entire system would have collapsed years ago. At the very least, one would expect that there would be less demand for shares of Delaware corporations than for shares of businesses incorporated in other states. Since the vast majority of large corporations with many shareholders continues to choose Delaware, it appears that investors do not perceive the perils to their interests that the critics profess to see [SB 33].

Although the point is not raised explicitly, it would be fair to observe that the state statutes generally have been concerned with structure, form, and procedures and have not tried to reconcile conflicting interests or to correct instances of managerial abuse in any systematic way. The enabling approach of state legislation has the obvious advantage of flexibility to accommodate a variety of changing business activities. But, have the drafters of legislation been remiss in failing to develop definitive rules of conduct reconciling the potentially conflicting interests of shareholders, management, and creditors?

I believe the answer is no. There are definite limits to the extent to which the law can or should try to define appropriate managerial activity. Legal rules operate not in a vacuum but in a world in which market transactions can and do influence conduct. And, in many instances, legal restraints as checks on management's actions are neither as efficient nor as effective as the restraints imposed by competitive market forces.

Here, arguments are important. For years, the courts and legislatures struggled with the problem of how much corporations should be permitted to pay out as dividends. The result was an absolute muddle, and a statutory structure that was as elaborate as it was easily evaded. Modern statutes impose relatively few restraints on dividend payouts, leaving creditors to protect themselves by bargaining for contractual restrictions. Creditors have done so, and the resulting individually negotiated agreements achieve better creditor protection with less interference with managerial discretion than any statutory provision of general applicability could ever offer. Second, the critics seem to assume that unless management is subject to a number of legal strictures, it will exercise its freedom to indulge its own preferences at the expense of shareholders. This ignores the existence of market forces, which provide powerful incentives for managers to accommodate shareholder interests [SB 17, SB 55].

Finally, some critics, most notably William Cary, seek to justify federal intervention on the grounds that the Delaware courts have a consistent promanagement bias and that Delaware decisions have had an undue influence on the development of state corporation law generally [89]. Cary suggests that the Delaware courts are so clearly identified with managerial interests that their independence is subject to question. He seeks to prove his thesis by examining a handful of Delaware cases that reach results with which many might disagree. Obviously, his data are too limited to have any significance. One could easily cite other Delaware decisions that do not demonstrate the promanagement bias he finds in the cases he selects. One could repeat this process for every other jurisdiction, including the federal courts, proving nothing except that the outcome of litigation is uncertain, and that not everyone likes every decision.

ADDITIONAL READINGS: 22, 92, 166, 214, 253, 284, 374.

THE FEDERAL CHARTERING ALTERNATIVE

30. Do Corporations Have No Inherent Rights, Only Government-given Privileges?

DONALD L. MARTIN
Law and Economics Center
University of Miami School of Law

Editor's Summary   The modern corporation descends from the joint-stock company, which resulted from the exercise of individual rights to contract and private property. Limited liability, legal personality, perpetual life, and other characteristics are not government-granted corporate privileges. Federal chartering will narrow the scope of legitimate contracting among consenting parties and will, consequently, diminish private property rights, while it transfers both resources and power to the government. Federal chartering would represent a long step in the further politicization of decisions that would otherwise be based on economic criteria; the socioeconomic control process that relies on voluntary transactions in largely decentralized and competitive markets would be replaced by political and bureaucratic forces catering to their constituencies. The motives for federal chartering are redistributions of power, rights, and wealth.

The large, modern corporation once again is under attack from sources that view it as a privileged organizational form, insulated from competition and armed with great economic and political powers [52, 145, 189, 327, 328]. The threat that the corporation poses for consumer sovereignty and for democracy is claimed to be so great that nothing less than radical revisions in corporate chartering are necessary to stem the growth of unchecked corporate power and action inconsistent with the *public interest*.

The latest proposal offered to achieve these ends is *federal chartering* legislation, under which corporations engaging, or intending to engage, in interstate commerce would be subject to a federal charter above and beyond the existing state incorporation requirements [328: 62–71]. Firms unwilling to comply with federal regulations and statutes could be denied a charter and, in addition, would continue to face the conventional penalties associated with violations of the law.

THE ARGUMENTS FOR FEDERAL CHARTERING OF CORPORATIONS

Corporate critics rationalize the entrance of the federal government into the incorporation process by asserting that the corporation, compared to other forms of economic organization, is distinguished by special privileges. These include limited liability, legal personality, and "perpetual life." These privileges, it is believed, allow corporations to wield great economic and political power to the detriment of consumers, workers, stockholders, and democratic institutions [SB 5, SB 49].

Although antisocial corporate actions may be the direct results of managerial activities, the privileges or rights that permit such transgressions, nevertheless, are said to be the *creations* of the state. Without government sponsorship, corporate detractors believe, corporate privilege would perish; the rights that distinguish corporations from other organizational forms and natural persons, consequently, are not inherent or inalienable [402: 700–713, 328: 62–71]. These special rights are said to arise from a contractual arrangement with the state. In its capacity as a contractual participant, the state is the public's guardian, or representative, for it is the public that gives life and privileges to the corporation [328: 62–71]. The corporation, in this view, is more like a public utility than a proprietary enterprise and therefore should be amenable to state monitoring and discretion.

The recently resurrected federal corporate charter concept dates back to mercantilist Britain where, in exchange for monopoly rights to a given market, certain joint-stock companies agreed to support the Crown and to conform to its demands. Corporate charters were synonymous with monopoly power, and the special relationship between the Crown and a favored company gave the company access to the Crown's and Parliament's law and courts for suits.

The corporation today, according to those who would subject it to federal, rather than state, regulation, is a modern version of its mercantilist ancestor [SB 27]. That is, the contemporary corporation, like its mercantilist ancestor, derives its monopoly powers from the privileges it receives from the state. Whereas the charter relationship between the corporation and the Crown was one of quid pro quo, today's reformers complain that governments now bestow special privileges on corporations in exchange for concessions that understate drastically the wealth and power that the state has made possible.

The current demand for more concessions from corporations is not in terms of bullion or other pecuniary booty; it is, nevertheless, a demand for more corporate resources to finance public wants. And, these demands are above and beyond state incorporation terms. By requiring corporations to obtain and adhere to a federal charter before they may enter into interstate commerce, the federal government could reduce the wealth and power of the larger corporations.

Suggested components of federal corporate charters include, for example, shareholder referenda on all "fundamental" transactions [213]. Although this policy is called corporate democracy, its effect is to narrow the scope of legitimate contracting between consenting parties, which implies a reduction in the scope of private property rights, relative to collective or political action, as a social control mechanism. Although this policy may appear to be a transfer of resources from corporate managers to shareholders, actually it is a transfer from shareholders to members of Congress, political lobbyists, and other special-interest groups. Under federal chartering, political criteria are substituted for market criteria in shaping shareholder participation in corporate management.

Another reform that federal chartering promises is "full disclosure," a concept that reflects the public utility view of the corporation. Just as conventional public utilities must (by law) release their books and other information to public scrutiny, so, it is argued, should all firms that receive special privileges from the government, since the public has a right to know the financial position and social impact of *its* largest corporations [213, 328: 132–179]. "Full disclosure," moreover, demands the identification of shareholders using *street names* and public access to the private corporate informaton that government agencies desire. Additional limitations on privacy at the corporate level imply a narrowing of private property rights, as well as a further transfer of resources to government [SB 22, SB 23, SB 24].

The chartering of corporations at the federal level, finally, would facilitate limitations on and reductions of firm size and market share, goals the founders of the modern federal charter concept have pursued for some time. Large firms in concentrated industries often have been charged with earning "excess" profits—and with being lethargic (a logical consequence of earning excess profits). Corporate privileges supposedly insulate them from competition and from the need to search for the most efficient management, production, and marketing techniques. The result of breaking up existing concentrations of power and of prohibiting the continued chartering of corporations that expand their market shares beyond "permissible limits" is expected to be increased competition in industry and enhanced efficiency [SB 40, SB 50, SB 51, SB 57].

THE CROWN-CHARTERED, MONOPOLISTIC CORPORATION ANALOGY

The case for the federal chartering proposal rests on two shaky pillars. The first is the assumption that modern corporations, especially large ones, are the direct descendants of the Crown-chartered corporations that enjoyed monopoly powers in the seventeenth and eighteenth centuries. If the analogy between the earlier and the modern corporations is false, as I show presently, the grounds for distinguishing between alternative forms of business organization as a criterion in developing social policy are highly suspect.

The second weak pillar of the federal chartering concept is the assertion that there are links between corporate size or market share, monopoly profits, and the absence of competitive incentives to operate efficiently. If the evidence cannot support the asserted links, and I show that it cannot, the case for divestiture and the supportive role federal chartering is supposed to play also must be suspect.

Let us examine the first shaky pillar. A careful reading of economic history shows that the so-called privileges enjoyed by modern corporations, unlike those enjoyed by the Crown-chartered corporations, are not a function of government patronage, as supporters of federal chartering maintain. Joint-stock companies in the eighteenth and nineteenth centuries could not incorporate because the Bubble Act of 1720 prohibited their incorporation. Yet, these same joint-stock companies enjoyed the advantages of limited liability, legal personality, and "perpetual life," which are three so-called distinguishing characteristics of the modern corporation. The emergence and survival of unincorporated joint-stock companies having these characteristics were the results of privately executed deeds of settlement among stockholders, as well as of notice of limited liability given to these companies' creditors.

Courts of equity recognized these deeds and expanded the law of agency so that the unincorporated joint-stock companies could have access to the courts, a privilege otherwise reserved for Crown-chartered corporations in common-law courts [9, 200]. Naturally, this privilege facilitated suits and settlements that were and are important mechanisms for solving personal disputes among owners and between owners and creditors. Although it was not until 1862 that joint-stock companies with limited liability were permitted incorporation under the law as a right rather than as a privilege, their unincorporated status did not appear to threaten their growth and prosperity during the approximately 150-year period that preceded the complete repeal of the Bubble Act [256].

This is remarkably compelling evidence that joint-stock companies with limited liability, the true precursors of modern corporations, were not the offspring of the state or of the Crown. They were, instead, the conscious expression of private parties who exercised their rights to property and contract. Like the equity courts of old, modern government, represented in this case by the respective state commissioners of corporations, records, validates, and enforces the articles of incorporation that constitute a contract exclusively between the persons that form a joint-stock company. The state is not a party to this contract, as it was to those of chartered corporations insulated from competition by the Crown.

The modern commissioner of corporations, like the modern registrar of deeds or of births, has no paternity interests in supervising the conduct and results of private arrangements. Modern state incorporation procedures merely are relatively less expensive means (compared to the situation when incorporation was outlawed) of facilitating the limited liability, legal personality, and continuity arrangements between private parties in joint-stock companies. Similarly, there is nothing particularly unique about corporate personality, and corporate personality does not depend upon state creativity. Legal personality permits a corporation to sue or to hold title to property as a unit. But, partnerships also are legal entities, and in any form of business organization trustees may be appointed to represent the owners in lawsuits or to accept or convey title to property [213].

Thus, the modern corporation is the direct descendant of the unincorporated joint-stock company that flourished in the eighteenth and nineteenth centuries in Britain and that managed to achieve limited liability, corporate personality, and continuity without special support or privileges from the state. It is doubtful, then, that the rationale used to apply federal standards to state corporations is a valid one. Corporations *do not* enjoy special privileges that can be supplied only through government chartering. Governments, moreover, are not parties to modern articles of incorporation, and the modern corporate organization is under no moral or logical obligation to support public policy *more* than other forms of business organization support it.

THE ATTACK ON CORPORATE SIZE AND CONCENTRATION

The second pillar on which federal chartering rests is the assertion that large corporations are so insulated from competition that their large profits permit them to ignore efficient management techniques. Of course, this appears to be an appropriate observation for regulated utilities and for government corporations such as the United States Post Office. If this were the case for most private corporations, however, firms with monopoly power would exhibit excess profits for *sustained* periods, thus demonstrating their insulation from competitive forces. The evidence points to the opposite conclusion. Even the most profitable firms are under constant attack from actual and would-be rivals in the same or closely related industries. Abnormally high rates of return, even in the more highly concentrated industries, are subject continually to the process of dissipation as the market sends signals to would-be competitors that higher-than-average rates of return can be had for those *firms that enter and compete with currently profitable corporations* [68, 72].

THE REAL, REDISTRIBUTION MOTIVE OF FEDERAL CHARTERING

If the case for "constitutionalizing" the corporation is based on two shaky pillars, what alternative explanation is there for the enthusiasm accorded the proposal for federal chartering? Perhaps the redistributive dynamics of our political system hold the answer. A popular way to appropriate wealth from others has been first to identify a subset of the population having some distinguishing characteristics; second, to deny that these characteristics have any positive net social value (indeed, claim that they are "antisocial"); and, third, to deny to the distinguishable group, by virtue of its antisocial nature, its legitimate or natural rights to property, liberty, or due process of law. That is, property rights and political rights exist for the group in question at the pleasure of the state. The state, then, is in a position to issue and withdraw rights that other less distinguishable groups enjoy as inalienable (until their time comes!).

Usually, the victim group has been distinguished because of religious convictions, national origin, race, or physical characteristics. Recently, a new set of characteristics has been introduced, one identified less with natural persons than with the forms of economic organization those persons choose to own and use. Large corporations have been singled out, and their identifying characteristics are the special privileges they are alleged to enjoy compared to those of other economic organizations.

Once the corporation has been distinguished from other organizational forms, and once its contractual rights have been attributed to the discretion of government rather than to the sanctity of the Constitution, it is but a short step to the appropriation of wealth through regulation. But, federal chartering is more than mere regulation. It is an attempt to reduce the scope of private property as a social economic control device [9]. It is an attempt to replace the use of voluntary exchange values in the market for alienable property by political directive. Only those having a comparative advantage in political competition stand to gain from such a change.

ADDITIONAL READINGS: 10, 222, 227, 284, 287.

31. Is Federal Chartering Necessary to Curb Corporate Power?

THOMAS D. MORGAN
College of Law
University of Illinois

Editor's Summary   Some critics allege that state law fails to provide adequate safeguards in the interest of minority shareholders. But, shareholders currently are free to purchase shares in a variety of corporations, many of which impose numerous and different restrictions on management. Federal chartering would eliminate the advantages of a wide range of different corporate laws and, as a consequence, injure those shareholders who prefer earnings to participation. If the Federal Trade Commission, the Equal Employment Opportunity Commission, the Justice Department, and all the other agencies that regulate corporations have not been able to curb so-called corporate abuses, how much additional coercive power would the "new" proposals require to accomplish the critics' purposes?

Corporations today are "chartered" (given their basic license to do business) by a single state. In a country as interrelated as the United States, such a practice initially may seem undesirable, or at least incongruous. Thus, it is perhaps not surprising that proposals continue to arise for federal chartering of corporations.

Federal chartering is not a new proposal. It has been advocated periodically both before and since the turn of the century [63, 405]. No matter how often it has been proposed, however, Congress never has come close to adopting it. Such a history seems revealing, especially when juxtaposed with current examples of special federally chartered corporations such as AMTRAK and the United States Postal Service.

FEDERAL CHARTERING'S DRAMATIS PERSONAE

Three advocates of and two proposals for federal chartering stand out in the current debate. William Cary is concerned that Delaware, the state in which more major corporations are chartered than in any other, "is both the sponsor and the victim of a system contributing to the deterioration of corporation standards" [89: 663]. Cary has collected a series of examples in which Delaware courts have, in his view, been insensitive to the rights of shareholders, particularly minority shareholders, and have emphasized flexibility for corporate management over full disclosure and strict accountability. (Professor Cary's solution is to come "up from Delaware" to a set of "federal standards of corporate responsibility," which allegedly would put intracorporate relationships—those among shareholders and between shareholders and managers—on a "fairer" basis.)

Donald Schwartz views the issues more broadly and seeks, "first, to constrain the power of corporations within the society, [and] second, to contain the power of corporate managers or at least to render the exercise of their power more effectively accountable" [384:1128; 385]. This proposal, in short, focuses on the use of the chartering process to establish substantive limits or obligations on corporations. Charter prohibitions, for example, allegedly could reduce corporate size without the need to prove a violation of the antitrust laws. Further, a charter could require managers to concentrate more on the effects of their decisions on "outside constituencies" and less on profits for shareholders [SB 5].

Ralph Nader and his associates make no substantive additions to the Schwartz proposals but give them substantial public visibility [328]. They have given added content to the Cary proposal by recommending various "protective" devices, such as mandatory cumulative voting and professional outside directors.

The Schwartz-Nader proposal to dictate the substantive practices of corporations through charters is both misdirected and disturbing. The Nader, Green, and Seligman book, for example, begins in characteristic fashion with a recitation of the litany of wrongs allegedly perpetrated by particular American firms. The wrongs often are wholly unrelated—for example, exposing employees to toxic chemicals, on the one hand, and using "inane, misleading, or deceptive" advertising on the other. Sometimes the charges are even contradictory. For example, American management is said to be insufficiently innovative, and also insufficiently cautious about the consequences of new technology.

FEDERAL CHARTERING AND CORPORATE ACTIVITIES

Even if these examples are valid, however, the proposed solution of federal chartering has nothing whatsoever to do with the elimination of these "evils." Each of the alleged wrongs is the subject of both state and federal regulation, often by several agencies at each level. Certainly not all of that regulation is sound; unquestionably much of it imposes costs that far exceed any benefits derived [SB 3, SB 8, SB 11, SB 23, SB 26, SB 60]. But, if more specific regulation is required and is cost-justified, it, too, can be imposed. Plainly, none of the problems or objectives that Schwartz or Nader and his associates cite, whether in the area of fuller disclosure, nondiscrimination, or industry deconcentration, has any relationship at all to the issue of what agency should license corporations to do business.

Stripped of rhetorical flourishes, this "substantive" side of federal chartering seems to be based on the unstated assumption that the enforcement policy and remedies available under a federal charter would be tougher than what is available today. Federal administrative law, for example, admits much more of agency "rule making" and adjudication that defines and, arguably, rewrites the underlying statute. Some of the SEC's most potent weapons—for example, Rule 10b-5 on insider trading—were created by the agency and not by Congress [SB 25, SB 26]. The flexibility to *avoid* being confined by the basic statute indeed may be one of the most important objectives of federal chartering advocates.

Proponents speak also of "revoking the charter" as a punishment for any firm that does not comply with the federal view of proper corporate behavior [SB 32]. Revoking the charter of General Motors, for example, would mean closing down all the company's operations—period—until the company "got in line." Some critics like the idea of giving representatives of "the people" that kind of authority. Of course, a federal chartering statute could be written that would deny any agency this arbitrary power. The courts possibly would intervene in extreme cases. However, federal chartering advocates express no particular concern about company civil liberties, and they seem to understand and welcome the coercive effect of this Draconian remedy.

FEDERAL CHARTERING AND CORPORATE STRUCTURE

The various proposals for federalizing the internal structure of corporations are more nearly responsible, but equally unwise. The fundamental reason for these proposals is that competition among states to charter corporations has led to a lowest common denominator of shareholder protection. Delaware, it is said, has won the contest for "most irresponsible" and thus continues to attract the nation's largest firms [22].

Once again, however, a proposal for federal chartering, by itself, implies nothing whatsoever about the content of a charter. As the critics themselves recognize, it is at least possible that Congress could enact the Delaware Corporation Act as federal law. What proponents seem to hope is that their influence will be much stronger in Washington than it is in state capitols so that "federal chartering" will be a way, in one stroke, to get critics' favorite substantive changes enacted into corporate law.

Such an analysis ignores the inherent advantage of a range of possible corporate laws covering every different kind of shareholder protection or lack of it [SB 21]. A responsible business planner will select the state of incorporation best suited to clients' needs. In Illinois, for example, every share must have a vote, and all corporations must use cumulative voting, just as Nader and his associates propose. But, other states do not have such requirements, and thus the range of choices afforded by state incorporation allows a planner to incorporate in Illinois, if that state's requirements are useful to the planner's clients, as they often are, or somewhere else, such as Delaware, if those requirements do not square with the clients' needs.

One might respond that federal "minimum standards" would not eliminate choice; they would only set basic limits. That response assumes that "minimums" truly will remain "low"; the history of regulation indicates, however, that once an agency is in the business of regulation, restraint is not a common virtue [325, 423].

Further, any minimum, by definition, will eliminate a range of choices thought to be "below" that floor. In general, the establishment of minima will mean that some degree of management flexibility will be eliminated. This will not trouble the corporate critics, but one can argue persuasively that the rise of management flexibility was an important advance in the development of the modern corporation, and not a cause for the gnashing of teeth. Company managers are specialists at trying to use resources effectively, and real economic costs may be imposed by narrowing their options through various shareholder "protection" schemes.

If, and to the extent that, corporate earnings are reduced because of restraints on management, shareholders will be forced to pay involuntarily for their protection. This might not be so bad if one could show that shareholders want additional protection. But, if shareholders really favored restrictive acts over "liberal" statutes like Delaware's, one would expect to see them pay a premium for stock in firms registered outside Delaware. Senior managers, in turn, who by the critics' own assumptions are eager to inflate the value of their stock options, would rush to incorporate in restrictive states. No such phenomenon, of course, has occurred. Shareholder protection, it seems, is valued far more by shareholders' "advocates" than by shareholders themselves [SB 5, SB 16, SB 17, SB 21].

Finally, responsible analysts should recognize that there already is an extensive "federal corporation law" consisting of the rules and procedural requirements of the Securities and Exchange Commission [164]. Virtually all the largest publicly held corporations about which Cary, Schwartz, and Nader and his associates are concerned issue stock or debt, and some do so on a reasonably frequent basis. Hence, they are subject to disclosure requirements that are virtually as imposing as those that Nader suggests. The antifraud provisions of the Securities Acts, likewise, regulate insider self-dealing in ways not unlike those suggested for federal chartering plans.

The SEC, of course, does not require cumulative voting, boards composed wholly of outside directors, or some of the social accounting information that various proposals would require. But, by imposing personal liability on corporate directors, attorneys, and accountants who sign a materially inaccurate registration statement, the Commission can give, and already has given, directors and skilled "outsiders" the same kind of federalized incentive for investigation and independent judgment to which the "new" federal system would aspire.

SUMMARY

Federal chartering, in short, would add another layer of regulation to an already top-heavy system. It cannot accomplish anything that direct regulation of particular evils could not achieve, and its "protection" is neither valued by the market nor likely to be cost-justified. Federal chartering, it seems, is neither new, nor innovative, nor wise.

ADDITIONAL READINGS: 44, 45, 47, 48, 52, 289.

32. Should Corporate Charters Be Reviewed Regularly for Renewal or Cancellation?

ARLEEN LEIBOWITZ
The Rand Corporation

Editor's Summary Periodic review and renewal of state or federal
corporate charters would encourage short-run, rather than long-run,
planning by firms. The uncertainty associated with renewal reviews
and the threat of cancellation would lead to distortions in investment
decisions as well as artificial and unnecessary fluctuations in stock
market prices. As a practical matter, it is unlikely that many renewals
would be denied. In its periodic reviews of radio and television
stations, the FCC has seldom refused to renew the licenses of the
present owners. It is even less likely that corporations' charters would
not be renewed, since it would be nearly impossible to distribute
corporate assets equitably, and since thousands of stockowners
(including union pension funds) would suffer losses. The costs of
defending against this possibility, nevertheless, would be substantial
and would be paid by consumers in the form of higher prices.

Richard Posner suggests that states typically grant corporations perpetual life "to obviate the need for a special agreement limiting withdrawal or dissolution" [356: 177]. Believing that corporate charters can control corporate activity, some people advocate short-term *federal* charters [328, 384, 385]. To assure that corporations live up to standards of corporate behavior embodied in the proposal, the charters would be subject to periodic review and renewal.

The federal chartering proposal has two serious faults. First, corporations would be limited to short-run, rather than long-run, planning. Second, charter review is unlikely actually to result in the revocation of corporate charters. Here, I examine both of these faults.

RENEWABLE AND REVOCABLE CHARTERS WILL DISTORT INVESTMENT

In making investment decisions, a firm must weigh the initial costs of, say, a new piece of equipment against the present value of the stream of expected future profits generated by that piece of equipment. To illustrate, consider a piece of equipment with a useful life of twenty years. Each year it produces output that can be sold for $100 more than the cost of the other inputs used. The present value of the income stream, assuming an interest rate of 5 percent, is $1,246.22. (For the interested reader, the calculation derives from the formula $V = (100/0.05) \times (1 - (1/1.05)^{20}$.) So, the firm should be willing to pay up to $1,246.22 for this piece of equipment.

Suppose the firm believes that there is a 50 percent probability of its charter being revoked after five years. Using a similar calculation, the expected present value of the income stream becomes only $839.59, because the last fifteen years of the profit stream have a 50 percent chance of not materializing. Because the expectations are reduced, the piece of equipment will be bought only if the price is $839.59 or less. Thus, the uncertainty associated with renewal causes an investment to become no longer economically worthwhile, even though it is justified under a longer longer horizon. The uncertainty that the possibility of nonrenewal generates leads, therefore, to distortions in investment activity.

RENEWABLE AND REVOCABLE CHARTERS WILL DISTORT SHARE PRICES

A related kind of distortion occurs with respect to stock prices. As the time for renewal nears, stock prices, which are related to the expected present value of returns, will fall because there is some finite possibility that the renewal will be denied and returns will cease. After renewal, stock prices will rise again. These artificial fluctuations in stock prices would be most undesirable. Even if renewals never are denied in practice, as long as there is the *threat* that they may be denied in the future, the distortions will exist.

Indeed, it is unlikely that periodic review would actually result in the revocation of corporate charters. Revocation is such a massive penalty that it is hard to imagine what activity could justify it. The FCC's periodic review of radio and television station licenses resulted in only fifty-five denials of renewal from 1934 to 1971, of which only three affected television stations [368: 160, 447]. Robinson and Gellhorn write: "Despite all of the formal requirements for obtaining renewal, the process has been regarded by many as ritualistic since only on rare occasions does the Commission deny renewals" [368: 159]. Even though few charters are likely to be revoked, furthermore, the costs of preparing and presenting evidence before the renewal commission are likely to be substantial. These costs will be passed on to consumers.

WHAT REVOCATION OF A CHARTER WOULD MEAN

Infrequent as the FCC's refusal to renew a broadcasting license has been, the denial of charter renewal is likely to occur even less often. What would the revocation of a charter mean for a corporation? Would the assets be split up and sold to the highest bidder, thereby imposing capital losses on thousands of stockowners? (Such a practice cannot result in a profit for stockowners; if it did, the potential purchasers of assets would already have bid for stock.) This outcome is unlikely. Could a commission legally force a change in the board of directors or the management? The renewal proceeding might be subject to real abuse by parties seeking to use the government as an instrument in takeover bids. Unscrupulous parties could bring false charges to receive from the government what they could not acquire with a tender offer.

CONCLUSIONS

One conclusion, then, is inescapable: corporate charter renewal would not be a viable method for regulating corporations. If there was a positive probability that a charter renewal request could be denied (that is, if charter revocation was a legal option), distortions in investment decisions, as well as in stock prices, would occur. This method would also open the door to serious abuses by parties wishing to wrest control of corporations from their present owners and managers. It is unlikely that renewals would be denied, however, because it would be nearly impossible to dispose equitably of corporate assets, and because thousands of stockowners (including union pension funds) would suffer losses in the process. The costs of defending against this possibility, nevertheless, would be substantial and would be paid by consumers in the form of higher prices.

ADDITIONAL READINGS: 213, 287.

33. Do Lenient State Incorporation Laws Injure Minority Shareholders?

ALLEN HYMAN
Southwestern University School of Law

Editor's Summary   Ralph Nader, William Cary, and others call for
federal chartering of corporations. These persons ignore the extensive
benefits that result from a variety of state laws, and they fail to
establish that there is any harm resulting from existing state
corporation laws. The competition for corporations among states
produces effective, efficient, and responsive state laws that operate in
the best interest of all stockholders. Federal chartering would harm
rather than help minority and majority stockholder interests.

Some legal commentators, believing that state corporation laws are too
"lax" and too "permissive," are alarmed at the competition among the
states for corporate residents. These commentators thus advocate federal
chartering of corporations to stem the growing "liberalization" of state
corporation laws. Delaware, the most successful "lax" and "permissive"
state, long has been the punching bag of legal combatants hostile to state
corporation law. Delaware today is the legal domicile of over one-half of
the firms listed on the New York Stock Exchange [6: 23–24].

THE CRITICS OF DELAWARE

Because it successfully attracts incorporations as a result of its "liberalization," Delaware is singled out as representing the worst in state corporation law. William Cary states the matter thus: "Delaware is both the
sponsor and the victim of a system contributing to the deterioration of
corporation standards . . . they have watered the rights of shareholders
vis-à-vis management down to a thin gruel" [89: 666]. Ralph Nader and
his associates, the major proponents of a federal chartering law, ask, "Why
federal chartering, such an old idea in 1976?. . . Because . . . state chartering laws, downgraded by the Delaware Syndrome, have failed to restrain
corporate abuses" [328: 252]. Neil Jacoby adds, "Federal chartering
could, however, establish a uniform national pattern of governance. It
could put a stop to the progressive permissiveness—'charter monger-
ing'—that has marked state chartering for many years" [226: 14].

The immediate questions raised in response to these writers are: What
is so wrong, so evil, and so undesirable about state corporation laws,
especially those of Delaware? What, in particular, generates this call for a

federal law? In what manner has state law failed us? And, whom does state law harm?

WHOM DO PRESENT CORPORATION LAWS HARM?

State laws obviously do not harm the state that enacts them. Those who criticize Delaware as a prime example of a state that has undesirable corporation laws are quick to point out that the state does quite well as a result of its corporate jurisprudence. Delaware receives approximately 16 percent of its state revenue from corporate filing and franchise fees [6: 20–34]. While Nader et al. claim that the amount is 23 percent, their estimate is inconsistent with my calculations derived from standardized state tax tables, which indicate that the percentage derived from corporations is 16 percent [328: 57, 60].

Does a lax corporate code harm the controlling or majority shareholders of a corporation? Hardly; the corporate managers are the ones who decide to move the corporation to Delaware in the first place. One can assume that the controlling shareholders favor the "permissive" law that allegedly gives them a considerable amount of discretion in organizing the internal corporate structure.

Who, then, is left? Who is harmed? Whom do Cary, Nader, and Jacoby wish to protect? They are concerned with the welfare of minority shareholders [167: 1078]. Detractors of state corporation codes believe that state law is inadequate because it operates, allegedly, to the disadvantage of minority shareholders.

Delaware's antagonists traditionally refer to a set of ten to twelve regulations that, they claim, harm minority shareholders. The provisions of these regulations are as follows: allow straight, rather than cumulative, voting; lower shareholder voting requirements for fundamental corporate changes; allow directors to determine their own salaries and bonuses; and, allow corporations to indemnify directors and officers for mistakes they make in handling corporate affairs.

In response, one cannot say categorically that these regulations are undesirable simply because someone asserts that they give management too much discretion. Greater managerial discretion may allow corporations to become more profitable—and thereby enable minority shareholders to receive greater earnings. Many other provisions of the Delaware Corporation Code, furthermore, are especially advantageous to minority shareholders. Minority shareholders can more easily sue controlling shareholders and directors in Delaware than in other states, and they have easier access to corporate records in Delaware than in other states. It is not evident, therefore, that Delaware's laws harm persons who own minority share interests in Delaware corporations.

NEGLECTED ECONOMIC THEORY IN
THE FEDERAL CHARTERING CASE

The strongest rebuttal to Nader, Cary, and Jacoby, however, stems from their own arguments. Their very formulation of the problem indicates a complete lack of appreciation for twenty years of intellectual development and research in the fields of finance, capital market theory, and economics. Since a set of laws was in existence when minority shareholders bought their shares (the laws still exist), one cannot argue realistically that these shareholders were harmed because they bought shares in Delaware corporations.

The market price of a share already reflects the impact of the laws in existence at the time of purchase. Current and past information is already reflected in current stock prices. The market price of all assets (commodities, government bonds, and stocks of companies incorporated in other states or countries) reflects the costs and benefits of the legal structure under which the equity is governed. Thus, the price of a share of stock in a corporation whose legal domicile is in Delaware and whose internal affairs are controlled by Delaware law should already reflect the effect of the Delaware law.

Therefore, one cannot possibly find out by analyzing the particular laws whether the "permissive" Delaware laws (as compared with the laws in more restrictive states) are beneficial or harmful to any particular class of Delaware shareholders. The effects of those laws are already captured in the market prices of Delaware corporations' stocks.

There is a method, however, by which one can statistically analyze Nader's claim. First, though, it is useful to clarify one important issue. If a firm incorporates in a particular state, its legal domicile, that state's corporation laws apply to and regulate the organizational structure and "internal affairs" of the firm. That is, the state in which this firm is incorporated regulates only the relationships between the controlling and minority shareholders, on the one hand, and management, on the other hand. The state's laws are not permissive in the sense that they allow the corporation to pollute the environment or violate antitrust laws [SB 3]. The laws *are* permissive in the sense that they allow shareholders wide discretion in governing their organizational affairs free from mandated state rules. But, the corporation is *still* governed by the laws of commercial practice in the states in which it does business. Federal and state antitrust laws and laws regulating environmental matters and labor practices still govern the corporation's business activities in the states in which it operates. The "lax" laws apply only to corporate internal organizational matters.

To analyze the "effect" of Delaware law upon minority shareholder interest, I examined the change in prices of corporate stocks traded on the

New York Stock Exchange around the date of the first public announcement that a particular corporation intended to change its place of incorporation to the state of Delaware, the most liberal and most permissive state as far as corporate law is concerned [224]. This examination substantiated the fact that prices of shares of corporations that announced they were moving to Delaware outperformed the Standard and Poor's average around the date of the announcement. It appears, therefore, that Delaware law does not operate to harm minority shareholder interest but instead actually benefits that interest.

THE COSTS OF LESS PERMISSIVE FEDERAL CHARTERING

If this evidence is not enough to deflate the arguments for a federal chartering law, consider the evolution of state corporation law. When early corporations were formed, and shares of stock first issued, the costs of ownership transfer (by selling stock in one corporation and purchasing shares in another corporation) were considerably higher than they are today. From 1810 to 1880, the internal affairs of corporations were controlled far more by state law than they are today, and state restrictions served a useful purpose. In the early nineteenth century, it was very difficult to get information about a stock before purchase. Since there was very little public information about earnings history, dividend history, and management activity, state law imposed many controls on corporate internal affairs. Though corporations may have been hampered because of the controls imposed by state law, the law allowed greater security for minority interests. Nader and others would like to have us reinstate the laws of the nineteenth century.

The cost of trading shares in market transactions, however, has fallen drastically over the last 150 years. Today, considerable information is available through voluntary corporate action or by SEC mandate. And, the cost of acquiring this information has fallen. Shareholders are much better protected through market transactions; they can easily, cheaply, and swiftly sell their holdings in one corporation and buy into another through stock exchange transactions.

Why should contemporary corporations be restricted in structuring their internal affairs? If a shareholder does not like what a corporation is doing, he or she can easily find another, more suitable firm [SB 21]. Stock markets have become very efficient. Individual shareholders can acquire information about a variety of investments much more cheaply than they could in the past.

Today, it makes little sense to legislate many restrictions upon the internal decision-making matters of corporations. A corporation could achieve the same result through its own corporate bylaws and articles of incorporation. Why not give managers the freedom to make good business decisions? If minority shareholders do not like the way managers are handling the affairs of their corporation, they can sell out and buy into another corporation. The sale of shares tends to depress prices and discipline poor managers.

Most shareholders have a greater desire to tend to their wealth interest through a modification of their portfolios rather than through participation in corporate political activity [SB 5]. One would predict that as the stock markets have become more efficient, and as investor information has become cheaper to acquire, shareholders would avoid corporate political activity, preferring individual market activity to protect and enhance their wealth.

It seems questionable that a decline in democratic shareholder activity in corporations and an increase in shareholder trading activity would trouble corporate law commentators. Delaware has pioneered, and other states are attempting to institute, sets of rules and regulations that give greater freedom and discretion to corporate managers. And, everyone is better off, minority shareholders as well as majority shareholders.

This new kind of corporate law is consistent with the minority shareholders' declining interest in participation in corporate decision-making activities. The new rules allow managers and controlling shareholders to respond more quickly to different business changes. In addition, the rules permit minority shareholders to modify their interests by buying and selling shares, rather than by engaging in corporate political activity (as Nader would like).

Basing their arguments on a fictitious charge of harm, proponents of federal chartering would have us believe that minority shareholders desire a federal corporation law. It appears, however, that minority shareholders who are residents of other states benefit as a result of permissive corporation laws. There is no question that there is greater flexibility and variety in state corporation laws than there ever conceivably could be under a single federal system. Implicit in the arguments of those who want a federal law is the claim that federal law is superior to state law and that those who live in Washington, D.C., know more about what is better corporation law than those who live in the individual states.

It is most inconsistent that those who advocate federal chartering in the name of individual liberty and individual rights for shareholders should try to promote liberty by emasculating state laws, and by installing their own personal laws at the federal level. State laws provide considerable variety and individual determination as they favor individual stockholder action. A centralized federal program would greatly harm stockholder rights.

ADDITIONAL READINGS: 22, 118, 384, 385.

PART FOUR

CORPORATE POWER
AND THE MARKET

┌───┐
│   │
│   **PRICE AND**   │
│   **OUTPUT DECISIONS**   │
│   │
└───┘

34. Are Administered Prices Socially Undesirable?

ROBERT W. CLOWER
Department of Economics
University of California, Los Angeles

Editor's Summary   Individual producers, wholesalers, retailers, and employers set "asked" or "bid" prices in the noncorporate sector, as well as in the corporate sector. Administered prices exist for most commodities because these commodities come in an almost endless variety. Hence, alternative pricing schemes would be too costly. Firms hold inventories of these commodities and sell at administered prices until their changes in inventories indicate that they should raise (or lower) prices. Prices in such markets are "rigid"—first, because changing posted prices is costly for both sellers and buyers. Second, since the rate of future sales is uncertain, sellers often tie their posted prices to their costs. Third, administered prices reduce buyers' search costs. Hence, rigid prices, idle capacity, and fluctuating output occur not because sellers insist on this arrangement but. rather, because most customers prefer it.

During the early years of the Great Depression, prices in some industries (for example, steel and automobiles) fell hardly at all, while prices in others (for example, agricultural products, crude petroleum, and textiles) fell by more than 50 percent. These disparities were too gross and prolonged to be explained satisfactorily by standard textbook principles of supply and demand. Either reported Bureau of Labor Statistics (BLS) price data conveyed a highly inaccurate impression of actual transaction prices, or standard price theory requires fundamental revision.

THE THESIS OF ADMINISTERED PRICES

In an influential report published in 1935, Gardiner C. Means puts forward a case for revision. He notes first that the prices of most commodities are determined in practice not by impersonal forces of demand and supply, as reflected in the bids and offers of traders in organized markets, but rather by the personal administrative actions of the sellers (or buyers) of particular products. Then, Means argues that the area of "price discretion" in many industries is large and that the prevalence of administered prices, especially in the corporate sector, adversely influences the overall performance of the economic system [308, 310, 311].

Means does not provide precise criteria for distinguishing between "administered" and "market" prices. Nor does he explain the rationale of discretionary pricing, or provide reasons why administered prices should be less responsive than market prices to changes in demand. These are serious omissions. Economists do not need Means to tell them that individual producers, wholesalers, retailers, and employers set all but a handful of commodity prices (more accurately, "asked" or "bid" prices), for this has been common knowledge for at least two centuries. The only relevant issue that remains is whether or not the ubiquitousness of administered prices fundamentally alters the normal working of "impersonal forces of supply and demand." Means's argument sheds no significant light on this question.

EVIDENCE ABOUT ADMINISTERED PRICES

Means's "administered price thesis," however, deserves to be taken seriously. Stigler and Kindahl do take it seriously in the most ambitious attempt to resolve some of the issues that Means poses [426]. They show that BLS price data generally reflect "quoted" or "list" prices, rather than prices at which actual trades take place. They show also that actual transaction prices for a large group of industrial products are significantly more flexible than reported BLS prices for the same products. Even their data indicate, however, that industrial prices tend to respond sluggishly to changes in demand. Other studies, proceeding along similar lines, bear out this finding. Hence, it is settled that transaction prices respond relatively slowly to changing economic conditions in administered price industries [269, 375].

"STICKY" PRICES AS SHOCK ABSORBERS

This stipulation, however, fails to resolve the central issue, for sellers (or buyers) in virtually all industries are price administrators. Restaurant owners, barbers, corporate and noncorporate department and grocery store managers, automobile dealers, refrigerator manufacturers, ice cream vendors, and university employment officers all set "asked" or "bid" prices at their own discretion, at levels that seem to them suitable for maximizing the net wealth of their enterprises over a long period of time. This observation holds for noncorporate and "competitive" business firms, as well as for corporate and "noncompetitive" business firms. Thus, administered pricing is in no way connected with corporate forms of business organization or with monopolistic or oligopolistic restrictions on output or entry per se.

The economic significance of administrative pricing, if any, is that it contributes to price rigidity [269]. Thus the question one must answer is not: "Does administrative pricing contribute to price rigidity?" I presume that it does, if only for the sake of argument. Rather, the question to answer is: "Do rigidities associated with administrative pricing, as compared with some other feasible, alternative method of pricing, adversely affect the allocation of resources and the stability of markets?"

It is not immediately obvious that "sticky" prices necessarily are a "bad thing." Just as shock absorbers contribute to the stability of an automobile driven over rough roads, so may price rigidities contribute to the stability of an economy often exposed to natural and man-made disturbances. Real economies, like real automobiles, do not always travel along smooth roads. If economic conditions are "rough," institutions will evolve that ensure sufficient absorption of shocks to allow the economy to survive. In analogous circumstances, an automobile without shock absorbers would simply fall apart. In considering the implications of administrative price rigidities, therefore, one should ask whether business people "rig" prices to promote their own interests, or whether they permit buyers and sellers to overcome problems of resource allocation inherent in an imperfect and uncertain world.

THE NECESSITY OF ADMINISTERED PRICES

By considering first commodities whose prices are "market"—determined—commodities such as basic agricultural products, government and corporate securities, gold, silver, and foreign exchange—one can gain some idea of why most prices are administered. Goods whose prices are seldom administered are homogeneous or easily standardized, and they are traded in considerable volume by many buyers and sellers. Neither buyers nor sellers have any reason to prefer doing business with particular persons on the other side of the market, and purchasers need not inspect goods before taking delivery. Hence, a seller who tries to sell above the going price finds few if any buyers, and a buyer who tries to purchase below the going price is ignored by potential sellers. Even in markets of this kind, individual dealers set prices, not machines or ghostly forces of "supply and demand." But, the "area of price discretion" in such markets is small or nonexistent.

Matters are quite different, of course, for the great bulk of all commodities traded in the modern world. Steel is a basic industrial raw material, but it comes in endless shapes, sizes, and varieties, many of which must be produced almost to order to meet the specifications of particular customers. Grocery products come in countless brands, qualities, and kinds of containers; one cannot effectively trade such goods except in conveniently located retail markets that carry stocks for immediate delivery. Restaurant meals might be priced by bids and offers communicated to brokers in a single national market, but no superior chef would find it either necessary or profitable to observe the prices in his or her establishment.

Central markets, more generally, do not and could not exist for commodities that are not standardized (branded goods, personal services), that require inspection before purchase or delivery (furniture, automobiles), that are purchased frequently in small lots (groceries, cigarettes, gasoline), or that are produced to order (tailored suits, machine tools, residential dwellings). In all such cases, the volume of trade of any *specific* commodity is extremely small compared with the total volume of trade in any *general* category. A central market for "automobiles" might make sense if automobiles come in just one variety; but, how would such a market accommodate the great number of makes and models that actually exist? Obviously the only viable form of market organization in this case and in similar cases is one that assigns primary responsibility for the pricing of specific products to particular sellers or buyers. This is a market characterized by administered prices.

THE BENEFITS OF "STICKY" PRICES

Prices in such a market should be relatively rigid—first, because it is costly for sellers (or buyers) to change posted prices. Catalogs must be reprinted, menus altered, and sales people and customers alerted, for example. For this reason of cost alone, administered prices generally are unresponsive to small or erratic changes in demand. Advertising and special sales and discounts take the place of price changes to lure customers if demand becomes slack; inventories are allowed to run down if demand becomes strong.

The second reason why prices in such a market should be relatively rigid is that sellers (or buyers) who set administered prices have no way of knowing in advance what sales (or purchases) at these prices will be. Past experience is their only guide, and this guide is often treacherous. Hence, prices often will be changed not in response to movements in demand (which are difficult to interpret) but, rather, in response to changes in costs. This kind of pricing can lead, of course, to serious and expensive errors, as well as to price movements that, to an external observer, appear misguided, if not perverse. Prices, for example, can go up as demand goes down. This kind of pricing can also lead to sticky prices, for where mistakes are inevitable, it is natural for price administrators to proceed cautiously, taking no action at all until they have compelling reasons to do so.

Armen Alchian suggests a third and undoubtedly crucial reason for the inflexibility of administered prices [8]. Alchian's contention is that sellers keep prices constant to reduce search costs to buyers. If sellers were continuously to adjust prices in response to every fluctuation in sales, buyers would be induced to search for relatively favorable prices before buying any products. This search would be a clear waste of time and effort if the prices actually paid after the search were much the same as would be paid by always purchasing from single sellers at constant prices. Variable prices would be particularly bothersome for industrial buyers; they would have great difficulty predicting their own production costs to be able to negotiate effectively with potential customers. Thus, by maintaining relatively rigid prices, sellers perform a highly useful economic service for their customers. Even though they might set better terms (resulting in costly search), they provide a ready market in which the customers can purchase goods on predictable terms that are, on the average, favorable.

Alchian illustrates his theory by noting that restaurant owners do not raise prices when the number of customers rises above normal or post lower prices outside their doors when customers inside are few. Prices could be adjusted hourly so that a restaurant always operates at or near full capacity. This practice would stabilize output, but potential customers would then have an incentive to shop around among competing restaurants before buying a meal, and this would be costly and inconvenient. Most customers are willing, and some are actually anxious, to pay slightly higher fixed prices (which are required when capacity often is excessive) to eliminate the need for search. Hence, rigid prices, idle capacity, and fluctuating output occur not because restaurant owners insist on this arrangement but, rather, because most customers prefer it.

SUMMARY

This brief explanation of administered prices by no means exhausts the subject. Nor does the analysis of this chapter decisively refute the belief that administered prices contribute to the misallocation of resources and encourage economic instability. The argument shows, nevertheless, that criticisms of administered prices rest on shaky facts and on inadequate analysis.

ADDITIONAL READINGS: 10, 188, 204, 431, 438.

35. Do Corporations Set Prices Arbitrarily High?

ROBERT TOLLISON
Department of Economics
Virginia Polytechnic Institute and State University

Editor's Summary   Corporations, like all other economic
agents, seek the best price—not the highest price—for their services.
The higher the price set by a corporation, the less it will sell. Hence,
the best price for a corporate product is the price that attracts a sales
volume associated with maximum long-run profits for the firm. In both
theory and practice, corporations set asking prices through search and
experiment. The apparent rigidity of list (asking) prices disappears
when actual transactions prices are examined. The other dimensions
of a transaction—product quality, delivery time, discounts, special
services—change often but are not reflected in published list prices.
Thus, the wholesale price index is a poor indicator of short-run price
changes for corporate products. Finally, price rigidity is not strongly
associated with industry concentration.

One misconception about how modern corporations set prices is that the
product prices of larger corporations fluctuate less than do those of
smaller firms. This misconception holds, further, that corporations arbitrarily announce and administer prices independent of the forces of
supply and demand. Hence, prices are not reliable and accurate market
signals. Rather, prices are believed to be rigid. And, they seldom fall.

ADMINISTERED PRICES, PRICE CHANGES, AND FIRM INCENTIVES

The belief that corporate prices rarely fall is a serious misconception
because it implies that when demand for the output of corporations falls,
corporations respond by reducing output and employment while holding
the line on prices. Stigler suggests that this view of corporate price setting
follows neither from economic theory nor from empirical evidence.

> Economists have long struggled to find a rational explanation for pro-
> longed price rigidity, which is in general as inadvisable for profit-maxi-
> mizing monopolists as it is impossible for "price taker" industries. Putting
> aside minor or special circumstances . . . they have failed to discover any
> such explanation. It appears that the real world has been equally remiss
> in supplying the phenomena they were seeking to explain [414: 8].

Gardiner Means initiated the furor over administered pricing by
observing that despite a sharp decline in aggregate demand between 1929

and 1933, some prices fell relatively little or not at all, while others fell substantially [311]. Means attributed the observed cases of price rigidity to administered pricing in concentrated industries with few firms. Hall and Hitch, as well as Sweezy, subsequently offered theoretical explanations for the pattern of price rigidity in Means's results [204, 431]. Means also applied the administered pricing argument to other time periods [309, 310]. Finally, Galbraith proposed an interpretation of Means's results in the context of inflation [188].

Price setting implies that a firm is searching for a price that is best from its point of view, that is, a price expected to maximize the firm's wealth. All economic agents seek the best price—not the highest price—for their services. The higher the price a firm's agent sets, the less the firm will sell. Hence, the best price is not the highest obtainable price (at which only one unit could be sold); the best price is that which is low enough to encourage the sales volume associated with maximum profit.

But, a firm must search for a best price, and it is easier to find the best price in some situations than in others. In a perfectly competitive market, firms simply take the best price as that given by the market. Larger firms must discover the best price through search, or through trial and error in the market. That some firms search for their best price leads to the misconception that in this process large firms can set any price they please. In both theory and practice, the price that a large or small firm "pleases" to set is the best (wealth-maximizing) price found through search and experimentation.

The concept of a best price for a firm must be linked to the nature of the firm's transactions in different markets. Most transactions are complicated and involve considerations of quality specifications, delivery time, quantity discounts, special services, and the like [SB 34]. The number of physical characteristics of industrial products alone is immense. Price "stabilization," in some cases, is a very sensible and efficient business procedure. Buyers of copper, for example, generally do not purchase ingots on a daily basis because this procedure costs the firms more than they gain. Copper typically is bought on contract at a fixed price to economize on the costs of transactions in the copper market [426]. Noncorporate examples of prices that do not vary over fixed contractual periods are many and include college tuition and apartment rentals. The prices of some products and services, therefore, are stabilized for very sensible economic reasons that have nothing to do with arbitrary actions by the firms that sell these products and services [438].

BUREAU OF LABOR STATISTICS INDEX PROBLEMS

Unfortunately for Means and for those who seek a theoretical justification of his arguments, most of the observed rigidity in his study derives from the source of his data on prices: the wholesale price index published by the Bureau of Labor Statistics. There are many shortcomings in the price index. Changes in this index, for example, are poor reflections of product quality changes. Sample sizes used by the Bureau of Labor Statistics leave much to be desired, since many Bureau of Labor Statistics price series are based on the reports of one or two sellers, although the frequency of price change in the wholesale price index is proportional to the number of reporting firms [298, 414].

The most important bias in the wholesale price index, however, is that it reports *list* prices rather than actual *transaction* prices. Originally, Means observed that manufacturers' prices for goods such as automobiles did not change over a yearly period. But, these were manufacturers' list prices, which remain unchanged for yearly periods because the cost to firms of redoing the paper work on week-to-week changes in prices is prohibitively expensive. Every automobile purchaser knows that transaction prices vary considerably from manufacturers' list prices, especially late in a model year.

Stigler and Kindahl constructed transaction price indices by sampling the prices paid by purchasing agents for several industrial commodities that, according to Means, are supposed to be priced administratively [426]. They found that out of a maximum of 295 possible price changes, the wholesale price index showed 127 changes (43 percent), while their series showed 236 changes (80 percent). Thus, the wholesale price index is a poor indicator of short-run price changes and is the main source of misinformation about price rigidity in the United States.

To return to the specific example of the automobile industry, a common view is that in recent years automobile firms have increased prices and cut back on production in the face of falling demand. Auto manufacturers thus seem to cause inflation and escape the discipline of the forces of supply and demand. A recent econometric study by Hoffer, Marchand, and Albertine, however, indicates that this is not the way automobile prices behave in the post-Korean War period in the United States [218]. Wholesale automobile prices in this period are determined by changes in factor costs and by changes in the anticipated domestic demand for new cars. These results are directly counter to the speculation that the automobile industry administers prices.

ADMINISTERED PRICES AND INDUSTRY CONCENTRATION

To complete the discussion, Means suggested also that administered pricing is practiced mainly in concentrated industries; conventional wisdom holds that prices are less flexible in industries with a few large firms. Unfortunately for this view, market power, as measured by market concentration ratios, is *not* strongly associated with price rigidity. Horace DePodwin and Richard Selden extensively examined the inflation of the period 1953–1959 and found little statistical correlation between the number (or size) of firms in an industry and the frequency (or amplitude) of price changes over this period [131]. There was no relationship between concentration and price changes in industries at the two-digit SEC code level. Approximately 1 percent of the price changes over this period was explained by concentration. Other studies by Weiss and Phlips essentially confirmed these conclusions [454, 350].

DePodwin and Selden concluded, as I conclude, that "it is time to put the administrative inflation hypothesis to rest" [131: 126].

ADDITIONAL READINGS: 269, 308, 375, 418.

36. Does Corporate Advertising Raise Prices?

ROBERT AYANIAN
Department of Economics
San Francisco State University

Editor's Summary   Some economists claim that advertising causes product prices to rise, while others claim that it causes prices to fall. The actual effect depends on the characteristics of particular products and particular markets. When similar goods are advertised at different rates in the same market, the heavily advertised goods seem to have higher prices. But, advertising makes changes in demand more responsive to changes in price. If advertising is prohibited, prices are definitely higher than they would be if advertising were permitted. Unadvertised goods have a "free ride" at the expense of similar, advertised goods; for example, private-label sugar is placed next to branded sugar on supermarket shelves. In all cases, however, advertising lowers consumers' search costs; advertising informs potential customers about the availability, prices, and locations of products.

The literature on the relationship of advertising to product prices and market power might lead to the conclusion that advertising is the great wild card of economics. With advertising, it appears, one can produce almost any result. First, there is theory to explain how advertising may raise the prices of advertised goods. Second, there is theory to explain how advertising may raise prices while lowering the total costs to consumers of advertised goods. Third, there is theory to explain how advertising may lower the prices of advertised goods. Along with these theories there is statistical evidence purporting to show that advertising raises the prices of advertised goods and that advertising lowers the prices of advertised goods. Because the literature on the economic aspect of advertising is considerable, I do not survey it here. Instead, I briefly review the main theoretical considerations at issue and critically examine the more persuasive statistical evidence.

THEORIES OF ADVERTISING AND PRICE

The logic behind the idea that advertising raises prices is simple and straightforward. Profit-seeking firms advertise because the additional revenues gained from this activity are at least as great as the associated additional costs. Those who believe that advertising raises prices believe also that the additional revenues come from higher prices for the firms' products. Increased demand for products induced by advertising allows firms to raise prices, and thereby realize additional revenues.

The view that advertising may raise prices while lowering total costs to consumers stresses the informational role of advertising. A consumer's total cost of purchase, in this view, is the product's price *plus* the "search costs." Search costs are the costs of ascertaining the characteristics of a product: What is it? Where is it? And, how does it compare with other products in price and performance?

Phillip Nelson suggests that the fact that a product is advertised is *in itself*, valuable information for consumers, besides the information provided within advertising messages. Nelson contends not only that consumers believe that advertised brands are better but also that consumers are right in this belief [331]. Advertising is most profitable for better products because initial purchases, induced by advertising, will be followed by repeated purchases induced by satisfaction with the products. Thus, extensive advertising of a brand gives potential new customers an indication that consumers generally find the performance of the product to be satisfactory.

Advertising, by providing information that lowers search costs, can result in lower total costs to consumers, even though the prices of advertised goods may be higher to pay for the advertising. Indeed, if advertising were not valuable to consumers, why would they be willing to pay for it by paying (putatively) higher prices for advertised goods? If advertising were not valuable, would not some firms sell unadvertised goods at lower prices and thereby drive out of business firms whose products were priced higher because of advertising? Thus, the survival of advertising in the marketplace suggests that advertising is valuable to consumers. One obvious reason why advertising is valuable to consumers is that it lowers search costs.

The hypothesis that advertising may lower prices may rest partially on the notion that advertising makes changes in the demand for a product more responsive to changes in price. Advertising thus creates a situation in which a firm realizes a larger sales increase from a price reduction or product improvement than it could in the absence of advertising. The firm might increase its net revenues through a price reduction, since the increase in total revenues arising from increased sales in response to the lowered price can be greater than the associated additional advertising costs.

Also, advertising can lead to lower prices if a firm can produce increased output at a lower unit cost as a result of economies of scale (the volume effect). A firm's average costs, in this case, are actually lower with advertising than without it if the economies realized in production and distribution exceed the additional advertising expenses. The earlier discussion of search costs, of course, remains relevant. Thus, it is possible for advertising to result in a significant reduction in total costs to consumers through a reduction in both prices and search costs. Hence, to find out what effect advertising has on prices, the researcher must know the characteristics of products and markets.

EVIDENCE ABOUT ADVERTISING AND PRICE

Empirical studies purporting to show that advertising results in higher prices are generally nonrigorous and impressionistic. One can often find references to the local supermarket, which typically sells little-advertised brands at prices that are lower than those for heavily advertised brands of similar items. A problem with such comparisons is that one does not know if the items compared really are the same in all relevant aspects. Price differences may arise from quality variations between advertised and unadvertised items. Thus, an unadvertised brand of green beans may be of lower average quality than a heavily advertised brand of green beans. Even if average quality is the same, consumers may perceive that variations in quality are greater for the unadvertised brand than for the advertised brand. Hence, the unadvertised brand is riskier, and therefore less desirable for the consumers.

Persuasive evidence that larger advertising expenditures are associated with higher prices was offered to the Senate Subcommittee on Monopoly in 1971 [446: 271]. This evidence, as Table 1 shows, indicated that Bayer charged higher prices, and had higher advertising expenditures, for adult

Table 1 Aspirin Advertising and Prices, 1968

	BAYER		ST. JOSEPH'S	
Item	*Advertising Expenditures (Million $)*	*Suggested Retail Price*	*Advertising Expenditures (Million $)*	*Suggested Retail Price*
FIVE GRAIN:	15.6		0.7	
50 Tablets		$0.63		$0.39
100 Tablets		$0.98		$0.59
200 Tablets		$1.73		$0.98
CHILDREN'S:	2.3		2.1	
36 Tablets		$0.39		$0.39

SOURCE: *Advertising of Proprietary Medicines* (Washington, D.C.: U.S. Government Printing Office, 1971), p. 271.

aspirin than St. Joseph, while with respect to children's aspirin, both advertised about the same and charged prices that were the same.

This evidence, however, is far from conclusive. First, the discussion on product quality and search costs becomes applicable here. Regarding quality, there is considerable room for variation among the nonaspirin components of aspirin tablets. Second, and more important, the numbers do not reveal what the price (or cost) of St. Joseph's aspirin would be *in the absence of Bayer's advertising.* An infrequently advertised or unadvertised brand may be a "free rider" on the advertising of a heavily advertised brand. For example, Bayer's advertising expenditures for adult aspirin may result in a general increase in the demand for aspirin, including an increase in the demand for unadvertised brands of aspirin; thus the unadvertised brands are allowed to survive and, perhaps, to prosper. Infrequently advertised and unadvertised brands have lower prices because their costs are lowered when they "ride free" on the heavily advertised brands' advertising. Unadvertised brands almost invariably are next to advertised brands on supermarket shelves, and it would seem strange in this context to speak of advertised brands as being next to unadvertised brands.

Fortunately, there is one excellent study dealing with the effect of advertising on price in situations in which the "free-rider" problem is absent. This study, "The Effect of Advertising on the Price of Eye-Glasses," by Lee Benham, examines the effect on eyeglass prices of state regulation of optometric advertising [42]. Benham found that in those states in which advertising was prohibited, the average price of eyeglasses to consumers was $37.48. Where advertising was permitted, the average price to consumers was only $17.98. Benham explained his results thus:

> In general, large-volume, low-price sellers are dependent upon drawing customers from a wide area and consequently need to inform their potential customers of the advantages of coming to them. If advertising is prohibited, they may not be able to generate the necessary sales to maintain the low price. ... At the same time, the likelihood that small-volume, high-priced retailers survive in the market will increase [42: 339].

This explanation of the price-reducing effect of advertising and the evidence Benham offered are most persuasive. Not only was the free-rider problem absent, but also, as Benham suggested, a price difference of this magnitude could not be accounted for by differences in the quality of the products or services provided. Clearly, advertising by sellers of low-priced eyeglasses lowered both the prices and the search costs paid by consumers, to the benefit of sellers and consumers alike.

SUMMARY

It is risky to generalize about the relationship of advertising to prices on the basis of the amount of evidence available. This pattern, however, is discernible: If similar goods are differentially advertised in the same market, larger advertising expenditures seem to be associated with higher prices. If advertising is prohibited, prices definitely are higher than they would be if advertising were permitted. Relative to a situation in which there is an effective regulatory constraint on advertising, therefore, it is clear that advertising unambiguously lowers prices: it lowers the prices of advertised goods, and it lowers even more the prices of similar goods that are not advertised. These unadvertised goods are allowed to "ride free" on the advertising of the advertised goods. Further, advertising lowers total costs to consumers through the reduction of search costs.

ADDITIONAL READINGS: 58, 59, 67, 330, 397.

37. Are Corporate Pricing Policies a Primary Cause of Inflation?

ROBERT L. CROUCH
Department of Economics
University of California, Santa Barbara

Editor's Summary   Corporations only *transmit* the inflationary forces unleashed by excessive monetary expansion. Inflation arises when the rate of growth in the supply of money exceeds the rate of growth in real gross national product. Thus, money per-unit-of-output increases and the excess demand for products causes the overall level of prices to rise. Without an increase in the money supply, any corporate temptation to raise prices would soon be suppressed, since the increase in prices would diminish the community's stock of real purchasing power. To rebuild real purchasing power, persons and corporations would be motivated to *decrease* their demand for other assets, current output, and factors of production. These deflationary forces would soon curb corporations' alleged tendency to unilaterally increase prices. Excessive monetary expansion has been permitted by the Federal Reserve System, which in turn has been seduced into such expansion by the importunate deficit spending and debt-increasing activities of the federal government.

The United States experienced its first peacetime bout of "double-digit" inflation in 1974, when consumer prices rose by over 12 percent. Since then, inflation has remained for most people a source of major concern, even though it has decreased to about one-half the 1974 rate.

What causes inflation? The two most common answers to this question are, first, that corporations cause inflation by exploiting their market power and continually raising prices and, second, that labor unions cause inflation by extorting wage increases from their employers in excess of productivity increases, thereby increasing costs and forcing corporations to increase prices in an attempt to preserve their profit margins [2].

I argue here that these two answers are wrong. Both corporations and labor unions are "carriers" of inflation, but neither is its cause. Inflation exists because the Federal Reserve System ("the Fed"), induced in large measure by the federal government's fiscal irresponsibility, permits excessive monetary expansion. First, I will explain how excessive monetary expansion causes inflation. Second, I will indicate why, in the absence of excessive monetary expansion, corporations and labor unions would not continually increase prices and wages. Thus, the inference is inescapable that excessive monetary expansion is a condition both necessary and sufficient for inflation to occur.

EVIDENCE ABOUT THE CAUSES OF INFLATION

The price of an individual product rises if there is a "shortage" of (or excess demand for) that product. Similarly, the overall level of prices will rise if, and only if, there is an excess demand for products in general. Such a situation can occur if a community's dollar purchasing power increases more rapidly than the quantity of goods to be purchased—that is, if there is "too much money chasing relatively too few goods." To be more precise, if the community's stock of money (its "purchasing power") increases more rapidly than its real gross national product ("goods to be purchased"), excess demand occurs, and prices rise.

The evidence indicates that, in the long run and on the average, our real gross national product increases by between 3 and 4 percent per annum. (This growth rate for real gross national product is attributable to growth in the quantities of the factors of production and to technological progress.) Consequently, if the supply of money (defined as currency held by the public and checking account deposits owned by the public at commercial banks) also increases by between 3 and 4 percent per annum, no excess demand for commodities in general occurs, and prices do not rise. If the supply of money increases by more than 3 or 4 percent per annum, however, prices rise. The greater the rate of increase in the money supply relative to real gross national product, moreover, the greater the excess demand, and the greater the increase in prices. This explanation of inflation, whose leading living articulator is Milton Friedman, is known as the quantity theory of money [175, 178].

How does this theory square with the facts? Figure 1, reproduced from Schwartz, presents some relevant evidence [383]. The change in the money supply per unit of real gross national product is plotted along the horizontal axis. The annual average of this statistic is calculated for forty countries for the period 1952–1969. The average annual change in prices for each of the forty countries over the same period is also calculated, and is plotted on the vertical axis of Figure 1. Thus, the dot in the upper right-hand corner of the figure (representing Brazil) indicates that the 30 percent average annual increase in money per unit of real gross national product from 1952 to 1969 was approximately matched by a 30 percent average annual increase in prices over the same period. Each dot in the figure reflects the experience of a different country. (The dot for the United States is included in the group in the lower left-hand corner.) The positive relationship between the two variables is obvious by inspection. The coefficient of correlation is .97.

It is worthwhile to ask what those who blame inflation on corporations and labor unions would make of these data. The average annual rate of inflation has been 30 percent in Brazil, while in the United States it has been a mere 3 percent. Can it be seriously suggested that Brazilian

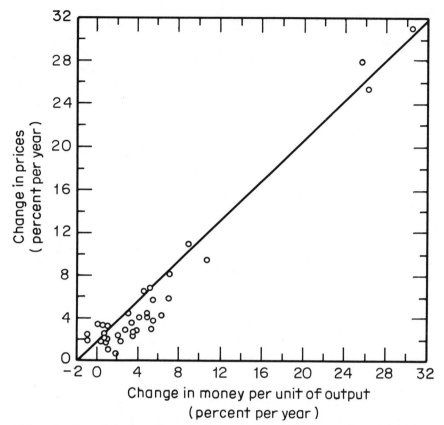

Figure 1 Rate of change of prices and money per unit of output in forty countries.
SOURCE: Anna J. Schwartz, "Secular Price Change in Historical Perspective," *Journal of Money, Credit and Banking*, 5 (February 1973). Reprinted by permission. Copyright © 1973 by the Ohio State University Press.

corporations are that much more predatory in their pricing practices and that Brazilian labor unions are that much more powerful than their American counterparts? The evidence indicates otherwise. Industrial concentration and the degree of unionization (which are standard measures, respectively, of corporate market power and union strength) are *greater* in the United States than in Brazil. Why, then, have prices increased less rapidly in the United States than in Brazil? We have already discovered the answer. The degree of monetary expansion in Brazil has been far more excessive than the degree of monetary expansion in the United States.

One can make a similar point in a different way by referring to Figure 2, which traces the United States consumer price index (CPI) from 1945

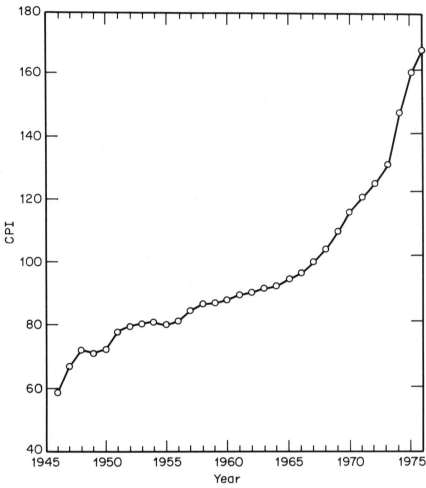

Figure 2   The CPI, 1945–1975.

to 1975. Prices rose rapidly immediately after the war. From 1948 to 1950, the CPI was virtually constant. If one blames the immediate postwar price increases on predatory price-gouging corporations and rampant union-ism, why did business and labor become supine from 1948 to 1950? The answer is that the postwar price increases had nothing to do with corpo-rate and union market abuse in the first place. Prices rose after the war because inflation had been *suppressed* by price controls during the war. When these controls were lifted, prices increased to their equilibrium level and *stabilized*.

One could make a similar argument in connection with United States price experience in the current decade. Between 1970 and 1972 prices rose by roughly 4 percent per annum. Then, the rate of inflation accelerated. In 1973 prices rose by 9 percent, and in 1974 they rose by 12 percent. In 1975 and 1976, the rate of inflation receded to around 6 percent. Is there the slightest piece of evidence that corporate market power to administer prices increased in 1973 and 1974 from what it had been earlier in the decade and then receded in 1975 and 1976? There is not. Industrial concentration simply does not vary in this way. (Indeed, it has hardly varied at all.) Neither, it might be added, does the degree of unionization vary in a way that would be consistent with the changes of prices in this decade. The degree of unionization did not surge in 1973 and 1974, and it has not waned since then. What *did* surge in 1973 and 1974 and wane in the next two years is the degree of monetary expansion. *That* (and, of course, the impact of higher energy prices) is what caused the rapid increase in prices in 1973 and 1974, as well as the more recent slowdown in the rate of inflation.

THE THEORY OF PRICE CHANGES AND INFLATION

The evidence is completely inconsistent, then, with the notion that corporate and union abuse of the power to set prices and wages is the cause of inflation. On reflection, that finding should not prove to be surprising, since elementary economic analysis would lead to the same conclusion.

Consider, for a moment, the suggestion that dominant firms with market power can cause inflation by continually increasing their prices. In the absence of an increase in the supply of money, price increases would cause the *real* value of the community's purchasing power to decline. As a result, the asset portfolios of wealthholders (both persons and businesses) would hold too small a proportion of money relative to other assets. In an attempt to rebuild the money component of their asset portfolios, people would cut back on their spending for currently produced output and decrease their demand for other assets, while corporations would decrease their demand for the factors of production. Thus, the aggregate demand for goods and services, assets, and factors of production would diminish. These *deflationary* phenomena would soon put a stop to any tendency businesses might have continually and unilaterally to keep prices spiraling upward. (An exactly analogous argument refutes the notion that unions precipitate a continually increasing spiral of wages and prices.)

The conclusion is inescapable that a process of continually increasing prices can be sustained if, and only if, the money supply is expanded at least as rapidly as prices are being increased so that society's stock of real purchasing power is not reduced. If this matching of rates of increase occurs, economists say that the upward movement of prices (which otherwise would soon stop) is *validated* by the monetary expansion.

HOW THE FED CREATES INFLATION

If inflation is attributable to excessive monetary expansion, it is pertinent to ask who has been responsible for that occurrence. The Fed, in the last analysis, controls the supply of money in the United States through its control over bank reserves by way of open-market operations. When the Fed buys government securities on the open market, it pays for its purchases with a check drawn on itself. The check is deposited in the seller's own bank, which, in turn, receives payment for the check by having its own account at the Fed credited. Since this account is part of the bank's reserves, open-market purchases by the Fed have the effect of increasing the reserves of commercial banks. This increase allows the banks to make more loans, buy more bonds, and increase the supply of money.

If the blame for excessive monetary expansion is to be placed anywhere, it must be placed on the Fed. The Fed initially buys excessive quantities of government securities, and this action causes excessive increases in bank reserves, which, in turn, lead to excessive monetary expansion.

But in all fairness, the record should show that the Fed has been under the importunate influence of the federal government in permitting this process to occur. Since 1945, the federal government has had a budget surplus in eight years and a deficit in the other twenty-five. Its *cumulative* deficit (that is, the increase in the national debt) has been almost $275 *billion.*

The government can market its debt by selling bonds to the private sector (individual persons, banks, insurance companies, pension funds, and so forth) or by selling bonds to the Fed. If it sells bonds to the private sector, immediate upward pressure on interest rates occurs because higher interest rates must be offered to induce the private sector to take the government securities into its portfolios. But, the government and the Fed are averse to high interest rates because "check" money is politically unpopular with Congress and with the people. Consequently, the government is disposed to seek other outlets for its debt, and, unfortunately, the Fed has been only too easily suborned into acquiring a disproportionately large fraction of that debt. Congress appears to hold the Fed responsible for interest rate increases. To assuage Congress, therefore, the Fed has been all too willing to avoid the *immediate* upward pressure on interest rates by acquiring government security issues for its own portfolio.

The figures speak for themselves. In 1946 the Fed held $23.2 billion in government securities; in 1974, the figure was $80.5 billion—nearly a fourfold increase. In 1946, the Fed held only 9 percent of the *total* outstanding government securities; by 1974, that figure had risen to 16 percent.

SUMMARY

We are led, in sum, to the conclusion that corporations and groups of workers (not only unionized groups) transmit the forces of inflation, since they post the prices at which they offer to exchange their goods or services. But, the Fed unleashes the forces of inflation by permitting excessive monetary expansion as it succumbs to the pressure to withhold more and more of the federal government's ever-increasing debt from the public security markets.

ADDITIONAL READINGS: 66, 114, 142, 160, 271, 308, 351, 388, 440.

38. Is Industrial Concentration the Cause of Inflation?

ROBERT D. TOLLISON
Department of Economics
Virginia Polytechnic Institute and State University

Editor's Summary   Inflation is a persistent rise in the general price level. The relative growth of the money supply is a necessary, if not sufficient, condition for inflation. Historical episodes of inflation occurred well before corporations and labor unions emerged as economic institutions. The degree of market power enjoyed by corporations and labor unions may explain why prices are *high,* but it cannot explain why prices and wages are *rising,* unless market power also is increasing. The evidence shows that there has been no significant increase in the degree of monopoly in the economy since 1899. And careful empirical studies do not show a relationship between industrial concentration and price changes. Hence, the belief that corporate and labor union concentration cause inflation has no substance.

A common political response to inflation is to blame corporations and labor unions for rising prices and wages. Lewis Engman, former chairman of the Federal Trade Commission, states, for example, that "inflation can be reduced by purging the economy of anti-competitive behavior" [148]. According to John Sheehan of the Federal Reserve Board, furthermore, "monetary policy can do little about an income-cost-push inflation without risking severe sectorial imbalances and unacceptable unemployment levels, bankruptcies and the like" [391: 10–11]. The solution, according to Sheehan, lies in the "vigorous application of the antitrust and other laws to break up the concentrations of price and wage setting corporate and labor power in our society" [391: 10–11].

Thus, corporations and labor unions are said to be using market power to inflate prices and wages. Market power, by implication, is both a necessary and sufficient condition for this inflationary activity. In the absence of market power, firms and unions would act competitively, and prices and wages would not rise! Obviously, the argument that corporations and unions initiate and perpetuate inflation has serious logical and factual flaws.

THE CAUSE OF INFLATION

Inflation is a persistent, and perhaps increasing, rate of increase of prices in general, as measured, for example, by the consumer price index (CPI).

Persistent increases in prices in general derive from increases in the supply of money relative to the supply of goods produced in an economy over an interval of time [SB 37]. As a first approximation, if the money supply expands at the same rate as the output of goods and services, the general price level will remain unchanged (but conceivably it could fall slightly because of productivity enhancement). The prices of some goods and services may rise or fall relative to the prices of others, but the average of all prices will remain constant if the supply of money is kept in the same proportion to total output. If the general price level does increase, the supply of money is increasing faster than the supply of goods. Because there are no additional goods that can be purchased with the additional dollars, those dollars are used by individual persons and firms and governments to bid against one another for the available output of the economy. As a consequence, prices rise and inflation occurs.

Recall that inflation refers to a persistent *rise* in the general price level. The cause is the excessive rate of growth of the money supply relative to the supply of goods and services. Recall also the importance of considering the rate of growth of the money supply *relative* to the rate of growth of the supply of goods and services. Obviously, a 10 percent rate of growth of the money supply could lead to quite different rates of growth (positive or negative) in prices, depending on the rate of growth of output. The relative growth of the money supply, in any event, is acknowledged widely as a necessary, if not sufficient, condition for inflation [366: 46].

INFLATION AND MARKET POWER

What does the market power of firms and unions have to do with the process of inflation? Historically, significant periods of inflation occurred long before there were legal entities called corporations or labor unions. Such interesting evidence aside, the more fundamental logical point is that the *level* of market power has nothing to do with the fact or degree of inflation. The level of market power can explain why prices are *higher* in some market structures than they would be under competitive conditions. But, recall that inflation refers to a *rising* general price level. Connecting market power to inflation in a cause-effect relationship would require linking *increases* in market power with *increases* in inflation.

Monopolists generally raise their prices when their costs increase; so do competitive firms. Thus, while a given degree of monopoly or "market power" can account for a differential price (higher than a competitive price), the existence of market power offers no explanation for *rising* prices (inflation) unless market power also is *increasing*.

There have been historical episodes, of course, in which market power has grown and stimulated wage and price increases. Milton Friedman cites a case in the 1930s, when the National Recovery Act, which sanctioned business cartels as well as the growth in the monopoly power of labor unions, led to substantial price and wage increases in the face of high unemployment levels [177]. More recently, over the period 1971–1976, the United States economy experienced a number of nonmonetary shocks (for example, wage and price controls and higher oil prices), which affected the pattern of relative prices. Many analysts claim that these shocks affected the rate of inflation, but a recent study by Denis Karnosky shows convincingly that the monetary explanation of inflation I review earlier holds up remarkably well in explaining aggregate price movements over this period [230].

Careful study of the evidence suggests that market power has *not* been growing in the United States over this century. In two famous studies of the growth of enterprise monopoly in the United States over the period 1899–1958, the evidence indicates that the amount of output produced by the monopolistic sector of the economy (defined as industries in which 50 percent or more of the sales are produced by the top four firms) actually *declined* somewhat over this period [4, 335: 88–93]. In 1899, output from the monopolistic sector of the economy represented 17.4 percent of national income, while 76.1 percent came from workably competitive industries, and 6.5 percent came from government. In 1958, the monopolistic sector accounted for some 11.5 percent of national income, while 66.4 percent came from workably competitive industries, and 21.5 percent came from government and regulated industries.

While clearly there were shifts of market power within these economywide figures, the overall trend suggests that market power did not increase over quite a long period of American economic history. These results make it impossible to show that increasing market power could have been a source of inflation. Market power, in reality, did not increase.

Several studies examine the role of concentration in directly causing inflation. Horace DePodwin and Richard Selden found that for the inflation of 1953–1959 there was no relationship between concentration and price change in two-digit industries. They also found that only 1 percent of price changes over this period was attributable to concentration [131]. Other papers essentially confirming these findings are the works of Leonard Weiss and Louis Phlips [454, 350].

MARKET POWER AND OPPOSITION TO UNION DEMANDS

Finally, do firms in concentrated industries contribute relatively more to inflation because they yield to larger wage concessions? Purportedly, these firms are able to make these concessions because they can pass the higher costs along to consumers in the form of higher prices. Scherer reviews the evidence on this question and shows, essentially, that there is no statistically reliable relationship between concentration and the rate of wage increase [375]. Thus, firms in concentrated industries do not appear to transmit the effects of growth in the money supply in a manner predictably different from that of firms in unconcentrated industries.

In sum, there is neither a logical nor factual argument for the claim that corporate market power causes inflation in the United States.

ADDITIONAL READINGS: 2, 10, 66, 160, 356.

39. Do Corporations Suppress Technical Innovations?

ROGER SHERMAN
Department of Economics
University of Virginia

Editor's Summary   Quantitative studies concerning research efforts and firm size indicate that larger firms conduct proportionately more research than smaller firms. But, research output does not go up more than proportionately with increases in firm size. These results are consistent with the belief that large organizations may benefit from economies of scale in conducting research, that they can bear the risks of engaging in research whose outcome is uncertain, and that they expect to realize the profits from an innovation in a substantial market. There is no evidence that larger corporations suppress innovations or that the rate of diffusion of innovation is slower in more concentrated industries.

Seldom do all corporations fall under the umbrella of the belief that corporations suppress innovation. Such a broad characterization cannot be sustained because corporations obviously carry out much innovation, and because it is very difficult to establish any reasonable bench-mark rate of innovation by a *noncorporate* body, a rate that must underpin any convincing empirical comparison. A more subtle and important belief is that large corporations or corporations that already have some monopoly advantage, compared with smaller corporations or those subject to more competition, suppress innovation.

THEORETICAL AMBIGUITIES ABOUT SUPPRESSION AND INNOVATION

The prominent research efforts of large business firms seem consistent with the early prediction of Joseph Schumpeter that very large firms would produce technical achievements, which in turn would bring economic progress [382]. Interestingly enough, this claim concerning *greater* research efforts by large corporations, rather than the belief in suppressed innovation, stimulated research aimed at discovering what effect firm size or monopoly power might have on an industry's progressiveness and innovation.

Corporate size, of course, is not necessarily equivalent to monopoly power. Large firms may have advantages if economies of large scale exist in conducting research, if the exploitation of discoveries can be more fruitful in firms that have many operations in which savings from new discoveries can be realized, or if the costs and risks of attempting innovation are so great that smaller firms cannot, or dare not, finance them. Large firms thus may appear to have opportunities for innovation that are denied smaller firms. But, some argue that large organizations are conservative, reluctant to try new ideas, and generally so stodgy that they are handicapped in conducting research.

Monopoly power, on the other hand, depends on a firm's control over its product market rather than on its size. Such market control often can give a firm more assurance that it alone will enjoy any gains from its discoveries, whereas a competitor must worry about the use of its discoveries by others unless it can win patent protection. A monopoly is more likely to have the funds to support research. But, the monopoly may not experience the driving force of competition that can spur it on to innovation. Thus, on the basis of a priori reasoning, the net effect of monopoly power on innovation is ambiguous. The actual effect on innovation of either large size or monopoly power is, of course, ultimately an empirical question.

RESEARCH, INNOVATION, AND FIRM SIZE

Empirical studies try to measure research activity in many ways, such as by counting the number of patents received, the number of research employees, or the expenditures for research and development. These measures can then be related to measures of firm size, such as sales or assets, in an effort to find out whether research is relatively more important in larger firms. Such studies show that larger firms indeed may conduct proportionately more research. But, the research output, such as the number of patents awarded, does not go up more than proportionately with increases in firm size, and the quality of the larger firms' patents, for example, is not judged to be any greater because of firm size. While there is a weaker research effort by smaller firms, this diminished effort is attributable principally to *very* much smaller firms, firms of fewer than 5,000 employees; above that size there is no generally larger effort by larger firms. So, perhaps a greater corporate size, certainly a size beyond that of most proprietorships and partnerships, is good for invention and innovation; but beyond that point there is no evidence to suggest that larger size is apt to yield proportionately more invention and innovation. Neither is there convincing evidence from these studies that larger firms suppress invention.

Monopoly power also has been examined for its effect on research effort. Here, comparisons become even more difficult. We cannot measure simply to find out if research effort is proportional to firm size; we must instead make more complicated judgments about the degree of monopoly power in different industries. In comparing industries, it is especially difficult to control successfully for all influences other than monopoly power. These influences include, for instance, the opportunity for technological change that may exist in each industry. Most studies represent monopoly power through an admittedly crude and unreliable surrogate, the industry concentration ratio. Research and development effort does seem to increase as industry concentration increases. The effect of concentration is not uniform, however, for although research effort usually is low when the concentration rate is below .10, it seems to increase no further when concentration passes above .50 or .55, and indeed research effort may decline beyond that range of concentration ratios. Similarly, with respect to entry barriers, a middle range of entry difficulty (requiring between $20 million and $100 million in investment, or roughly between 4 and 10 percent of a market to enter) is the range where more research and development activity is observed.

SUPPRESSION OF INNOVATION

Thus far, I have examined influences on research effort or rate of invention. Now I will consider the question of whether some corporations directly suppress innovation itself. Edwin Mansfield had experts identify the major innovations since 1918 in bituminous coal, steel, and petroleum refining industries, and he traced the innovations back to the firms responsible for them in an effort to detect any effect of firm size directly on the rate of innovation [290, 291]. Mansfield found that the four largest firms innovated proportionately *more* in coal and petroleum but proportionately *less* in steel. He also found that larger firms tended to be more innovative if the investment needed to innovate was great, or if the ultimate profitable user of an innovation would tend to be large. Using those same data, Oliver Williamson showed that the ratio of innovations to firm size (the latter measured by production capacity) is negatively related to concentration, meaning that any relatively greater innovativeness of larger firms declines as monopoly power in their industry (again represented only crudely by concentration) becomes greater [461: 67–73].

DIFFUSION OF INNOVATION

A question closely related to innovation is that of diffusion: how quickly is an innovation diffused throughout firms and industries before the new idea comes into widespread use? This question was studied very effectively by Zvi Griliches in the case of hybrid corn [199]. He found that corn

growers introduced hybrid corn in a manner consistent with profit maximization. (He also found the social rate of return from this innovation
and diffusion to be enormous.) Edwin Mansfield, using methods like
those of Griliches, studied this question too, focusing on the diffusion of a
dozen innovations in the bituminous coal, brewing, coal, railroad, and
steel industries [290]. He judged the diffusion process to be a slow one,
since often it took twenty years before all the major firms in an industry
installed an innovation. The rate of diffusion was higher, though, for the
more profitable innovations. The rate differs by industry for several
plausible economic reasons, and it appears to be slightly faster in less
concentrated industries, although no very conclusive result is available on
that point. Suppression might be suspected because there are many
situations in which a large firm does not innovate but copies very quickly
an innovation that occurs in its industry. However, aside from examples
like the Gillette Company's quick introduction of a new razor blade after
the Wilkinson Sword was introduced, there is no persuasive quantitative
evidence to support such a suspicion.

Available evidence does not support the belief that large corporations,
or corporations with monopoly power, actually suppress innovations in a
general way. Nor does the evidence suggest that large firms are relatively
better at conducting research, innovating, or copying others' innovations
than small, competing firms. Instead, the evidence suggests that firms
make decisions that will yield the most profit over time, and in that finding
there lies no evidence of a pervasive practice that suppresses innovation.
Suppression may occur, nevertheless, not so much in management practices as in the manipulation of patent applications to achieve the maximum monopoly value from any discovery.

The patent is a well-established international institution for granting a
property right in a concrete and practical idea. The property right
typically extends the power of a government to guarantee to an inventor
exclusive control over his or her invention. But, when such a right can be
assigned, corporations (as well as other forms of business organization)
may seek patents "strategically" to strengthen their positions in markets
relative to the positions of other corporations. Courts can sometimes
recognize and curtail this practice, particularly when patents are bought
rather than developed internally by firms. Nevertheless, corporations
have used their research and development resources to accumulate vast
numbers of patents, almost certainly to protect their positions by making it
difficult for others to patent substitute processes. And, it is possible that as
a result of such corralling of possible new developments, some will be
suppressed, although a competitive atmosphere would bring them out for
society's benefit.

CONCLUSION

The question of whether corporations suppress innovation is very hard to respond to, in part because finding the optimal time for introducing an invention for maximum social benefit is not a simple matter. Competing enterprises do not always choose a time to introduce an invention for maximum social benefit. Indeed, suppression conceivably can bring social benefits. Antitrust laws that attack monopoly practices may lessen the incentive to engage in research and development, too, and so governmental remedies for suppression often are not at all obvious. Measures should be instituted to prevent a corporation from trying illegally to suppress an innovation simply because it will lessen monopoly power. The available evidence indicates, however, that no general claim of suppression against a large group of corporations appears to have any standing.

ADDITIONAL READINGS: 37, 185, 189, 228, 243, 272, 302, 329, 346, 363, 365, 370, 371, 375, 378, 395, 449, 450.

40. Does Monopoly Power Cause Extensive Welfare Losses?

KENNETH CLARKSON
Law and Economics Center
University of Miami School of Law

Editor's Summary   The welfare losses attributable to corporate activity generally can be traced to direct government regulations, to private responses to government constraints, or to misinterpretations of corporate actions. Government regulations, including mandatory crosshauling rules, cost-plus contracts, and similar constraints, are the primary forces causing inefficiency in corporations. Various estimates of the welfare loss from *pure* monopoly pricing are extremely small— about 1 percent of GNP. Thus, the greatest welfare losses result from government action or inaction.

$\mathbf{A}$ common belief among critics of the corporate sector is that corporations are responsible for extensive welfare losses to society. These losses are believed to be a direct consequence of the monopolistic or oliogopolistic power allegedly shared by most of the large United States corporations. (Welfare, in economics, is a measure of a person's subjectively determined well-being, wealth, or happiness. While welfare may not be directly measurable, it is possible to compare two situations to find out if one situation represents an increase or loss of welfare in comparison with the other situation. Welfare, in this sense, bears no relationship to "welfare programs," Food Stamps, and so forth.)

WELFARE LOSSES IN THEORY

In traditional economic models, welfare losses arise if a firm can sell more output at a lower price and just cover the cost of the last item sold. Most enterprises charge a single, uniform price for a product. If that price is lowered, volume expands. But, all sales, new and old, are made at the new, lower price. Consequently, the expected change in total revenue that results from lowering price must include the forgone revenues associated with sales at the higher price. The net change in revenue, commonly referred to as marginal revenue, then becomes the important variable in decision making, since a wealth-maximizing firm would compare the marginal revenue to the marginal cost of providing the increased quantity or quality of output.

A wealth-maximizing monopolist expands production only if it pays. But, the monopolist does not expand production as much as a comparable competitive firm. This results in higher prices and lower outputs than would be generated by perfectly competitive markets. The net result is a welfare loss to society.

MEASURING WELFARE LOSSES

Various researchers, including Arnold Harberger and David Kamerschen, estimate that the total welfare loss from "monopolistic" resource misallocation is considerably less than 1 percent (approximately 0.001) of gross national product [207, 229]. Demsetz, furthermore, shows that if one identifies goods and services according to their characteristics, welfare losses are considerably less. Demsetz argues that previous estimates neglect differences in the quality, service, and other characteristics of the goods produced and sold [128].

Perhaps more important than the welfare losses associated with monopolistic resource misallocation are reported losses from pricing distortions in regulated sectors; inefficiencies from deficient incentives for controlling costs under government contracts; losses from enterprises insulated from competition; the costs of certain legal regulations such as crosshauling; and losses from excess capacity attributable to industrial cartelization. Frederic Scherer estimates that total welfare losses, including losses from wasteful promotional efforts and from operations at less than optimal scale, are approximately 6.2 percent of gross national product [375: 408]. Table 2 shows Scherer's estimates by general major category.

THE REAL CAUSES OF WELFARE LOSSES

A closer examination reveals, however, that one can attribute welfare losses to direct government controls, to private responses to governmental constraints, or to a misinterpretation of private actions. One can link direct government controls, for example, to deadweight losses (0.6 percent of GNP, according to Table 2) from pricing distortions in the regulated sector [28]. Kessel investigates the consequences of milk market regulations established by state and other authorities [233]. One can show that distortions in such cases are linked directly to government controls and administrative procedures. Too, one can attribute most of the costs associated with crosshauling and other transportation inefficiencies to rules and regulations governing interstate transportation. The Interstate Commerce Commission, the Civil Aeronautics Board, and other administrative agencies promulgate such regulations.

Table 2

	Percentage of GNP, Circa 1966
Deadweight welfare losses due to monopolistic resource misallocation: unregulated sectors	0.9
Deadweight losses due to pricing distortions in the regulated sectors	0.6
Inefficiencies due to deficient cost control by market sector enterprises insulated from competition	2.0
Inefficiencies due to deficient cost control by defense and space contractors	0.6
Wasteful promotional efforts	1.0
Operations at less than optimal scale for reasons other than differentiation serving special demands	0.3
Cross-hauling costs and transportation costs associated with distorted locational decisions	0.2
Excess and inefficient capacity due to industrial cartelization and the stimulus of collusive profits	0.6
TOTAL LOSSES DUE TO MARKET POWER	6.2

SOURCE: Frederic M. Scherer, *Industrial Market Structure and Economic Performance* (Chicago: Rand McNally, 1970). Reprinted by permission. Copyright © 1970 by Rand-McNally.

Private responses to governmental constraints also contribute to inefficiencies usually blamed on private-sector actions. Cost overruns by defense contractors and others engaged in the delivery of goods and services to public-sector agencies, for example, derive from the nature of the contractual relationship governing the provision of goods and services. Frederic Scherer, Kenneth Clarkson, and others identify such deficiencies [375, 96]. Many of the inefficiencies in this category stem from the nature of ownership rights in the industry. Many nonprofit enterprises, for example, produce products and services at costs that are higher than those for their for-profit counterparts. These higher costs result from the nature of the incentive structures defined by the nonprofit organizations [97]. In other cases, such as excess capacity from industrial cartelization, welfare losses derive from responses to government constraints even if such constraints are supposed to protect the public welfare. The American Medical Association, for example, through entry restrictions and the prohibition of advertising, acts effectively as a cartelized industry [234, 333: 46–52].

Finally, many of the alleged private abuses, such as "wasteful" advertising or promotional efforts or efforts resulting in "excess" capacity, are really actions that promote economic welfare. Recent studies indicate that advertising, promotion, and research and development expenditures create intangible capital [SB 35, SB 36, SB 51]. Advertising, for example, establishes brand names with associated service warranties and other desirable consequences. Advertising also provides information for existing and potential customers and competitors [67]. With regard to excess capacity, a full analysis of the relationships among the rate of production, the total production plan, and the cost of adjusting to fluctuating demands implies that many industries will hold inventories in the form of "excess" capacity because "excess" capacity is necessary for increased production in periods of high demand. Thus, instead of creating inefficiencies, such actions help stabilize the flow of goods and services to members of society.

CONCLUSION

Although the evidence is not complete, many of the factors that are believed to contribute to market imperfections and welfare losses are clearly overstated. Where such losses do occur, often they can be directly or indirectly traced to existing governmental laws or administrative procedures. Hence, the conclusion that the private sector is responsible for excessive welfare losses is clearly unwarranted.

ADDITIONAL READINGS: 49, 103, 193, 254, 359, 442.

CORPORATE COMPETITION AND MARKET POWER

41. How Important Is Predatory Pricing?

M. BRUCE JOHNSON

Department of Economics
University of California at Santa Barbara

Editor's Summary   The strategy of pricing below cost to drive smaller rivals out of business is neither analytically nor empirically relevant in the American economy. Economic analysis suggests that predatory pricing is an expensive mistake unless a predator firm has complete control over entry into its industry. Actual cases of predatory pricing are so rare as to lead one to wonder why the belief in predatory pricing persists in the public debate about business activity.

The antibusiness rhetoric of contemporary critics has an allegation for every conceivable situation. If a corporation charges a higher price than its competitors charge for similar products, the allegation is "profiteering" or "price gouging." If corporations charge the same price, they are accused of collusion. One would think that if a corporation charged less than its competitors charged, it would be praised for participating in the competitive process to the benefit of consumers. But, the critics are not easily persuaded; if a corporation charges a lower price than its competitors charge, it is accused of predatory pricing.

The empirical evidence about the existence of predatory pricing is meager, flimsy, and virtually nonexistent. The theory of predatory pricing, moreover, suggests that the issue is largely irrelevant. Proved cases of predatory pricing, finally, are so rare as to lead one to ask why the issue persists in public debate.

THEORETICAL VIEWS OF PREDATORY PRICING

Predatory pricing is thought to occur if a firm sells its products at uneconomical (below-cost) prices for the deliberate purpose of driving out or keeping out rivals. Such an attempt to monopolize is illegal under the provisions of Section 2 of the Sherman Act. Clearly, the firm that instigates predatory pricing must have greater financial staying power than its rivals, and the owners must believe that there is a high probability that the current losses they experience in the predatory pricing campaign will be exceeded by the profits they will earn after the rivals have been destroyed or forestalled from entry. The first condition is referred to as the "deep-pocket" syndrome. The owners of the predator firm must have greater actual or potential wealth at their disposal, or they must be able to subsidize their predatory campaign by charging higher, nonpredatory prices in other isolated markets. Thus, the logic of the case for predatory pricing leads one to look at the largest firms in an industry.

The critics assert that large corporations will use predatory pricing and other tactics to drive their smaller competitors out of business. The rationale is that once the smaller firms leave the industry, the giant corporations can raise their prices to the initial (or even higher) levels to reap abnormally high profits. It does not take much insight to realize that predatory pricing, to be successful, must be accompanied by effective entry barriers; once rival firms have been driven out of an industry, the predator must be able to prevent their reentry or the entry of any new rivals. In the absence of effective entry controls, predatory pricing must be an expensive failure. Frederic M. Scherer summarizes this problem.

> To generalize, no matter how deep a large firm's pocket is, price warfare aimed at driving small but equally efficient rivals from the market will not be attractive, and is therefore improbable, unless barriers to new entry can be maintained during the post-war period at levels sufficiently high to permit the realization of profit margins considerably greater than they would be if rivals were permitted to survive [376: 868].

PREDATORY PRICING AND WEALTH MAXIMIZATION

Predatory pricing is a peculiar tactic for a corporation to use if it wants to maximize its profit or wealth. The tactic involves self-imposed, short-run losses for the predator as well as for its rivals. The short-run losses, of course, are guaranteed, whereas the long-run gains, if any, are probabilistic.

Smaller firms have inherent advantages in relation to a large predator. First, smaller firms suffer smaller absolute losses. Second, it is quite possible that smaller firms can temporarily suspend operation as they await the return of higher prices; meanwhile, the predator continues to bear the losses of its below-cost pricing policy.

Even if the predator is successful in driving the smaller firms out of business, the physicial assets of the smaller firms are not destroyed; these assets can be purchased and used by other rivals. Indeed, if the assets are purchased at distressed prices during the peak of the predatory action, the new rivals have an extremely attractive cost base from which to compete with the predator. It appears that the predator would have to continue below-cost pricing for a period of time sufficiently long to wear out completely the existing physical capital. Even if the predator is willing to bear the enormous expense of below-cost pricing while its rivals' existing productive assets depreciate, still other rivals can enter with new capital equipment when the predator, having eliminated the existing rivals, raises its prices.

There is overwhelming evidence to suggest that predatory pricing is not consistent with a wealth-maximizing strategy for a corporation. A large firm could easily avoid the short-run (and long-run?) losses stemming from a predatory price war and also secure long-run gains sooner if it simply merged with its smaller rivals, or bought them out. Economic theory would lead us to forecast mergers with much higher frequency than we would predatory pricing. The assets of the inefficient, high-cost, smaller rivals would shift to the more efficient large firm, and, in the absence of complete monopoly, this would result in lower product prices for consumers.

EVIDENCE ABOUT PREDATORY PRICING

Assuming that a firm does engage in predatory pricing, how, short of sitting in the boardroom, could one tell? What pricing actions would lead one to conclude unambiguously that a firm is indeed engaging in predatory pricing? Obviously, the observation that a firm is selling its product below average cost does not suffice as evidence of predatory pricing, since setting a "low" price is consistent with a desire to advertise: to inform consumers about the existence of a product. Short-run losses from below-cost pricing can be regarded as an investment by a firm.

The pattern of a firm's rate of output (sales) also does not suffice as evidence of predatory pricing. It might be argued that below-cost pricing accompanied by an increase in a firm's output is evidence of predatory pricing. A necessary condition for acceptance of this test would be that total industry demand had not changed. Even so, the observed output pattern is hardly detrimental to consumers; the firm in question tries to secure business at the expense of its rivals with price cuts. Consumers pay lower prices for the products of the initiating firm and, assuming the lower prices are matched, for the products of rival firms. Only if the rival firms are driven out of the industry and no new rivals can enter and replace them can consumers possibly be injured. There is a real danger that a preoccupation with predatory pricing could lead to antitrust enforcement that would severely damage the competitive process.

An examination of famous historical predatory price incidents supports the preceding chain of argument. In a study of the Rockefeller Standard Oil Company in the context of predatory pricing, John McGee finds that Standard Oil typically purchased its rivals at very attractive prices, contrary to the popular folklore of the time. He concludes that "Standard Oil did not use predatory price discrimination to drive out competing refiners, nor did its pricing practice have that effect" [303: 168]. Historical cases of alleged predatory pricing are so few as to be individually famous. For example, it was commonly believed that the Gunpowder Trust, an explosives industry combination that spanned forty years, made extensive use of predatory pricing tactics to ruin new entrants or force them to sell out to the trust. Kenneth Elzinga, in his analysis of this particular case, finds only evidence of competitive practices [147]. Where price-cutting occurred, it was typically initiated by the supposed "victim."

Close examination of the evidence suggests that the historical episodes of alleged predatory pricing are more folklore than fact. Generally speaking, predatory pricing has ceased to be of practical importance in antitrust litigation, perhaps because the alleged practice is theoretically unsound and empirically irrelevant. It seems that the popular preoccupation with the possibility of predatory pricing and related tactics creates its own unnecessary costs; it is very likely that the threat of antitrust action prompts large, efficient firms to hold back on initiating price cuts.

There has been a resurgence of allegations about the occurrence of predatory pricing in connection with cross-subsidization between markets served by conglomerates. The analysis, however, is as valid for a conglomerate as it is for a specialized firm. Unless the conglomerate has a systematically lower internal rate of discount, and unless that difference in discount rates between conglomerates and nonconglomerates is large, the conclusion stands: predatory pricing is a theoretical curiosity rather than an empirical reality.

ADDITIONAL READINGS: 10, 17, 18, 245, 246, 377, 425, 433, 462.

42. Can Corporations Limit New Entry?

ROBERT D. TOLLISON
Department of Economics
Virginia Polytechnic Institute and State University

Editor's Summary   While the theory and the measurement of
barriers to entry are still in flux, these barriers appear to be less
important than originally thought. Government regulations, such as
those affecting the banking, motor trucking, taxicab, airline, and public
utility industries, create the major barriers to new entry. Evidence
about the relationship between barriers to entry and profits is
inconclusive.

Do corporations (especially those in industries with only a few firms)
limit new competition in their industries so that they may charge higher
prices and make higher profits? The people who believe so, for the most
part, tend to base their beliefs on very shortsighted surveys of industrial
structure. In the long run, the market share of dominant firms in most
industries declines because of new entry. As Frederic Scherer points out,
for example, United States Steel dominated the steel industry at the turn
of the century, yet by 1968 its market share of ingot capacity had fallen to
21 percent [375]. Similar histories involve rayon, cars, corn products,
refining, farm implements, synthetic fibers, and aluminum extrusions.
Corporations are sometimes accused of consciously limiting entry—for
example, by buying the available quantities of scarce raw materials—and
sometimes they are accused of doing so unconsciously through the sheer
greatness of their size and the amount of money that it takes to build their
large, efficient plants.

REVIEWING THE ARGUMENT ABOUT COMPETITION

The concept of entry barriers rests on the work of Joe Bain, who stresses
the role of such aspects as economies of scale, capital requirements,
superior factors of production, and advertising in barring the entry of
new firms into an industry [29]. Theoretical elaborations of Bain's concept are found in the work of Franco Modigliani and Paolo Sylos-Labini
[320, 432]. The gist of these extensions to Bain's work is that potential
entrants force oligopolists (with entry barriers) to charge lower prices than
otherwise would be charged. Subsequent empirical work, such as that by
William Comanor and Thomas Wilson, focuses on elaborating Bain's

original finding that entry barriers and concentration ratios are positively correlated with the rates of return of corporations [105, 32]. This point of view is quite popular. This chapter asks if this view of the modern corporation makes sense.

THE NATURE OF BARRIERS TO ENTRY

A barrier to entry is a cost of production that entering firms, but not existing firms, must bear. In other words, according to the usual convention in economics, the size distribution of firms in an industry is determined by demand and cost conditions. In this context, it is useful to examine the analytical basis of several of the so-called barriers to entry.

Economies of scale are often believed to bar the entry of new firms into an industry. Economies of scale occur if a firm's average cost of output (goods produced) declines over a long range of levels of output. Suppose only one firm can operate profitably, since over some range of output its revenues from that output exceed the cost of that output. If, however, there are two firms, each with half of the industry sales, and each facing the same costs, neither firm can operate profitably. Is entry in this case limited by demand or by economies of scale? The point is simply that demand and cost conditions determine market structure in an industry. Under the conditions discussed here, the entry of new firms will not eliminate monopoly or oligopoly, and monopoly profits will persist until technology or demand changes. Net entry, in this case, is not efficient.

The importance of economies of scale in creating industry concentration varies widely from industry to industry. For local public utilities, economies of scale are so important as to lead to natural monopolies. In the manufacturing sector of the economy, however, there are very few industries in which the minimum efficient size of a firm is as large as 5 percent of that industry's output [417]. Consequently, one must explain small numbers of firms in an industry on grounds other than those of economies of scale.

The existence of superior resources is often taken as an indication that one firm can limit the ability of other firms to produce a certain product. The existence of a limited amount of high-quality natural resources in an industry, for example, may restrict the expansion of the number of firms in that industry. There are many famous cases of this kind in the extractive industries, such as the diamond, potash, radium, bauxite, nickel, and sulfur industries. It is not typically true, however, that the supply of high-quality natural resources remains limited. There tend to be subsequent discoveries of comparable, or even higher-quality, resources. Indeed, a steeply rising supply price for a resource does not imply an oligopolistic organization of an industry. More often than not, the mining industries, in which this phenomenon is believed to occur most often, have been organized as compulsory cartels rather than as a small number of oligopolies [425].

GOVERNMENTALLY INDUCED ENTRY BARRIERS

Sometimes, entrepreneurial ability is lumped into the category of superior factors of production. This means, in effect, that firms with superior entrepreneurs have lower costs. If rents are included in costs, over time only the firms with superior entrepreneurs will survive. That the superior firms have lower costs is desirable, however, since it is precisely these firms that should survive from an economic point of view.

Finally, government restrictions are a very effective means of controlling entry, especially if entry is based on franchising or licensing [SB 40]. For instance, a franchise or license is required from the government to open a bank, to start an airline, to broadcast on radio or television, or to produce the services of local public utilities. Often, these are areas that would have had only a few firms in the market anyway because of economies of scale. Local public utilities fall into this category of "natural" monopolies. The government limits entry in many fields, however, where competition among a large number of firms might have worked very effectively. The examples of banking, motor trucking, and taxicabs come readily to mind. There is no problem explaining these barriers to entry because they result from politicians' selling favors to business people [361].

Another form of exclusive franchise that the state provides is a patent [272]. A patent grants exclusive rights to a process or product for seventeen years. A patent is a peculiar form of a monopoly grant by the state. One reason why a patent is granted is that it is quite risky and expensive to invent new ideas and products, yet quite easy and inexpensive to copy them. Thus, competitive copying of inventions leads persons and firms to invest less in inventive activity than we normally would wish. If inventors cannot get a significant share of value from their research, there will be a suboptimal amount of investment in inventive activity. Patents enable inventors to capture the social value of their research.

Patents also confer a limited monopoly privilege on inventors. The patent system, therefore, involves a trade-off between two kinds of bad effects: first, without patents less than the optimal amount of invention is produced; second, with patents monopoly in the production of the items patented is obtained for a period of seventeen years. While there are many problems with this imperfect system, and while there are difficulties in making this kind of trade-off, the existing patent system does seem to work reasonably well in encouraging inventive activity.

Many historical monopolies in the United States were based on patents. Aluminum, rayon, cellophane, xerography, and Scotch tape were the subjects of cases in which patent rights granted limited monopolies. Even patent rights, however, do not prohibit the reproduction of new products in the form of very close substitutes. Thus, patents do not contribute in a major way to creating concentrated industries.

(The amount of capital required to build a plant of minimum efficient size and the amount spent on advertising in an industry have also been treated as barriers to entry [105]. Other chapters examine the role of capital requirements and advertising as entry barriers [SB 44, SB 46].)

ENTRY BARRIERS AND PROFIT RATES

While there is evidence of a relationship between barriers to entry and profit rates, the basis of this evidence is only beginning to be clearly understood in theoretical and empirical terms [105]. Many of the observed relationships between profit rates and measures of entry barriers and concentration have been brought into question on purely empirical grounds. Subsequent examinations have shown that these relationships deteriorate over time; thus, one could explain earlier measures in *disequilibrium* terms, not in terms of *persistent* monopolistic returns [68, 69].

Additional research has shown that the use of accounting profits in the earlier studies biased the studies significantly toward finding relationships between concentration and entry barriers on the one hand and profits on the other hand [95]. Thus, the empirical case for linking concentration and entry barriers to higher-than-average profit rates in the economy is quite unstable. Furthermore, there is no adequate theory of the firm that can be used to relate the number of firms and market structure to profit rates. Much of the recent theory concerning oligopolistic action stresses that it is extremely difficult for firms to collude and set monopoly prices [424]. Indeed, much of this recent theory suggests the instability of oligopolistic coordination [SB 53].

CONCLUSION

Both empirically and theoretically the concept of barriers to entry is an unsettled area of research in economics. At the simplest level, differences in cost and demand conditions influence the number of firms in an industry. That is about all that one can conclude.

ADDITIONAL READINGS: 30, 31, 126, 320, 419, 420, 423, 442.

43. Should All Mergers Be Government-Approved?

ALLEN HYMAN
Southwestern University School of Law

Editor's Summary   The argument that mergers lead to monopolies is false. In-depth analysis shows that the growth of a firm prior to merger best explains the size of the merged company, not the merger itself. Firms become large because they are efficient; if mergers stop, firms are going to become large anyway, but they are going to do so in a less efficient way. It is difficult to comprehend why there is concern with mergers when this country already has a rigorous antimerger law. Any merger that would tend to prohibit competition in any sector of the country is subject to attack under this law. Unfortunately, this law has been used to prohibit mergers that would render firms more efficient. The less able competitors of merging firms seek to prohibit their rivals from becoming better businesses; sometimes the courts agree. Those who oppose mergers may not realize that antimerger policy has done far more to harm competition than to encourage it.

Those who are hostile to corporate mergers argue that the laws that regulate mergers are inadequate. These "reformers," to support their campaign to strengthen the antimerger laws, rely upon studies that, they claim, tentatively indicate increasing concentration in American industry. They also assert that without additional merger regulation, the day will soon come when monopolies dominate our economy [328: 205–212]. They contend, further, that "the road to monopoly has been paved by mergers" [328: 205].

THE MERGER-MONOPOLY THEORY

The merger-monopoly theory holds that companies classified as large, either in an absolute sense or in comparison with other companies in their same industry, are by their size alone able to get monopoly power. Since large size allegedly is achieved through merger, a prohibition of mergers would, in theory, restrict the formation of monopolistic firms.

Typical of antimerger proposals based on this theory is the recently proposed (but unsuccessful) amendment to the antitrust laws, which would provide the government antitrust agencies with additional powers to prevent mergers [445: 205–210]. This proposed amendment would require federal courts to grant preliminary injunctions prohibiting mergers without requiring proof that a merger would generate anticompetitive effects. The proposed law would establish a presumption that mergers are harmful. In the case of any proposed merger challenged by the government, the firms wishing to merge would have to demonstrate that their merger is not anticompetitive. This traditional analysis concerning mergers and monopoly has come under considerable attack during the last several years as a growing number of analysts and commentators have realized that this simplistic antimerger theory cannot be supported either in theory or in fact.

THE DESIRABLE EFFECTS OF MERGERS

There is a growing awareness that mergers generate many desirable economic effects. Even commentators hostile to mergers agree that the existence of the market for ongoing companies provides an owner-manager with an important incentive to build up and run a business [231: 127]. Mergers provide a low-risk opportunity for existing firms to enter new businesses, and merger is a far more desirable alternative than bankruptcy for a troubled firm. Most important, mergers provide a way of disciplining managers of corporations; inefficient managers, whose company is looked upon for potential take-over by more efficient managers, have the most to fear in a stock acquisition, proxy fight, or merger take-over [282, SB 20]. Often they are the ones who try to use the antitrust laws to insulate themselves from take-over by a more efficient firm [*Missouri Portland Cement Company v. Cargill, Inc.*, 498 F. 2d 851 (1974)]. Contrary to the presumption that mergers are anticompetitive is the finding that mergers produce competitive firms, allow an efficient transfer of capital, and permit firms to take advantage of changing technology and efficiencies.

There is even some evidence to suggest that the incentive behind a merger is, in part, the desire to create economies in the provision of services supplied exclusively by regulated industries. Firms will merge, for example, to take advantage of economies of scale in providing transportation facilities internally. Mergers that receive hostile treatment from proponents of government merger regulation are generated in part by the desire of a firm to provide its own transportation services. Self-provision of these services is superior to purchasing the services at cartel prices from government-created and regulated industries, whose exclusive franchise was created in part by past efforts to prohibit mergers.

Consistent with the arguments already offered are the results of studies that demonstrate that merged companies do not grow significantly faster than other companies and that acquisitions by larger companies are not more likely to accelerate the growth of acquired companies. Some studies also demonstrate that the best explanation for the growth of a merged company is the premerger growth of the acquired company [196].

Prohibiting mergers does not stop the growth of large firms, for more efficient firms will continue to expand as a result of their superior efficiency. Thus, the prohibition of mergers will have no permanent impact on the size of firms; it will only keep the more efficient firms from growing in the most efficient manner as they are forced to use more costly options.

MERGER PROHIBITIONS PROTECT INEFFICIENT FIRMS

It is difficult to justify additional regulation of mergers, since the United States already has the strongest and most complete antimerger law among the industrialized countries. The principal federal law regulating mergers, Section 7 of the Clayton Act, allows public and private prosecution of mergers if it can be demonstrated that there is "a lessening of competition or a tendency to create a monopoly in any line of commerce in any section of the country" [38 Stat. 731 (1914), 15 U.S.C.A. Section 18]. This section contains the provisions of the Celler-Kefauver Act of 1950 [64 Stat. 1129 (1950)]. As a result of the federal courts' liberal interpretation of Section 7, hundreds of lawsuits, both public and private, are filed each year to seek remedies.

Those who seek greater regulation of mergers fully support the many federal court decisions that embrace the antimerger philosophy. These same commentators argue that the courts should be even more restrictive in their approval of merger consolidations and combinations.

Reappraisals of the many court decisions that prohibit mergers in the name of antimonopoly demonstrate that court administration of antimerger policy often does more to hamper competition than to help it. The many antimerger decisions are at times inconsistent, but often they seem directed toward protecting existing firms from newly formed, more efficient businesses.

The courts have prohibited mergers that, they claimed, would have led to lower prices [*Brown Shoe Company v. United States*, 370 U.S. 294, 82 S. Ct. 1502, 8 L. Ed. 2d 510 (1962)], and they have prohibited mergers that would have provided more competition in certain industries [*Treadway Company, Inc., v. Brunswick Corporation*, 364 F. Supp. 316 (1973)]. The courts until most recently have penalized more efficient firms by awarding damages to their competitors, who allegedly suffered losses because of the mergers that formed the more efficient firms in the first place [*Calnetics Corp. v. Volkswagen of America*, 353 F. Supp. 1219 (1973)]. The growing consensus is that the antimerger laws have been used very successfully by the least-efficient firms to hinder the efforts of their most competitive rivals.

It is unfortunate that those who call for greater regulation of mergers not only underestimate the cost of such additional regulation in terms of lost efficiency but also do not realize that, in the name of regulation, far more has been accomplished to harm competition than to help it.

ADDITIONAL READINGS: 11, 68, 72, 126, 165, 211, 285, 287, 354, 355, 357, 360, 361, 393.

44. Does the Large Corporation's Access to Capital Markets Discourage Entry?

R. DAVID RANSON
Partner, H. C. Wainwright & Company
Boston, Massachusetts

Editor's Summary   If large corporations had easier access to financial capital, the largest firm would have the greatest advantage and would eventually dominate both its industry and the entire economy. But, concentration levels in American industry during the 1950s and 1960s were little or no higher than in the 1900s. The success of large firms may be more appropriately measured by profit rates than by concentration. But, since capital in large blocks is a factor of production different from capital in small sums, high returns to large blocks of capital are properly included in product prices. The consistently pluralistic character of our economy suggests that no particular class of firms has more than a fleeting competitive advantage over other classes.

$\mathbf{D}$o corporations have easier access to capital than other business firms? If there is such a competitive advantage, does it provide an increased tendency for industries to be dominated by relatively few firms? Although many people instinctively answer "yes" to both questions, a step-by-step examination of the logic behind these answers makes them appear far less certain than at first sight.

Why should corporations have easier access to capital than other kinds of business enterprise? Presumably the secret is not in the corporate legal form itself, since any business is free to incorporate at modest cost. If there were an unambiguous advantage in the corporate form, no business would fail to use it. Perhaps what the assertion that corporations have easier access to capital markets really means is that large business firms, which are virtually always corporations, have easier access to capital by virtue of their *size*.

EVIDENCE ABOUT CAPITAL MARKET ACCESS

What is the evidence about this assertion? Irving Schweiger's study of the "adequacy" of small business financing since World War II finds that the expansion of both equity funds and loan funds is "considerably greater percentage-wise" for smaller firms than for large businesses; Schweiger claims that the "overall view of small business as being weak, unprofitable, and lacking access to capital funds" is "incorrect" and suggests that "common misconceptions about the financing of small business have resulted in part from the faulty statistics available" [387: 346–347].

A recent and popular text simply asserts that the financial size advantage exists, as if it were too self-evident to question. "[C]apital market imperfections may contribute to concentration in industries which demand a very high capital investment for successful operation, since small firms may be unable to raise the necessary funds" [375: 102]. The only evidence this text cites is circumstantial and prejudges the issues: "In five industries analyzed by Bain, entry at an efficient scale necessitated a commitment of at least $100 million. The need to raise such a large sum was clearly an obstacle to the entry of small new enterprises" [375: 230; 30]. (The text fails to mention Schweiger's study.)

DIFFERENTIAL ACCESS IS DEFINITIONAL

Can a cause-and-effect relationship between financial size advantage and industrial concentration be proved? Not easily, because there is a truism involved. An industry in which a small number of the largest firms play a predominant role is, by definition, a concentrated industry. One cannot know whether a purely financial advantage or some other factor led to high concentration. Even complicated statistical tests would find the answer to be elusive. The statistical correlation between financial size and market share is likely to be close, even if the implied hypothesis is wrong.

THE LOGIC OF DIFFERENTIAL ACCESS

To evaluate the hypothesis that large firms have better access to capital markets, one must ask first not whether the hypothesis is factual but whether it is logical. How is the process supposed to work? More favorable treatment in the financial markets is the presumed meaning of "easier access to capital." This could mean that a large firm pays a lower interest rate than a small firm on a comparable loan, or that a large firm faces less stringent conditions on the use of the funds borrowed, or even on the arrangements for repayment. Or, it could mean that a large firm can obtain a loan while, in otherwise identical circumstances, a small firm is turned down and must search elsewhere. The large firm's unit costs, in any event, would be lower as a consequence.

If a small firm faces this kind of disadvantage, it will find it hard to compete. A small firm is less able than a large one to justify capital projects. As market demand grows, a large firm can add to its capacity more cheaply than a small firm can, since its more plentiful and cheaper capital allows it to outbid the small firm when purchasing new machinery and other resources. So, the small firm remains on the edge of the industry while the large one grows. Concentration develops.

THE EVIDENCE REFUTES THE HYPOTHESIS OF DIFFERENTIAL ACCESS

This reasoning sounds logical. Indeed, the trouble is that the logic is too powerful, leading beyond the result alleged in this chapter's initial questions to more extreme and less plausible predictions. In a contest between two large firms for control of an industry, luck and managerial skill and error, as well as financial advantage, all are important. But, the larger firm, on the average, would win. The process would continue until a single firm (by virtue of financial advantage) dominates each industry. Indeed, the process leads beyond this result: until one firm dominates the entire economy.

The mechanism described thus far, to be precise, does not necessarily predict *high* concentration. The resulting level of concentration depends on how rapidly the process operates and on how long it has already been under way. What the logic does seem to predict, however, is that concentration levels will tend to *rise* as time passes. Empirical evidence does not confirm this prediction. According to most estimates, average concentration levels in American industry in the 1950s and 1960s were little or no higher than in 1900 [4; 334; 335; 375: 61–63; 393].

When closely analyzed, the same logic leads to a still more extreme prediction than a trend leading ultimately toward complete concentration. As long as financial advantages of size are evident to the participants, they will not wait for nature to take its course. Firms, both large and small, can merge to achieve easier access to capital and to avoid unnecessary financial costs. Although there are legal obstacles to mergers between firms that already have a large share of the same market, other firms are free to merge, and they will do so as long as the incentive exists. The logic thus leads to the conclusion that new firms will either combine to become large or fail to survive. There will be no permanent place in the economy for small firms, a paradoxical result.

WHY SMALLER FIRMS SURVIVE

The key to the paradox is the recognition that a firm need not go so far as to merge with others to gain financial size advantages. As in other situations in which size is an advantage, firms can form a consortium to borrow on their behalf. Small and large firms, for example, bid jointly on oil field development leases. To a lender, a consortium of small firms is essentially indistinguishable from just another large firm. Or, if necessary, a small firm can purchase a controlling interest in a bank with gross assets many times the size of those of the firm itself. In this way, the small firm can make up whatever financial disadvantage it faces alone. This insight is one good reason to doubt the truth of the hypothesis that financial size advantage leads to concentration.

There is another, more profound reason to doubt the same hypothesis. In a world in which a particular person or firm has an enduring and unbounded competitive advantage over others, a pluralistic economy would not be possible. After a short time, the entity with the greatest competitive advantage would own everything. There would be no room for a firm that is even "slightly" less competitive than the most efficient firm.

Although some firms are more successful than others, concentration appears to be very stable over long periods of time. It is as if there were an equilibrium level of concentration around which actual industry conditions merely fluctuate. And, it is a condition of equilibrium that, at the margin, one firm's competitive power must be equal to every other firm's competitive power. Success, as measured by profit rate, may be a function of the production of capital of different sizes, not a function of firms of different sizes.

> Capital in large lots would be a different factor of production from capital in small sums. A billion dollars in capital would be more productive in its best employment than the total of one thousand lots of a million dollars each. Given the imperfection of capital markets, the high returns to large lots of capital are social opportunity costs, and are properly included in product price [203: 330].

In other words, observation suggests that our economy, by and large, is not only pluralistic but also consistently pluralistic. This evidence refutes the contention that any particular class of firms has more than a fleeting competitive advantage over other classes. In the most fundamental sense, every surviving firm has equal access to capital.

ADDITIONAL READINGS: 415, 419.

45. Does Limited Liability Subsidize Corporations at the Expense of Society?

ROGER E. MEINERS
Law and Economics Center
University of Miami School of Law

Editor's Summary   The benefits of limited liability of corporation shareholders are grossly exaggerated. As long as business loans are negotiated on an individual basis, the interest rate and collateral for each loan will be independent of the liability rule and form of business organization. The role of limited liability as it affects involuntary (tort) creditors is best analyzed as an issue of appropriate insurance coverage rather than as an issue of appropriate capitalization of firms. Regardless of the system of liability, insurance coverage is not free. And, customers must pay for corporate liability, limited or unlimited, in the form of higher prices.

$\mathbf{T}$he view that limited liability of corporation shareholders is of central importance to the corporate form of organization has persisted over the years. Legal scholars pay homage to the concept in casebooks, in treatises, and in articles [180; 212: 96; 407: 2–2]. Corporations thus seem to have an advantage not available to other forms of business organization. Some observers believe that since limited liability allows corporations to acquire credit at a cost lower than the cost to noncorporate organizations, society must absorb the expenses of risky corporate ventures [252]. Also, limited liability is claimed to produce inequitable results in connection with involuntary (tort) creditors. Major problems are believed to occur in cases of one-person corporations and subsidiaries of existing corporations. Consequently, limited liability is commonly believed to provide corporations with a subsidy at the expense of the general public.

THE NATURE OF LIMITED LIABILITY

Limited liability implies that corporation shareholders are liable only to the extent of their respective capital contributions. In a sole proprietorship or a partnership, all personal assets of the investors are potentially available to creditors. A corporation's creditors, however, will, as a rule, only be able to capture the funds invested directly in the corporation. The creditors will not be able to reach shareholders' other assets.

This general rule is inapplicable if there is a defect in the formation of a corporation, which is now quite rare, or if a court finds some reason to "pierce the veil" of a corporation. That may be done in a variety of circumstances—for example, if there is inadequate capitalization of the corporate entity, or if a shareholder allows his or her funds to be comingled with those of the corporation. In general, "when the notion of legal entity is used to defeat public convenience, justify wrong, protect fraud, or defend crime, the law will regard the corporation as an association of persons" [*U.S. v. Milwaukee Refrigerator Transit Co.*, 142 F. 2d 247, 255 (1905)].

LIMITED LIABILITY, CREDIT MARKETS, AND THE RIGHT TO CONTRACT

The liability rule, in practice, is not likely to be significant in credit markets. Since loans are contracted on an individually bargained basis, the costs of doing business as a proprietorship should be nearly the same as the costs of doing business as a corporation. Only the forms used in the agreement and the magnitude of the credit investigation may differ. But, there is little reason to believe that the differences are significant. Thus, in a competitive credit market, the same loan emerges for any form of business organization. And, the results would remain unchanged even in a world of unlimited liability for corporation shareholders.

(Often, in making loan agreements, creditors insist that individual persons incorporate. The corporate form avoids certain probate problems and has other advantages that the creditors believe represent a net benefit. If limited liability reduces the creditors' chances for repayment, it would be unlikely that they would find the corporate form of organization preferable to the proprietorship.)

If limited liability reduced the collateral backing of a debtor, a bank could insist on a higher interest rate for the same money loaned and thus cover the added risk. The borrower, in that case, would be paying a premium for doing business as a corporation. The interest rate would not be altered, however, if, despite the limited liability, a person contracted to make *himself* or *herself* liable for the corporate debts. It is also possible, of course, for a person, as a sole proprietor, to contract with a bank for limited liability. The person could agree to collateralize the same assets that would be pledged if he or she incorporated with a specified amount of capital. The bank might be willing to approve such a loan, but it would charge a higher interest rate reflecting the added risk.

Accordingly, the credit result may be the same under either liability rule. Because each loan is made on an individual basis, and because the interest rate is determined specifically for each loan, the collateral can vary for each loan no matter what the liability rule, *so long as free contracting is allowed.* When a person contracts to limit his or her liability or has it limited by law, market conditions cause that person to pay a premium for the limited liability. Protection for some of the person's assets works as an insurance policy, and a premium is paid for that "policy." People may prefer to purchase insurance for some assets by paying a higher interest rate to a lender, but the real cost of credit remains the same. Hence, the belief that limited liability allows corporations to acquire credit at a cost lower than the cost to noncorporations stems from a lack of understanding of how competitive credit markets operate.

LIMITED LIABILITY, INSURANCE, AND TORT-FEASORS

The confusion that exists with respect to the case of the involuntary (tort) creditor of a corporation stems from a similar lack of understanding of the real issue. Limited liability again is seen as a subsidy for the corporate form of organization, and concern centers on smaller enterprises.

In the case of a one-person corporation, a person who may have been fully responsible as a sole proprietor can limit his or her liability to the extent of personal investment in the company. Suppose that person's corporation has fewer assets than the proprietorship. Tort victims will be disadvantaged if they are unable fully to collect a judgment against the corporation.

In the case of subsidiaries, an existing corporation can limit its liability and protect some of its assets, since tort claimants can reach only the assets of the subsidiaries [50]. As in the case of the one-person corporation, the main problem here is presented in terms of "undercapitalization." "State corporation statutes clearly do not require corporate entities to be capitalized adequately as a prerequisite to engaging in most types of business activities. . . ." [252: 592]. It is believed that this "undercapitalization" encourages entrepreneurs to protect their assets from tort victims by using the corporate device. This protection forces society to subsidize corporations.

"Undercapitalization," of course, is not peculiar to corporations. A proprietorship or partnership can be "undercapitalized" in the sense that it cannot pay very much in a tort case. Most persons are "undercapitalized" in the same sense; if there were tort judgments against them, they would not be able to pay a large award. Since there are many more "undercapitalized" persons than "undercapitalized" corporations, it is not clear why such corporations should be singled out for concern.

The *real* concern seems to be with the current asset value of a corporation, not with its initial capitalization. A taxi company could own a thousand taxicabs but have a very low asset value at the time of a tort claim. A one-person taxi corporation could have a higher net value at a certain point in time than the thousand-cab company. Larger corporations, of course, tend to have higher net values than smaller corporations. Thus, in general, large tort awards are easier to collect from large corporations. If the concern is that a company might not be able to pay a tort award at some point in time, however, a rule of "adequate" capitalization would have to require that some minimum level of adequate capital be met constantly, or a firm would lose its corporate status.

The real issue is not one of undercapitalization, but one of underinsurance. A company with very little capital could buy insurance to cover most tort claims that might arise. The same is true of most persons. Since the concern is that some persons could be injured and left without insurance to cover losses, or without a solvent company to sue for damages, the rule of limited liability plays only a small role in a widespread problem. The policy issue, therefore, appears to revolve around the question of who should bear the immediate cost of general accident insurance.

In reality, many firms, corporations, and proprietorships carry insurance to protect their assets from tort claims. A mandatory rule of adequate insurance would eliminate the perceived problem of "undercapitalized" corporations. However, it is difficult to think of a logical reason why such a rule should not apply equally to all other forms of business organization, and even to all persons.

Ignoring these considerations, though, think about a world of limited liability for corporations as compared with a world of unlimited liability for corporations. Assume that with limited liability tort claimants are, indeed, likely to collect less from the average corporation in the average tort claim. Taxicabs *individually* incorporated, for example, would be less concerned with protecting corporate assets with insurance than would be the case if all taxicabs were owned by a single corporation. That corporation would have more assets against which a tort claimant could collect than the single-taxi corporations. In a competitive taxicab market the result would be that individual taxis would charge a lower fare than taxis that were part of large corporations.

This is the key aspect about the provision of insurance. Insurance is not free, no matter how it is purchased. A person buys a little insurance every time he or she rides in a taxi owned by a large corporation (which must charge a higher fare to cover its insurance costs). The person pays for that insurance just as if he or she were riding in a taxi that had no insurance protection and no assets to back the taxi owner. In that case the rider could self-insure, that is, bear the costs of an accident in a lump sum. Or, the rider could purchase insurance from an insurance company, which would cover the rider's costs in case there were an accident. In terms of economic efficiency it is not clear why one system of liability is better than another.

If limited liability of shareholders does indeed lead to less coverage of accidents by tort-feasors than would hold true in a world of unlimited liability, it means merely that one party rather than another purchases the insurance. If there were unlimited liability, corporations would provide more insurance, and persons would have to purchase slightly less. The cost of the insurance purchased by corporations would be reflected in the prices of the goods sold by corporations. Consumers would buy insurance indirectly rather than directly, as they would under limited liability, which would accompany lower prices, reflecting the corporations' lack of insurance.

OTHER BENEFITS OF THE CORPORATE BUSINESS FORM

The primary reasons for the existence of the corporate form of organization are not related to the rule of limited liability. There are many attributes of corporate organization that make it preferable to other forms of organization, and that will hold under any rule of shareholder liability. These attributes include perpetual life, a separate legal entity, the ability to exchange ownership rights cheaply and efficiently, the ability to raise capital through a sale of stock, management by experts without shareholder participation, majority rule (or rule by any specified percentage), the ability to raise funds in ways other than through the sale of stock, and flexibility in the range of operations [SB 16, SB 21, SB 30]. (Today, tax considerations are very important in determining which form of business organization to choose. This development is recent, however, and does not affect the preceding argument.) The common-law contractual origins of the corporation provide the incentives to use the corporate form of organization. With free contracting, a statutory rule of limited liability is of little consequence.

ADDITIONAL READINGS: 11, 90, 227, 284, 358.

46. Is Corporation Product Advertising a Barrier to Entry?

HARRY BLOCH
Department of Economics
University of Denver

Editor's Summary   Since new entrants use advertising widely as they try to establish their products, and since that advertising may have long-lasting effects on consumer loyalties, any blanket restriction on advertising would serve the interests of established firms by insulating these firms' customers from the knowledge provided by the advertisers of new products. The immediate effect of a blanket restriction on advertising would be to discourage entry. Evidence about the effects of advertising on entry is mixed.

The immediacy of advertising's role in daily business operations often makes it difficult for persons involved in these operations to appreciate the assertion that their advertising acts as a barrier to entry. A lack of appreciation of this assertion could stem from a failure to consider product advertising in the context appropriate to the assertion. Joe S. Bain, in his study of barriers to entry, evaluates the *condition of entry* into an industry in terms of "the extent to which established sellers can persistently raise their prices above a competitive level without attracting new firms to enter the industry" [30: 5; 252]. One must view the effect of advertising on the condition of entry from the perspective of potential rivals rather than from that of existing rivals. Product advertising, which is an accepted part of the rivalry between existing sellers, may appear as a serious deterrent to potential entrants.

EXPLANATIONS OF HOW ADVERTISING RESTRICTS ENTRY

There are several explanations of how product advertising deters entry. One explanation is that product advertising promotes brand loyalty; thus, potential entrants must attract customers either through lower prices or through heavier advertising, which means higher costs. As a result of the lower prices or higher costs for potential entrants, established firms can charge prices above their costs without encouraging entry. The issue in this explanation is whether there is a difference between the effort required to break down brand loyalties and the effort required to establish such loyalties originally. If existing firms spend as much in promoting brand loyalty as new entrants must spend to switch loyalties to their products, no price or cost advantage accrues to the established firms, and there is no barrier to entry. Hence, this first explanation is wrong.

Another explanation of how advertising serves as a barrier to entry is that advertising expenditures represent a long-term commitment to altering consumer buying patterns. The benefit to a firm from such expenditures occurs over a long period of time. Thus, new entrants must be . prepared to make investments in their advertising programs. As the future benefits to be derived from an advertising program are an intangible asset, it is usually necessary to finance investments in advertising by using risk capital. The amount of risk capital necessary for a successful advertising program might be so large that some firms cannot enter into competition in an industry because they cannot raise sufficient amounts of risk capital. While this argument has some commonsense appeal, there is no direct evidence to support it, and there are many cases in which new firms establish themselves in industries whose existing firms advertise heavily. Hence, this second explanation is wrong.

A third explanation of how advertising serves as a barrier to entry is that there are economies of scale in advertising. The existence of economies of scale means that the cost of an advertising program increases less than in proportion to the impact of the program; that is, the cost per unit of advertising impact declines as the scale of the advertising program grows. Economies of scale can arise either because the effectiveness of advertising messages increases as the number of messages increases or because the price of advertising messages falls as the number of messages purchased increases. The existence of economies of scale acts as a deterrent to entry because it becomes necessary for new entrants to achieve a substantial size before their average costs are as low as those of the large established firms. A potential entrant must consider the possible adverse effect of its entry, at a substantial size, on the price structure in the industry. Even though current prices are higher than the costs of established firms, the prospect of a price decline following entry may deter the potential entrant.

Direct evidence is available concerning the merits of the argument that the price of advertising messages falls as the quantity purchased increases. The evidence, however, is somewhat contradictory. Three studies find no significant evidence of quantity discounts in the advertising media [57, 162, 347]. A more recent study finds a suggestion of the presence of quantity discounts on network television rates, but this study rests on the questionable assumption that all television programs provide equal quality advertising vehicles [104: 53–61].

MEASURING THE EFFECTS OF ADVERTISING ON ENTRY

Aside from the explanation about quantity discounts in the advertising media, all the other explanations of how advertising acts as a barrier to entry depend upon some assertion about the effects of advertising on consumers. The assertions are that advertising is more effective for established firms than for new entrants, that there is a substantial minimal size for a successful advertising campaign, and that advertising effectiveness increases with the number of advertising messages. Empirical verification or contradiction of these assertions is virtually impossible because measurement of the effects of advertising is generally highly imprecise. Advertising can impact on sales long after the original expenditure. Also, differences in content lead to great variations in the effectiveness of advertising. In view of these difficulties, it is not surprising that economists rely on indirect methods for empirically assessing the impact of advertising on the condition of entry.

The most common indirect method for finding out whether advertising acts as a barrier to entry is suggested by Bain's evaluation of the condition of entry. This method involves the use of profit rates as indicators of the presence of barriers to entry. The condition of entry is measured by the extent to which prices can be raised above average costs; thus the existence of barriers to entry should be reflected in larger differences between prices and costs or, alternatively, in higher reported profit rates.

An inspection of any listing of the profit rates of large corporations leads to the conclusion that firms that engage in heavy advertising are overly represented among those firms with the highest profit rates. The conclusion is amplified by statistical studies, which find a strong positive relationship between advertising intensity and reported profit rates [30: 190–201; 105; 159]. In these studies, the strong positive relationship between advertising intensity and reported profit rates remains even when the influence of other factors, such as the rate of growth of industry sales and the degree to which industry sales are dominated by a few large firms, is separated statistically.

Advertising expenditures are treated as a current expense in the calculation of reported profit rates. Yet, as noted earlier, advertising has a long-term impact with respect to switching consumer loyalties, and the future benefits from a firm's advertising program are an intangible asset. The value of this asset can be quite high for a firm that spends great amounts on advertising over long periods of time. Excluding the value of this asset from the firm's accounts means understating the value of stockholder investment in the firm. Besides leading to an understatement of stockholder investment, the expensing of advertising has the effect of understating reported profit whenever current expenditures on advertising exceed depreciation of the intangible advertising asset. Most growing firms are increasing the value of their investment in advertising by having current expenditures that exceed depreciation on past expenditures; thus, for most firms both reported profit and reported stockholder investment are understated by the expensing of advertising.

The net effect of the understatements of reported profit and stockholder investment on a firm's reported profit rate (reported profit divided by stockholder investment) depends on the firm's reported rate of return and the growth rate of its advertising expenditures [437: 123; 453: 423]. An examination of specific data for forty established food manufacturing firms showed that the net effect of expensing advertising was that the reported profit rates of thirty-nine of the forty firms were overstated [59: 285]. A general rule would be that the expensing of advertising leads to the overstatement of the reported profit rates of established firms, although it might very well lead to the understatement of the reported profit rates of new entrants, who are making large investments in advertising, and who have not yet accumulated a large advertising asset.

Two alternative explanations of the positive relationship between advertising intensity and reported profit rates now can be distinguished. One explanation is that advertising acts as a barrier to entry that allows established firms to earn excessive profits without inducing entry. A second explanation is that the reported profit rates of established firms that advertise heavily are inflated by inappropriate accounting methods. (There is no relationship between reported profit rates and advertising intensity when the effects of inappropriate accounting are removed.)

Efforts to find out empirically which of the two alternative explanations is correct adopt a common approach. This approach is to calculate adjusted profit rates by removing the effects of the inappropriate accounting of advertising expenditures from the reported profit rates. The same kind of statistical analysis applied to the relationship between advertising intensity and reported profit rates is then applied to the relationship between advertising intensity and adjusted profit rates. Some studies that use adjusted firm profit rates find no statistically significant relationship between advertising intensity and adjusted profit rates [59]. By contrast, other studies that use adjusted industry profit rates find a strong, positive, and statistically significant relationship between advertising intensity and adjusted profit rates [104: Chap. 8; 453]. One can trace the difference in findings between studies using firm profit rates and those using industry profit rates to a difference in the treatment of the effects of each firm's advertising on other firms in the same industry. The relative merits of the different treatments remain an area of controversy, but I provide elsewhere a strong case for preferring the treatment implied in the use of firm data [59: 270].

Examining the relationship between advertising intensity and profit rates is one indirect method of estimating the effect of product advertising on the condition of entry. Another indirect method is to examine the effect of product advertising on the strength of loyalties to the brands of established sellers. If heavy product advertising in an industry increases the strength of loyalties to existing brands, new entrants will have a more difficult time getting established in industries in which products are heavily advertised. If heavy advertising by established firms leads to increased brand switching by consumers, the prospects for potential entrants are improved—as long as these entrants are prepared to commit risk capital for the establishment of their new brands. Lester Telser examines the stability of brand shares for a group of branded food products and for a group of branded toiletries and finds that the food products have more stable brand shares than the toiletries, even though they are less heavily advertised [435].

PUBLIC POLICY TOWARD ADVERTISING

Proponents of the position that advertising acts as a barrier to entry are inclined to view in a favorable light public policy that restricts advertising. The evidence I cite here concerning the influence of advertising on the condition of entry is largely indirect and contradictory. A possible explanation for the contradictory evidence is that the influence of advertising on the condition of entry varies among industries. In some industries heavy advertising by established firms might ease entry, while in other industries it might discourage entry. Any public policy that imposes blanket restrictions on advertising is ill-advised if this explanation for the contradictory evidence is correct.

Another consideration in formulating public policy toward advertising is the distinction between the effects of advertising by established firms and the effects of advertising by new entrants. While contradictory evidence is available with respect to the effects of advertising by established firms on the condition of entry, it is clear that new entrants use advertising widely in successfully establishing their products. Since advertising has long-lasting effects on consumer loyalties, any blanket restriction on advertising would serve the interests of established firms by protecting the loyalties of their customers from the attack of new-product advertising.

The immediate effect of a blanket restriction on advertising would be to discourage entry. The length of time over which this effect lasts would depend on the rate at which the impact of advertising on consumer loyalties decays. Estimates of the decay rate of the impact of advertising vary widely, depending on the method of estimation used and the kind of product advertised. But, rates as low as 15 percent per year are not uncommon [1: 662–664; 58: 47–52; 434: 498]. With a 15 percent decay rate, more than one-half of the original impact of advertising still remains after four years, and more than one-quarter of the original impact still remains after eight years. This suggests that blanket restrictions on advertising might give established firms a significant advantage over new entrants for as long as a decade.

ADDITIONAL READINGS: 27, 67, 74, 161, 397, 436.

47. Is Planned Obsolescence a Serious Problem?

DANIEL K. BENJAMIN
Department of Economics
University of Washington

Editor's Summary   Any product could be made more durable, but
only for a higher price. Because consumer tastes are incredibly
diverse, there is no single level of product durability that is optimal for
all consumers. One dimension of competition among business firms
involves experimentation with various degrees of product durability.
Consequently, consumers are offered a wide range of durability and
prices for products. No one has ever documented a case in which
firms refused to produce goods of greater durability when customers
were willing to pay the costs of added durability. If an error is made,
competition among firms forces the mistaken firm to correct its error or
go out of business.

Since the publication of Vance Packard's *The Waste Makers*, the term
"planned obsolescence" has become common in discussions of the durability and quality of products [340]. The list of persons claiming that
corporations plan obsolescence into their products includes John Kenneth
Galbraith, Ralph Nader, and various officials of Consumers Union. While
the proponents of this claim seldom specify what they mean by "planned
obsolescence," three notions seem to predominate: first, corporations fail
to make products that last as long as they conceivably could last; second,
products are made to last for a shorter time than they *should* last; and
third, firms deliberately make products that are less durable than consumers expect.

PLANNED OBSOLESCENCE AS
THE UNDEREMPLOYMENT OF TECHNOLOGY

Proponents of the first notion of planned obsolescence usually base their
arguments strictly on technological considerations. They observe (or at
least assert) that the engineering know-how exists to permit the manufacture of some product so that it will last X years. Since the actual lifetime of
the product is less than X years, they conclude that the shorter period of
durability injures consumers and society as a whole.

The fundamental flaw in this argument is simple: the argument
the *cost* of producing more durable goods. Simply because it is possible to
put a man on the moon does not imply that the Sea of Tranquility is the
appropriate place for most people to take their next vacation. Similarly,

even though one can make a light bulb that lasts a century, to do so may not be efficient.

Generally, the durability of any product can be increased only by incurring additional costs. From the standpoint of businesses, consumers, and society, extra durability should be added only if the benefits of doing so exceed the extra costs. Consider a product that can be made to last an additional year at a cost of $10, and suppose that potential purchasers would pay only $6 for the added durability. The producer of this product would not choose to make the more durable version, since doing so would yield a loss of $4 per unit. If consumers were somehow forced to purchase the more durable version at a premium of $10, the firm would willingly comply. But, consumers would then suffer a loss of $4. Whoever pays the bill loses if the costs of extra durability exceed the benefits. In this example, production of the more durable version would yield something worth only $6 at the expense of other things worth $10; thus there would be a loss of $4. A firm's decision not to produce an item more durable than the version for which consumers are willing to pay serves not only its own interests but the interests of consumers and society as well.

PLANNED OBSOLESCENCE AS ECONOMIC STUPIDITY

The second notion of planned obsolescence supposes that consumers are willing to pay for more durable goods but that businesses refuse to provide them. Thus, as Vance Packard believes, a firm "is vulnerable to criticism . . . if it sells a product with a short life expectancy when it knows that for the same cost, or only a little more, it could give the consumer a product with a much longer useful life" [340: 49]. Supposedly, the firm adopts this strategy to increase profits; plainly, however, this argument implies that the firm fails to act in its own interest.

If consumers would pay more than it costs to produce added durability, a firm could always increase its profits by increasing durability. The desire to increase durability so as to increase profits would persist until the incremental cost of added durability equals the incremental amount that consumers are willing to pay. Hence, a firm would not knowingly choose to produce a product whose life expectancy could be increased at a cost that is less than what a consumer (and thus society) is willing to pay.

Even if a firm is mistakenly forgoing profits by producing an inappropriately short-lived item, competition will force it to correct its error or go out of business. A competing firm will offer for sale a more durable version of the item. Since consumers will prefer the more durable version, any other firm that fails to produce an equally durable version will find itself without customers. Again, only goods having the durability consumers prefer will be produced.

It might seem that this argument fails to hold in the case of "unique" products for which no close substitutes exist. One must remember, however, that the market value of any firm is the capitalized value of its profit stream. If a firm is forgoing profits by producing short-lived products, its market value will be relatively low. Hence, it will pay outsiders to buy control of the firm at the depressed market value; they will reap the full value of the profits that they can obtain by making the products more durable. Again, the private incentive of the business person coincides with the interests of consumers and society as a whole.

PLANNED OBSOLESCENCE AS CHEATING THE CUSTOMER

The third notion of planned obsolescence asserts that firms try to cheat their customers by producing goods whose durability is less than what customers expect. Consumers, of course, understand this possibility, which is precisely what motivates firms to offer guarantees for their products. Even in the absence of explicit guarantees, however, short-run profits from cheating will be offset by long-run losses. A firm that tries to deceive its customers about the true durability of its products will soon develop a reputation for cheating. The firm will lose customers, and even those who remain will pay much lower prices for the products: prices low enough to compensate them for the risk of deception. Competition from other firms also will tend to prevent "planned obsolescence" of this sort; competing firms will hasten to offer superior guarantees and to advertise the inferior durability of the cheater's products. This is not to say that cheating never occurs. The point is, simply, that cheating does not pay as a systematic policy.

SUMMARY

Allegations of planned obsolescence are made freely and often. Yet no one has ever documented an instance in which firms refused to produce goods of greater durability in the face of customers who were willing to pay the costs of added durability. In light of the flaws in the planned obsolescence arguments, this lack of documentation is hardly surprising. Both the profit motive and the forces of competition operate to ensure that "planned obsolescence" is, and will remain, but an intellectual curiosity.

ADDITIONAL READINGS: 43, 238, 343, 430.

48. Does Advertising Persuade Consumers to Buy Things They Do Not Need?

ROBERT AYANIAN
Department of Economics
San Francisco State University

Editor's Summary   The concept of consumer "needs" defies definition, since there is no clear distinction between physical needs and psychic needs. All kinds of goods are important to people in both primitive and modern societies. The evidence indicates that commodities like food and drugs are more heavily advertised than commodities like candy, chewing gum, paper products, and photographic equipment. Consequently, the proposition that advertising persuades consumers to buy frivolous rather than needed items is meaningless.

One of the most basic yet elusive popular views about business is that corporate advertising persuades consumers to buy things they do not "need." This belief seems to be a popular distillation of John Kenneth Galbraith's view of advertising, for to Galbraith, advertising is the sine qua non of American society as we know it, and advertising is a despot. In Galbraith's words, "advertising and its related arts thus help develop the kind of man the goals of the industrial system require—one that reliably spends his income and works reliably because he is always in need of more" [189: 210].

This situation arises, according to Galbraith, because of the very success of the industrial system that has freed us from concern with physical needs. With growing material prosperity, psychic needs (unlike physical needs, which are neither objective nor compelling) become predominant and make Americans increasingly susceptible to persuasion through "advertising and its related arts." American industry has seized the opportunity to "develop the kind of man the goals of the industrial system require. . . ."

Galbraith believes this need not have happened. "In the absence of the massive and artful persuasion that accompanies the management of demand, increasing abundance might well have reduced the interest of people in acquiring more goods. They would not have felt the need for multiplying the artifacts—autos, appliances, detergents, cosmetics—by which they were surrounded" [189: 209]. To summarize Galbraith's views in one sentence, *corporate advertising persuades people to buy things they do not need.*

THE UBIQUITY OF "ARTIFACTS"

The critics of advertising fail to realize that people in all societies have always concerned themselves with more than mere physical survival. "That man does not live by bread alone" was believed and practiced long before the industrial revolution. Cosmetics are used by all primitive societies, and paintings decorate the walls of prehistoric caves. Even baboons groom themselves. If people have an instinct for grooming, the desire for cosmetics can hardly be a creation of television advertising!

The notion that rising material prosperity makes people more "manageable" with respect to the goods they consume is not supported by our knowledge of primitive societies. Indeed, in a primitive society virtually everything a person does is "managed" by custom, tradition, or tribal law. The process of civilization and industrialization in the West has largely been one of expanding the options open to people. It is astonishing that Galbraith should propound the opposite view at a time when growing numbers of people are actively living "alternative life-styles"; when it is getting harder and harder to find a Republican or even a Democrat, let alone Galbraith's "reliable man"; when our whole society seems at times to be coming apart at its cultural seams.

THE UBIQUITY OF PSYCHIC WANTS

Similarly, the idea that physical needs are objective and compelling while psychic needs are not is strange. There is no basis for claiming that cosmetics, which mean the difference between feeling lovely and feeling dumpy, are any less important than another hunk of meat. Indeed, people in both primitive and developed societies show consistently by their actions that all kinds of goods are important. Trying to rank needs from physical to psychic is useless because there is no clear distinction between purely physical needs and purely psychic needs. Physical needs do not arise in abstraction from our minds and emotions, nor do psychic needs arise in abstraction from our bodies. People are integrated beings, as current developments in both humanistic psychology and medical biofeedback demonstrate conclusively. Human needs are an integration of physical and psychic requirements and desires, just as water is an integration of hydrogen and oxygen.

EVIDENCE ABOUT GALBRAITH'S VIEWS OF ADVERTISING

Consider Galbraith's views of advertising and its relationship to American society in more detail. Harold Demsetz subjects several of Galbraith's key propositions to empirical tests [124]. Two of these tests pertain directly to the effects of advertising. One proposition Demsetz tests is that advertising produces high sales growth rates for corporations: "Once the safety of the technostructure is insured by a minimum level of earnings, there is then a measure of choice as to goals. . . ." And, "There is little doubt as to how, overwhelmingly, this choice is exercised: It is to achieve the greatest possible rate of corporate growth as measured in sales" [189: 171]. In Galbraith's view, then, the principal method of achieving high sales growth rates is intensive advertising.

Demsetz studies a sample of 70 firms, including 30 of the 200 largest United States corporations, for the period 1958–1970. He correlates a common index of advertising intensity—the ratio of a firm's advertising outlays to its sales revenues—with the ratio of the firm's annual sales growth rate to its annual profit rate. Galbraith's proposition implies that the index of advertising intensity is correlated positively with the rate of sales growth relative to profit rate.

Demsetz finds that the index of advertising intensity is negatively correlated with a firm's relative sales growth rate. This finding, of course, is precisely the opposite of what Galbraith's proposition implies. While the accounting treatment of advertising investment as a current expense may bias the annual profit rates of intense advertisers upward, thereby biasing downward their relative sales growth rates, Demsetz's finding clearly offers no support for Galbraith's view.

A second proposition Demsetz tests is that advertising produces stability for a corporation. In this test Demsetz studies 375 industries to see if there is a positive correlation between advertising intensity and stability of an industry's sales and employment. There is not. Demsetz concludes that "the phenomenon of advertising and Galbraith's world view cannot be reconciled, and the role of advertising in modern society must be sought elsewhere" [124: 74].

Following Demsetz's statistical approach, I examine empirically the proposition "Corporate advertising persuades people to buy things they do not need." This is difficult to do because no one knows precisely what "need" means. Indeed, economists avoid this term in favor of the more intelligible term "want" so that they will know what they are talking about. This approach, however, is unavailable here, since Galbraith would not want his theory summarized as "Corporate advertising persuades people to buy things they do not *want.*"

Taking a somewhat freewheeling approach to hypothesis testing, I try to capture the essence of the popular distillation of Galbraith's view: advertising expenditures by the major United States corporate advertisers are greatest for goods that are least needed by the American people and least for goods that are most needed. Using data from the *Advertising Age* listing of the 100 largest (in dollars) United States domestic advertisers for 1975, I rank eleven more-or-less well-defined product groups by total advertising expenditures for all firms within each group. Table 3 shows

Table 3   Need Ranking Asserted by Galbraith's Proposition

Need Ranking	Product Group	1975 Advertising[a] Expenditures (Million $)
MOST NEEDED:	Candy, Chewing Gum	46
	Paper Products	46
	Photographic Equipment	86
	TVs, Radios, Appliances	159
	Cosmetics	236
	Cigarettes	398
	Beer, Liquor, Soft Drinks	473
	Soaps, Cleansers, Detergents	616
	Cars, Gas, Tires	818
	Drugs	906
LEAST NEEDED:	Food	1,243

[a]SOURCE: *Advertising Age*. Reprinted with permission from the August 23, 1976, issue of *Advertising Age*. Copyright 1976 by Crain Communication Inc.

products ranged from "most needed" to "least needed" according to Galbraith's proposition.

Proposition: Advertising expenditures by the major United States corporate advertisers are greatest for goods that are least needed, or not needed, by the American people and least for goods that are most needed. needed.

I invite the reader to form his or her own conclusion as to whether or not people need the products at the top of the table more than they need those at the bottom. But, if these results are judged simply by Galbraith's assertion that food is needed, whereas cosmetics, detergents, appliances, and automobiles are not, Galbraith's proposition stands refuted.

SUMMARY

The proposition that corporate advertising persuades people to buy things they do not need cannot mean, for example, that food and drugs are more important than candy and chewing gum. The results in the table imply precisely the opposite. But, if the proposition cannot mean that, what can it mean? Presumably it means nothing at all. Clearly the vast majority of advertising in American society is for goods that the American people both want and need.

ADDITIONAL READINGS: 42, 58, 59, 67, 330, 331, 446.

49. Do Corporations Overwhelm Consumers and Voters?

DOUGLAS K. ADIE
Department of Economics
Ohio University

Editor's Summary   Corporate detractors' preoccupation with the size of the larger corporations blinds them to the checks and balances of the competitive environment within which these firms operate. Mere size does not imply power unless it is the result of special government protection. Advertising should nearly always be honest. Consumer tastes limit corporate discretion. Capital markets and internal incentives control managerial activity. And, labor's mobility checks any corporate abuses.

Some detractors of corporations claim naïvely that by accumulating great wealth, corporations have gained independence from consumers, stockholders, bondholders, employees, and voters [189, 198, 274]. Some corporations indeed have amassed great wealth. But, how independent are corporations to pursue their own ends? What is the source of this autonomy? And, to what extent do corporations use this alleged power to oppose the interests of employees and voters? When corporations are operating *efficiently,* their actions are not detrimental to employees and voters. Consumers, stockholders, and owners of capital, in their legal and economic relationships with a corporation, can compel the corporation to follow efficiency criteria. If corporations are subject to the constraints of the competitive system, they have little room for discretionary actions that overwhelm employees and voters.

DOES ADVERTISING OVERWHELM CONSUMERS?

Vance Packard and others argue that since advertising hypnotizes consumers and voters and causes them to purchase goods and services they really do not want, corporations are free from consumer control [35, 339]. These writers believe that consumers' decisions are illegitimate because corporate advertising molds wants from infancy; hence, people become the easy prey of profit-greedy corporations. Others argue, in extreme opposition to this view, that wants are immutable and spring from an unchanging human nature. By this opposing argument, advertising is ineffective in the long run because consumers will spend their income only on what they wish to buy [SB 48]. What, then, is the role of advertising?

Phillip Nelson argues that although corporations are primarily interested in selling more products, they do provide information to consumers through advertising [330]. For products that can be tested before purchase, advertising provides information that one can verify directly; consumers can hardly be misled if they can detect the difference between advertised and actual qualities before purchase. Potential customers will detect misleading corporate advertising, and the guilty corporation will suffer a decline in its credibility.

In the case of products that cannot be tested before purchase, it is important for consumers to discover information about the products through advertising and brand names. Advertising is not distributed randomly over brands and media, and it is more likely to be seen by those whose tastes the brands best serve. Consumers assume quite confidently that the satisfaction value per dollar from an advertised brand is higher, since the firm wishes to protect the reputation of its brand name. The major control that consumers have in this case is reflected in their decision to repeat—or not repeat—the purchase of the brand.

Besides advertising, people use the recommendations of relatives, friends, and consumer magazines to make purchases. The greater the frequency of purchase (for gasoline, for example) and the higher the cost (of automobiles, for example), the less will be a consumer's reliance on advertising alone to make a decision. Since corporations plan to remain in business, they have an incentive to advertise accurately; the circumstances under which advertisers have the greatest temptation to deceive or mislead are those in which consumers are least likely to rely upon them and in which their credibility is the hardest to establish.

That total expenditures for advertising, as a percentage of gross national product, declined from 2.52 percent in 1929 and 1933 to 2.33 percent in 1966 suggests that advertising has become less important in our society, or that firms have become more efficient communicators. That only 16 percent of total advertising expenditures is for television while 73 percent is for the distribution of literature suggests, moreover, that informing potential customers may be more important than manipulating them [*Printer's Ink*, 25 August 1967].

Television advertising people regard their work as primarily creative rather than manipulative. That their success is far from universal is attested to by the 80 percent of new products that fail each year. Not only are viewers not manipulated by commercials; they also find commercials occasionally irritating and invariably easy to ignore. Five-year-old children are cynical about commercials. When it comes to manipulating minds, says Stephen Greyser, "television advertising people just aren't that fancy." Commercials can only arouse an interest which is already there. Americans, for instance, do not like body odor. Donald Kanter argues that "advertising didn't put that anxiety into the culture" [*Wall Street Journal,* 1 November 1976: 1, 22]. If a scented soap has the smell of rotten garbage, the most seductive commercial cannot make it a commercial success.

Wants need not be immutable to be legitimate. Is anyone born with an innate taste for good music or good literature? As people develop through different stages of their lives, their wants change. Consumers are informed by advertising, by experience, by education, and by their peers of the choices available to them. By anticipating these wants, advertising does not necessarily make them synthetic.

From this brief consideration of the role of advertising, it appears that consumers strongly direct the economic system and its corporations. Entrepreneurs and managers, while determining the range of goods from which consumers can choose, and while bearing the financial responsibility for their decisions, are under the command of consumers who choose among suppliers. This relationship limits to a considerable degree the area for corporate discretionary action.

HOW GOVERNMENT ENHANCES CORPORATE POWER

If competitive forces are prevented from operating—for instance, under government regulation—corporate power over employees and voters can grow [SB 16, SB 21, SB 42]. If stockholders' rights to profits are restricted or absent, for example, as in a public utility or a nonprofit or publicly owned corporation, managers may enjoy freedom to divert corporate resources to their own purposes. Stockholders, if they exist, do not bear the costs of this discretionary action if the corporation is already earning its upper legal limit, since they cannot receive extra benefits themselves. Many of the large corporations in this category are public utilities.

If legislation is enacted to control corporate power, vast new powers may be created that are virtually unreviewable by the legislatures or by the courts. The result may be that the government creates wealth for large corporations by establishing and preserving their market privileges, by enforcing cartel pricing, and by undertaking, subsidizing, or insuring risky ventures. Failing corporations may be rescued by tax benefits, defense contracts, or nationalization. The voting public, in these cases, pays the bills through taxes or through increased consumer expenditures. There is little or no recourse.

Monopoly power gained through government also enables managers to capture profits in cost-enhancing activities that can be detrimental to employees' and voters' interests. Armen Alchian and Reuben Kessel find that in the banking and insurance industries, in which government regulations protect monopoly power, racial prejudice in hiring is enhanced; if the firms in these industries were subjected to competition, managers who discriminated would be outcompeted by those who did not [12]. So, the voices of employees and voters can be overwhelmed by corporations with government-protected monopoly positions; and, this is most likely to occur in regulated industries.

THE DISCIPLINE OF INTERNAL INCENTIVES AND CAPITAL MARKETS

Despite some monopoly power in product markets, corporate activity still might be restrained by the discipline of capital markets and by internal incentives. If the management of a firm sacrifices wealth for growth, for instance, the value of the firm's stock will become relatively low, the firm will have difficulty getting bank loans, and it may suffer lower bond ratings. If stocks become undervalued, an aggressive management elsewhere can acquire the assets, effect a merger, or threaten the firm's management with a take-over bid [SB 20, SB 21, SB 43]. Shorey Peterson argues, accordingly, that the capital market is an effective control mechanism that encourages corporations to pursue efficiency as a goal and that limits corporate discretion [348].

Corporate managers are also influenced by internal incentives to pursue efficiency as a goal. Managers are likely to have stock options, rights, or bonuses that are correlated with profits. Thus, wielding discretionary power instead of maximizing wealth does not yield permanent gains for managers but results in lower pecuniary salaries as other managers compete for the more attractive jobs [SB 55]. Hence, internal incentives for management encourage the pursuit of efficiency rather than the free exercise of discretionary power and thus limit the corporate potential for overwhelming the voices of employees and voters.

THE POWER OF LABOR

Detractors of the corporation justify the rise of the labor union movement on the grounds that employees lack an opportunity to participate in decision making. Stephen Marglin believes that corporate managers make employees acquiesce to work that destroys human personality, while Galbraith blames upper and middle management for adverse working conditions [293, 189]. Both hail the Yugoslav firm as the prototype of the employee-controlled firm, even though it does not differ substantially from a large corporation that maximizes profit per worker [184].

Although corporate managers generate options and evaluate them, they are not superior disciplinary agents. Their power over employees is not nearly as great as that depicted by the caricature of the corporate "boss." They continually renegotiate employment terms that must be acceptable to employees, since each employee is free to quit. The worst a corporation can do to an employee is to fire and sue him or her. This does not represent enough power to overwhelm an employee except in circumstances in which the employee's alternative opportunities are severely limited [SB 7, SB 8].

SUMMARY

While advertising influences consumers' decisions, it does not free corporations from the influence of consumers. Competition in the product market forces firms to pursue efficiency; but even in the absence of competition, the need to resort to the capital market for funds, the threat of a take-over, and internal incentives push managers to pursue efficiency. Both restrictions on distributing profits and government regulations are the most important conditions allowing corporations to overwhelm employees and voters. While many aberrations impede the functioning of the corporate system, the belief that corporate power and wealth overwhelm the voices of individual employees and voters, as a condemnation of the corporate system, hardly seems justified.

ADDITIONAL READINGS: 7, 11, 34, 52, 181, 186, 187, 207, 223, 229, 292, 294, 295, 315, 317, 324, 331, 338, 339, 390.

50. Are Large Corporations Inefficient?

HAROLD DEMSETZ
*Department of Economics, UCLA
and the Hoover Institution*

Editor's Summary   Large firms are said to be inefficient and bound
up in red tape because their very size insulates them from competition.
Red tape occurs most often in governmental agencies or in nonprofit
institutions. Since large private firms do face competition and manage
to survive and grow under competitive pressures, their observed
success is unlikely to be linked to inefficiency. Indeed, statistical
evidence tends to support the proposition that large firm size is
associated with efficient operation. Large firms in concentrated
industries tend to be relatively low-cost firms. Efficiency, not
concentration, explains why large firms make greater profits than small
firms in a given industry.

The notion that size and inefficiency are linked is attributable partly to
common exposure to bureaucratic red tape and partly to the belief that
large size insulates a corporation from the pressures of competition. The
bureaucratic red tape that people experience most often is encountered
when interacting with governmental agencies and with other large not-
profit-maximizing organizations, such as the University of California.

THE REASONS FOR SIZE

It is not clear that such experiences are validly generalized to include
profit-maximizing organizations. Nor is it clear that bureaucratic complexities are not without compensating efficiencies elsewhere in the large

organizations. Purchasers of a commodity *may* buy from a large organization, even though they know that any complaints they have about their purchase must pass through a longer organizational chain before they get satisfaction. They may be convinced that ultimately they are more likely to get satisfaction from the large firm than from a smaller firm. Or, their confidence in the product may be sufficiently high (or the product's price may be sufficiently low) to warrant accepting the possibility of being forced to complain to a large organization. There are obvious compensating advantages in such cases that offset the costs of interacting with a large organization.

Large firms, of course, do face competition. Any market power they may have is severely limited, and there is no reason to expect that power to be used in a manner that raises production costs. Large firms not only continue to meet substantial competition but also succeed in growing larger in the face of such competition. This kind of success is unlikely to be associated with inefficiency.

SETTING NADER ET AL. STRAIGHT

The myth that size and inefficiency are linked is rampant, especially in works of advocacy that seek significant alterations in policy toward corporations. A current example is *Taming the Giant Corporation,* which is devoted to an attack on the corporation [328]. The belief that size and inefficiency are linked is important in that book. Not only do the authors attack the large corporation for its alleged errant activity; they also attack those who believe that there is evidence that large corporations are efficient. Thus, the authors of *Taming the Giant Corporation,* in two sentences, simultaneously criticize the large corporation and this writer.

> Conservative economist Harold Demsetz, speaking for another school of criticism, argues that "Embracing the market concentration doctrine through legislation is thus very likely to penalize the success and superior performance upon which depends the progress and wealth of this nation." Demsetz wrongly assumes that if a firm is big it must be efficient, when quite often the precise opposite is the case [328: 230].

The quotation actually contains three assertions: that I am a conservative economist; that I have spoken for a school of criticism; and that I have incorrectly *assumed* that bigness and efficiency are correlated.

Perhaps this is to be expected in a work devoted to advocacy. That advocacy is the purpose is obvious even to the most naïve. I am clearly labeled "conservative" in an obvious attempt to warn the reader that my political philosophy influences my statements, but no labels are assigned to John Blair, Gardiner Means, John Kenneth Galbraith, and Joe Bain, among others, when their opinions are quoted in the same chapter as is mine. I have no knowledge, furthermore, of a school of thought or criticism bearing on the issue of corporate size. My peers at UCLA, Chicago, Harvard, and MIT do not divide into any clear intellectual camps on this issue. While on another occasion I would rise to challenge these assertions, it is more appropriate here to move to the substantive issue: that "Demsetz wrongly assumes that if a firm is big it must be efficient, when quite often the precise opposite is the case."

I did not *assume* that bigness and efficiency are correlated; nor did I claim that if a firm is big it *must* be efficient. Rather, I gathered broad-based statistical evidence concerning two alternative explanations of the correlation between profit rate and market concentration that several earlier studies uncovered. This evidence, not any assumption of mine, supports hypotheses in which the general superior efficiency of larger firms in concentrated industries plays an important role, and it casts suspicion on explanations not assigning this role to large firms. The usual alternative, a belief that the correlation between profit rate and concentration derives solely from the greater ease of implicitly or explicitly colluding in more concentrated markets, is such a suspicious explanation [SB 42, SB 53].

The data underlying the statistical evidence include information from all American census industries, but no single industry or firm is separated for special analysis. In no way can one interpret such data to imply that if a firm is big, it *must* be efficient; nor did I claim such an implication. The evidence supports a general relationship between firm size and efficiency, but not necessarily one that is correct for each and every large firm.

DEFLATING THE COLLUSION HYPOTHESIS

The authors of *Taming the Giant Corporation* enthusiastically embrace the simple collusion hypothesis.

> A monopoly or well-coordinated cartel could obviously charge a higher-than-competitive price and make it stick since the consumer would lack a cheaper alternative. Yet when a few firms dominate an oligopolistic industry, a system of mutually beneficial "parallel pricing" or "price leadership" can achieve the same results [328: 213].

This explanation implies that *all or most* firms in more concentrated industries earn higher profit rates than their counterparts in unconcentrated industries. A successfully colluding industry, or one that practices parallel pricing or price leadership in the manner the authors depict, is an industry that will deliver higher profit rates to most of its constituent firms.

But, an examination of the data leads to a conclusion that is strongly inconsistent with this implication. Firms in concentrated industries do not tend to earn higher profit rates than firms in unconcentrated industries once one controls for the size of the firms in the study. The correlation between profit rate and market concentration for firms of a given size is very weak and often negative. But, the largest firms do tend to earn higher profit rates than smaller firms, and there tends to be a greater frequency of larger firms in the more concentrated industries. Hence, if firm size is ignored, the correlation between profit rate and market concentration appears larger than it really is.

I presented part of the evidence bearing on this problem in a table on the page facing the one from which the authors took their quotation of me [129: 178–179]. They chose to ignore the evidence. Table 4 is an up-to-date version of that table; its content is in full agreement with the substantive content of the original table.

Table 4 presents correlations between profit rate and concentration for firms in five different size categories and for each of five years. Each entry shows the size and direction of a correlation for an asset class. Theoretically, the correlation coefficient can vary from +1, which indicates that profit rate and concentration increase in direct proportion, to −1, indicating that an increase in concentration is associated with a proportional reduction in profit rate. Most of the entries in the table are insignificantly different from a correlation coefficient of 0, signifying no reliable association between the two variables.

Many of the positive correlations between profit rate and concentration that several earlier studies uncovered can be attributed to variations in the size of firms, with concentrated industries containing relatively more large firms, and not to the degree to which markets are concentrated. If size of firm is ignored, the correlation between profit rate and concentration becomes much more significant for each year.

Table 4 Correlations between Profit Rate and Concentration by Asset Size of Firms

Asset Size ($000)	Year				
	1958	1963	1966	1967	1970
0–500	−.09	−.19†	−.09	−.01	−.38*
500–5,000	.08	−.00	−.06	−.07	−.01
5,000–50,000	.16	.11	.04	−.05	−.00
50,000–100,000	−.06	.01	.09	.10	−.03
100,000 and up	−.00	.16	.16	.16	.28†

*Statistically significant at 1 percent error level.

†Statistically significant at 5 percent error level.

Table 5 Rates of Return[a] by Size of Firm and Industry Concentration

Four-Firm Concentration Ratios (1963 or 1970)	Average of 1963 and 1969 Rates of Return by Asset Size			
	Under $500,000	$500,000 to $5,000,000	$5,000,000 to $50,000,000	Over $50,000,000
10–20%	6.9%	9.7%	10.9%	10.2%
20–30	5.3	8.9	9.6	9.7
30–40	5.1	8.7	9.9	10.4
40–50	4.6	9.1	10.0	8.8
50–60	4.8	10.3	10.2	13.2
Over 60[b]	−1.3	10.0	10.9	20.3

[a]Profit before taxes and interest—total assets.

[b]Three industries.

SOURCE: Harold Demsetz. *The Market Concentration Doctrine* (Washington, D.C.: American Enterprise Institute, 1973).

This general pattern of correlations cannot be explained easily by the kind of simple collusion or conscious parallelism hypothesis that Nader et al. endorse. According to this theory, a firm of given size should enjoy a higher profit rate if it is in an oligopolistic industry, as opposed to an unconcentrated industry. Clearly, the evidence fails to support this expectation.

Besides the weak correlation between profit rate and concentration for firms of a given size, the data indicate a strong tendency for the profitability of large firms, relative to the profitability of smaller firms, to be greater, the more concentrated the industry. This relationship appears in Table 5, which is based on census and IRS data for 95 industries in 1963 and 69 (redefined by the IRS) comparable industries in 1969. Previous studies of the correlation between concentration and profit rate generally relied on census and IRS data for industry classifications, implicitly assuming that, in the main, firms classified in the same industry really compete in the same market. If this is so, the table indicates that the relative cost of serving a market is lower for large firms than for small firms if the market is highly concentrated.

THE REAL CAUSES OF LARGE SIZE

In the apparent absence of legal barriers to entry, and in the presence of competitive rivalry, the persistent concentration of industry's output in a few firms would derive mainly from these firms' superiority in producing and marketing products. The cost advantage that gives rise to concentration may be reflected in economies of scale that are generally available to all firms that achieve large size. Or, that advantage may be associated uniquely with the superiority of particular firms. Such firms grow relative to others, and as a result of either kind of cost advantage, markets having such firms will become more concentrated at the same time that the superiority of these firms generates high profit rates for them. Even though large firms in a concentrated industry can generally achieve lower unit costs (and, hence, higher profit rates) than smaller firms operating in the same industry, at the margin the capacity of these superior firms may be strained so that their prices will be high enough to allow smaller, higher-cost firms to survive at "more normal" profit rates. To bring smaller, less efficient firms into production, prices must be high enough to cover their unit costs, which means that the large, superior firms will record relatively high profit rates.

This explanation is consistent with the two statistical facts presented in the tables: the absence of a positive correlation between profit rate and market concentration for small- and moderate-size firms (such firms do about as well in concentrated industries as they do in unconcentrated industries), and the presence of greater differentials between the profit rates of large and small firms in concentrated industries than in unconcentrated industries. It is possible to construct more complex collusion models that are more in agreement with these facts. But, it is difficult to do so unless the larger firms in concentrated industries have a cost advantage. Hence, one can conclude *from the evidence* that the larger firms in concentrated industries tend to be relatively low-cost firms. While the issues that such evidence raises currently are being debated, to my knowledge there has not been any refutation of the evidence itself.

There is a great variety of evidence concerning firm size and efficiency. I have used a large mass of data describing census industries for those years in which such data are roughly comparable. I used no special selection criteria, and anyone can duplicate the experiment. It is also possible to provide evidence by pointing to the example of a particular case or by quoting a particular expert. Such evidence is not without value, but it must be mined deeply and carefully, and the method of selection must be clearly revealed if it is to have a significant impact. Failing these tasks—and the authors of *Taming the Giant Corporation* clearly do fail—the way is always open to critics to present counterexamples or counterquotations.

By way of example, consider how the authors attack concentration in the automobile industry.

> Reasons of efficiency do not compel General Motors to control over 50 percent of the domestic auto market . . . George Romney, then president

of American Motors, told a Senate Committee in 1958 that a small auto company could efficiently produce 180,000 to 220,000 cars a year. Bain put it at 300,000 to 600,000 cars and Lawrence White, fifteen years later ... at 400,000 to 800,000 [328: 217].

The reader is entitled to wonder about the variance in these estimates, about why the structure of the auto industry has persistently moved toward a greater concentration, and, also, about the failure of the authors to present other opinions and estimates to the contrary [301]. Plenty are available. In a *Los Angeles Times* story (November 14, 1976) about the rough times being experienced by American Motors, the current president of American Motors, Roy D. Chapin, Jr., describes the various measures his company must take now that buyers are shunning the small cars American Motors specializes in producing. The picture presented is one of touch and go, with bankruptcy lurking in the background. The story ends with an astute observation by Walter J. Kirschberger, an auto industry analyst with Paine, Webber, Jackson and Curtis: "What [American Motors is] trying to do in the auto market may be just impossible. [That is] to compete in just one segment of the market (small cars) and be in the 'right' segment all the time. So far, they have shown it can't be done."

This observation, that large automobile firms experience less risk by virtue of their more varied product mix, largely escaped the notice of Romney, Bain, and White when they estimated the minimum number of cars required to achieve low production costs. And, a great number of the references and quotations carefully selected by the authors of *Taming the Giant Corporation* can be deflated. But that is a task for someone else.

ADDITIONAL READINGS: 30, 31, 32, 68, 70, 72, 80, 103, 163, 359, 415, 422, 442.

51. Do Corporations Earn Excessive Profits?

KENNETH CLARKSON
Law and Economics Center
University of Miami School of Law

Editor's Summary   Corporations are often accused of reaping excessive profits. But, aggregate, real, after-tax profits have changed little in the past twenty-five years, and profits as a percentage of gross national product have declined substantially during this period. A large percentage of the variations in profits among industries and firms, furthermore, stems from traditional accounting practices. The extensive tests relating profits to particular industry characteristics are so plagued by specification errors, measurement errors, and sampling biases that the results provide little evidence concerning the specific factors that might contribute to overall profitability. Profitability and monopoly power, in sum, loom too large in public debates about corporations.

For many years, the alleged evils of capitalism and corporate organization have been associated with the word "profits." Researchers have used economic and statistical analysis to investigate the relationships among profitability, firm size and entry barriers, risk, advertising, executive compensation, and business combinations [32, 105, 163, 203, 276, 304, 428]. Hall and Weiss, for example, find that larger firms generally are more profitable than smaller firms [203]. Many researchers, including Joe Bain, show that entry barriers contribute to profitability [32]. Several studies also find a positive correlation between risk bearing and profitability [158]. And, some studies reveal a positive relationship between advertising and profitability, between executive compensation and profitability, and between business combinations and profitability.

Other studies, concentrating on specification errors, measurement errors, and sampling biases, find no relationship between entry barriers and profitability, advertising and profitability, and combinations achieved through consolidation and concentration rates [68, 69, 133, 161, 337]. Existing studies, in sum, do not provide conclusive evidence about specific factors that might contribute to overall profitability.

THE DECLINE OF PROFITS

Rather than investigate individual studies and proposed relationships between market structure and profitability, one can investigate the overall operating environment that constrains individual firms and their profita-

Table 6 Nominal and Real After-Tax Profits, 1950–1976

Year	Nominal After-Tax Profits (Billions of Dollars)	Real After-Tax Profits (Billions of Dollars)*	After-Tax Profits As a Percentage of Receipts†	After-Tax Profits As a Percentage of GNP
1950	15.7	35.1	7.1	5.5
1951	15.5	32.1	4.8	4.7
1952	16.0	32.5	4.3	4.6
1953	15.2	30.6	4.3	4.2
1954	17.0	34.1	4.5	4.6
1955	22.6	45.4	5.4	5.7
1956	20.9	41.4	5.3	5.0
1957	20.6	39.4	4.8	4.7
1958	18.5	34.5	4.2	4.1
1959	24.6	45.4	4.8	5.1
1960	23.9	43.5	4.4	4.7
1961	24.1	43.3	4.3	4.6
1962	30.9	55.0	4.5	5.5
1963	33.4	58.7	4.7	5.6
1964	39.0	67.7	5.2	6.1
1965	46.2	78.8	5.6	6.2
1966	48.9	81.1	5.6	6.5
1967	46.8	75.5	5.0	5.9
1968	46.4	71.8	5.1	5.3
1969	41.8	61.4	4.8	4.5
1970	33.4	46.3	4.0	3.4
1971	39.5	52.5	4.1	3.7
1972	50.5	65.0	4.3	4.3
1973	50.4	61.0	4.7	3.9
1974	32.4	35.4	5.5	2.3
1975	42.4	42.4	4.6	2.8
1976	53.9	50.9	5.5	3.2

*Based on CPI index where 1975 = 100.0.

†Manufacturing corporations only.

SOURCE: *Economic Report of the President*, 1977.

bility. Here, the results are far more conclusive. Since 1950, real after-tax profits (adjusted for price level changes) have fallen substantially with respect to gross national product, despite the relative stability of after-tax profits as a percentage of receipts. Table 6 shows individual after-tax profits (in nominal dollars) for the years 1950–1976 (column 2) and after-tax profits adjusted for changes in the price level (column 3). Columns 4 and 5 of the table show after-tax profits as a percentage of receipts and as a percentage of gross national product. In the last two dozen years, after-tax profits as a percentage of GNP have fallen by roughly 50 percent of their former levels. Between 1950 and 1956, the ratios of after-tax profits to GNP averaged 4.9 percent, which is 1.5 percentage points, or approximately 45 percent, higher than the average for 1970–1976.

VARIATIONS IN PROFITS

Some detractors of corporations, at this point, may agree that overall profitability has declined but continue to argue that individual firms or industries are earning excessive profits [SB 50]. There is variation in profitability among various industries as well as among firms within individual industries. Profit variation is, of course, one of the fundamental distinguishing characteristics of a market system. Variations in profits serve as a mechanism from which business people receive signals to move resources from lower-valued (less profitable) ventures to higher-valued ones [SB 21].

THE FUNCTION OF PROFITS

Profits provide the major instrument of consumer control over producers. Temporary variations in profits often are the consequence of a major shift in consumer demand for one product relative to others. Suppose a change in preferences leads to an increase in the demand for a commodity. Until existing production can be expanded, individual consumers will bid for the existing production and inventories, thus creating higher prices and, in most cases, higher profits. These profits, in turn, provide the signal for individual manufacturers to expand production and for new enterprises to enter and begin producing the now more highly valued good. Subsequently, resources move to those industries with brisk sales and higher profits; this shift results in greater production, lower prices, and improved resource allocation. Thus, the "public interest" (the outcome of lower prices and increased production) coincides completely with the business person's self-interest in seeking higher profits.

THE SOURCES OF PROFITS AND PROFIT VARIATIONS

Variations in profits are relatively easier to understand than the actual profit levels themselves. Existing theories of the forces causing variations in profits can be placed into three major categories: first, profits are implicit factor returns to entrepreneurs or to other resources; second, profits result from uncertainty; and third, profits result from monopoly.

In the first case, profits are merely implicit factor returns to business people and represent a payment for their special skills and forgone options. Thus, a business person who earns $25,000 a year by operating a retail trade establishment may actually incur losses by not becoming an airline pilot and accepting a wage of $30,000 a year. Inherent in each of the factor-return explanations is the direct relationship between innovation and entrepreneurship, with profits providing the motivating force leading to new products, processes, and other technological achievements that yield positive net benefits to society [382].

Most accounting profits reflect implicit factor returns. High accounting profits, in many cases, are a direct consequence of intangible capital that does not appear as capital on the balance sheet [95]. Profits may vary, depending on the method of financing an organization. If a firm is financed entirely by bonds, there could be relatively small profits, since interest is a deductible expense in determining profits for tax purposes. If an enterprise is largely equity-funded, on the other hand, profits may appear to be relatively large, even though the firm may be engaged in exactly the same activities (with identical sales and costs of operation) as the bond-financed firm.

The second explanation of profit variation is related to the uncertainty of future outcomes. Profits, according to this explanation, represent a payment for persons who engage in differing degrees of risk-bearing activities. Thus, profits become a payment from those persons who are risk-averse (those who do not want to bear the consequences of highly variable future outcomes) to those persons who are willing to bear risk and, hence, expect to receive profits as a compensation for bearing risk [242].

The third theory of profit variation views profits as the reflection of any permanent wedge between unit revenues and cost. Profits, in this sense, represent a return to specific entry barriers (such as government licenses or certification), or to a legally enforced cartel, or even to collusive actions.

CONCLUSION

The overall decline in profitability over the last two decades, as well as the inclusive evidence regarding profits and existing measures of noncompetitive power, compel the conclusion that corporate profitability and monopoly power are overemphasized in public policy decisions.

ADDITIONAL READINGS: 69, 72, 91, 419, 442.

52. Are Corporate Profits a "Pot of Gold" That Can Eliminate Social Ills?

DONALD F. GORDON
Department of Economics
Simon Frazer University

Editor's Summary   Contrary to popular belief, corporate profits amount to only 2.5 percent of each sales dollar. If the government expropriated the entire $33 billion paid to stockholders in 1975, the proceeds would amount to a mere 2 percent of all personal income. Dividend recipients, moreover, include colleges and universities, charitable organizations, nonprofit foundations, and persons of modest means. If pension funds' share of dividends is subtracted, the pot of gold amounts to $20 billion a year, a sum sufficient to grant a once-and-for-all increase in labor income of 2 percent. If the entire corporate pot of gold were drained, total social expenditures by the government could be increased by only 7 percent.

The bulk of people in the Western world for many centuries attributed much of the everyday evils and disasters of life to the existence of witches and demons in league with the devil. While perhaps more prevalent among the illiterate, the belief was shared by a goodly measure of educated opinion. It was thought that some control of these evils could be achieved by eliminating witches and demons; thus, up through the eighteenth century many persons suffered excruciating tortures and executions in the application of this public policy.

THE MYTH OF TODAY AND THE MYTH OF YESTERDAY

There is a substantial sense in which corporations have come to play the same role as the witches and demons of earlier times. The bulk of the population believes either that corporations are directly responsible for the majority of real or alleged social ills or that corporations represent a pot of gold, so to speak, that one can tap to eliminate most of these evils. From politicians running on about "obscene profits" to sober neoconservatives worrying about the "power" of "corporate capitalism," there is a crescendo of impatience in calling for public policies to drain this pot of gold, just as earlier there was an increasing demand for a public policy to eliminate witches. The analogy with witches and demons is persuasive, since the pot of gold theory is virtually as much a figment of the imagination as was the former devil theory [SB 51]. One important difference is that today more of the relatively better-educated people believe the pot of gold myth.

Today's myth seems much more irrational. Given the appalling ignorance from which few could escape in earlier times, the hypotheses concerning witches and demons were not entirely implausible or even unscientific. Scientific merit is always relative to existing knowledge. If a plague decimated the population, or if a loved one died mysteriously, who could say, with the then existing state of knowledge, that it was irrational to ascribe the event to the dark satanic forces that possessed, say, an eccentric neighbor? The beliefs of the bulk of educated opinion concerning the place of the corporation, on the other hand, are much less understandable, as they could be destroyed after spending a few minutes with the *Statistical Abstract of the United States* [411].

PUBLIC ATTITUDES TOWARD CORPORATE PROFITS

In 1975, George Gallup's organization polled juniors and seniors in high schools and in colleges and universities on their understanding of the level of corporate profits as a percentage of sales. High school students believed that profits account for 30 percent of each sales dollar, while those with four more years of education put the figure at 45 percent. The Department of Commerce, of course, reported profits from the sales of all United States corporations at 2.5 percent for 1973. Thus, four more years of education appear to have increased the misconception concerning the order of magnitude of an elementary economic fact!

The Opinion Research Council found in 1973 that a cross section of American adults believed that of the total corporate earnings and employee costs summed together, employees received 25 percent and corporate owners 75 percent. The true figures for that year were the reverse: 88 percent for employees and 12 percent for owners. If it is any consolation, the Canadian and West German publics hold very similar myths.

The figure used in the Gallup survey (earnings as a percentage of sales) is, for many purposes, not a relevant number. If, for instance, labor costs amounted to x percent of an automobile repair bill, one would not be likely to judge that percentage as fair or unfair unless one knew how much labor receives per hour. Similarly, one would want to know how much an investor receives per dollar invested before assessing the fairness or justice of the monetary rate of return.

There is some sense, nevertheless, in focusing on the ratio of profits to sales. The members of the public may understand the concept, or at least think they do, so that they answer the interviewers. The ratio, more importantly, is probably a crude indication to the members of the public of the amount by which their real incomes could rise or the amount of new funds available for government programs, if somehow there were no "profit system."

THE FALLACY OF EXPROPRIATION

Suppose, for example, that the 45 percent profit rate on sales is a crude gauge of what our educated young think is the size of the pot of gold: the corporate share of all output. This figure implies that if we could somehow, without cost, expropriate the corporate share of all output, we could raise the output for other purposes by some 82 percent (45/55). By implication, such a hypothetical transfer could raise the other parts of personal income by over $970 billion (using 1975 figures)—surely enough to both abolish all social evils and provide "us" (as opposed to the corporations) with a whopping rise in real income. Of course, this is all fantasy. The implications of the Opinion Research Council figures are even more ludicrous; the figures suggest a potential raise for corporate employees of 300 percent, if the employees can simply expropriate the alleged corporate earnings.

One can gain some perspective on these fantasies by asking what indeed would be available to reformers if they could remove, at no cost, what they want from whatever pot of gold is really available. In asking this question, I am concerned neither with labor versus capital nor with the distribution of income between the rich and the rest of us. There are few cries for the expropriation of interest payments as "usury" for the sake of enlarging social or environmental programs. Nor do there seem to be complaints about high incomes as such; for example, there is general acceptance of the high incomes of actresses and star athletes. The corporations (presumably, the owners of the corporations), however, are the modern versions of the demons and witches.

Suppose, then, that we simply nationalized all corporations. Leaving aside the questions of operating efficiency, future equity capital, or the justice of the whole scheme, what then would be available for other purposes? In 1975 the total after-tax earnings of all United States corporations was $65.3 billion. Corporate taxes, of course, have already been expropriated and cannot be twice confiscated. The owners of corporate stocks, however, received only $33.1 billion in dividends. This $33.1 billion (or 2.6 percent of all personal income) is a reasonable and tangible measure of the wealth and power of corporate capitalism.

These dividends are all that the stockholders receive because they account for the entire pot of gold. Undistributed profits *are* reinvested, and in some cases an individual stockholder may sell his or her shares in the future for a capital gain because of these reinvested earnings. The stockholder can add this gain to his or her dividends in calculating personal advantage. But, that is not true for all shareholders taken together, for when one owner sells out, another puts in an equal amount (less commissions). Dividends, therefore, are the *only* gains taken out of firms by corporate owners as a group.

There are other aspects of these reinvested earnings and potential capital gains. It is doubtful if those who attack corporate capitalism really would wish to reduce these investments, since they are the basis for more productive jobs in the future. Over the past decade real wage increases in the United States have been drastically lower than those in any other industrial nation, the next closest being over five times what they have been here. The reinvested earnings have also been somewhat modest: only $10 billion in 1975, when some $23 billion is subtracted from the $65 billion to reflect inventory replacement and true depreciation. Finally, anyone who still believes that the available flow should include capital gains as well as dividends should consider that from 1965 to 1975 the real return after allowing for inflation on all stocks in the Standard and Poor Index was *minus* 20 percent. By this line of reasoning there is a negative pot of gold, whatever that is. (As of April 1977, there has been an approximately zero gain in the stock market averages since the end of 1975.)

It is doubtful that the opponents of corporations would consider the entire $33.1 billion (or 2.6 percent of 1975 personal income) as really available for other purposes. Currently about one-third of dividends goes to pension funds, and surely the old-age pensions of wage and salary workers are not part of the pot of gold! There are also, of course, millions of other direct and indirect owners in relatively modest circumstances, not to mention colleges and universities, and charitable and philanthropic foundations.

Suppose that we somewhat arbitrarily take $20 billion, or 1.8 percent of personal income in 1975, as a reasonably high estimate of the amount available. By itself this may appear to be a large figure, even an obscene one. But, one gains a different perspective by considering the figure's relative magnitude. In 1975, for example, $20 billion could have provided a once-and-for-all increase in labor income (including a modest allowance for the self-employed) of 2 percent. That sum is about 4.2 percent of all government expenditures for the year 1974 and less than half of the *increase* in those expenditures from 1973 to 1974. It is about 7 percent of the total social welfare outlays of all governments for 1975 and only 42 percent of the *increase* in those outlays from 1974 to 1975.

Thus the corporate pot of gold hypothesis, albeit widely held, is a myth. No matter how one measures it, if we expropriated all the "surplus" income of the great and not-so-great corporations—that is to say, if we removed entirely the spark plug of the whole free enterprise system— there would remain very little available for other purposes.

THE FAILURE OF THE ECONOMISTS

As a teacher of economics for over thirty years, I believe the economics profession has a lot to answer for by way of errors of omission concerning this abysmal misconception about the very basis of our economy and society. (Our colleagues in the humanities and other social sciences have perhaps contributed through errors of commission.) We have excellent analytic textbooks, but they lack crucial empirical content. When I have discussed data such as this before undergraduates (in very recent classes, I should add), I have had the impression I was being met with complete incredulity.

It is only reasonable to suppose that misinformation regarding the most elementary facts has had a powerful effect on attitudes toward a whole host of public policies. The typical student may consider economic efficiency and even economic freedom to be worthy goals; surely, however, these goals are weak competition for the myth that there is a huge pot of gold, a huge slush fund, capable of creating a minor utopia, if only public policy could tap the corporation.

ADDITIONAL READINGS: 95, 221, 300, 412.

53. Can Corporations Collude to Achieve Higher Profits?

M. BRUCE JOHNSON
Department of Economics
University of California at Santa Barbara

Editor's Summary   Large corporations are the targets of price-fixing allegations because of their size and visibility in an economy plagued by government-sponsored inflation. Price-fixing is virtually impossible unless a cartel can ensure that its members will abide by the agreement and that no new rivals can enter the industry. Consequently, price-fixing agreements can be enforced and entry blocked primarily through the good efforts of government regulatory agencies such as the Interstate Commerce Commission, the Civil Aeronautics Board, and the Department of Agriculture (through its Milk Marketing Orders).

$\mathbf{A}$dam Smith said it long ago: "People of the same trade seldom meet together, even for merriment and diversion, but the conversation ends in a conspiracy against the public, or in some contrivance to raise prices" [402: 128].

THE BACKGROUND OF PRICE-FIXING PROHIBITIONS

Economic and legal thought in the United States have judged collusion or conspiracy to fix prices to be the cause of serious social losses. An effective price conspiracy can distort the allocation of resources by leading to higher prices and lower rates of output than would prevail under competition. Section 1 of the Sherman Act, the 1890 basis of our contemporary antitrust law, prohibits "every contract, combination . . . or conspiracy in restraint of trade or commerce among the several states." Subsequent court decisions interpret the language of Section 1 to mean that all agreements among competing firms to fix prices, to restrict or pool output, to share markets on a prearranged basis, or otherwise to restrict the force of competition are illegal per se. Thus, the courts do not apply the "rule of reason" and examine the economic results of an alleged conspiracy: conspiracies to fix prices are illegal per se regardless of the effectiveness and consequences of a conspiracy, contract, or combination.

THE "MARKET" FOR ANTITRUST ACTIVITY

It is useful in this connection to consider the "market" for antitrust activity [SB 57, SB 58, SB 59, SB 60, SB 61]. The *demand* for government civil and criminal lawsuits against price-fixers, on the one hand, has increased in recent years for a variety of reasons. First, price-fixing charges are an apparently popular and plausible element in the package of antibusiness rhetoric that contemporary reformers use. Second, the size of large corporations in concentrated industries makes them obvious and easy targets. Third, the inflation of the 1970s has served to focus attention on the prices of corporate products, even though corporations are the mechanisms that transmit inflation rather than the causes of inflation [SB 37].

On the *supply* side, the increasing complexity of pervasive government regulations and controls makes corporations increasingly vulnerable to federal and state crackdowns, whether they be of an economic or political nature. The capricious and inconsistent legislation passed by Congress and the arbitrary rules and regulations promulgated by the myriad federal and state agencies place corporations in the same position as individual taxpayers: if the government wants to "get" them, it can.

WHY PRICE-FIXING FAILS

The time has come to assess the analytical importance of price-fixing as a viable, if illegal, business strategy. Other things being equal, the incentives for collusion are clear: higher prices and higher profits. It is also clear, however, that one can create and maintain an effective conspiracy to fix prices only at very high costs.

As a matter of law, it takes but *two* firms to conspire. Their combined market share is irrelevant to the fact of conspiracy. As a matter of economic analysis, however, it takes *all* the rivals in an industry to make an *effective* conspiracy. Any collection of firms that agrees to raise prices must enlist the support and agreement of all rivals in the industry. Otherwise, firms outside the conspiracy can exploit the situation by underpricing or underbidding the cartel and, hence, achieve increases in sales and market share. A conspiracy without complete participation by all firms in the industry shortly will fail, since the conspirators will suffer declining sales and profits.

If all the members of an industry agree to participate in a price-fixing arrangement, they must also agree on the "best" price to charge for their respective products. Agreement is extraordinarily difficult to reach, since each firm judges the best collusive price differently: each firm has its own cost structure, its own estimate of the responsiveness of sales to price changes for its product, and its own growth forecast. There is no reason to believe that the participants in a price conspiracy will bare their souls, open their books, and exchange all technical and cost data [SB 23, SB 24, SB 25, SB 26].

A price conspiracy, indeed, is inherently unstable because its participants are natural rivals, not partners. If the firms remain independent (as opposed to consolidated through a merger), each will jealously guard its own cost and technical data. Hence, negotiations over the "best price" will be complicated because few of the cards will be on the table.

Agreement pertaining to the allocation of business among the firms in a conspiracy and among the customers is also difficult to reach. Obviously, each member of a cartel prefers more business to less. If the allocation of sales is made on straightforward geographic lines, the danger of attracting the attention of the Justice Department is increased substantially. Hence, allocation schemes must be clever, complicated, and ostensibly unsystematic.

Joe Sims, a deputy antitrust chief, illustrates the government's preoccupation with the form rather than the substance of price-fixing in a statement quoted in *Business Week* [27 December 1976: 29]: "Merely following someone else's price rise is never an antitrust violation." Yet, *Business Week* reported that "Justice is now ready to sue over related actions—even a public announcement of a price change—which it views as a bid for tacit agreement by other producers."

Still other difficulties exist for conspirators. The participants must be wary of setting a price so high as to lose substantial sales to firms that produce goods that are close substitutes. The larger the number of firms in a conspiracy, in general, the more difficult it is for the conspirators to reach agreement on the best price and the best allocation of sales.

Everything else aside, the sine qua non of a successful price conspiracy is an effective mechanism for monitoring, policing, and enforcing cartel activity by the participants. The mere signaling of price information is irrelevant if every participant in a cartel has an incentive to cheat. A firm may agree to "hold the line" on the cartel price, but it will be strongly tempted to offer secret price concessions, hidden discounts, extra service, faster delivery times, and better quality. For a collusive agreement to be effective, therefore, some means of detecting, proscribing, and punishing cheating must be devised and implemented. Otherwise, the separate self-interests of the cartel participants will provide strong incentives to cheat with impunity.

EVIDENCE ABOUT PRICE-FIXING

The official record of revealed attempts to fix price supports these conclusions. Testimony from the great electrical conspiracy trial of the early 1960s indicates that meetings among the conspirators were characterized by acrimonious debate and accusations of cheating. Much time and energy were devoted to persuading conspiracy members to "get back in line."

The antitrust laws make it virtually impossible to establish an effective enforcement mechanism in a price-fixing cartel. Obviously, if one of the participants "breaks" the agreement, no legal remedies are available to the other participants. The cheater recognizes that the wrath of fellow conspirators cannot lead to deliberate public exposure and litigation. Price competition from rivals outside the conspiracy or from potential entrants attracted by the higher cartel prices, furthermore, is completely beyond the scope of the conspiracy's persuasive discipline. Since these rivals can charge a price just under the cartel's umbrella price and thereby capture a significant portion of industry sales, an additional destabilizing force works against the conspiracy. Members of the cartel will struggle over how to divide up a shrinking market.

The enforcement of illegal price-fixing agreements is most easily monitored if immediate price information is available to all. This condition is met in the case of sealed bidding for government contracts. Typically, the government calls for bids and opens those bids simultaneously at a public meeting. All bids are announced. The lowest bid wins, and there is no rebidding or renegotiation. Hence, firms in the bidding industry have strong incentives to engage in prior collusion because the government does not play one bidder off against another. (This competitive bidding is common in private markets.) The bids are revealed so that cheating by bidders can be detected instantly by members of the conspiracy. This is an ideal situation in which firms can collude to the extent that the government unwittingly makes possible the relatively easy policing of cheaters by conspiracy members.

Many of the famous price conspiracy cases of the past involved sealed bidding for government contracts. The famous electrical equipment conspiracy case of 1962 involved the sale of large power transformers, generators, and switchgear equipment to government agencies under a sealed-bid process. This contract system does not guarantee collusion, but it certainly invites it. However, even in this case the conspiracy broke down because of cheating on large contracts.

As a practical (that is, political) matter, antitrust actions against alleged price conspirators will continue. Aside from formal agreements between conspirators, the only evidence of effective collusion by secret conspirators would be the expenditure of resources on a mechanism to monitor and sanction cheaters and prevent the entry of new firms. Only the existence of such expenditures or the associated activity would be reliable evidence of collusion to fix prices. Because of its inherently surreptitious nature, evidence of collusive activities is scarce. In a study of several price-fixing agreements, Bjarke Fog finds that it is extremely difficult for firms to reach agreement on the best price for their cartel [165]. Participants view the motives of their fellow conspirators with considerable distrust and suspicion. Fundamental disagreements arise over what is the best short-run versus long-run policy for the conspiracy. Fog, in effect, finds that firms with different cost functions, different growth forecasts, and different responsiveness of sales to price changes prefer quite different price strategies for their cartel.

Fritz Voight finds a similar pattern in German cartels; the analysis and results are consistent with the participants' account of the electrical equipment conspiracy in the United States [452: 204]. Finally, more general evidence presented by Peter Asch and J. J. Seneca indicates that firms accused of price-fixing tend to be less profitable than other firms [23]. The authors find a consistently negative and statistically significant relationship between firm profitability and the presence of collusion. Naturally, these results are subject to interpretation, but they do indicate provisionally that it is very hard to initiate and maintain a successful, effective price conspiracy.

HOW GOVERNMENT FIXES PRICES

Earlier remarks suggest that a price-fixing conspiracy is very difficult to initiate and virtually impossible to run successfully unless a cartel has an effective means of ensuring that its members will abide by the agreement and that no new rivals can enter the industry. The odds, therefore, are overwhelmingly against a cartel operating in the unregulated, free market in contemporary America.

A growing number of industries, however, have been able to enlist the support of the government in their efforts to fix prices and otherwise monopolize their respective areas of business. Members of the trucking industry, for example, gather together in rate bureaus to fix prices and carve up the market among themselves, while the Interstate Commerce Commission looks on with an approving eye and enforces the agreements reached at the price-fixing sessions. Domestic trunk airlines, as another example, have the Civil Aeronautics Board as their enforcement mechanism; no new competition has been allowed to enter the industry since the CAB began operations in 1938. The market is carved up among the existing members of the airline cartel, and all rates are sanctioned and enforced by the CAB. Producers of milk in many metropolitan area milksheds, as a third example, have the Department of Agriculture (and, occasionally, the President of the United States) to fix milk prices and ensure that no member of the cartel deviates from the set prices. The list goes on.

Many business people, in large and small corporations alike, seem to prefer the quiet, orderly life. Competition, they claim, is ruinous and leads to chaos in the market. Unfortunately, a growing number of business leaders would prefer that their organizations become public utilities rather than remain as private firms competing in the open market. Consider, for instance, the comments of Thornton Bradshaw, president of the Atlantic Richfield Refining Company, a major domestic oil company:

> The free market mechanism never has worked for oil because there has always been too much oil or too little. . . . Letting OPEC set U.S. oil prices is tantamount to handing over control of our national future to other nations. . . . Therefore, I am reluctantly drawn to the third alternative— the permanent management of crude oil prices by the U.S. government. Under such a plan the government would first set a goal for crude oil production and then set a price that makes it possible to meet that goal [64: 103–104].

It goes without saying that Mr. Bradshaw would expect the government to set a price for oil that would eliminate "destructive, chaotic" competition and ensure a "satisfactory, predictable" level of profits for a newly formed, government-sponsored domestic oil cartel.

THE PARADOX OF PRICE-FIXING REGULATION

Price-fixing may indeed generate social costs and other undesirable consequences for the general public. Yet, it is paradoxical that the courts have ordered some convicted price-fixers to confess their sins in public speeches before public service and business groups while, at the same time, executives of some airline and oil companies are applauded for making speeches that extol the virtues of the price-fixing authority that they have or that they seek to acquire through government-sponsored cartels. This very real contradiction stems from our government's schizophrenic and political attitude toward business.

Adam Smith said it long ago: "[T]hough the law cannot hinder people of the same trade from sometimes assembling together, it ought to do nothing to facilitate such assemblies; much less to render them necessary" [402: 128].

ADDITIONAL READINGS: 121, 130, 209, 361, 404, 429, 442.

54. Are Corporations' Rates of Return Excessive?

KENNETH CLARKSON
Law and Economics Center
University of Miami School of Law

Editor's Summary   Rate of return is commonly defined as the ratio of
accounting profits to net worth or assets. Data on rates of return are
often cited in antitrust actions and in deconcentration proposals as
evidence of monopoly power. The casual use of these ratios is
unfortunate, since the relationship between concentration and rates of
return has not been proved or disproved. Until the debates on
statistical techniques and on the inclusion or exclusion of certain
variables such as intangible capital are settled, one should use extreme
caution when linking rates of return with noncompetitive actions. In a
competitive economy, high rates of return may be temporary and are
associated with efficiencies.

When the 1968 White House Task Force on Antitrust Policy recommended new legislation to supplement the antitrust statutes, its members
based their case on a number of rate-of-return studies. They proposed to
limit concentration and to control other factors that, they believed, contribute to high rates of return on capital.

> The adverse effects of persistent concentration on output and price find
> some confirmation in various studies that have been made of return on
> capital in major industries. . . . It is the persistence of high profits over
> extended time periods and over whole industries rather than in individ-
> ual firms that suggest artificial restraints on output and the absence of
> fully effective competition [68: 113].

More proposals, such as the "Antitrust, Pre-Merger Notification Act" (to
amend the Clayton Act, 15 U.S.C. 12 *et seq.*) and the "Antitrust Civil
Process Act" (to amend 15 U.S.C. 1311), also are concerned with potential
corporate actions that "may substantially lessen competition" or that "tend
to create a monopoly" and result in higher rates of return.

STUDIES OF RATES OF RETURN

Implicit in these recommendations is the view that there is an identifiable,
determinate relationship between the loose "indicators" of monopoly
power (concentration, entry barriers, advertising) and rate of return.

Monopoly power, in this context, is measured by the deviation of the average rate of return in an industry above some competitive norm [194: 444–445]. The rate of return, in most cases, is defined as the ratio of accounting profits (obtained from the income statement) to net worth or assets (obtained from the balance sheet).

Many studies, including those of Joe Bain, H. Michael Mann, and George Stigler, investigate the statistical relationships among rates of return, levels of concentration, and other "indicators" of monopoly power [32, 276, 415]. Bain's original study, using data from the late 1930s, finds a small correlation (.28) between rates of return and concentration and reveals that the average rate of return among the most-concentrated industries is higher than among the least-concentrated industries. When certain industries are excluded to improve the statistical confidence of the final results, however, the relationship is reversed: highly concentrated industries have lower average rates of return than less concentrated industries! More recent tests by Stigler show no statistical relationship between rates of return and various "indicators" of monopoly power [415].

The original Bain and Stigler studies are representative of the more than four dozen tests of the relationship between profitability and concentration. Based on a simple tally of the number of studies to date, the "vote" would seem to support the case for a positive relationship between concentration and rate of return [455].

PROBLEMS WITH PREVIOUS STUDIES

A more careful examination of each study with respect to its individual robustness, however, points to a different conclusion: the relationship between concentration and rate of return has not been satisfactorily proved or disproved. Much of the debate centers on poor statistical techniques, differences between static and dynamic profit rates, disequilibrium forces, the instability of results with respect to the inclusion or exclusion of certain industries with poor data or statistical characteristics, and weighted versus unweighted concentration rates.

Brozen, for example, shows that the single-period rates of return reported in the original Bain study are subject to substantial variation over time [68, 69]. Such variation confirms an alternative hypothesis that rates of return tend toward equality in the long run but are subject to temporary disequilibrium forces that may cause substantial temporary increases (or decreases) in *observed* rates of return. Brozen tests this hypothesis using Mann's study, which shows high rates of return [70]. Table 7 reveals that higher rates of return do tend toward equilibrium over time.

Table 7 Movement of Average Accounting Rate of Return on Net Worth for Nineteen Concentrated Industries Classified by Barriers to Entry, 1950–1960 to 1961–1966

	1950–1960*	*1961–1966*†
High Barriers Class Mean (Eight Industries)	16.1%	13.1%
Substantial Barriers Class Mean (Seven Industries)	11.3%	8.9%
Moderate-to-Low Barriers Class Mean (Four Industries)	12.7%	10.0%
ALL MANUFACTURING CORPORATIONS	11.1%‡	11.2%‡

*H. Michael Mann. "Seller Concentration, Barriers to Entry, and Rates of Return in Thirty Industries, 1950–1960." *Review of Economics and Statistics* 48 (August 1966): 296–307.

†Computed from data in H. Michael Mann, "A Note on Barriers to Entry and Long-Run Profitability," *Antitrust Bulletin,* and from his 1950–1960 data in "Seller Concentration, Barriers to Entry, and Rates of Return in Thirty Industries, 1950–1960."

‡*Economic Report of the President,* 1969, p. 310.

SOURCE: Yale Brozen. "Barriers Facilitate Entry." *The Antitrust Bulletin* 14 (Winter 1969). Reprinted by permission. Copyright © 1969 by Federal Legal Publications.

Nearly every study reveals difficulties with the actual data base used to test the relationships between rates of return and market power. Attempts to use different variables (such as those found in the Kilpatrick study and in studies based on firm rather than industry data) also fail to show significant relationships [235]. Finally, the overall predictive ability of empirical rate-of-return studies is very poor in the sense that large portions of the observed differences in rates of return are not explained.

More important, the accounting profit rate these studies use, whether computed on a base of net worth or on a base of assets, does not correspond to the underlying economic decision variables. Accounting variables, in general, rarely are economic decision variables. Solomon identifies these difficulties, and Bloch, Ayanian, and Clarkson estimate the associated biases [26, 59, 95, 406]. When unrealized income and increased capitalization of expenditures from intangible capital (such as advertising and research, whose returns begin at some future period) are properly accounted for, profit measurements in industries with higher-than-average rates of return are altered substantially. Table 8 shows that these simple corrections account for a substantial portion of the dispersion in

Table 8 Average Industry Accounting and Corrected Rates of Return on Net Worth, 1959–1973

Industry	No Depreciation or Capital Accumulation	Advertising and Research Capitalization and Depreciation*
Pharmaceuticals	18.29%	12.89%†
Electrical Machinery	13.33	10.10
Foods	11.81	10.64
Petroleum	11.23	10.77
Chemicals	10.59	9.14
Motor Vehicles	10.46	9.22
Paper	10.49	10.12
Rubber Products	10.11	8.69
Office Machinery	10.48	9.90
Aerospace	9.23	7.38
Ferrous Metals	7.55	7.28
AVERAGE	11.20%	9.60%
VARIANCE	7.50%	2.50%

*Advertising and promotion depreciate for three years; basic research accumulates five years longer than development; basic research depreciates for ten years and development for five years.

†The depreciation period for the pharmaceutical industry is fifteen years for basic research and ten years for development. This different cycle, however, changes the average by less than one-half of 1 percent.

SOURCE: Kenneth W. Clarkson. *Intangible Capital and Rates of Return* (Washington, D.C.: American Enterprise Institute, 1977).

unadjusted rates of return among industries. Bain's earlier analysis of the profit rate as a measure of monopoly power should have provided a warning.

> The unadjusted accounting rate of profit, as computed by the usual methods from balance sheets and income statements, is *prima facie* an absolutely unreliable indicator of the presence or absence either of monopoly power or of excessive profits. ... The relationship between price and accounting average cost tells us nothing about the degree of monopoly power and little about the extent of excess profit [33: 291].

Economic theory, of course, predicts that there will be differences among firms' and industries' economic rates of return, both in the short run and in the long run, even after making the appropriate "corrections" for advertising and for research and development.

ACCOUNTING FOR DIFFERENCES IN RATES OF RETURN

Differences in average rates of return in various industries are the result of many factors. First, the rates observed in any one period may be transitory, the result of disequilibrium in one or more markets. Second, there may be differences in fringe benefits and other nonpecuniary characteristics, which would cause observed pecuniary rates of return to differ under competitive market conditions. Third, the greater the risk associated with an industry, the greater the expected rate of return must be to attract capital in the financial markets. Fourth, there are differences in resource use efficiency, and those differences may cause variations in rates of return if superior resources are distributed "unequally" and earn rents that are not completely capitalized on the books of firms owning them. Fifth, some industries will be subject to, or will lobby for, specific legislation that creates entry barriers which, in turn, cause higher rates of return than are observed in other "unregulated" industries. Firms with patent protection, moreover, may show, over short periods of time, rates of return in excess of those achieved by firms without patents. Sixth, at any particular moment in time the positive costs of acquiring information and adjusting to new relative prices and demand conditions will contribute to differences in rates of return in industries as well as in individual firms. Disequilibrating forces will become less important over longer time periods, but other autonomous shocks come into play.

Considering these qualifications, it is highly unlikely that observed rates of return would be equal for firms in a particular industry or for firms across all industries. And, one cannot conclude that a high observed rate of return is sufficient evidence of monopoly power.

ADDITIONAL READINGS: 422, 424.

55. Can Corporate Executives Set Their Own Wages?

W. MARK CRAIN
Department of Economics
Virginia Polytechnic Institute and State University

Editor's Summary   Corporate detractors argue that executives have considerable leeway in establishing their compensation and that pay is set at excessive levels. The relatively high level of involuntary turnover of top corporate management, however, suggests that the market for managerial services is quite competitive. The market for executives is not subject to entry restrictions, and executives have little, if any, ability to set their own wages. Executive pay is determined primarily by company profits. This is precisely the result expected if executive action is consistent with overall economic welfare.

Casualness about facts abounds among detractors of the corporate sector of the American economy. Such casualness is not limited to drawing unflattering inferences about the pricing, production, and taxpaying practices of this sector but is extended to include more personal criticisms of those who make decisions in the private sector.

There are two separate sets of criticisms of corporate executives. One set of criticisms centers on the argument that in modern corporations top-level executives have considerable discretionary power, which is not subject to strict oversight by the actual owners. As "evidence" in support of this argument, some suggest that the remuneration of corporate executives seems to be quite independent of any performance criterion. *Business Week* reported, for example, that "increases in corporation profits tapered off last year but pay raises for chief executives kept right on growing" [25 August 1975: 19].

A second set of criticisms is more general and centers on the argument that the salaries of corporate executives are "excessive" and are therefore evidence of a perverse scheme of income distribution in the United States. "Managers award themselves stupendous salaries, stock options, bonuses and other benefits. The managerial elite of the top corporations are almost always wealthy men. One need only think of names like Thomas Watson, George Humphrey, David Packard, Charles Wilson, and Robert McNamara" [342: 16].

This chapter considers these two arguments concerning top-level decision makers in the corporate sector of the American economy. First, I offer some general information on the salaries and average time in office of corporate presidents and examine the market for executive services.

Second, I investigate the determinants of executive compensation within the framework of some basic economic analysis. Third, I offer some remarks on the conclusions that one may draw from a closer examination of the pay of corporate executives.

THE MARKET FOR EXECUTIVE SERVICES

Table 9 shows the average salaries and time in office of the chief executive officers of some 500 corporations in the United States. While the average salary of a corporation president undoubtedly is several times higher than the salary of the average wage earner in the United States, that it is "excessive" remains to be demonstrated.

"Excessive," to an economist, registers a picture of market prices being above some competitive bench-mark level. To begin the investigation, then, I characterize the general market in which managerial services are supplied and demanded so that we can examine and interpret the term "excessive." If we allege, for example, that the price of wheat is excessive, we would certainly begin by investigating the structure of the wheat market, seeking evidence to the effect that the supply of wheat relative to demand is restricted at the prevailing price. In virtually all market situations, of course, a necessary condition for prices to persist above the competitive level is the existence of some barrier to new or potential suppliers of the product or service in question. The first and perhaps most telling aspect of any market is the degree to which factors of production, in our case corporate managers, are able to enter (voluntarily) and exit (involuntarily). This simple mechanism of competitive markets provides an essential force that serves to eliminate excess returns.

Quantity adjustment through entry and exit thus provides a fruitful insight into the degree of competitiveness in the market for managerial

Table 9   Average Tenure and Salaries of Chief Executive Officers

Year	Tenure	Salary (in nominal dollars)
1970	8.28	181,449
1971	8.23	190,555
1972	7.79	233,788
1973	7.98	259,103
1974	7.59	276,239

SOURCE: *Forbes Magazine* 107 (15 May 1971):165–182; 109 (15 May 1972):205–240; 111 (15 May 1973):225–263; 113 (15 May 1974):126–167; 115 (15 May 1975):234–272.

services. Several recent studies of this question reveal that quantity adjustment is indeed a very important characteristic of this market [110, 122]. It appears, in effect, that the positions of even those executives at the very top of the corporate ladder are rather tenuous in that owners (stockholders) are not reticent about hiring and firing. The relatively high level of involuntary turnover of corporate management suggests that supply in the market for executive talent is not subject to entry restrictions and, indeed, is responsive to changes in pay offered. Thus, it is implausible to suspect that corporations would pay anything but the "going" market price for executives of the caliber they demand. Any single corporate executive would not have significant "wage-setting" power, since there appears to be a substantial pool of potential executives from which corporate owners can draw.

It is interesting to contrast the turnover of executives in private corporations with the turnover of executives in publicly owned enterprises. Evidence indicates that managers in publicly owned enterprises enjoy significantly more job security than those in the private sector. De Alessi suggests that the reason for the relative insularity of managers in public enterprises is that the "owners" of such enterprises, citizen-taxpayers, are not likely to detect and police managerial activity [122: 646]. The inability to transfer property rights or ownership shares in public enterprises effectively eliminates the incentive that owners of private firms have to monitor managerial performance.

Elected politicians, interestingly, do not seem to be as closely disciplined by market pressures as are executives in private corporations. For example, in 1972 the average number of years in office of members of the United States House of Representatives was over 11.2 [111].

COMPENSATION AND PERFORMANCE

Salary variations do exist, of course, in the market for managerial services. Bushels of wheat have different market values because of quality differentials. By analogy, quality differences among corporate executives may be the most important determinants of compensation differences, especially in a competitive market for executives. Thus, we can address the argument of the second set of criticisms, that executive salaries are not tied to performance or productivity, by examining the evidence concerning the responsiveness of salaries to some standard indicators of industrial performance.

The evidence about the exact determinants of managerial pay is not without conflict; nevertheless, standard performance criteria significantly affect remuneration. The disagreement among economists who investigate this issue concerns the particular kind of firm performance or objective that is most rewarded, not whether or not productivity affects salary differences [38, 93, 304, 344, 367]. More recent evidence suggests that a firm's profit picture (measured either by its reported earnings or by the market value of its common stock) is the most important factor in explaining variations in the salaries of corporate executives [112, 261, 297].

Finally, as standard economic theory would predict, managers of larger firms would be expected to be paid more than their counterparts in smaller firms because the value of wealth affected by their decisions is greater [10]. This relationship also has been examined, and the empirical evidence substantiates the prediction quite convincingly. The observed relationship between the capital or asset value of firms and the compensation of their executives provides more evidence that the pay differences that do exist result from quality differences, and that managerial factors tend to be allocated efficiently among firms.

CONCLUSION

Corporate executives are subject to the fundamental forces of supply and demand much like thousands of other factors of production employed by the corporate sector of the economy. A close examination of the market for managerial services suggests that there are no significant entry barriers and that the observed differences in compensation are well explained by quality differences. Corporate executives, in sum, are much like wheat when it comes to making dough.

ADDITIONAL READINGS: 81, 113, 258, 259, 260.

56. Is Corporate Executive Compensation Excessive?

ROBERT THOMAS
Department of Economics
University of Washington

Editor's Summary   Critics of executive pay levels argue that
corporate executive compensation is lavish and excessive; they
suggest that becoming rich is a crime and a waste. Most Americans,
however, believe that the opposite is true: achieving wealth reflects an
ability to perform well in the marketplace. The evidence concerning
corporate executives squares with this view. Corporate executives
tend to be well prepared, experienced, hardworking, beyond middle
age, vigilant, and very competitive. Their wages are determined by
market forces as corporations compete for the best executives.
Corporate executives are highly paid because their value to firms is
high in terms of the amount of stockholder wealth their decisions
affect.

$\mathbf{R}$alph Nader stands at the end of a long line of critics who assail the high
incomes of top corporate executives. Nader and his associates suggest that
"in the absence of judicial limitations, excessive remuneration has become
the norm" [328: 115]. They observe that the average top executive in each
of the fifty largest industrial corporations earns more salary in a year than
many of the corporate employees earn in a lifetime. Salaries are only part
(albeit the major part) of the compensation the top executives receive.
Bonuses, lavish retirements, stock options, and stock ownership combine
to swell the incomes of corporate chief executives by another 50 to 75
percent of the executives' direct remunerations. Nader and his associates
conclude that the top corporate executives receive "staggeringly large
salaries and stock options" [328: 118].

THE ATTACK ON EXECUTIVE INCOME

Those who criticize the level of compensation that corporate executives
receive are critical of any persons who are, or who become rich. The top
executives of our major corporations *do* become rich. *Fortune* magazine,
in a survey of the chief executives of the 500 largest industrial corporations, discovered that the median income in 1976 was $209,000 a year and
that when only the 100 largest corporations were considered, the median
salary was $344,000 a year [May 1976: 172].

Most Americans, however, do not consider becoming rich to be a crime. Indeed, the opposite is true. Achieving wealth reflects a high level of performance in providing through the market what the economy desires.

Nader and his coauthors recognize this admiration for performance and attack the level of executive compensation on other grounds. They suggest that the chief corporate executives are not entrepreneurs who risk their own capital in the search for profits, but functionaries who perform essentially the same tasks as government employees. The chief corporate executives "serve as the bureaucrats of private industry" [328: 118].

The difference between industry and government is that the boards of directors of large corporations allegedly are more lax in discharging their responsibilities to their shareholders (by constraining excessive executive salaries) than the members of the Congress of the United States and the various elected officials of state and local governments who serve as the watchdogs for the public interest. The managements of large corporations take advantage of this laxness to request and receive excessive compensation. Moreover, this is not an isolated phenomenon confined to an occasional corporation. Nader reports that it "has become the norm" [328: 115].

WHY EXECUTIVES ARE WELL PAID

In response, consider first who a chief corporate executive is, and examine the responsibilities a chief corporate executive must discharge. The typical top executive in each of the 500 largest industrial corporations is a white Protestant male aged sixty. He got his top position at age fifty-five; he averages between fifty-five and sixty-four hours a week on the job, takes three weeks of vacation each year, and earns a salary of $209,000 a year. He has attended graduate school, and he has worked for more than two companies during his business career. He owns less than $500,000 worth of stock in the company for which he works, and during the past decade he has seen his salary rise less rapidly, in percentage terms, than the salaries of his employees. In short, he is well prepared, experienced, hardworking, and beyond middle age.

Two things distinguish each of these 500 persons from several thousand others who have similar qualities. First, each is paid more. Second, each has been chosen as the person responsible for his company's present and future.

The Fortune 500 Company corporate executive directs a company whose sales in 1975 averaged almost $1.75 billion, whose assets totaled $1.33 billion, and which provided employment for almost 29,000 people [81: 172]. This executive directs the firm in a manner that allows it to earn an 11.6 percent return on its total investment. Such a rate of return is not guaranteed simply because a corporation is large. The opportunities to lose money are many; the managements of 28 of the 500 largest industrial corporations managed to show a loss in the recovery year of 1975. It is possible, moreover, to lose big: Singer reported a loss of $451.9 million in that year, and Chrysler $259.5 million. A chief executive who heads a management team that can avoid such losses and constantly succeed in earning a profit is obviously very valuable to the shareholders of a corporation. He is valuable not only to his employers but also to other corporations; thus his own firm pays him handsomely to retain his services.

Many pages of our national magazines devoted to business news— *Business Week, Forbes, Fortune*—report the movements of business executives from one firm to another. These shifts are induced by substantial increases in salary, often, according to one publication, of 30 percent or more [*Business Week*, 4 October 1971: 62]. Some excellently managed corporations, such as IBM, General Motors, Procter and Gamble, and Xerox, are known in industry as "executive breeders" [Ibid.: 57]. Xerox admitted in its 1976 proxy statement that its management was increasingly becoming "a target for other corporations seeking talented executives," and it proposed a new incentive plan for its executives [Ibid.]. This request for increased executive compensation was not self-serving on the part of Xerox's management; it stemmed in part from the prior move of twelve Xerox executives to a rival copier manufacturer.

The high salaries and fringe benefits that talented executives in large corporations receive stem not from laxness on the part of the boards of directors but, rather, from the boards' vigilance. Corporations must pay their executives, as well as any other employees, what they could earn by working for a rival firm, or lose them. Competition among corporations for the best people sets the level of executive compensation. If one person is to be placed in charge of a billion dollars in shareholder assets, which can easily be lost through mismanagement, even the $766,085 a year that the highest-paid corporate executive in the United States receives might not appear excessive to shareholders, especially if that salary is what it takes to get the services of the best available person.

There are many examples of corporations that are well rewarded for paying the price necessary to get the best person to remedy a bad situation. In one recent case, a firm that once tried to produce computers, and whose stock had sold for as high as $173 a share, fell on hard times; in 1973 it lost $119 million on sales of $177 million and had $300 million in long-term debts [*Forbes*, 15 October 1976: 78]. A new chief executive, who by 1976 had made the firm profitable once again, received $200,000 a year, performance incentives that earned him another $400,000, and stock options that made him a millionaire on paper. Clearly the compensation this executive received meets the Nader criterion for being "excessive." Yet, the Bank of America thought it was a worthwhile investment to guarantee his salary in an attempt, which proved successful, to ensure the eventual repayment of the large loans it had made to the firm. Individual shareholders also applauded the move; as a result of the executive's efforts, the value of a share has increased from $2 to over $21. In this one instance, the efforts of the new chief executive succeeded in increasing the market value of the company ten times.

A talented executive is highly paid because he is very productive. He earns for his firm additional net revenue at least equal in value to his compensation. If he did not, his firm would let him go. If his firm does not pay him what he is worth to others, it will lose him to a rival. The same holds true for any other valuable input in our economy and accounts as well for the high incomes received by talented persons in other fields [SB 55].

SALARIES OF OTHER PERSONS

Consider, for a moment, the salaries paid to entertainers. The fastest way to become a millionaire is not to become a corporate executive, but to become a big rock 'n' roll star or a superstar in professional sports. In 1973, for example, there were an estimated fifty music performers earning between $1 million and $6 million a year [*Forbes,* 15 April 1973: 28]. These thirty-five persons and fifteen groups made, annually, between three and seven times the salary paid to America's highest-paid executive. While the musicians performed, that highest-paid executive directed, and was responsible for, a company that employed 376,000 persons, had sales of over $11 billion and assets of over $10 billion, and earned almost $400 million in profits. Rock stars, moreover, earn their fortunes sooner than business executives; most start their careers as teenage idols; few have their best earning years after thirty. The average chief executive in each of the 500 largest industrial corporations does not attain that degree of success until the age of fifty-five.

Or, examine the compensation paid to the superstars in professional sports. The most interesting stories on sports pages now are not reports of games but stories about the fabulous salaries received by star athletes: $3 million to Julius Erving, $1.5 million each to O. J. Simpson and Pele, $500,000 to Kareem Abdul-Jabbar, $450,000 each to Tiny Archibald and Joe Namath, $400,000 to Catfish Hunter, $360,000 to Bob Lanier, $325,-000 to Bill Bradley, $302,000 to Spencer Haywood, $250,000 to John Havlicek, $237,500 to Rick Barry, $230,000 to Tom Seaver, and $225,000 to Dick Allen [*Fortune,* May 1976: 170]. More names from golf, hockey, and tennis could easily be added to the list. The reported incomes of these superstars are probably understated, since they exclude payments for endorsements and the like. These people, furthermore, work only part of the year, while the average chief executive has a forty-nine-week season.

When considered in the light of the compensation paid to extremely talented persons in other areas, the rewards earned by corporate executives do not appear excessive. A competitive economy ensures that highly productive persons command high rewards.

ADDITIONAL READINGS: 38, 93, 110, 122, 258, 259, 260, 261, 297, 304, 342, 344, 367.

57. Should American Industry Be Deconcentrated?

WARREN F. SCHWARTZ
School of Law
University of Virginia

Editor's Summary   Economic analysis provides no theory to verify empirical data linking industry structure with economic performance or with the amount of political and social power firms in an industry command. On the contrary, highly atomistic industries like agriculture, trucking, and the "independent" segment of the oil industry have long been successful at extracting economic and political concessions from government. Concentration appears to be neither a necessary nor a sufficient condition for socially adverse industry performance. If the purpose of deconcentration is to promote small business because it is a "good" thing, consumers and taxpayers will subsidize small-business entrepreneurship in several ways. First, society as a whole will be poorer if firms cannot direct resources to their most valuable uses. Second, deconcentration will require substantial public and private resources as the proposals are administered. Third, the legal system will make costly mistakes.

An appraisal of any proposal to broaden the criteria for antitrust action should begin with a careful specification of the ends that the amendment is designed to achieve. Often, advocates of change combine ill-defined social objectives with the notion of enhanced efficiency as ends that will be accomplished through the enactment and enforcement of far-reaching antitrust legislation. It is important, therefore, to sort out the various objectives the proposed legislation might serve, to find out the extent to which each objective will indeed be accomplished, and to establish the magnitude of the social costs that will be incurred in trying to secure the benefits allegedly available through enforcement of the new law. To illustrate this method of appraisal, I apply it here to a proposed amendment to the antitrust law.

The single most important proposal advanced to broaden the antitrust laws is that an industry should be "deconcentrated" whenever a "small" number of firms together have a "large" share of the market. Deconcentration proposals contemplate that existing "large" firms may be broken up into smaller firms or otherwise required to divest themselves of assets so that they serve a materially smaller portion of the market. These remedies would be available even though there is no evidence of wrongful conduct leading to concentration in the industry.

POLITICAL POWER AND INDUSTRY CONCENTRATION

A plausible case (though highly questionable as both a theoretical and empirical matter) can be made for a deconcentration bill on the grounds of enhancing efficiency by increasing competition. The issue can be examined rationally as to whether such a bill would do more good by reducing the incidence of monopoly pricing, with its attendant misallocation of resources, than harm by inducing inefficient industry structure and action and by consuming large amounts of resources in the public and private sectors for litigating the "appropriate" deconcentration remedy [SB 38, SB 40, SB 43, SB 50, SB 51, SB54].

When the specter of social or political power wielded by the "large" corporations is raised, however, and no systematic statement of the linkage between market share (or absolute size) and the exercise of such power is made, the debate loses much of its rationality. Any bill that in any degree diminishes the market share or absolute size of "large" firms is assigned independent value by its proponents on the grounds that it more widely distributes social and political power.

The evidence as to what factors make it possible for a firm or group of firms to exercise political or social power, however, supports no confident conclusion as to whether the changes in industry structure that a deconcentration bill would make have any significant bearing on the amount of power that firms in an industry command. Plainly, separate firms can collaborate to achieve political ends. While such collaboration becomes more costly as the number of firms grows, there may be advantages in having a "large" number of separately owned firms pursuing the same political ends. If concentration facilitates monopoly pricing, moreover, firms in a concentrated industry require less government support than those in an atomistic industry to accomplish the same objectives.

No theory with verifying empirical data exists, in any event, that links the structure of an industry with the amount of political or social power commanded by firms in the industry. Anecdotal evidence, such as with respect to agriculture, trucking, or the "independent" segment of the oil industry, suggests that there is no *simple* relationship between industry structure and political power. These highly atomistic industries have often been very successful politically. Indeed, large groups of persons, such as those in the labor and environmentalist movements, also have achieved extremely advantageous legislative treatment.

SMALL ENTREPRENEURS ARE RIGHTEOUS

Another set of objectives of deconcentration centers on the assertion that "small" business is a "good" thing, independent of its ability to provide customer satisfaction. The notion, presumably, is that an *entrepreneur* is happier and better able to contribute to society than if he or she were employed as a *manager* of a "large" corporation. There is no reason, of course, why voters cannot choose to impose costs on themselves as consumers and taxpayers to subsidize increased entrepreneurship by others. The plea with respect to this issue is a simple one. If a deconcentration bill is passed to buy for others the opportunity to be entrepreneurs (or if other legislation is enacted with similar effect), care should be taken to be very clear about the consequences of such action, in terms of both the benefits it creates and the costs to consumers in higher prices and to taxpayers in supporting the government apparatus required to implement the program.

DECONCENTRATION AND ECONOMIC EFFICIENCY

Appraisal of the deconcentration proposals as a matter of economic efficiency is a more complex question. Two basic difficulties plague efforts to make this judgment. First, the relationship between industry structure and the likely incidence of monopoly pricing is extremely unclear as a matter of both theory and empirical evidence [SB 50, SB 51, SB 54]. Various theories do posit concentration as one factor that is relevant for predicting the occurrence of monopoly pricing. But, a number of other industry characteristics, such as the degree of diversity or standardization of products or the degree of concentration in the buying side of the market, also are significant in deciding how great departures from competitive behavior are likely to be. There is no theory that systematically assigns importance to these various factors. What is completely lacking, therefore, is any basis for concluding that a given "deconcentration" of industry will yield a particular benefit in the form of price and output changes that are closer to those that would emerge in a competitive market.

The second basic difficulty is that the efficiencies that "large" firms realize are difficult to conceptualize and measure. These efficiencies derive not from economies of scale in the use of facilities and equipment but from the elusive improvements that can be achieved when resources are placed under the control of a single management. These improvements are attributable, ultimately, to a better flow of information about the possible uses to which the resources can be put [11]. The evaluation of the improvements depends on unresolved issues concerning the consequences of subjecting resources to different forms of internal control within a single firm, as compared to having their uses determined by competition among independent owners of them [227]. Plainly, though, "large" firms are found in circumstances in which it is extremely unlikely that one can explain their existence in terms of facilitating monopoly pricing. Large firms *do* achieve significant efficiences, even if we cannot quantify these efficiencies with any real confidence.

SUMMARY

The gains from a deconcentration statute in the form of decreased social and political power for the "large" corporations and greater efficiency in the functioning of presently "concentrated" industries are highly problematical. If it is worth it, deconcentration, no doubt, can be used to subsidize entrepreneurship.

The costs of implementing the deconcentration scheme must be emphasized. These costs are of three kinds. First, society as a whole will be poorer if firms cannot marshal and manage resources so as to put them to their most highly valued uses. Second, the deconcentration proposals will require substantial resources in the public and private sectors to resolve the host of issues that will be encountered in implementing the program. Third, any legal system will make mistakes. Considering how little we understand about efficient industrial organization and how far-reaching the effects of deconcentration remedies might be, the opportunities for costly error are very great.

Thus, a particular deconcentration proposal must be evaluated carefully to find out if the benefits it will produce will exceed the costs of implementation. Although one cannot exclude the possibility that a proposal will be formulated that will pass this test, it is now doubtful that the case for this far-reaching change (and for others that turn on similar judgments) can be persuasively established.

ADDITIONAL READINGS: 48, 126, 194, 231, 354, 361.

58. Does the Lack of Funds Hinder Antitrust Enforcement?

TIMOTHY J. MURIS
University of Miami School of Law

Editor's Summary Increased public antitrust activity would be desirable if it would increase competition. Yet, many supporters of increased antitrust expenditures fail to realize that some FTC and Justice Department prosecutions have done more to harm competition than to help it. The FTC has filed complaints charging, for example, that companies sold their products too cheaply! Firms often are punished for being too successful. Increased spending for antitrust efforts could aggravate the problems caused by the failure of antitrust authorities to provide a reasonable, consistent basis for their policies and decisions. Until the federal agencies provide a rational approach, many of their activities will continue to be counterproductive and will generate costly uncertainty.

In his 1965 essay entitled "What Happened to the Antitrust Movement?" historian Richard Hofstadter concludes that "antitrust has become almost exclusively the concern of small groups of legal and economic specialists, who carry on their work without widespread public interest or support" [206: 24]. How times have changed! Today, leaders of both political parties, representatives of consumer groups, and many academicians enthusiastically support antitrust, arguing that substantial increases in funding are necessary to guarantee adequate enforcement (see, for example, Schifrin's article in the *Washington Post*, "Climate Now Right for Antitrust Revival" [22 December 1974: E2]).

Why the renewed interest in antitrust? The major catalyst appears to be the severe economic problems of recent years. Increasing antitrust enforcement, we are told, will increase consumer welfare by improving economic performance and reducing prices. Since the case for increasing antitrust activity rests on economic grounds, this chapter considers whether those grounds justify an increase in antitrust funding. In short, this chapter decides whether increasing the antitrust activities of the FTC and of the Department of Justice will increase consumer welfare.

To answer this question, it is useful to separate antitrust cases into two categories. One category comprises practices that firms allegedly have used to eliminate competition among themselves; the other category includes practices that a firm (or, occasionally, a group of firms) allegedly has used to exclude or eliminate competitors [357].

Almost all economists conclude that the first category of cases, usually termed "collusive practices," often reduces consumer welfare. Thus, the antitrust laws properly outlaw these practices (for example, price-fixing and mergers to form a monopoly). The same cannot be said, however, of the second category of cases, the so-called exclusionary practices. Many economists and legal scholars conclude that these activities (for example, tie-in agreements and low-pricing campaigns) do not harm consumers except in the rarest of circumstances [62, 136].

THE PROBLEM OF COLLUSIVE PRACTICES

FTC and Justice Department cases against collusive practices have produced important consumer benefits. Antitrust actions may have helped stop mergers to form monopolies, and they have reduced the amount and harmful effects of price-fixing [416, 419]. Current antitrust enforcers are expanding their efforts by challenging collusive schemes of professionals (for example, doctors, lawyers, and real estate brokers) that limit or eliminate price competition and advertising. Further, antitrust authorities are increasingly criticizing and, where possible, attacking the considerable amount of government-sponsored collusion. The Justice Department, for example, has long tried, with partial success, to persuade the Civil Aeronautics Board to become more responsive to the interests of consumers. And, the FTC is trying to preempt state laws that cost consumers millions of dollars a year by prohibiting the price advertising of certain services, such as those relating to eye care and funerals [42].

Even if the entire antitrust budget were spent on efforts to eliminate collusion, however, a significant percentage of the expenditures would not necessarily aid consumers, since many cases involve industries in which the potential for successful collusion is negligible [360, SB 60]. Many collusion cases, for example, involve industries characterized by many firms and ease of entry—conditions not conducive to successful price-fixing [SB 53]. These cases occur because antitrust law focuses on the attempt to collude, not on the successful act, and thereby diverts resources from more important cases without producing benefits in return. One can find attempts to collude reprehensible yet still refuse to spend tax money on cases involving collusion attempts that are not likely to succeed.

THE PROBLEM OF EXCLUSIONARY PRACTICES

Even under the present allegedly small budget, the government brings many cases against exclusionary practices [360, 422]. Current cases pending against distributional restraints, vertical integration, and price discrimination continue to figure prominently in enforcement, particularly at the

FTC. Specific examples include challenges to contractual covenants that require franchisers and shopping center tenants to follow standardized practices designed, in part, to ensure uniform or high product quality. There are also complaints alleging that ITT Continental and General Foods are selling their products too cheaply. Since exclusionary cases normally do not improve consumer welfare (and since, as I shall argue, they may harm consumers), the current antitrust budget could profitably be diminished, unless these cases are dropped in favor of suits benefiting consumers.

OTHER PROBLEMS OF ANTITRUST ENFORCEMENT

Besides funding cases that will not benefit consumers, increased spending could exacerbate at least three other problems of current antitrust enforcement. First, many cases, particularly those involving exclusionary practices, actually reduce consumer welfare. Attempts to stop the all-but-nonexistent practice of "predatory" pricing (such as the cases against ITT Continental and General Foods) decrease the supply of beneficial low pricing by increasing its cost [245]. Enforcement of the Robinson-Patman Act, that creature of the anticompetition spirit of the Great Depression, is almost entirely anticonsumer. Many cases even directly attack business efficiency. For example, in *Brown Shoe Co. v. United States* [370 U.S. 294, 82 S Ct. 1502, 8 L.E.D. 2d 510 (1962)], the Supreme Court found a merger to be illegal in part because its vertical aspects lowered prices to consumers, giving the merged firm an "unfair" advantage over its nonintegrated competitors. Unfortunately for consumers, the examples in this paragraph by no means exhaust the areas of harmful antitrust enforcement.

Second, increased antitrust spending may harm consumers because much of the current support of antitrust rests on the belief that industrial concentration and heavy advertising reduce consumer welfare. As shown elsewhere in this sourcebook, this is a belief that many economists dispute [SB 41, SB 42, SB 43, SB 44, SB 46, SB 50, SB 51, SB 53, SB 57, SB 60, SB 61]. Thus, government cases to break up firms in industries such as oil and cereals may be misguided. Further, the solution that some FTC officials propose for the advertising "problem"—namely, trademark licensing—will hurt consumers [*Borden, Inc.* 3 CCH Trade Reg. Rptr., Sec. 21, 114 (1976)]. Under trademark licensing, a manufacturer of a specified leading brand would be forced to allow its competitors to use its trademark. If Brand X, for example, was the leading seller, competing brands would be allowed to call their products Brand X. This practice will punish firms for past success and confuse consumers. And unless the Commission can somehow continually monitor product quality to guarantee that all brands competing with Brand X meet the standards of Brand X, this practice will create an incentive to cheat on product quality and take advantage of the reputation that Brand X has among consumers. Probably, this social engineering, which is implicit in deconcentration and trademark licensing, would only increase with increased funds. (As Wesley J. Liebeler once remarked, the philosophy implicit in trademark licensing is "we are one nation; we will have one brand of beans.")

Finally, increased antitrust spending could aggravate the problem resulting from the failure of antitrust authorities and judges to provide reasoned and understandable bases for their policies and decisions [355]. This failure causes great uncertainty among business people and attorneys as to what courses of action are legal. As former FTC Commissioner Lowell B. Mason remarked, "What a young [antitrust] law student needs most after a diploma and a shingle and a client is a good pair of eyebrows and broad shoulders. Then when his client asks him how to stay out of trouble with the government, he can raise the first and shrug the second. . . " [296: 20]. Such uncertainty is yet another cost of current enforcement.

CONCLUSION

Thus, even under the current budget, part of antitrust activity harms, or at least does not benefit, consumers. Cases against practices that do not normally hurt consumers and that may even help them, cases in industries in which there is a limited possibility for successful collusive practices, cases based on highly disputable economic theory, and cases that increase uncertainty as to what conduct is legal without providing compensating benefits are not in the public interest. Considering the emphasis on such cases, a lack of funds cannot be said to hamper enforcement. If some current funds are wasted, why is there need for more?

Might not one argue, however, that increased funding could support cases whose benefits outweigh the harms that other cases cause? If such potentially beneficial cases do exist, they can currently be funded by simply substituting them for the many nonbeneficial cases now brought. Antitrust authorities should receive additional funds only if they demonstrate that all existing resources are used in cases that increase consumer welfare and that they cannot pursue additional beneficial cases without additional funds. Before antitrust administrators ask for more money, they must first put their own house in order.

ADDITIONAL READINGS: 62, 126, 159.

59. Should the Federal Trade Commission's Activities Be Strengthened and Enlarged?

WESLEY J. LIEBELER
The School of Law
University of California at Los Angeles

Editor's Summary Any decision to strengthen and enlarge a government agency's activities should be based on a comparison of the costs and benefits of that action. If more resources devoted to the FTC are not expected to produce benefits as great as those available from expansion elsewhere, the expansion should not take place. Observers accuse the Commission of "inadequate planning, failure to establish priorities, excessive preoccupation with trivial matters, undue delay and unnecessary secrecy." The Commission has never agreed on any goal or structure of goals to guide its activities. The purposes of the Commission, consequently, have never been articulated. Without a statement of purposes or goals, no system of priorities or effective planning controls can be implemented. The FTC cannot measure the benefits created or the costs imposed by its actions and programs. Without a benefit-cost analysis, there are no rational grounds for the argument that the Commission's activities should be strengthened and enlarged.

$\mathbf{P}$rivate firms strengthen and enlarge their operations only if they expect that the additional investment will produce returns at least equal to the costs of that investment. This can occur only if consumers are willing to buy the output of the enlarged operations at prices that cover costs. The justification of private investment, therefore, is based ultimately on the willingness of others to give up part of their wealth in voluntary market transactions in exchange for the output in question.

MEASURING GOVERNMENTAL ACTIVITY'S COSTS AND BENEFITS

There is no such fundamental check on the value of investment in additional *governmental* activity. Since consumers do not ordinarily purchase the output of government agencies, there are no transactions that reflect their judgment as to its value. This makes it hard to tell whether an additional dollar invested in a "strengthened and enlarged" governmental activity, whether by the Federal Trade Commission or by some other agency, will produce a dollar's worth of benefit to the general welfare.

Stated more precisely, the relevant question is whether or not a dollar invested in additional governmental activity will produce as great a return as a dollar invested elsewhere. If it does not, it should not be so invested. Difficult though it may be, however, that question must be answered if rational decisions concerning resource allocations are to be made.

Measurability remains a necessary condition. Two appropriate quotations begin the Federal Trade Commission's 1976 *Budget Overview*. The first quotation is from George Stigler: "If we cannot measure the effects of policies, the society is incapable of rational behavior—rational behavior is behavior appropriate to the ends in view, and means cannot be appropriate if their effects are unknown." The second quotation is from Frederic Scherer: "Difficult though the task may be, costs and benefits must be assessed in formulating rational public policies" [82: E1].

Those who argue that the Federal Trade Commission's activities "should be strengthened and enlarged" are claiming that additional resources devoted to that agency would produce benefits that would exceed the value of those resources if they were used elsewhere. Proponents of that conclusion could *begin* to demonstrate its accuracy by coming forward with a reasonably clear statement of what the Commission is expected to do with the additional resources.

THE BAD REPUTATION OF THE FTC

Pleas for the Commission's expansion, however, are not ordinarily accompanied by any such specification. In the absence of that specification, insight into the question of the desirability of additional investment in the Federal Trade Commission may• be gained by examining the Commission's past performance.

Until recently, the Commission was generally regarded as a dismal failure. In 1969, following a stinging indictment of the Commission by "Nader's Raiders," a special American Bar Association committee appointed at the request of the President to examine the Commission's performance reported:

> Over the past 50 years, a succession of independent scholars and other analysts has consistently found the FTC wanting in the performance of its duties by reason of inadequate planning, failure to establish priorities, excessive preoccupation with trivial matters, undue delay and unnecessary secrecy [109; 16: 59].

In the ABA committee's view, the FTC had "mismanaged its own resources, elevated to important positions a number of staff members of insufficient competence," and failed to "establish and adhere to a system of priorities." The result of the last failure was "a misallocation of funds and personnel to trivial matters. . ." [109: 59–60].

Richard Posner, in a dissent, argued that "the Commission has continuously done so badly over so long a period of time that it is difficult any longer to regard its failings as accidental and remediable." He proposed:

> ... a policy of (a) freezing the Commission's appropriations at their present level and (b) withholding from it any new responsibilities. It is scandalous to allow so dubious an enterprise to continue to wax in size and power. The procedure that I suggest would at least force the agency and its supporters to attempt to justify its existence and actions. If no justification were forthcoming, the freeze would be maintained and the forces of inflation and economic growth would gradually effect a practical repeal of the regulatory scheme [16: 98].

In spite of the bleak picture, the ABA committee's majority members believed that the Commission could be reformed. They recommended an increased emphasis on localized consumer fraud, a realignment of antitrust enforcement resources, and greater discretion to issue complaints and open and close investigations on the staff level. Most important, they strongly urged the Commission "to establish goals, priorities, and effective planning controls." The Office of Program Review was to be expanded and invigorated "to take primary responsibility for proposing to the Commission ways and means of coordinating future operations." The committee did not go into great detail in suggesting just what the goals and priorities should be. It concluded that "if change does not occur, there will be no substantial purpose to be served by its [the Commission's] continued existence" [16: 62].

THE CONTINUING FAILURE OF THE FTC

Such was the situation in 1969. The burden was on those who argued even for the Commission's continued existence. But since then the Commission has been given extensive new powers, and its budget has been vastly increased. In significant part its old reputation has been rehabilitated. Yet, this rehabilitation has happened without any serious attention to the question of how much the Commission really has changed since the justification for its continued existence was questioned in 1969.

In terms of the ABA committee recommendations, the Commission has failed to develop any meaningful consumer fraud program on the local level. And it has not notably increased the power of the staff to issue complaints (the staff can never do this) or open and close significant investigations. While it is not clear how implementing these recommendations would necessarily improve the Commission's effectiveness, they were made by the ABA committee, and they have not been adopted.

If the committee's recommendation as to antitrust matters was a suggestion that the Commission deemphasize enforcement of the Robinson-

Patman Act, some progress has been made on a formal level. Robinson-Patman enforcement has decreased, but the Commission continues to bring cases under Section 5 of its act that are based on Robinson-Patman principles, and these cases have largely the same adverse effects as those brought formally under the Robinson-Patman Act [262, SB 51, SB 53, SB 54]. There is no more evidence now than there was in 1969—when there was none—to suggest that the Commission's antitrust enforcement activities do not impose significant costs on society, let alone that they produce benefits even approaching their costs. A statement that much of the Commission's antitrust activity is positively harmful, primarily because of its deep-seated hostility to efficiency, may seem extreme to some. There is considerable reason to believe, however, that such is the case [319].

The *Fiscal 1975 Mid-Year Budget Review,* prepared by the FTC Office of Policy Planning and Evaluation, discussed twenty-two separate matters then being pursued by the Bureau of Competition. An estimate of benefits had been calculated for only two of these matters; as to one of them, the Planning Office estimated that success by the Bureau of Competition would raise consumer prices by about 580 percent. This is not to say that all programs were without value. It *is* to say that benefits had been estimated in only two cases and that the production of negative benefits sometimes occurs. In that report, the Planning Office recommended that a proposed budget of approximately 112 man-years for the Bureau of Consumer Protection be reduced to about 68 man-years [85; 86; 82: E1; 83: D1; 84: D1].

The Commission did take formal action on the recommendation that the Office of Program Review be expanded and invigorated so that it can propose "goals, priorities, and effective planning controls." It created an Office of Policy Planning and Evaluation, and, in a related move, it adopted a program budget handled primarily by the executive director. It has thereby created machinery that provides at least the opportunity to compare the relative value of different Commission programs and shift resources among them.

THE DIM FUTURE PROSPECTS OF THE FTC

The existence of this formal machinery, however, in no way suggests that decent results will be forthcoming [398: 1298]. One can imagine the enthusiasm with which *any* institution, let alone one as encrusted as the FTC, could be expected to welcome the work of an office whose charge is to push new goals, priorities, and effective planning controls. Administrative agencies do not want clearly stated goals and priorities, and they want effective planning controls even less. Such devices limit and constrain the choices of individual commissioners and staff members; they interfere with "dis retion." Thus, the influence of the Policy Planning Office and the impact of the program budget on the Commission's choice of policy options have not been great.

The Commission has never agreed on any goal or structure of goals. The purpose or purposes of Commission action have never been articulated in even a marginally operational way. Without a statement of purpose acceptable to the parties involved, there can be no system of priorities, and there most certainly cannot be any effective planning controls. Perhaps there could be a system under which the Commission could control the extent to which the staff observes the budget, which is not always the case now. But, there could never be a system under which a meaningful comparison between different programs could be made, or under which the worth of any one program could be measured.

In truth, the Federal Trade Commission does not have any way in which to measure the benefits created, or the costs imposed, by its various programs. It does not even have a standard that it is willing to use, even in a general way, to make such judgments. The indications are that if the value of the Commission's activities were measured in terms of the effects on the welfare of consumers, those activities would be found wanting.

There has never been even a modestly serious attempt to demonstrate that the benefits flowing from the work of the FTC exceed the costs of such efforts. Thus there can be no serious argument that the activities of the FTC should be strengthened and enlarged.

ADDITIONAL READINGS: 62, 136, 357, 360, 416.

60. Does Antitrust Activity Increase Economic Welfare?

ROBERT D. TOLLISON
Department of Economics
Virginia Polytechnic Institute and State University

Editor's Summary   Monopoly pricing imposes a welfare cost: a deadweight loss because resources are misallocated and neither consumers nor monopoly shareholders benefit. The ranking of industry groups according to the potential gains from antitrust activity is quite different from the ranking according to antitrust cases actually brought from 1945 to 1970. The evidence suggests that the desire to eliminate welfare loss from monopoly pricing and output cannot explain past antitrust activity.

In the enforcement of the Sherman Antitrust Act against price-fixing conspiracies, great emphasis is placed on finding evidence of a price agreement. Some observers believe that this *legal* approach to antitrust action ignores the *economic* effects of price-fixing [SB 53]. The approach seems to lead antitrust officials to prosecute parties in unstable local bread cartels in Michigan, while ignoring the price and output effects of more persistent collusions elsewhere in the economy.

APPROACHES TO THE MONOPOLY PROBLEM

Economists have studied the social costs of monopoly and the gains from its elimination [207]. There has been very little work, however, linking the economists' estimates of the costs of monopoly to the practical allocation problems faced by federal antitrust agencies [265]. Nor have economists used their estimates of monopoly costs across different industries to evaluate the efforts of antitrust agencies.

As a basic approach, suppose that the Antitrust Division rationally weighs the economic benefits and costs from bringing cases against firms in particular industries and then proceeds most often against those industries in which the benefits of legal action most exceed the costs. Although antitrust decisions may be constrained by political, procedural, or legal factors, I attend here to the economic costs and benefits of antitrust activity.

EFFECTS OF MONOPOLY

The economic benefits from antitrust cases are represented most simply by the concept of the welfare loss from monopoly [265, SB 40]. Predictably, a monopolist produces less to secure a higher price and greater profits. Monopoly pricing and production redistributes income from consumers (who pay higher prices for goods) to monopolists (who receive excess profits), and in the process, monopolistic activity imposes on all members of society a "deadweight" loss in social welfare.

The excess profit and deadweight welfare loss effects of converting a competitive industry into a pure monopoly are important to distinguish. The excess profits that monopoly shareholders earn are not lost to the system if the monopoly is formed. These returns are transferred, or redistributed, from consumers to monopoly shareholders.

In converting a competitive industry into a monopoly, however, there is also a second effect of wealth lost by all members of society. One can see why this is called a "welfare loss." It is a loss in the sense that it simply vanishes when the monopoly is formed; it is captured by neither monopoly shareholders nor consumers. It is lost consumer surplus and represents the *net* social cost of the formation of the monopoly in this case. (Consumer surplus is the amount above the actual sum paid for a product that a consumer would be willing to pay for a given amount of the product rather than go without it.) There are several special assumptions that accompany the depiction of the welfare loss from monopoly, but there is no need to complicate matters here by going into these assumptions.

HOW TO ALLOCATE ANTITRUST DIVISION RESOURCES

Welfare loss provides a simple measure of the net economic gains from resource reallocation arising from the demonopolization of industries. If the potential benefits from antitrust action are equated with this welfare measure, other things being equal, antitrust activity against firms in industries should be correlated positively with the relative magnitude of the welfare loss for different industries. Although there may be no relationship between these potential economic benefits and the actual effects of successful antitrust cases, if the Antitrust Division is concerned with securing benefits of this sort, there *should* at least be a link between this measure of benefits and the distribution of cases brought across industries.

The costs of bringing antitrust cases are more difficult to represent. These costs include the economic costs involved in bringing cases to successful completion, such as investigation and courtroom expenses (for both the Antitrust Division and each company, compounded over the time involved) and any indirect costs of the actions. One way to measure such costs is to estimate the actual outlays of time and money for specific cases, using information such as the internal records of the Antitrust Division. Since this information is not available, there is no way directly to measure costs. Consequently, I assume here that the cost of a case is the same for any industry. This assumption converts the problem of allocating antitrust resources into one that relies on pure benefit criteria for deciding where to bring legal actions. The result, therefore, will be only a first approximation of a model of optimal antitrust activity.

EVIDENCE ABOUT ANTITRUST DIVISION ACTIVITY

Welfare losses can be estimated from data on excess profits and sales and from an assumed range of the responsiveness of sales to changes in price. Since I consider antitrust cases brought over the period 1945–1970, the year 1956 (the approximate midpoint of this period and of a business cycle within this period) is the base year I use to estimate welfare losses.

Table 10 ranks 20 two-digit SIC manufacturing industries on the basis of the estimates of welfare losses. That is, the ranking is based on the relative welfare losses from monopoly power within each industry group. If the costs of bringing cases were the same across industries, this ranking would provide an approximate set of priorities for antitrust activity. Presumably, society would gain more if federal antitrust agencies were to operate against industries according to a ranking of this sort rather than, say, spread cases equally across industries or randomly bring cases as evidence comes to the attention of the relevant governmental agency.

If antitrust enforcement activities are measured in terms of the total number of cases brought against different industries, one can form an approximate impression of actual antitrust priorities over the last twenty-five years. Table 10 also presents the number of cases the Antitrust Division brought against different manufacturing industries between 1945 and 1970 and ranks the industries according to the number of cases brought.

This table does not show a very close relationship between actual antitrust activities, 1945–1970, and the priorities that the welfare loss analysis prescribes. A casual examination of this table indicates that there are some important differences between antitrust activity and welfare rankings. The data suggest that in terms of the economic model, the Antitrust Division has underprosecuted in the industries of paper; tobacco; petroleum; transportation equipment; stone, clay, and glass; and primary metals, in that order. The data also suggest that the Antitrust Division has, in a relative sense, overprosecuted in the industries of food, apparel, miscellaneous manufacturing, fabricated metals, electrical machinery, and instruments, again in that order.

With unlimited resources, and with the knowledge that bringing any case will reduce monopoly power, the Antitrust Division can press cases wherever it sees evidence of monopoly. In the "real world," however, in which the Division has a very limited budget, and in which cases represent rather mild methods of alleviating monopoly excesses, the Division must

Table 10 Antitrust Division Cases Brought Against Manufacturing Industries, 1945–1970

Industry Group	Rank by Welfare Losses	Antitrust Cases Brought, 1945–1970	Rank by Cases Brought
Petroleum and Coal Products	1	26	7
Chemicals	2	41	3
Machinery (except Electrical)	3	53	2
Primary Metal Products	4	26	8
Pulp and Paper Products	5	10	15
Transportation Equipment	6	25	11
Stone, Clay, and Glass Products	7	24	12
Printing and Publishing	8	25	10
Instruments and Related Products	9	28	6
Fabricated Metal Products	10	35	4
Electrical Machinery	11	28	5
Food and Kindred Products	12	66	1
Tobacco Manufacturing	13	0	20
Rubber Products	14	16	14
Lumber and Wood Products	15	5	17
Furniture and Fixtures	16	8	16
Miscellaneous Manufacturing	17	26	9
Textile Mill Products	18	1	19
Leather and Leather Products	19	5	18
Apparel and Related Products	20	16	13

SOURCE: *B. and P.A. Report* 4 (Summer 1972). Reprinted by permission. Cornell University Graduate School of Business and Public Administration.

use its resources where it can make the most economic headway. This could require, for example, that the Division bring all its cases against one or two industries in which it can secure the largest welfare gains. Bringing most of its cases (about 15 percent) against the food industry, which ranks twelfth in estimated welfare losses, probably represents a misallocation in terms of this model. At the same time, bringing only ten cases (2 percent) against the paper industry, which ranks fifth in welfare gain possibilities, probably represents a misuse of scarce resources according to the model.

Going beyond the general relationship between welfare losses and antitrust activities, one can estimate statistically the effect of economic industry characteristics on antitrust activity. Using data on antitrust cases and industry sales, excess profits, total assets, and concentration (a measure of monopoly power), Long, Schramm, and Tollison discovered evidence of the importance of certain economic variables in explaining the Antitrust Division's activities [265]. Of the composite measures of the potential benefits from antitrust action tested, welfare losses alone or together with excess profits appeared to play only a minor role in explaining antitrust activity. Thus, economic variables do not appear to explain antitrust activity significantly. However, in the models tested in which economic variables were examined separately, "sales" appeared as a strong explanatory variable throughout, while the "profits" variable performed well in some specifications. In models introducing concentration, the authors found some evidence to support the view that concentration enters the antitrust problem in deciding where to bring cases. These results tend to support the view that the Antitrust Division does look at certain economic variables in making its calculations about bringing cases, although not necessarily because of the relationship between these variables and welfare loss measures.

While economic variables may influence antitrust decisions, Long, Schramm, and Tollison stressed that all the models tested explained at best 50 to 60 percent of the variance in cases brought across industries. Much of the explanation for antitrust activity clearly lies outside their models. This finding indicates the need for additional work in specifying and testing models such as those discussed here and in developing methods to improve the allocation of existing antitrust resources. These are important issues worthy of further research; indeed, such research would blend nicely with the recent increased efforts of the Federal Trade Commission to develop statistical information on its activities.

ADDITIONAL READINGS: 10, 147, 246, 303, 356, 360, 416, 425, 433, 462.

61. Should Criteria for Antitrust Action Be Broadened?

ALLEN HYMAN
Southwestern University School of Law

Editor's Summary   Politicians and self-appointed analysts argue that it is time to "deconcentrate" industries. This policy would do far more harm than good. One can define any industry as being concentrated, depending upon how one defines the market area and the number of firms in the industry. Firms may be large (and therefore classified as monopolists) because of their superior efficiency and because their products are highly salable. So, when persons either in or out of government call for a law that would dissolve concentrated industries, they might well be calling for a law that would outlaw the most efficient and productive sector in our society.

There is no controversy more fundamental to the continuing debate concerning modification of the antitrust laws than that over the regulation of what are termed "concentrated industries" [31]. Both the 1973 legislative proposals and the currently pending modification of the antitrust laws are attempted cures for what is termed "the decline of competition in industries with oligopoly or monopoly power" [Antitrust Improvement Act of 1976, Part II: 168–170].

PROPOSALS TO "DECONCENTRATE"

Concentrated industries not only are often accused of being monopolies but also are repeatedly said to cause inflation and unemployment. According to some, these industries can even " . . . impair the ability of federal or state government to operate effectively and democratically" [328: 223].

An industry is labeled "concentrated" if a few, rather than many, firms account for a given percentage of the domestic sales of a particular product. The 1968 White House Task Force on Antitrust Policy, which proposed a law that would have required the Attorney General and the Federal Trade Commission to investigate the structure of markets that appear to be oligopolistic, in its Neal Report defined an oligopoly or concentrated industry as one "where the largest four firms accounted for 70 percent of the domestic industrial output . . . during the previous four or five years." And, the Industrial Reorganization Act of 1973 (the Hart proposal) would presume that an industry is a monopoly "if any four or fewer corporations accounted for 50 percent (or more) of sales in any line of commerce in any section of the country in any year out of the previous three years" [194: 445].

The proponents of these two antitrust proposals readily accept as valid the beliefs about "concentrated" industries I mention earlier. Other chapters in this volume respond to some of these beliefs. These other chapters cite the many studies that clearly demonstrate that no correlation exists between industrial concentration and price changes or wage levels [SB 37, SB 38]. The analysis here is directed toward the alleged relationship between concentration and monopoly power, the same relationship that is the focus of the arguments of those who would render unlawful the *existence* of a "concentrated industry."

Those who strongly suggest that antitrust action should be broadened base their proposals on statistical studies demonstrating that there is some very small correlation between profit rates of return in an industry and the degree of concentration in the industry [SB 50]. These critics, more importantly, accept the very questionable assumption that the higher rates of return in concentrated industries result not from superior efficiency or economies of scale but from tacit collusive arrangements that are more easily accomplished in industries with few, rather than many, firms.

Many statistical investigations demonstrate a positive relationship between concentration rates in particular industries and rates of return. The correlation appears weak and tentative, and other studies demonstrate a lack of correlation, but on balance the majority of the investigations conducted demonstrate some limited correlation between rate of return and industry concentration [32, 69].

PROBLEMS IN DEFINING THE MARKET

Yet, if one analyzes the actual statistical surveys, it becomes apparent that there are major deficiencies in the studies themselves. The studies, for example, use accounting data that tend to overstate the profits of the larger and more successful firms. Industries defined acccording to these studies are so designated by United States census standard industrial codes that do not necessarily correspond to actual product markets. One of the most disturbing deficiencies is that the data exclude the imports of foreign firms; that is, the concentration data measure solely the domestic productive sector, rather than the sales sector, of a particular market.

In contrast to this reliance on pure concentration ratios, the courts in many antitrust cases have realized that the presence of imports affects one's view in describing a market as concentrated or not concentrated. For example, in *United States v. Bliss and Laughlin, Inc.* [202 F. Supp. 334 (1962)], the court, in denying a request for a preliminary injunction to prevent an acquisition by the defendant corporation, noted that the existence of imports (which have increased from 761 tons in 1957 to approximately 8,983 tons in 1960) is proof in part that the merger of two domestic corporations will not result in a lessening of competition in an industry. In many other cases involving mergers, the courts have considered the existence of imports as an important factor in deciding whether a market is too concentrated. In cases involving the alleged monopolization of boat, salt, and typewriter markets, the courts have looked not only at domestic production but also at the *total* sales, including imports.

A simple example demonstrates how the arbitrary use of the domestic productive sector greatly biases the measure of concentration. If one classified the automobile industry in terms of the domestic output of all new automobiles, the market would appear highly concentrated; the four largest domestic firms would account for over 95 percent of the market. If one viewed the industry in terms of all new automobiles sold in the United States, both foreign and domestic, the concentration rate would be considerably lower, and the four largest firms would account for approximately 75 percent of the market. If one included used cars in the definition of the automobile market, the concentration rate would fall drastically, and the four largest firms would probably account for no more than 30 to 40 percent of all sales.

The authors of concentration/profit studies might argue that my concern over the exclusion of imports from their studies overstates a deficiency, since some may have tried to exclude from their samples those industries with large import sectors. Yet, these same authors would probably agree with the argument that concentration is dependent on how one defines an industry (a somewhat subjective procedure, as indicated by the ways in which the authors themselves chose and defined the industries they studied) and that the levels of concentrations in their studies are biased upward.

The resulting effect of this bias is that even those who are responsible for the surveys do not find that the statistical results are conclusive enough to support deconcentration proposals [194]. If one can "find" any level of concentration one desires by appropriately defining a "market," it is perhaps startling that these limited studies should form the basis of legislative proposals that would greatly broaden the antitrust laws and substantially modify the entire structure of industry in this country.

WHICH COMES FIRST: PROFITABILITY OR CONCENTRATION?

Even if one were to accept the validity of the statistical surveys that purport to demonstrate a relationship between concentration and profit rates, one is left with the vitally important question of whether the higher rates of return are the result of collusive agreements, or whether these superior rates of return are generated by superior efficiency and economies. If the higher rates of return result from superior efficiency, one is left with proposals that would dissolve or cripple this country's most efficient business firms. Consider a slightly more complex question: even if higher profits are the result of some monopoly position, they might in part be the result of superior efficiency as well; therefore, any measures directed toward reducing monopoly power might be very costly as they result in reduced efficiency [300: Chap. 6].

Harold Demsetz finds that the rates of return of the smaller firms in concentrated industries are less than those of the larger firms in these industries [125]. Demsetz argues that if the more concentrated industries indeed are cartels, the smaller firms in those industries should participate in the cartels' profits and also "earn" higher rates of return. The lower rates of return of the smaller firms in concentrated industries serve as evidence, therefore, that the greater rates of return derive in part from economies of scale rather than from some degree of monopoly power.

CONCLUSION

Regardless of the final outcome of this debate, at present there is little conclusive evidence to support the kinds of deconcentration laws proposed during the last ten years. The uncomfortable conclusion remains that an antitrust law that includes a deconcentration policy would render unlawful the existence of the most productive sector of our economy.

ADDITIONAL READINGS: 4, 30, 35, 49, 62, 72, 91, 129, 203, 354, 357, 360, 375, 417.

BIBLIOGRAPHY

1. Abdel-Khalik, A. Rashad. "Advertising Effectiveness and Accounting Policy." *Accounting Review* 50 (October 1975):657–670.

2. Ackley, Gardner. "Administered Prices and the Inflationary Process." *American Economic Review, Papers and Proceedings,* 49 (May 1959):419–430.

3. Adams, Av. *Tort Fair Employment and the Equal Employment Opportunity Commission: A Study of Compliance under Title VII of the Civil Rights Act of 1964.* Washington, D.C.: United States Equal Employment Opportunity Commission, Aug. 31, 1972.

4. Adelman, Morris. *Economic Concentration.* Testimony in the U.S. Senate, Subcommittee on Antitrust and Monopoly, Hearings. Washington, D.C., 1964. (See entry under United States Congress.)

5. Adie, Douglas. *An Evaluation of Postal Service Wage Rates.* Washington, D. C.: American Enterprise Institute, 1977.

6. Advisory Committee on Intergovernmental Relations. *Federal-State-Local Finances: Significant Features of Fiscal Federalism.* Washington, D. C.: U.S. Government Printing Office, 1974.

7. Alchian, Armen A. "Corporate Management and Property Rights." In *Economic Policy and the Regulation of Corporate Securities,* edited by Henry G. Manne, pp. 337–360. Washington, D.C.: American Enterprise Institute, 1969.

8. ———. "Information Costs, Pricing, and Resource Unemployment." In *Microeconomic Foundations of Employment and Inflation Theory,* edited by Edmund S. Phelps, pp. 27–52. New York: Norton, 1970.

9. ———. "On Corporations: A Visit with Smith." Paper presented to the Mont Pelerin Society, 26 August 1976, at St. Andrews, Scotland.

10. ———, and Allen, William R. *University Economics.* 3d ed. Belmont, Calif.: Wadsworth, 1972.

11. ———, and Demsetz, Harold. "Production, Information Costs, and Eco-

nomic Organization." *American Economic Review* 62 (December 1972):777–795.

12. ———, and Kessel, Reuben A. "Competition, Monopoly, and the Pursuit of Pecuniary Gain." In *Aspects of Labor Economics,* edited by H. B. Lewis et al., pp. 156–183. Princeton: Princeton University Press, 1962.

13. Alexander, Tom. "It's Time for New Approaches to Pollution Control." *Fortune,* November 1976, pp. 128–131.

14. American Bar Association–American Legal Institute Model Business Corporation Act, Sections 49, 52.

15. Andrews, Kenneth. "Public Responsibility in the Private Corporation." *Journal of Industrial Economics* 20 (April 1972):135-145.

16. *Antitrust Law and Economics Review* 56 (Spring 1970).

17. Areeda, Phillip, and Turner, Donald F. "Predatory Pricing and Related Practices under Section 2 of the Sherman Act." *Harvard Law Review* 88 (February 1975):697–733.

18. ———. "Scherer on Predatory Pricing: A Reply." *Harvard Law Review* 89 (March 1976):891–900.

19. Arrow, Kenneth. *Social Choice and Individual Values.* 2d ed. New York: Wiley, 1963.

20. ———. "Social Responsibility and Economic Efficiency." *Public Policy.* 303 (Summer 1973).

21. ———. "The Theory of Discrimination." In *Discrimination in Labor Markets,* edited by Orley C. Ashenfelter and Albert E. Rees, pp. 3–23. Princeton: Princeton University Press, 1973.

22. Arsht, S. Samuel. "Reply to Professor Cary." *Business Lawyer* 31 (February 1976):1113–1123.

23. Asch, Peter, and Seneca, Joseph J. "Is Collusion Profitable?" *Review of Economics and Statistics* 58 (February 1976):1–12.

24. Ashenfelter, Orley C., and Rees, Albert E., eds. *Discrimination in Labor Markets.* Princeton: Princeton University Press, 1973.

25. Austin, Douglas, and Fishman, Jay. *Corporations in Conflict—The Tender Offer.* Ann Arbor: Masterco Press, 1970.

26. Ayanian, Robert. "The Profit Rates and Economic Performance of Drug Firms." In *Drug Development and Marketing,* edited by Robert B. Helm. Washington, D.C.: American Enterprise Institute, 1975.

26a. ———. "Advertising and Rate of Return." Mimeographed. 1974.

27. Backman, Jules. *Advertising and Competition.* New York: New York University Press, 1967.

28. Bailey, Elizabeth. *Economic Theory of Regulatory Constraint.* Lexington, Mass.: Heath, 1973.

29. Bain, Joe S. "A Note on Pricing in Monopoly and Oligopoly." *American Economic Review* 39 (March 1949):448–464.

30. ———. *Barriers to New Competition.* Cambridge, Mass.: Harvard University Press, 1956.

31. ———. "Economies of Scale, Concentration, and the Condition of Entry in 20 Manufacturing Industries." In *Readings in Industrial Organization and Public Policy,* edited by Robert B. Heflebower and George W. Stocking. Homewood, Ill.: Irwin, 1958.

32. ———. "Relation of Profit Rate to Industry Concentration: American Manufacturing, 1936–1940." *Quarterly Journal of Economics* 65 (August 1951):293–324.

33. ———. "The Profit Rate as a Measure of Monopoly Power." *Quarterly Journal of Economics* 55 (February 1941):271–293.

34. Baran, Paul. "A Marxist View of Consumer Sovereignty." In *Economics: Mainstream Readings and Radical Critiques,* edited by David Mermelstein. New York: Random House, 1970.

35. ———, and Sweezy, Paul. *Monopoly Capital.* New York: Monthly Review Press, 1966.

36. Barnet, Richard J., and Müller, Ronald E. *Global Reach: The Power of the Multinational Corporations.* New York: Simon and Schuster, 1974.

37. Barzel, Yoram. "Investment, Scale, and Growth." *Journal of Political Economy* 79 (March–April 1971):214–231.

38. Baumol, William J. *Business Behavior, Value, and Growth.* rev. ed. New York: Harcourt Brace Jovanovich, 1967.

39. ———. *The Stock Market and Economic Efficiency.* New York: Fordham University Press, 1965.

40. Becker, Gary S. *The Economics of Discrimination.* 2d ed. Chicago: The University of Chicago Press, 1971.

41. Bell, Daniel. *The End of Ideology.* New York: Free Press, 1960.

42. Benham, Lee. "The Effect of Advertising on the Price of Eyeglasses." *Journal of Law and Economics* 15 (October 1972):337–352.

43. Benjamin, Daniel K., and Kormendi, Roger C. "The Interrelationship between Markets for New and Used Durable Goods." *Journal of Law and Economics* 13 (October 1974):381–402.

44. Benston, George J. *Corporate Financial Disclosure in the U.K. and the U.S.A.* Lexington, Mass.: D. C. Heath, 1976.

45. ———. "The Effectiveness and the Effects of the SEC's Accounting Disclosure Requirements." In *Economic Policy and the Regulation of Corporate Securities,* edited by Henry G. Manne. Washington, D.C.: American Enterprise Institute, 1969.

46. ———. "The Federal Trade Commission's Line of Business Program: A Benefit-Cost Analysis." In *Goverment Information Needs and Business Disclosure.* New York: Columbia University Center for Law and Economic Studies, 1977.

47. ———. "Required Disclosure and the Stock Market: An Evaluation of the Securities Exchange Act of 1934." *American Economic Review* 63 (March 1973):132–155.

48. ———. "The Value of the SEC's Accounting Disclosure Requirements." *Accounting Review* 44 (July 1969):515–532.

49. Bergson, Abram. "On Monopoly Welfare Losses." *American Economic Review* 63 (December 1973):853–870.

50. Berle, Adolph A. "Subsidiary Corporations and Credit Manipulation." *Harvard Law Review* 41 (May 1928):874–893.

51. ———. *The Twentieth-Century Capitalist Revolution.* New York: Harcourt Brace Jovanovich, 1954.

52. ———, and Means, Gardiner C. *The Modern Corporation and Private Property.* rev. ed. New York: Harcourt Brace Jovanovich, 1968.

53. Bishop, Joseph W. "Sitting Ducks and Decoy Ducks: New Trends in the Indemnification of Corporate Directors and Officers." *Yale Law Journal* 77 (May 1968):1078–1103.

54. Black, Duncan. "The Decisions of a Committee Using a Special Majority." *Econometrica* 16 (January 1948):245–261.

55. ———. *The Theory of Committees and Elections.* New York: Cambridge University Press, 1963.

56. Blandi, Joseph G. *Maryland Business Corporations, 1783–1852.* Baltimore: Johns Hopkins, 1934.

57. Blank, David M. "Television Advertising: The Great Discount Illusion, or Tonypandy Revisited." *Journal of Business* 41 (January 1968):10–38.

58. Bloch, Harry. "Advertising, Competition, and Market Performance." Ph.D. dissertation, University of Chicago, 1971.

59. ———. "Advertising and Profitability: A Reappraisal." *Journal of Political Economy* 82 (March–April 1974):267–286.

60. Blumberg, Phillip I. "Selected Materials on Corporate Social Responsibility." *The Business Lawyer* 27 (July 1972):1275–1299.

61. Bock, Betty. "Line of Business Reporting: A Quest for a Snark?" *The Conference Board Record* 12 (November 1975):18–22.

62. Bork, Robert H., and Bowman, Ward S. "The Crisis in Antitrust." *Columbia Law Review* 65 (March 1965):363–376.

63. Brabner-Smith, John W. "Federal Incorporation of Business." *Virginia Law Review* 24 (December 1937):159–166.

64. Bradshaw, Thornton. "My Case for National Planning." *Fortune,* February 1977, pp. 103–104.

65. Brewster, Kingman, Jr. "The Corporation and Economic Federalism." Edward S. Mason editor, *The Corporation in Modern Society,* pp. 72–85. Cambridge, Mass.: Harvard University Press, 1959.

66. Bronfenbrenner, Martin, and Holzman, Franklyn D. "Survey of Inflation Theory." *American Economic Review* 53 (September 1963):593–661.

67. Brozen, Yale, ed. *Advertising and Society.* New York: New York University Press, 1974.

68. ———. "The Antitrust Task Force Deconcentration Recommendation." *Journal of Law and Economics* 13 (October 1970):279–292.

69. ———. "Bain's Concentration and Rates of Return Revisited." *Journal of Law and Economics* 14 (October 1971):351–369.

70. ———. "Barriers Facilitate Entry." *The Antitrust Bulletin* 14 (Winter 1969):851–854.

71. ———. "Business Leadership and Technological Change." *The American Journal of Economics and Sociology* 14 (October 1954):13–30.

72. ———. "Concentration and Profits: Does Concentration Matter?" *The Antitrust Bulletin* 19 (Summer 1974):381–399.

73. ———. "Determinants of Entrepreneurial Ability." *Social Research* 21 (Summer 1954):339–364.

74. ———. "The Persistence of 'High Rates of Return' in High-Stable Concentration Industries." *Journal of Law and Economics* 14 (October 1971):501–512.

75. ———. "The Social Impact of Technological Change." *Journal of Engineering Education* 41 (November 1950):148–154.

76. ———. "Technological Change, Ideology and Productivity." *Political Science Quarterly* 70 (December 1955):522–542.

77. ———. "Technology and the Structure of Society." Mimeographed.

78. Buchanan, James M., and Tullock, Gordon. *The Calculus of Consent: Logical Foundations of Constitutional Democracy.* Ann Arbor: The University of Michigan Press, 1962.

79. Bunting, Robert L. *Employer Concentration in Local Labor Markets.* Chapel Hill: The University of North Carolina Press, 1962.

80. ———. "A Note on Large Firms and Labor Market Concentration." *Journal of Political Economy* 74 (August 1966):403–406.

81. Burck, Charles G. "A Group Profile of the Fortune 500 Chief Executive." *Fortune,* May 1976, p. 173.

82. Bureau of National Affairs. *Antitrust and Trade Regulation Reporter* 692 (Dec. 10, 1974).

83. Bureau of National Affairs. *Antitrust and Trade Regulation Reporter* 693 (Dec. 17, 1974).

84. Bureau of National Affairs. *Antitrust and Trade Regulation Reporter* 694 (Dec. 24, 1974).

85. Bureau of National Affairs. *Antitrust and Trade Regulation Reporter* (Special Supplement) 723 (July 22, 1975).

86. Bureau of National Affairs. *Antitrust and Trade Regulation Reporter* 758 (Apr. 6, 1976).

87. Business International. Survey reported in *Commerical and Financial Chronicle,* May 1976, p. 32.

88. Cadmin, John W. *The Corporation in New Jersey: Business and Politics, 1791–1875.* Cambridge, Mass.: Harvard University Press, 1949.

89. Cary, William L. "Federalism and Corporate Law: Reflections upon Delaware." *Yale Law Journal* 83 (March 1974):663–705.

90. Cataldo, Bernard F. "Limited Liability with One-Man Companies and Subsidiary Corporations." *Law and Contemporary Problems* 18 (Autumn 1953):473–504.

91. Chamberlin, Edward. *The Theory of Monopolistic Competition.* 8th ed. Cambridge, Mass.: Harvard University Press, 1962.

92. Chirelstein, Marvin A. "Corporate Law Reform." In *Social Responsibility and the Business Predicament,* edited by James W. McKie. Washington, D.C.: The Brookings Institution, 1974.

93. Ciscel, David H. "Determinants of Executive Compensation." *Southern Economic Journal,* April 1974, pp. 613–617.

94. Clark, Victor. *History of Manufacture in the United States.* New York: McGraw-Hill, 1929.

95. Clarkson, Kenneth W. *Intangible Capital and Rates of Return.* Washington, D.C.: American Enterprise Institute, 1977.

96. ———. "The Right Way, the Wrong and the Government Way." *Res Publica* 2 (Fall 1974):14–19.

97. ———. "Some Implications of Property Rights in Hospital Management." *Journal of Law and Economics* 15 (October 1972):363–384.

98. Coase, Ronald. "The Nature of the Firm." *Economica* 4 (November 1937):386–405.

99. ———. "The Problem of Social Cost." *Journal of Law and Economics* 3 (October 1960):1–44.

100. Cochran, Thomas C. *Business in American Life: A History.* New York: McGraw-Hill, 1972.

101. Collins, Daniel W. "SEC Product Line Reporting and Market Efficiency." *Journal of Financial Economics* 2 (June 1975):125–164.

102. Comanor, William S. "Racial Discrimination in American Industry." *Economica* 40 (November 1973):363–378.

103. ———, and Leibenstein, Harvey. "Allocative Efficiency, X-Efficiency and the Measure of Welfare Losses." *Economica* 36 (August 1969):304–309.

104. ———, and Wilson, Thomas A. *Advertising and Market Power.* Cambridge, Mass.: Harvard University Press, 1974.

105. ———, and Wilson, Thomas A. "Advertising Market Structure and Performance." *Review of Economics and Statistics* 49 (November 1967):423–440.

106. Cook, Donald C., and Feldman, Myer. "Insider Trading under the Securities Exchange Act." *Harvard Law Review* 66 (February 1953):612–641.

107. Cooper, Richard N. "Trade Policy Is Foreign Policy." *Foreign Policy* 9 (Winter 1972–1973):18–36.

108. Cootner, Paul, ed. *The Random Character of Stock Market Prices.* Cambridge, Mass.: The M.I.T. Press, 1964.

109. Cox, Edward F.; Fellmeth, Robert C.; and Schulz, John E. *The Nader Report on the Federal Trade Commission.* New York: R. W. Baron, 1969.

110. Crain, Mark; Deaton, Thomas; and Tollison, Robert. "On the Survival of Corporate Executives." *Southern Economic Journal* 43 (January 1977): 1372–1375.

111. ———. "The Determinants of Tenure in the U.S. House of Representatives." Mimeographed. Virginia Polytechnic Institute and State University, 1976.

112. ———, and Tollison, Robert. "Managerial Incentives in Regulated and Nonregulated Firms." Mimeographed. Virginia Polytechnic Institute and State University, 1976.

113. ———. "State Budget Sizes and the Marginal Productivity of Governors." *Public Choice,* (Fall 1976):91–96.

114. Crouch, Robert L. *Macroeconomics.* New York: Harcourt Brace Jovanovich, 1972.

115. Cyert, Richard M., and Hedrick, Charles L. "Theory of the Firm: Past, Present, and Future; An Interpretation." *Journal of Economic Literature* 10 (June 1972):398–412.

116. Dahl, Robert. "Governing the Giant Corporation." In *Corporate Power in America,* edited by Ralph Nader and Mark Green, pp. 10–24. New York: Grossman, 1973.

117. ———. *After the Revolution: Authority in a Good Society.* New Haven: Yale University Press, 1970.

118. Davis, Joseph S. *Essays in the Earlier History of American Corporations.* Vol. 2. New York: Russell and Russell, 1965.

119. Davis, Lance E. "Capital Immobilities and Finance Capitalism: A Study of Economic Evolution in the United States, 1820–1920." *Explorations in Entrepreneurial History* 1, ser. 2 (Fall 1963):88–105.

120. ———. "The Investment Market, 1870–1914: The Evolution of a National Market." *Journal of Economic History* 25 (September 1965):355–399.

121. Day, Richard H. "A Note on the Dynamics of Cost Competition within an Industry." *Oxford Economic Papers* 20 (November 1968):369–373.

122. De Alessi, Louis. "Managerial Tenure under Private and Government Ownership in the Electric Power Industry." *Journal of Political Economy* 82 (May 1974):645–653.

123. ———. "Private Property and Dispersion of Ownership in Large Corporations." *Journal of Finance* 28 (September 1973):839–851.

124. Demsetz, Harold. "Advertising in the Affluent Society." In *Advertising and Society,* edited by Yale Brozen. New York: New York University Press, 1974.

125. ———. "Industry Structure, Market Rivalry, and Public Policy." *Journal of Law and Economics* 16 (April 1973):1–9.

126. ———. *The Market Concentration Doctrine.* Washington, D.C.: American Enterprise Institute, August 1973.

127. ———. "Perfect Competition Regulation, and the Stock Market." In *Economic Policy and the Regulation of Corporate Securities,* edited by Henry G. Manne, pp. 4–5. Washington, D.C.: American Enterprise Institute, 1969.

128. ———. "The Welfare and Empirical Implications of Monopolistic Competition." *Economic Journal* 74 (September 1964):623–641.

129. ———. "Two Systems of Belief about Monopoly." In *Industrial Concentration: The New Learning,* edited by Harvey J. Goldschmid, H. Michael Mann, and J. Fred Weston, pp. 164–184. Boston: Little, Brown, 1974.

130. ———. "Why Regulate Utilities?" *Journal of Law and Economics* 11 (April 1968):55–65.

131. DePodwin, Horace J., and Selden, Richard T. "Business Pricing Policies and Inflation." *Journal of Political Economy* 71 (April 1963):116–127.

132. Devine, Eugene J. *An Analysis of Manpower Shortages in Local Government.* New York: Praeger, 1970.

133. Dewing, A. "A Statistical Test of the Success of Consolidations." *Quarterly Journal of Economics* 36 (November 1921):84–101.

134. Dick, Daniel T., and Medoff, Marshall H. "Filtering by Race and Education in the United States Manufacturing Sector: Constant Ratio Elasticity of Substitution Evidence." *Review of Economics and Statistics* 58 (1976):148–155.

135. Diebold, John. "Multinational Corporations: Why Be Scared of Them?" *Foreign Policy* 12 (Fall 1973):79–95.

136. Director, Aaron, and Levi, Edward H. "Law and the Future: Trade Regulation." *Northwestern University Law Review* 51 (May–June 1956):281–296.

137. Dodd, Edwin M. *American Business Corporations Until 1860.* Cambridge, Mass.: Harvard University Press, 1954.

138. Dolan, Edwin G. "Alienation, Freedom, and Economic Organization." *Journal of Political Economy* 79 (1971):1087–1094.

139. Domar, Evsey D. "Poor Old Capitalism: A Review Article." *Journal of Political Economy* 82 (November–December 1974):1301–1313.

140. Dorfman, Robert, and Dorfman, Nancy S. *Economics of the Environment.* New York: Norton, 1972.

141. Due, John F. "Studies of State-Local Tax Influences on Location of Industry." *National Tax Journal* 14 (June 1961):163–173.

142. Duesenberry, James S. "The Mechanics of Inflation." *Review of Economics and Statistics,* (May 1950):144–149.

143. Dykstra, Daniel J. "The Revival of the Derivative Suit." *University of Pennsylvania Law Review* 116 (November 1967):74–101.

144. *Economic Report of the President 1977.* Washington, D.C.: U.S. Government Printing Office, 1977, pp. 277–284.

145. Eicher, Alfred S. *The Megacorp and Oligopoly.* New York: Cambridge University Press, 1976.

146. Eisenberg, Melvin A. "Access to the Corporate Proxy Machinery." *Harvard Law Review* 83 (May 1970):1489.

147. Elzinga, Kenneth. "Predatory Pricing: The Case of the Gunpowder Trust." *Journal of Law and Economics* 13 (April 1970):223–240.

148. Engman, Louis. "Address before 1974 Fall Conference." Detroit, Mich.: Financial Analysts Federation, Oct. 7, 1974.

149. Epstein, Edwin M. *The Corporation in American Politics.* Englewood Cliffs, N.J.: Prentice-Hall, 1969.

150. ———. "Dimensions of Corporate Power, Part I." *California Management Review* 16 (1973):9–23.

151. ———. "Dimensions of Corporate Power, Part II." *California Management Review* 16 (1974):32–47.

152. *Equal Employment Opportunity Commission Annual Reports.* Washington, D.C.: United States Equal Employment Opportunity Commission, 1966–67 and 1972–73.

153. "Extortionate Corporate Litigation: The Strike Suit." *Columbia Law Review* 34 (November 1934):1308–1347.

154. Fama, Eugene F. "Efficient Capital Markets: A Review of Theory and Empirical Work." *Journal of Finance* 25 (May 1970):383–417.

155. ———. "Risk, Return, and Equilibrium." *Journal of Political Economy* 79 (January–February 1971):30–55.

156. ———; Fisher, Lawrence; Jenson, Michael; and Roll, Richard. "The Adjustment of Stock Prices to New Information." *International Economic Review* 10 (February 1969):1–21.

157. ———, and Laffer, Arthur B. "Information and Capital Markets." *Journal of Business* 44 (July 1971):289–298.

158. ———, and MacBeth, James D. "Risk, Return, and Equilibrium: Empirical Tests." *Journal of Political Economy* 81 (May–June 1973):607–636.

159. Federal Trade Commission. *On the Influence of Market Structure on the Profit Performance of Food Manufacturing Companies.* Washington, D.C.: U.S. Government Printing Office, 1969.

160. Fellner, William. "Demand Inflation, Cost Inflation, and Collective Bargaining." In *The Public Stake in Union Power,* edited by Phillip D. Bradley. Charlottesville: University Press of Virginia, 1959.

161. Ferguson, James M. *Advertising and Competition: Theory, Measurement, Fact.* Cambridge, Mass.: Ballinger, 1974.

162. ———. "Anticompetitive Effects of the FTC's Attack on Product-Extension Mergers." *St. John's Law Review* 44 (Spring 1970):392–415.

163. Fisher, I. N., and Hall, G. R. "Risk and Corporate Rates of Return." *Quarterly Journal of Economics* 83 (February 1969):79–92.

164. Fleischer, Arthur. "'Federal Corporation Law': An Assessment." *Harvard Law Review* 78 (April 1965):1145–1179.

165. Fog, Bjarke. "How Are Cartel Prices Determined?" *Journal of Industrial Economics,* 5 (November 1956):16–23.

166. Folk, Ernest L. "Some Reflections of a Corporation Law Draftsman." *Connecticut Bar Journal* 42 (March 1968):409–435.

167. ———. "State Statutes: Their Role in Prescribing Norms of Responsible Management Conduct." *The Business Lawyer* 31 (February 1976):1031–1090.

168. "Fortune Directory of 500 Largest Industrial Corporations." *Fortune,* May 1975, pp. 208–241.

169. Frech, Harry E., III. "The Property Rights Theory of the Firm: Empirical Results from a Natural Experiment." *Journal of Political Economy* 84 (February 1976):143–152.

170. Freeman, Richard. "Education and Racial Discrimination." In *Discrimination in Labor Markets,* edited by Orley C. Ashenfelter and Albert E. Rees. Princeton: Princeton University Press, 1973.

171. Friend, Irwin, and Herman, Edward S. "The SEC through a Glass Darkly." *Journal of Business* 37 (October 1964):382–405.

172. Friedman, Milton. *An Economist's Protest.* Glen Ridge, N.J.: Thomas Horton and Daughters, 1972, pp. 177–184.

173. ———. *Capitalism and Freedom.* Chicago: The University of Chicago Press, 1962.

174. ———. "Social Responsibility of Business." *The New York Times Magazine,* 14 September 1970. Reprinted in Friedman, Milton. *An Economist's Protest.* Glen Ridge, N.J.: Thomas Horton and Daughters, 1975, pp. 177–184.

175. ———, ed. *Studies in the Quantity Theory of Money.* Chicago: The University of Chicago Press, 1956.

176. ———. "The Uses of Corruption." *Newsweek,* 22 March 1976, p. 73.

177. ———. "What Price Guideposts?" In *Guidelines: Informal Controls and the Market Place,* edited by George P. Schultz and Robert Z. Aliber, pp. 17–39. Chicago: The University of Chicago Press, 1966.

178. ———, and Schwartz, Anna J. *A Monetary History of the United States 1867– 1960.* Princeton, N.J.: Princeton University Press, 1963.

179. Fromm, Erich. *Marx's Concept of Man.* New York: Ungar, 1961.

180. Fuller, Warner. "The Incorporated Individual: A Study of the One-Man Company." *Harvard Law Review* 51 (June 1938):1373–1406.

181. Furubotn, Eirik G. "Bank Credit and the Labor Managed Firm: The Yugoslav Case." *Canadian-American Slavic Studies* 8 (1974):38–106.

182. ———. "Worker Alienation and the Structure of the Firm." In *Governmental Controls and the Free Market: The U.S. Economy in the 1970's,* edited by Svetozar Pejovich, pp. 195–225. College Station, Tex.: Texas A&M University Press, 1976.

183. ———, and Pejovich, Svetozar, eds. *Economics of Property Rights.* Cambridge, Mass.: Ballinger, 1974.

184. ———, and Pejovich, Svetozar. "Property Rights and the Behavior of the Firm in a Socialist State: The Example of Yugoslavia." *Zeitschrift fur National- okonomie* 30 (1970):431–454.

185. Galbraith, John Kenneth. *American Capitalism.* Boston: Houghton Mifflin, 1952.

186. ———. "A Review of a Review." *The Public Interest* 9 (Fall 1967):109–118.

187. ———. *Economics and the Public Purpose*. Boston: Houghton Mifflin, 1973.

188. ———. *Hearings before the Subcommittee on Antitrust and Monopoly, United States Senate, 1957*. Washington, D.C.: U.S. Government Printing Office, 1957.

189. ———. *The New Industrial State*. Boston: Houghton Mifflin, 1967.

190. "Georgia Power Case: Another Federal Agency Comes of Age, Or, 'My God! Our Employer-Client's Testing Practices Are Being Challenged by the EEOC!'" *Marquette Law Review* 57 (1974):515–557.

191. Goldman, Marshall I. "The Convergence of Environmental Disruption." *Science*, 2 October 1970, pp. 37–42.

192. ———. *Ecology and Economics: Controlling Pollution in the 70's*. Englewood Cliffs, N.J.: Prentice-Hall, 1972.

193. ———. "Product Differentiation and Advertising: Some Lessons from Soviet Experience." *Journal of Political Economy* 68 (August 1960):346–357.

194. Goldschmid, Harvey J.; Mann, H. Michael; Weston, J. Fred; eds. *Industrial Concentration: The New Learning*. Boston: Little, Brown, 1974, pp. 178–179.

195. Goodkind, Conrad G. "Blue Sky Law: Is There Merit in the Merit Requirements?" *Wisconsin Law Review* (November 1976):79–123.

196. Gort, Michael, and Hogarty, Thomas F. "New Evidence on Mergers." *Journal of Law and Economics* 13 (April 1970):167–184.

197. Green, Mark, and Nader, Ralph. "Economic Regulation vs. Competition: Uncle Sam the Monopoly Man." *Yale Law Journal* 82 (April 1973):871–889.

198. Greer, Edward. "The Public Interest University." In *Economics: Mainstream Readings and Radical Critiques*, edited by David Mermelstein. New York: Random House, 1970.

199. Griliches, Zvi. "Research Costs and Social Returns: Hybrid Corn and Related Innovations." *Journal of Political Economy* 66 (October 1958):419–431.

200. Grodin, Joseph R. *Union Government and the Law: British and American Experiences*. New York: Institute of Industrial Relations, 1961.

201. Gunderson, Gerald *A New Economic History of America*. New York: McGraw-Hill, 1976.

202. Hacker, Louis. *American Problems of Today*. New York: Crofts, 1938.

203. Hall, Marshall, and Weiss, Leonard. "Firm Size and Profitability." *Review of Economics and Statistics* 49 (August 1967):319–331.

204. Hall, R. L., and Hitch, Charles J. "Price Theory and Business Behavior." *Oxford Economic Papers* (May 1939):12–45.

205. Hammett, Carol G. "Attorneys' Fees in Shareholder Derivative Suits: The Substantial Benefit Rule Reexamined." *California Law Review* 60 (January 1972):164–190.

206. Handler, Milton; Blake, Harlan M.; Pitofsky, Robert; and Goldschmid, Harvey J. *Cases and Materials on Trade Regulation*. Mineola, N.Y.: Foundation Press, 1975.

207. Harberger, Arnold. "Monopoly and Resource Allocation." *American Economic Review, Papers and Proceedings* 44 (May 1954):77–87.

208. Hardin, Garrett. "The Tragedy of the Commons." *Science*, 13 December 1968, pp. 1243–1248.

209. Hay, George A., and Kelley, Daniel. "An Empirical Survey of Price Fixing Conspiracies." *Journal of Law and Economics* 17 (April 1974):13–38.

210. Hayes, Samuel L., III, and Taussig, Russell A. "Are Cash Takeover Bids Unethical?" *Financial Analysts Journal* 23 (January–February 1967):107–111.

211. ——, and Taussig, Russell A. "Tactics of Cash Takeover Bids." *Harvard Business Review* 45 (March–April 1967):135–148.

212. Henn, Harry G. *Corporations*. 2d ed. St. Paul, Minn.: West, 1970.

213. Hessen, Robert. "Creatures of the State? The Case against Federal Chartering of Corporations." *Barron's,* 24 May 1976, p. 7.

214. Hetherington, J. A. C. "Fact and Legal Theory: Shareholders, Managers, and Corporate Social Responsibility." *Stanford Law Review* 21 (January 1969):248–292.

215. ——. "Insider Trading and the Logic of the Law." *Wisconsin Law Review,* (Summer 1967):720–737.

216. Hindley, Brian. "Separation of Ownership and Control in the Modern Corporation." *Journal of Law and Economics* 13 (April 1970):185–221.

217. Hirschman, Albert O. *Exit, Voice and Loyalty: Responses to Decline in Firms, Organizations, and States*. Cambridge, Mass.: Harvard University Press, 1970.

218. Hoffer, G.; Marchand, J.; and Albertine, J. "Pricing in the Automobile Industry: A Simple Econometric Model." *Southern Economic Journal* 43 (July 1976):948–951.

219. Horwitz, Bertrand, and Kolodny, Richard. "Line of Business Reporting and Security Prices: An Analysis of an SEC Disclosure Rule." *Bell Journal of Economics* 8 (Spring 1977):234–249.

220. Hughes, Jonathan R. T. "Eight Tycoons: The Entrepreneur and American History." *Explorations in Entrepreneurial History* 1, ser. 2 (Spring/Autumn 1964):213–231.

221. ——. *The Vital Few*. Boston: Houghton Mifflin, 1966.

222. Hunt, Bishop C. *The Development of the Business Corporation in England, 1800–1867*. Cambridge, Mass.: Harvard University Press, 1936.

223. Hutt, William. *The Strike-Threat System*. New Rochelle, N.Y.: Arlington House, 1973.

224. Hyman, Allen. "Economics of State Corporation Law: The Delaware Controversy." Working paper. University of Miami, Mar. 2, 1977.

225. Imel, Blake, and Helmberger, Peter. "Estimation of Structure-Profit Relationships with Application to the Food Processing Sector." *American Economic Review* 61 (September 1971):614–627.

226. Jacoby, Neil. Review of *Taming the Giant Corporation,* by Ralph Nader et al., in *Wall Street Journal,* 10 January 1977.

227. Jenson, Michael C., and Meckling, William H. "Theory of the Firm: Managerial Behavior, Agency Costs and Ownership Structure." *Journal of Financial Analysis* 3 (October 1976):305–360.

228. Jewkes, John; Sawers, David; and Stillerman, Richard. *The Sources of Invention.* 2d ed. New York: Norton, 1969.

229. Kamerschen, David. "An Estimation of the Welfare Losses from Monopoly in the American Economy." *Western Economic Journal* 4 (Summer 1966):221–236.

230. Karnosky, Denis S. "The Link between Money and Price—1971–1976." *Federal Reserve Bank of St. Louis Bulletin,* June 1976, pp. 17–23.

231. Kaysen, Carl, and Turner, Donald F. *Antitrust Policy: An Economic and Legal Analysis.* Cambridge, Mass.: Harvard University Press, 1959.

232. Kazman, Samuel. "The Economics of the 1974 Federal Election Campaign Act Amendments." *Buffalo Law Review* 25 (Winter 1976):519–543.

233. Kessel, Reuben. "Economic Effects of Federal Regulations of Milk Markets." *Journal of Law and Economics* 10 (October 1967):51–78.

234. ———. "Price Discrimination in Medicine." *Journal of Law and Economics* 1 (October 1958):20–53.

235. Kilpatrick, Robert W. "The Choice among Alternative Measures of Industrial Concentration." *Review of Economics and Statistics* 49 (May 1967):258–260.

236. Kindleberger, Charles P. *International Corporation: A Symposium.* Cambridge, Mass.: The M.I.T. Press, 1970.

237. Kirkpatrick, Miles W., et al. "ABA Report on the FTC: A Summary." *Antitrust Law and Economics Review* 3 (Spring 1970):58–65.

238. Klein, Benjamin. "The Competitive Supply of Money." *Journal of Money, Credit, and Banking* (November 1974):423–453.

239. Kneese, Allen V. *Pollution, Prices, and Public Policy.* Washington, D. C.: The Brookings Institution, 1975.

240. ———. "Water Quality Management by Regional Authorities in the Ruhr Area." *Papers and Proceedings of the Regional Science Association* 11 (1963).

241. Knepper, William E. "Officers and Directors: Indemnification and Liability Insurance—An Update." *Business Lawyer* 30 (April 1975):951–967.

242. Knight, Frank. *Risk, Uncertainty, and Profit.* Boston: Houghton Mifflin, 1957.

243. Knight, Kenneth E.; Koznetsky, G.; and Baca, Helen R. *Industry Views of the Role of the Federal Government in Industrial Innovation.* Austin: University of Texas Graduate School of Business, 1976.

244. Kolko, Gabriel. *Railroads and Regulation: 1887–1916.* Princeton: Princeton University Press, 1965.

245. Koller, Roland H. "The Myth of Predatory Pricing: An Empirical Study." *Antitrust Law and Economics Review* 4 (Summer 1971):105–123.

246. ———. "Predatory Pricing in a Market Economy." Ph.D. dissertation, University of Wisconsin, 1969.

247. "Korn/Ferry International Board of Directors Annual Study 8." Cited in *The Outside Director of the Public Corporation,* February 1976.

248. Kreinen, Mordechai E. *International Economics: A Policy Approach.* 2d ed. New York: Harcourt Brace Jovanovich, 1975.

249. Kripke, Homer. "The SEC, the Accountants, Some Myths and Some Realities." *New York University Law Review* 45 (December 1970):1151–1205.

250. Laffer, Arthur, and Ranson, R. David. "A Formal Model of the Economy." *Journal of Business* 44 (July 1971):247–270.

251. ———, and Zechner, R. "Some Evidence on the Formation, Efficiency, and Accuracy of Anticipation of Nominal Yields." *Journal of Monetary Economics,* July 1975, pp. 327–342.

252. Landers, Jonathan M. "A Unified Approach to Parent, Subsidiary, and Affiliate Questions in Bankruptcy." *University of Chicago Law Review* 42 (Summer 1975):589–652.

253. Latty, Elvin R. "Why Are Business Corporation Laws Largely 'Enabling'?" *Cornell Law Quarterly* 50 (Summer 1965):599–619.

254. Leibenstein, Harvey. "Allocative Efficiency vs. 'X-Efficiency'." *American Economic Review* 56 (June 1966):392–415.

255. Lev, Baruch, and Mandelker, Gershon. "The Microeconomic Consequences of Corporate Mergers." *Journal of Business* 45 (January 1972):85–104.

256. Levi, Leone. *The History of the British Commerce and of the Economic Progress of the British Nation, 1763–1878.* 2d ed. London: J. Murray, 1880.

257. Levy, David. "Marxism and Alienation." *New Individualist Review* 5 (Winter 1968):34–41.

258. Lewellen, Wilbur G. *Executive Compensation in Large Industrial Corporations.* New York: National Bureau of Economic Research, 1968.

259. ———. *The Ownership Income of Management.* New York: National Bureau of Economic Research, 1971.

260. ———. "Recent Evidence on Senior Executive Pay." *National Tax Journal* 28 (June 1975):159–172.

261. ———, and Huntsman, Blaine. "Managerial Pay and Corporate Performance." *American Economic Review* 60 (September 1970):710–720.

262. Liebeler, Wesley J. "The Robinson-Patman Act—Let's Repeal It." *Antitrust Law Journal* 45 (Spring 1976):18–43.

263. Livermore, Shaw *Early American Land Companies.* New York: The Commonwealth Fund, 1939.

264. Long, Norton E. "The Corporation and the Local Community." *The Annals of the American Academy of Political and Social Science* 343 (September 1962):118–127.

265. Long, William; Schramm, Richard; and Tollison, Robert. "The Economic Determinants of Antitrust Activity." *Journal of Law and Economics* 16 (October 1973):351–364.

266. Lorie, James, and Brealey, Richard, eds. *Modern Developments in Investment Management.* New York: Praeger, 1972.

267. ———, and Hamilton, Mary T. *The Stock Market: Theories and Evidence.* Homewood, Ill.: Dow Jones–Irwin, 1973.

268. ———, and Niederhoffer, Victor. "Predictive and Statistical Properties of Insider Trading." *Journal of Law and Economics* 11 (April 1968):35–53.

269. Lustgarten, Steven. *Industrial Concentration and Inflation.* Domestic Affairs Study 31. Washington, D.C.: American Enterprise Institute, June 1975.

270. Macaulay, Stewart. "Non-Contractual Relations in Business: A Preliminary Study." *The American Sociological Review* 28 (February 1963):55–67.

271. Machlup, Fritz. "Another View of Cost-Push and Demand-Pull Inflation." *Review of Economics and Statistics* 42 (May 1960):125–139.

272. ———. "Patent." In *International Encyclopedia of the Social Sciences* II, edited by David L. Sills, pp. 461–472. New York: Macmillan, 1968.

273. Malkiel, Burton G., and Malkiel, Judith A. "Male-Female Pay Differentials in Professional Employment." *American Economic Review* 63 (September 1973):693–705.

274. Mandel, Ernest. "Workers under Neo-Capitalism." In *Economics: Mainstream Readings and Radical Critiques,* edited by David Mermelstein, pp. 159–172. New York: Random House, 1970.

275. Mandelker, Gershon, "Risk and Return: The Case of Merging Firms." *Journal of Financial Economics* 1 (1974):303–335.

276. Mann, H. Michael. "Seller Concentration, Barriers to Entry, and Rates of Return in Thirty Industries, 1950–1960." *Review of Economics and Statistics* 48 (August 1966):296–307.

277. Manne, Henry G. "Accounting and Administrative Law Aspects of Gerstle v. Gamble-Skogmo, Inc." *New York Law Forum* 15 (Summer 1969):304–331.

278. ———. "CSR: Wrong Pew, Wrong Church, and Wrong Doctrine." *The Alternative* (December 1975):26–28.

279. ———. "Insider Trading and the Administrative Process." *George Washington Law Review* 35 (March 1967):473–511.

280. ———. "Insider Trading and the Law Professors." *Vanderbilt Law Review* 23 (1970):547–590.

281. ———. *Insider Trading and the Stock Market*. New York: Free Press, 1966, pp. 8–10.

282. ———. "Mergers and the Market for Corporate Control." *Journal of Political Economy* 73 (April 1965):110–120.

283. ———. "The Myth of Corporate Responsibility—Or, Will the Real Ralph Nader Please Stand Up?" *The Business Lawyer* 26 (November 1970):533–543.

284. ———. "Our Two Corporation Systems: Law and Economics." *Virginia Law Review* 53 (March 1967):259–284.

285. ———. "Some Theoretical Aspects of Share Voting." *Columbia Law Review* 64 (December 1964):1426–1445.

286. ———, ed. *Economic Policy and the Regulation of Corporate Securities*. Washington, D.C.: American Enterprise Institute, 1969.

287. ———, ed. *The Economics of Legal Relationships: Readings in the Theory of Property Rights*. St. Paul, Minn.: West, 1975.

288. ———, et al. *Wall Street in Transition: The Emerging System and Its Impact on the Economy*. New York: New York University Press, 1974, pp. 23–103.

289. ———, and Wallich, H. *The Modern Corporation and Social Responsibility*. Washington, D.C.: American Enterprise Institute, 1972.

290. Mansfield, Edwin. *Industrial Research and Technological Innovation*. New York: Norton, 1968.

291. ———. *Technological Change*. New York: Norton, 1971.

292. Marcuse, Herbert. *One Dimensional Man*. Boston: Beacon Press, 1964.

293. Marglin, Stephen A. "What Do Bosses Do? Part I." *The Review of Radical Political Economics* 6 (Summer 1974):60–112.

294. ———. "What Do Bosses Do? Part II." *The Review of Radical Political Economics* 7 (Spring 1975):20–37.

295. Marris, Robin. "Galbraith, Solow, and the Truth about Corporations." *The Public Interest* 11 (Spring 1968):37–46.

296. Mason, Lowell B. Speech at Marquette University, 11 April 1950. Quoted in Flemming, Harold. *Ten Thousand Commandments: A Story of the Antitrust Laws*. Englewood Cliffs, N.J.: Prentice-Hall, 1951, p. 20.

297. Masson, Robert. "Executive Motivations, Earnings, and Consequent Equity Performance." *Journal of Political Economy* 79 (November–December 1971):1278–1292.

298. McAllister, H. E. "Price Statistics of the Federal Government." Staff Paper Number 8 in Joint Economic Committee, *Government Price Statistics.* Washington, D.C.: U.S. Government Printing Office, Jan. 21, 1961.

299. McEachern, William A. "Corporate Control and Risk." *Economic Inquiry* 14 (June 1976):270–278.

300. McGee, John S. *The Defense of Industrial Concentration.* New York: Praeger, 1971.

301. ———. "Economies of Size in Auto Body Manufacture." *Journal of Law and Economics* 16 (October 1973):239–273.

302. ———. "Patent Exploitation: Some Economic and Legal Problems." *Journal of Law and Economics* 9 (October 1966):135–162.

303. ———. "Predatory Price Cutting: The Standard Oil (N.J.) Case." *Journal of Law and Economics* 1 (October 1958):137–169.

304. McGuire, J.; Chiu, J.; and Elbing, A. "Executive Incomes, Sales, and Profits." *American Economic Review* 52 (September 1962):753–761.

305. McKean, Roland N. "Collective Choice." In *Social Responsibility and the Business Predicament,* edited by James W. McKie. Washington, D.C.: The Brookings Institution, 1974.

306. McLure, Charles E., Jr. "Taxation, Substitution, and Industrial Location." *Journal of Political Economy* 78 (January-February 1970): 112–132.

307. McManus, John C. "The Costs of Alternative Economic Organizations." *The Canadian Journal of Economics* 8 (August 1975):334–350.

308. Means, Gardiner C. *Administered Inflation and Public Policy.* Washington, D.C.: Anderson Kramer Associates, 1959.

309. ———. *Hearings before the Subcommittee on Antitrust and Monopoly,* United States Senate, 1957. Washington, D.C.: U.S. Government Printing Office, 1957.

310. ———. "The Administered-Price Thesis Reconfirmed." *American Economic Review* 62 (June 1972):292–306.

311. ———. *Industrial Prices and Their Relative Inflexibility.* U.S. Senate Document 13, 74th Cong., 1st sess., 1935.

312. Medvin, Norman. "How Big Oil Influences Government." *American Federationist* 81 (December 1974):16–19.

313. Meiselman, David. *The Term Structure of Interest Rates.* Englewood Cliffs, N.J.: Prentice-Hall, 1962.

314. Mermelstein, David, ed. *Economics: Mainstream Readings and Radical Critiques.* New York: Random House, 1970.

315. Millibrand, Ralph. "Professor Galbraith and American Capitalism." *The Socialist Register.* London: Merlin Press, 1968.

316. Mintz, Morton, and Cohen, Jerry. *America, Inc.* New York: Dell, 1973.

317. Mishan, Ezra J. "The Myth of Consumers' Sovereignty." In *Economics: Mainstream Readings and Radical Critiques,* edited by David Mermelstein, pp. 729–754. New York: Random House, 1970.

318. ———. "Pareto Optimality and the Law." *Oxford Economic Papers* 255 (November 1967):235–288.

319. Mitchell, Edward, ed. *Vertical Integration in the Oil Industry.* Washington, D.C: American Enterprise Institute, 1976.

320. Modigliani, Franco. "New Developments on the Oligopoly Front." *Journal of Political Economy* 66 (June 1958):215–232.

321. Mofsky, James S. "Adverse Consequences of Blue Sky Regulation of Public Offering Expenses." *Wisconsin Law Review* (1972):1010.

322. ———. *Blue Sky Restrictions on New Business Promotions.* New York: Matthew Bender, 1971.

323. ———, and Tollison, Robert. "Demerit in Merit Regulation." *Marquette Law Review* 60 (Winter 1977):367–378.

324. Moore, John. "Managerial Behavior in the Theory of Comparative Economic Systems." In *The Economics of Property Rights,* edited by Eirik Furubotn and Svetozar Pejovich, pp. 327–340. Cambridge, Mass.: Ballinger, 1974.

325. Morgan, Thomas D. *Economic Regulation of Business.* St. Paul, Minn.: West, 1976.

326. Musgrave, Richard A., and Musgrave, Peggy B. *Public Finance in Theory and Practice.* New York: McGraw-Hill, 1973.

327. Nader, Ralph, and Green, Mark, eds. *Corporate Power in America.* New York: Grossman, 1973.

328. Nader, Ralph; Green, Mark; and Seligman, Joel. *Taming the Giant Corporation.* New York: Norton, 1976.

329. Nelson, Richard R.; Peck, Merton J., and Kalachek, Edward D. *Technology, Economic Growth, and Public Policy.* Washington, D.C.: The Brookings Institution, 1967.

330. Nelson, Phillip. "Advertising As Information." *Journal of Political Economy* 82 (July–August 1974):729–754.

331. ———. "The Economic Value of Advertising." In *Advertising and Society,* edited by Yale Brozen, pp. 43–66. New York: New York University Press, 1974.

332. Noll, Roger G., ed. *Government and the Sports Business.* Washington, D. C.: The Brookings Institution, 1974.

333. North, Douglas, and Miller, Roger. *The Economics of Public Issues.* New York: Harper & Row, 1976.

334. Nutter, G. Warren. *The Extent of Enterprise Monopoly in the United States: 1899– 1939.* Chicago: The University of Chicago Press, 1951.

335. ——, and Einhorn, Henry A. *Enterprise Monopoly in the United States: 1899– 1958.* New York: Columbia University Press, 1969.

336. Oaxaca, Ronald. "Sex Discrimination in Wages." In *Discrimination in Labor Markets,* edited by Orley C. Ashenfelter and Albert E. Rees. Princeton: Princeton University Press, 1973.

337. Ornstein, Stanley I. "Concentration and Profits." *Journal of Business* 45 (October 1972):519–541.

338. Orr, Daniel. *Property, Markets, and Government Intervention.* Pacific Palisades, Calif.: Goodyear, 1976.

339. Packard, Vance. *The Hidden Persuaders.* New York: McKay, 1957.

340. ——. *The Waste Makers.* New York: Simon and Schuster, 1963.

341. Palmer, John. "The Profit Performance Effects of the Separation of Ownership from Control in Large U.S. Industrial Corporations." *Bell Journal of Economics and Management Science* 4 (Spring 1973):293–303.

342. Parenti, Michael. *Democracy for the Few.* New York: St. Martin's, 1974.

343. Parks, Richard W. "The Demand and Supply of Durable Goods and Durability." *American Economic Review* 64 (March 1974):37–55.

344. Patton, A. *Man, Money, and Motivation.* New York: Columbia University Press, 1961.

345. Peles, Yoram. "Rates of Amortization of Advertising Expenditures." *Journal of Political Economy* 79 (September–October 1971):1032–1058.

346. Pessemier, Edgar. *New Product Decisions.* New York: McGraw-Hill, 1966.

347. Peterman, John L. "The Clorox Case and the Television Rate Structures." *Journal of Law and Economics* 11 (October 1968):321–422.

348. Peterson, Shorey. "Corporate Control and Capitalism." *Quarterly Journal of Economics* 79 (February 1965):1–24.

349. Phelps, Edmund S., ed. *Microeconomic Foundations of Employment and Inflation Theory.* New York: Norton, 1970.

350. Phlips, Louis. "Business Pricing Policies and Inflation—Some Evidence from E.E.C. Countries." *Journal of Industrial Economics* 18 (November 1969):1–14.

351. Pitchford, J. D. "Cost and Demand Elements in the Inflationary Process." *Review of Economic Studies* 24 (February 1957):139–148.

352. Pittman, Russell. "The Effects of Industry Concentration and Regulation on Contributions in Three 1972 U.S. Senate Campaigns." *Public Choice* 27 (Fall 1976):71–80.

353. Poole, R. Clifton. "Blue Sky Laws and the Registration of New Issues on Common Stock: An Empirical Study." Richmond, Va.: University of Richmond, 1976.

354. Posner, Richard A. *Antitrust Law: An Economic Perspective.* Chicago: The University of Chicago Press, 1976.

355. ———. "Antitrust Policy and the Supreme Court: An Analysis of the Restricted Distribution, Horizontal Merger, and Potential Competition Decisions." *Columbia Law Review* 75 (March 1975):282–327.

356. ———. *Economic Analysis of Law.* Boston: Little, Brown, 1972.

357. ———. "A Program for the Antitrust Division." *University of Chicago Law Review* 38 (Spring 1971):500–536.

358. ———. "The Rights of Creditors of Affiliated Corporations." *University of Chicago Law Review* 43 (Spring 1976):499–526.

359. ———. "The Social Costs of Monopoly and Regulation." *Journal of Political Economy* 83 (August 1975):807–827.

360. ———. "A Statistical Study of Antitrust Enforcement." *Journal of Law and Economics* 13 (October 1970):365–419.

361. ———. "Theories of Economic Regulation." *Bell Journal of Economics and Management Sciences* 5 (Autumn 1974):335–358.

362. "A Proposal for the Designation of Shareholder Nominees for Director in the Corporate Proxy Statement." *Columbia Law Review* 74 (October 1974):1139–1174.

363. National Bureau of Economic Research Conference. *Rate and Direction of Inventive Activity: Economic and Social Factors.* Princeton: Princeton University Press, 1962.

364. Reid, Samuel R. *Mergers, Managers, and the Economy.* New York: McGraw-Hill, 1968.

365. *Report of the National Commission on Technology, Automation, and Economic Progress.* Washington, D.C., 1966.

366. Ritter, Lawrence S., and Silber, William L. *Money.* New York: Basic Books, 1970.

367. Roberts, David R. *Executive Compensation.* New York: Free Press, 1959.

368. Robinson, Glen O., and Gellhorn, Ernest. *The Administrative Process.* St. Paul, Minn.: West, 1974.

369. Robinson, Joan. *The Economics of Imperfect Competition.* New York: St. Martin's, 1969.

370. Rosenberg, Nathan. *Technology and American Economic Growth.* New York: Harper & Row, 1972.

371. ———, ed. *The Economics of Technological Change.* Baltimore: Penguin, 1971.

372. Samuelson, Paul. "Proof that Properly Anticipated Prices Fluctuate Randomly." *Industrial Management Review* 6 (Spring 1965):41–50.

373. Say, Jean Baptiste. *A Treatise on Political Economy.* New York: A. M. Kelley, Publishers, 1964.

374. Schelling, Thomas C. "Command and Control." In *Social Responsibility and the Business Predicament,* edited by James McKie. Washington, D.C.: The Brookings Institution, 1974.

375. Scherer, Frederic M. *Industrial Market Structure and Economic Performance.* Chicago: Rand McNally, 1970.

376. ———. "Predatory Pricing and the Sherman Act: A Comment." *Harvard Law Review* 89 (March 1976):869–890.

377. ———. "Some Last Words on Predatory Pricing." *Harvard Law Review* 89 (March 1976):901–903.

378. Schmookler, Jacob. *Invention and Economic Growth.* Cambridge, Mass.: Harvard University Press, 1966.

379. Scholes, Myron S. "The Market for Securities: Substitution versus Price Pressure and the Effects of Information on Share Prices." *Journal of Business* 45 (April 1972):179–211.

380. Schotland, Roy A. "Unsafe at any Price: A Reply to Manne, Insider Trading and the Stock Market." *Virginia Law Review* 53 (1967):1425–1478.

381. Schulman, Stephen H. "The Costs of Free Speech in Proxy Contests for Corporate Control." *Wayne Law Review* 20 (November 1973):1–39.

382. Schumpeter, Joseph. *Capitalism, Socialism, and Democracy.* New York: Harper & Row, 1947.

383. Schwartz, Anna J. "Secular Price Change in Historial Perspective." *Journal of Money, Credit, and Banking* 5 (February 1973):243–269.

384. Schwartz, Donald E. "A Case for Federal Chartering of Corporations." *Business Lawyer* 31 (February 1976):1125–1159.

385. ———. "Federal Chartering of Corporations: An Introduction." *Georgetown Law Journal* 61 (October 1972):71–88.

386. ———. "Towards New Corporate Goals: Co-existence with Society." *Georgetown Law Journal* 60 (October 1971):57–109.

387. Schweiger, Irving. "Adequacy of Financing for Small Business Since World War II." *Journal of Finance* 13 (September 1958):323–347.

388. Selden, Richard T. "Cost-Push versus Demand-Pull Inflation." *Journal of Political Economy* 67 (February 1959):1–20.

389. Sethi, S. Prakash, ed. *The Unstable Ground: Corporate Social Policy in a Dynamic Society*. Los Angeles: Melville, 1974.

390. Sharpe, Myron E. *John Kenneth Galbraith and the Lower Economics*. White Plains, N.Y.: International Arts and Sciences, 1973.

391. Sheehan, John. "Remarks before the Washington Forum." Boca Raton, Fla., Nov. 9, 1974, pp. 10–11.

392. Shepherd, William G. "Market Power and Racial Discrimination in White Collar Employment." *The Antitrust Bulletin* 14 (Spring 1969):142–161.

393. ———. "Trends of Concentration in American Manufacturing Industries: 1947–1958." *Review of Economics and Statistics* 46 (May 1964):200–212.

394. ———, and Levin, Sharon G. "Managerial Discrimination in Large Firms." *Review of Economics and Statistics* 55 (November 1973):412–422.

395. Sherman, Roger. *The Economics of Industry*. Boston: Little, Brown, 1974.

396. Silberman, Jonathan, and Durden, Garey. "Determining Legislative Preferences on the Minimum Wage: An Economic Approach." *Journal of Political Economy* 84 (April 1976):317–329.

397. Simon, Julian. *Issues in the Economics of Advertising*. Urbana: The University of Illinois Press, 1970.

398. Singer, James U. "Consumer Report: FTC Planning Office Plays Larger Role in Decision Making." *National Journal* 7 (September 1975):1298–1302.

399. Singh, Ajit. *Takeovers: Their Relevance to the Stock Market and the Theory of the Firm*. N.Y.: Cambridge University Press, 1971.

400. Smiley, Robert. "The Effect of the Williams Amendment and Other Factors on Transactions Costs in Tender Offers." *Industrial Organization Review* 3 (1975):138–145.

401. ———. "Tender Offers, Transactions Costs and the Theory of the Firm." *Review of Economics and Statistics* 58 (February 1976):22–32.

402. Smith, Adam. *The Wealth of Nations*. New York: Modern Library, 1937.

403. Smith, James D., and Welch, Finis. "Black-White Wage Ratios: 1960–1970." *American Economic Review*, in press.

404. Smith, Richard A. "The Incredible Electrical Conspiracy." *Fortune*, May 1961, p. 161.

405. Snapp, Dorrance D. "National Incorporation." *Illinois Law Review* 5 (February 1911):414–422.

406. Solomon, Ezra. "Alternative Rate of Return Concepts and Their Implications for Utility Regulation." *Bell Journal of Economics and Management Science* 1 (Spring 1970):65–81.

407. Sowards, Hugh L. *Corporation Law*. New York: Matthew Bender, 1974.

408. ———, and Mofsky, James. "Factors Affecting the Development of Corporation Law." *University of Miami Law Review* 23 (1969):476–494.

409. Sowell, Thomas. "'Affirmative Action' Reconsidered." *Public Interest* 42 (Winter 1976):47–65.

410. Spann, Robert, and Erickson, Edward. "The Economics of Railroading: The Beginning of Cartelization and Regulation." *Bell Journal of Economics and Management Science* 1 (Autumn 1970):227–244.

411. *Statistical Abstract of the United States 1976.* Washington, D.C.: U.S. Government Printing Office, 1976, pp. 504–523.

412. Stein, Herbert. "Examination of the Economic Situation and Outlook." *Hearings by Joint Economic Committee.* Washington, D.C: U.S. Government Printing Office, July 30, 1974, pp. 115–118.

413. Steiner, Peter O. *Mergers: Motives, Effects, Policies.* Ann Arbor: The University of Michigan Press, 1975.

414. Stigler, George. "Administered Prices and Oligopolistic Inflation." *Journal of Business* 35 (January 1962):1–13.

415. ———. *Capital and Rates of Return in Manufacturing Industries.* Princeton: Princeton University Press, 1963.

416. ———. "The Economic Effects of the Antitrust Laws." *Journal of Law and Economics* 9 (October 1966):225–258.

417. ———. "The Economies of Scale." *Journal of Law and Economics* 1 (October 1958):54–71.

418. ———. "The Kinky Oligopoly Demand Curve and Rigid Prices." *Journal of Political Economy* 55 (October 1947):432–449.

419. ———. Capitalism and Monopolistic Competition: the Theory of Oligopoly. *American Economic Review* 40 (May 1950):23–47.

420. ———. *The Organization of Industry.* Homewood, Ill.: Irwin, 1968.

421. ———. "Public Regulation of the Securities Markets." *Journal of Business* 37 (April 1964):117–142.

422. ———. "Report of the Task Force on Productivity and Competition." *Antitrust Law and Economics Review* 2 (Spring 1969):13–36.

423. ———. "The Theory of Economic Regulation." *Bell Journal of Economics* 2 (Spring 1971):3–21.

424. ———. "A Theory of Oligopoly." *Journal of Political Economy* 72 (February 1964):44–61.

425. ———. *The Theory of Price.* New York: Macmillan, 1966.

426. ———, and Kindahl, James K. *The Behavior of Industrial Prices.* New York: National Bureau of Economic Research, Columbia University Press, 1970.

427. ———. "Industrial Prices, as Administered by Dr. Means." *American Economic Review* 63 (September 1973):717–721.

428. Stocking, George, and Watkins, Myron. *Monopoly and Free Enterprise.* New York: Twentieth Century Fund, 1951.

429. Stone, Christopher D. *Where the Law Ends: The Social Control of Corporate Behavior.* New York: Harper & Row, 1976.

430. Swan, Peter L. "Durability of Consumption Goods." *American Economic Review* 60 (December 1970):884–894.

431. Sweezy, Paul M. "Demand under Conditions of Oligopoly." *Journal of Political Economy* 46 (August 1938):568–573.

432. Sylos-Labini, Paolo. *Oligopoly and Technical Progress.* Cambridge, Mass.: Harvard University Press, 1962.

433. Telser, Lester G. "Cutthroat Competition and the Long Purse." *Journal of Law and Economics* 9 (October 1966):259–277.

434. ———. "Advertising and Cigarettes." *Journal of Political Economy* 70 (October 1962):471–499.

435. ———. "Advertising and Competition." *Journal of Political Economy* 72 (December 1964):537–562.

436. ———. "The Demand for Branded Goods as Estimated from Consumer Panel Data." *Review of Economics and Statistics* 44 (August 1962):300–324.

437. ———. "Discussion." *American Economic Review, Papers and Proceedings* 59 (May 1969):121–123.

438. ———. "When Are Prices More Stable Than Purchase Rates?" *Revue d'economie politique* 81 (1971):273–301.

439. Theobold, Robert. *The Economics of Abundance.* New York: Pitman, 1970.

440. Thorp, Willard, and Quandt, Richard. *The New Inflation.* New York: McGraw-Hill, 1959.

441. Tucker, Robert. *Philosophy and Myth in Karl Marx.* N.Y.: Cambridge University Press, 1961.

442. Tullock, Gordon. "The Welfare Costs of Tariffs, Monopolies, and Theft." *Western Economic Journal* 5 (June 1967):224–232.

443. United States Bureau of Labor Statistics. "Geographical Profile of Employment and Unemployment, 1974." *Monthly Labor Report #452.*

444. United States Congress, Senate Committee on Banking and Currency. *Stock Exchange Practices.* 73d Cong., 2d sess., 1934, Sen. Rept. 1455.

445. United States Congress, Senate Committee on the Judiciary. *Improvement Act of 1976. Part II—Minority Views.* To accompany S. 1284, 94th Cong., 2d sess., 20 May 1976.

446. United States Congress, Senate Subcommittee on Monopoly. *Advertising of Proprietory Medicines.* 92d Cong., 1st sess., 1971.

447. United States Federal Communications Commission Annual Report. Vol. 37, p. 148 (1971). In *The Administrative Process,* edited by Glen Robinson and Ernest Gellhorn. St. Paul, Minn.: West, 1974.

448. United States Securities and Exchange Commission. *Costs of Flotation of Registered Issues 1971–1972.* Washington, D.C.: U.S. Government Printing Office, 1974.

449. Vaughn, Floyd L. *The United States Patent System.* Norman: University of Oklahoma Press, 1956.

450. Vernon, John M. *Market Structure and Industrial Performance: A Review of Statistical Findings.* Boston: Allyn and Bacon, 1972.

451. Vernon, Raymond. *Sovereignty at Bay: The Multinational Spread of U.S. Enterprises.* New York: Basic Books. 1971.

452. Voight, Fritz. "German Experience with Cartels and Their Control during Pre-War and Post-War Periods." In *Competition, Cartels, and Their Regulation,* edited by John P. Miller, p. 204. Amsterdam: North Holland, 1962.

453. Weiss, Leonard W. "Advertising, Profits, and Corporate Taxes." *Review of Economics and Statistics* 51 (November 1969):421–430.

454. ———. "Business Pricing Policies and Inflation Reconsidered." *Journal of Political Economy* 74 (April 1966):177–187.

455. ———. "The Concentration-Profits Relationship and Antitrust." In *Industrial Concentration: The New Learning,* edited by Harvey J. Goldschmid, H. Michael Mann, and J. Fred Weston, pp. 184–231. Boston: Little, Brown, 1974.

456. Welch, Finis. "Education and Racial Discrimination." In *Discrimination in Labor Markets,* edited by Orley C. Ashenfelter and Albert E. Rees. Princeton: Princeton University Press, 1973.

457. Weston, J. Fred, and Mansinghka, Surenda K. "Tests of the Efficiency Performance of Conglomerate Firms." *Journal of Finance* 26 (September 1971):919–946.

458. Williamson, Oliver E. *Corporate Control and Business Behavior: Managerial Objectives in a Theory of the Firm.* Englewood Cliffs, N.J.: Prentice-Hall, 1964.

459. ———. "Corporate Control and the Theory of the Firm." In *Economic Policy and the Regulation of Corporate Securities,* edited by Henry G. Manne, pp. 281–336. Washington, D.C: American Enterprise Institute, 1969.

460. ———. "The Economics of Internal Organization: Exit and Voice in Relation to Markets and Hierarchies." *American Economic Review, Papers and Proceedings* 66 (May 1976):369–385.

461. ———. "Innovation and Market Structure." *Journal of Political Economy* 73 (February 1965):67–73.

462. Yamey, B. S. "Predatory Price Cutting: Notes and Comments." *Journal of Law and Economics* 15 (April 1972):129–142.

463. Yeager, Leland B., and Tuerck, David G. *Foreign Trade and U.S. Policy.* New York: Praeger, 1976.

464. Zellner, Harriet. "The Determinates of Occupational Segregation." In *Discrimination and the Division of Labor,* edited by Cyntha B. Lloyd. New York: Columbia University Press, 1975.

LEGAL REFERENCES

Blair v. Lamb, 314 F.2d 618 (2d Cir. 1963).

Brown Shoe Co. v. United States, 370 U.S. 294, 82 S. Ct. 1502, 8 L.Ed. 2d 510 (1962).

Calnetics Corp. v. Volkswagen of America, 353 F. Supp. 1219 (C. D. Calif. 1973).

City of Valparaiso v. Hagen, et al., 153 Ind. 337, 54 NE 1062 (1899).

Cohen v. Beneficial Industrial Loan Corporation, 337 U.S. 541, 69 S.Ct. 1221, 92 L. Ed. 1528 (1949).

Dartmouth College v. Woodward, 17 U.S. 518, 4 L.Ed. 629 (1819).

Dodge v. Ford Motor Company, 204 Mich. 459, 170 N.W. 668 (1919).

Federal Trade Commission v. Rubberoid Co., 343 U.S. 470 72 S. Ct. 800, 96 L.Ed. 1081 (1952).

Fletcher v. Peck, 10 U.S. 87, 3 L.Ed. 162 (1810).

J. I. Case Co. v. Borak, 377 U.S. 426, 84 S. Ct. 1555, 12 L. Ed. 2d, 423 (1964).

Jones v. Tri-County Electric Cooperative, 512, F.2d 1 (5th Cir. 1975).

Knapp v. Bankers Securities Corp., 230 F.2d 717 (3d Cir. 1956).

Marsh v. State of Alabama, 326 U.S. 501, 66 S. Ct. 276 (1946).

Daniel McAleer v. American Telephone and Telegraph Company [416 F. Supp. 435 (D.C. 1976)].

Missouri Portland Cement Co. v. Cargill, Inc., 498 F.2d 851 (2d Cir. 1974).

Platt Bros. & Co. v. City of Waterbury, 72 Conn. 531, 45 A. 154 (1900).

Proprietors of the Charles River Bridge v. Proprietors of the Warren Bridge, 36 U.S. 420, 9 L.Ed. 773 (1873).

Stone v. F.C.C., 466 F.2d 316 (D.C. 1972).

Treadway Co., Inc. v. Brunswick Corp. 364 F. Supp. 316 (N.J. 1973).

United States v. Bliss and Laughlin, Inc. 202 F. Supp. 334 (S.D. Calif. 1962).

United States v. Milwaukee Refrigerator Transit Co., 142 F. 247, (E.D. Wis. 1905).

United States v. Texas Gulf Sulfur. 401 F.2d 833 (2d Cir., 1968), *cert. denied,* 394 U.S. 976 (1969).

NAME INDEX

SUBJECT INDEX

LB (line-of-business) reporting
 requirements, 111–115
Less-developed countries, multinational corporations and,
 29–30
Liability:
 of corporations, 87–89
  (*See also* Limited liability)
 of managers for third-party injuries,
  86–91
Limited liability, 17
 credit markets and, 224–225
 insurance and, 226–227
 involuntary (tort) creditors and, 223,
  225–227
 joint stock companies with, 154–155
 nature of, 223–224
 19th-century incorporation laws and,
  143
 right to contract and, 224–225
Lincoln Electric, 46
Line-of-business (LB) reporting
 requirements, 111–115
Liquidation of assets, takeover
 bids and, 98
List prices, 174, 180
Litigation (*see* Antitrust activity; Liability; Shareholders, remedies
 available to)
Loans, limited liability and, 224–225
Local government (municipalities):
 bribery of officials of, 67
 corporate influence on, 63–65
 monopsonistic labor market and, 40
 pollution and, 16, 18, 65

Management:
 compensation of, 79
  liability of managers and, 88
  (*See also* Executives, salaries and
   other compensation of)
 control of the corporation by:
  proposals to weaken, 82–83
  (*See also* Shareholders, control of
   the corporation and)
 incompetence of, constraints on, 36
 insider trading (*see* Insider trading)
 insurance for, 87, 88, 95–96
 liability of, for third-party injuries,
  86–91
 mergers and, 216

Management (*Cont.*):
 monitoring of: as constraint on
   power of managers, 78–80
  diffuse stock ownership and, 102–
   105
 power of, 77
  competition as constraint on, 79
  over employees, 243–244
  illusion of, 78
  market constraints on, 78
  monitoring by owners as
   constraint on, 78–80
 separation of ownership from: civil
   rights of employees and, 35–36
  job discrimination and, 49
 of takeover-bid target companies, 98,
  100
 (*See also* Board of directors; Executives; Officers, corporate)
Managers (*see* Management)
Market:
 power of managers constrained by,
  78, 79
 (*See also* Capital markets; Credit
   markets; Labor market;
   Stock market)
Market concentration (*see* Industry
 concentration)
Market power:
 job discrimination and, 49–52
 rates of return and, 269
 of unions and corporations, 195–197
 (*See also* Industry concentration;
   Monopoly)
Marsh v. State of Alabama, 37–38, 40–41
Mercantilism, 135–136
 federal chartering of corporations
  and, 152–153
Mergers:
 antimerger law, 215–218
 capital market access and, 221
 desirable effects of, 216–217
 monopoly and, 215–216
 (*See also* Takeover bids)
Merit regulation, state, 126–129
 (*See also* Blue sky laws)
Minorities, discrimination against (*see*
 Job discrimination)
Missouri Portland Cement v. Cargill, Inc.,
 216
Monetary policy, efficient market
 hypothesis and, 109

Money supply, inflation and, 188–193,
195
Monitoring:
of employees: carelessness, 10, 11
civil rights, 37, 41–42
of managers: as constraint on power,
78–80
diffuse stock ownership and, 102–
105
of production, 9–11
(*See also* Government regulations
and restrictions)
Monopoly:
in American economic development,
137–139
corporate chartering and, 137–139
discrimination and, 50
firm size and, 198–199
inflation and, 194–197
mergers and, 215–216
national, railroads and, 137–138
patents and, 213–214
public utilities, 212, 213
rates of return and, 267–268
technological innovation and, 198–
201
welfare loss from, 204, 294–297
(*See also* Antitrust activity; Industry
concentration; Market power;
Price-fixing)
Monopoly charters, state incorporation
laws and, 136, 137, 141–144, 154–
155
Monopsonistic labor market, 40
Multinational corporations:
currency manipulation and, 27–28
domestic development and, 29–30
domestic jobs and, 28–29
resource allocation and, 26–31
tax avoidance by, 29
Municipalities (*see* Local government)

National Environmental Policy Act
(1969), 18
National Petroleum Council, 59
Natural resources as entry barrier,
212–213
Needs of consumers, advertising and,
236–239
New York Business Corporation Act,
146

Obsolescence, planned, 233–235
Officers, corporate:
liability of, for third-party injuries,
86–91
(*See also* Management)
Oil industry, 283
Oil prices, proposal that government
set, 266
One-person corporations, limited
liability and, 225
Owners:
monitoring of management by, 78–
80, 272
separation of management and: civil
rights of employees and, 35–36
job discrimination and, 49
(*See also* Property rights;
Shareholders)

Parallel pricing, 247
(*See also* Price-fixing)
Pariah countries, trade with, 71–74
Partnerships, 142, 155
Patents, 201, 213–214
Payoffs:
forms of government and, 66–67
for political favors, 59–60
(*See also* Bribery)
Physical needs, 236, 237
Planned obsolescence, 233–235
Planning, renewable and revocable
charters and, 163–164
Platt Bros. & Co. v. City of Waterbury, 18
Policy Planning Office of FTC, 292,
293
Political influence (*see* Political power)
Political power, 59–62
as commodity, 59–60
competitiveness of market for, 60–
62
government as enhancing, 242–243
industry concentration and, 282–283
in local communities, 63–65
Political system, analogy between
corporations and, 21–25
Pollution:
common law and, 18–19
common property rights and, 14–16
government regulations and, 18–20
local government and, 18, 65
managers and, 80